FROM THESE BARE BONES

From These Bare Bones

Raw materials and the study of worked osseous objects

edited by

Alice Choyke and Sonia O'Connor

Proceedings of the Raw Materials session at the 11th ICAZ Conference, Paris, 2010

Oxbow Books
Oxford and Oakville

Published by
Oxbow Books, Oxford, UK

© Oxbow Books and the individual authors, 2013

ISBN 978-1-78297-211-2

A CIP record for this book is available from the British Library

This book is available direct from:

Oxbow Books, Oxford, UK
(Phone: 01865-241249; Fax: 01865-794449)

and

The David Brown Book Company
PO Box 511, Oakville, CT 06779, USA
(Phone: 860-945-9329; Fax: 860-945-9468)

or from our website
www.oxbowbooks.com

Library of Congress Cataloging-in-Publication Data

International Council for Archaeozoology. Conference (11th : 2010 : Paris, France)
  From these bare bones : raw materials and the study of worked osseous objects / edited by Alice Choyke and Sonia O'Connor.
     pages cm
  "Proceedings of the Raw Materials Session at the 11th ICAZ Conference, Paris, 2010."
  Includes bibliographical references.
  ISBN 978-1-78297-211-2
  1. Bone implements, Prehistoric--Congresses. 2. Bone carving, Prehistoric--Congresses. 3. Tools, Prehistoric--Congresses. 4. Art, Prehistoric--Congresses. 5. Excavations (Archaeology)--Congresses. I. Choyke, Alice Mathea, editor, author. II. O'Connor, Sonia A., editor, author.
III. Title.
  CC79.5.B64I56 2010
  930.1--dc23
                      2013044841

Front cover image: The elephant ivory comb (site 1988–89.24 sf4139) and bone gaming die (site1976–81.7 sf12286) in this picture are included by kind permission of the York Archaeological Trust. Photography by Sonia O'Connor and Tom Sparrow. Back cover image: Bone finds from a Middle Neolithic burial at Ajvide, Gotland, Sweden. Photo by Kristiina Mannermaa.

Printed and bound in Great Britain by
Berforts Information Press

Contents

Social Aspects of Raw Material Selection

New Methods of Materials Identification

Contributors

STEVEN P. ASHBY
Department of Archaeology,
University of York,
The King's Manor,
York Y01 7EP, UK.
Steve.ashby@york.ac.uk

CORNELIA BECKER
Institute for Prehistoric Archaeology,
Free University Berlin,
Altensteinstr. 15,
D-14195 Berlin, Germany.
cobecker@zedat.fu-berlin.de

NATACHA BUC
CONICET-INAPL,
Instituto Nacional de Antropología y Pensamiento
   Latinoamericano,
3 de Febrero 1378,
Buenos Aires, Argentina.
natachabuc@gmail.com

ROXANA CATTÁNEO
IDACOR-CONICET, Museo de Antropología,
Facultad de Filosofía y Humanidades,
Universidad Nacional de Córdoba,
Av. H. Yrigoyen 174,
5000, Córdoba, Argentina.
roxanacattaneo@gmail.com

ALICE M. CHOYKE
Medieval Studies Department,
Central European University,
1051 Budapest,
Nador u. 9. Hungary.
Choyke@ceu.hu

MATTHEW J. COLLINS
BioArCh,
Departments of Biology, Archaeology and Chemistry,
Wentworth Way,
University of York,
York YO10 5DD, UK.

LÍDIA COLOMINAS
Laboratori d'Arqueozoologia, Departament de Prehistòria,
Universitat Autònoma de Barcelona,
Bellaterra, 08193. Spain.
now
McDonald Institute for Archaeological Research,
University of Cambridge,
Downing Street, Cambridge CB2 3ER, UK.
lc547@cam.ac.uk and lidialidia_@hotmail.com

JIMENA CORNAGLIA FERNÁNDEZ
CONICET-CEIA,
Centro de Estudios Interdisciplinarios en Antropología,
Universidad Nacional de Rosario-Facultad de Humanidades y Artes,
Entre Ríos 758,
2000 Rosario, Santa Fe, Argentina.
jimenacornaglia@hotmail.com

LETICIA I. CORTÉS
CONICET, Museo Etnográfico,
Facultad de Filosofía y Letras,
Universidad de Buenos Aires, Moreno 350,
1091, Buenos Aires, Argentina.
leticiacortes@gmail.com

MARINA ALMEIDA ÉVORA
NAP – Núcleo de Arqueologia e Paleoecologia,
Faculdade de Ciências Humanas e Socials da
   Universidade do Algarve, Campus de Gambelas,
8005-139 Faro, Portugal.
marevora@gmail.com

REBECCA FARBSTEIN
Department of Archaeology and Centre for the Archaeology of
   Human Origins, University of Southampton,
Southampton SO17 1BF, UK.
r.a.farbstein@soton.ac.uk

OLIVER W. HOUNSLOW
BioArCh, Departments of Biology, Archaeology and Chemistry,
Wentworth Way,
University of York,
York YO10 5DD, UK

ANDRÉS D. IZETA
IDACOR-CONICET, Museo de Antropología,
Facultad de Filosofía y Humanidades,
Universidad Nacional de Córdoba,
Av. H. Yrigoyen 174,
5000, Córdoba, Argentina.
andresizeta@gmail.com

CAMILLE JÉQUIER
Università di Ferrara,
Sezione di Scienze Preistoriche ed Antropologiche,
Corso Ercole I d'Este 32,
44121 Ferrara, Italy.
camille.jequier@gmail.com and jqcll@unife.it

HEIDI LUIK
Department of Archaeobiology and Ancient Technology,
Institute of History,
Tallinn University,
6 Rüütli St.,
10130 Tallinn, Estonia.
heidi.luik@tlu.ee

KRISTIINA MANNERMAA
University of Helsinki, Department of Philosophy,
History, Culture and Art Studies, Archaeology,
University of Helsinki,
P.O. Box 59,
00014 Helsinki, Finland.
kristiina.mannermaa@helsinki.fi

LAURA MARCHIONNI
División Arqueología, Facultad de Ciencias Naturales y Museo,
Universidad Nacional de La Plata y CONICET,
Paseo del Bosque s/n°,
1900, La Plata, Argentina.
lau_marchionni@yahoo.com.ar

JACQUELINE MEIER
University of Connecticut,
Department of Anthropology,
354 Mansfield Road Unit 2176 Storrs,
CT 06269-2176, USA.
Jacqueline.s.meier@gmail.com or Jacqueline.meier@uconn.edu

LAURA MIOTTI
División Arqueología, Facultad de Ciencias Naturales y Museo,
Universidad Nacional de La Plata y CONICET,
Paseo del Bosque s/n°,
1900, La Plata, Argentina.
lmiotti@fcnym.unlp.edu.ar

KATHERINE MOORE
University of Pennsylvania Museum,
3260 South Street,
Philadelphia, PA 19104, USA.
kmmoore@sas.upenn.edu

SONIA O'CONNOR
Archaeological Sciences,
University of Bradford,
Richmond Road,
Bradford BD7 1DP, UK.
s.oconnor@bradford.ac.uk

MARCO PERESANI
Università di Ferrara,
Sezione di Scienze Preistoriche ed Antropologiche,
Corso Ercole I d'Este 32,
44121 Ferrara, Italy.

RIITTA RAINIO
University of Helsinki,
Department of Philosophy, History, Culture and Art Studies,
   Musicology,
Museokatu 25 A 8,
FIN-00100 Helsinki, Finland.
riitta.rainio@helsinki.fi

MATTEO ROMANDINI
Università di Ferrara,
Sezione di Scienze Preistoriche ed Antropologiche,
Corso Ercole I d'Este 32,
44121 Ferrara, Italy.

M. CRISTINA SCATTOLIN
CONICET, Museo Etnográfico,
Facultad de Filosofía y Letras,
Universidad de Buenos Aires, Moreno 350,
1091, Buenos Aires, Argentina.
cscattolin@gmail.com

VIVIAN SCHEINSOHN
Instituto Nacional de Antropología y Pensamiento
   Latinoamericano (INAPL),
Consejo Nacional de Investigaciones Científicas y Técnicas
   (CONICET),
Universidad de Buenos Aires (UBA),
3 de Febrero 1370 – (1426) Capital Federal, Argentina.
scheinso@retina.ar

JOANNA P. SIMPSON
BioArCh,
Departments of Biology,
Archaeology and Chemistry,
Wentworth Way,
University of York,
York YO10 5DD, UK.

ELISABETH A. STONE
Department of Anthropology,
MSC01-1040, Anthropology 1,
University of New Mexico,
Albuquerque, NM 87131, USA.
elisabethastone@gmail.com

ZSUZSANNA TÓTH
Eötvös Loránd Science University,
Institute of Archaeological Sciences,
Múzeum Krt. 4b, 1088 Budapest, Hungary.
zsuzsanna.toth11@gmail.com

SELENA VITEZOVIĆ
Archaeological Institute,
Kneza Mihaila 35/IV,
11 000 Belgrade, Serbia.
selenavitezovic@gmail.com

LAUREN WHALLEY
BioArCh,
Departments of Biology, Archaeology and Chemistry,
Wentworth Way,
University of York,
York YO10 5DD, UK.

Preface

This book is one of the volumes of the published proceedings of the 11th meeting of the International Council of Archaeozoology (ICAZ), which was held in Paris (France) 23–28 August 2010. ICAZ was founded in the early '70s and has ever since acted as the main international organisation for the study of animal remains from archaeological sites. The main international conferences are held every four years, and the Paris meeting – the largest ever – follows those in Budapest (Hungary), Groningen (the Netherlands), Szczecin (Poland), London (UK), Bordeaux (France), Washington D.C. (USA), Konstanz (Germany), Vancouver (Canada), Durham (UK) and Mexico City. The next meeting will be held in Argentina in 2014. The Paris conference – which was attended by about 720 delegates from 56 countries – was organised in 30 thematic and one general session, which attracted, in addition to archaeozoologists, scholars from related disciplines such as bone chemistry, genetics, morphometrics, anthropology, archaeobotany, mainstream archaeology *etc*. This conference was also marked by the increasing involvement in the international community of more numerous countries of Latin America and of South and East Asia.

As nearly 800 papers have been actually presented to the Paris conference, either as oral or poster presentations, it was not possible to organize an exhaustive publication of the proceedings. The session organizers were free to decide to publish or not the proceedings of their session and to choose its form. The Conference Organizers however, proposed to help publishing separately the sessions either in the form of open access digital volumes, published by the Service des Publications scientifiques du Muséum National d'Histoire Naturelle, Paris (http://www.mnhn.fr/museum/foffice/science/science/DocScientifique/publications/presentation.xsp?i=1) or in the form of peer reviewed volumes of the international journal *Anthropozoologica*. The list of the proceedings of the 11th ICAZ conference is regularly updated and posted on the web site of ICAZ.

We would also like to take this opportunity to thank the Muséum National d'Histoire Naturelle, the Université Pierre et Marie Curie and the ICAZ Executive Committee for their support during the preparation of the conference, and all session organisers – some of them being now book editors – for all their hard work. The conference would not have met such a success without help of the Alpha Visa Congrès Company, which was in charge of the management and of part of the material organization. Further financial help came from the following sources: la Région Ile-deFrance, the Bioarch European network (French CNRS, Nat. History Museum Brussels, Durham, Aberdeen, Basel and Munich Universities), the LeCHE Marie Curie International Training Network, granted by the European Council, the Institute of Ecology and Environment of the CNRS, the Institut National de Recherche en Archéologie Préventive (INRAP), the European-Chinese Cooperation project (ERA-NET Co-Reach), the Centre National Interprofessionnel de l'Economie Laitière (CNIEL) and its Observatory for food habits (OCHA), theVille de Paris, the Société des Amis du Muséum, the French Embassies at Beijing and Moscow, the lab "Archaeozoology-Archaeobotany" (UMR7209, CNRS-MNHN), the School of Forensic, Lancaster, the English Heritage and some private donors.

Jean-Denis Vigne, Christine Lefèvre
and Marylène Patou-Mathis

INTRODUCTION

From These Bare Bones: Raw materials and the study of worked osseous objects

Alice Choyke and Sonia O'Connor

A fundamental component of the study of worked osseous objects is the identification of the raw materials chosen to make them, an aspect sometimes under-emphasized in traditional bone tool studies. Although often the answer is obvious, assuming there is an archaeozoologist at hand, sometimes the objects have degraded to the point where identification becomes problematic or all identifying features of the original skeletal element have been completely removed by extreme working of the surface. Differentiating bone from antler often becomes difficult. Even deciding whether objects are made from either of these materials or even ivories and other teeth may be problematic. As the way in which these materials decay during burial and upon excavation can vary greatly, correct identification is crucial to the investigation of objects, their conservation and future curation. Above all, understanding raw material selection opens research gateways onto our understanding of human-animal interaction in the past both on pragmatic as well as symbolic levels.

The choices made by artisans vary by cultural tradition. In fact, such technical choices, starting with the choice of raw material (*e.g.* Lemonnier, 1993), provide a way for groups of people to distinguish themselves from others. There is a complex inter-play between the physical characteristics of the raw material which makes them more appropriate for certain kinds of use and the strong, social reinforcing power of tradition described by Bourdieu (1977) as the *habitus*, familiarity, and practice. Conversely, sudden changes in raw material choices can be a signal of social change or disruption. Not all choice in manufacturing is related to efficiency, but rather a desire on the part of individuals within the group to conform or sometimes express dissent. Nevertheless, in general,

changes in utilitarian bone tool forms and raw materials, especially at the household level, tended to be both slow and conservative. It should also not be forgotten that, just as meat preferences from parts of the animal body may signal beliefs about particular species, so choice of skeletal elements themselves may also be loaded with culturally specific meanings (*e.g.* Birtalan 2002).

It is these themes that formed the central tenets of the Raw Materials Session on 24th August, 2010 at ICAZ 2010 in Paris. The peer-reviewed papers presented in this volume were developed from the oral and poster presentations accepted for this session and include one invited paper. They have been divided into three general sections depending on the main thrust of the argument in individual papers and come from both Europe and South America. Clearly, no paper here deals exclusively with aspects surrounding raw material acquisition, exploitation and selection. Within each of the three thematic sections, the editors have tried to group papers together by geographical region and then chronologically since the timeline of archaeological events in these far-flung parts of the world make direct comparison difficult but exciting at the same time. The paper by Choyke, co-editor of this volume, acts as an introduction to the many ways bone as a raw material can potentially be researched. Each bone tool assemblage raises its own questions and has its own research trajectory within the field of raw material studies that can profitably be combined with other methodologies connected to manufacture technologies, use, curation and discard patterns – all reflecting on culturally idiosyncratic attitudes towards animals and the permeability of the cognitive boundaries between human and animal.

Raw material selection and curation within tool types

The first section deals largely with the huge number of choices in the skeletal elements from animal species exploited by people. The first three papers in this volume deal with raw material issues from the remote past but in quite different ways. Palaeolithic research into raw material choices must overcome the hurdle of distinguishing patterns with relatively few tools from time intervals of thousands of years. Despite these methodological problems interesting trends can still be revealed.

The paper by Jequier, Romandini and Peresani directly concerns the study of retouchers from the well-known Upper Palaeolithic Fumane Cave site near Verona in Italy. Retouchers made from osseous materials are sometimes difficult to distinguish from faunal materials exhibiting natural modifications and, in fact, some researchers even call into question whether they exist as a tool type at all. Here, the authors convincingly argue that there were changes in the selection of raw materials between gross chronological layers at the site for retouchers with patterned use wear on them. This change does not seem to be linked to simple availability. Évora also introduces the small Upper Palaeolithic bone tool repertoire in her article from twelve cave and rock-shelter sites in Portugal. Although she looks at a full range of tool types, these are limited by a variety of natural and methodology based taphonomic factors affecting survival as well as collection of these objects. The final paper dealing with Upper Palaeolithic raw materials by Elisabeth Stone comes at the issue of raw materials from a direction that has only recently begun to receive more attention from scholars; that of perishable technologies recognizable in use-wear on bone tools. Use-wears from ethnographically attested objects from a number of North American native groups were compared to wears that were experimentally produced and wears from a group of pointed bone tools from Entrefoces and El Perro, two small sites from northern Spain occupied at the very end of the Late Upper Palaeolithic. Stone finds that superficially identical awls were used in contact with materials from both plants and hides reflecting branches of artisanal activity that have 'disappeared' from the archaeological record.

The topic of patterns in the selection of raw materials continues with two papers from different regions and times in Argentina. The paper by Scheinsohn deals with the first native American 'colonizers' of two different regions in Patagonia, the islands in the straits of Magellan and more inland areas. While the bone tools on the islands seem to be associated with a littoral adaptation and are very variable with regards to their raw material and design, the rarer bone tools from the continental parts of the region display much greater raw material selection for a limited number of bone tool types. She concludes that in this latter area at least, people first came here in this early occupation with a firm notion of the use of targeted skeletal elements and species to produce specific tools for use in particular

activities. Izeta and his co-authors deal with household material from the Formative period, a more established period of settled agriculturalists but from a part of Argentina that has been less well studied from the point of view of bone tools. They found a developed bone tool industry reflecting a standardized use of camelid metapodials to manufacture awls for basketry and/or weaving in the southern Calchaquíes valleys, northwestern Argentina, much like what Moore found in her study of Formative material from Bolivia (see this volume). The bone tools from this area have parallels with similar tools from other settled groups elsewhere in the Americas as well. These tools also shed some light on domestic activities connected to now vanished objects made from plant fibres.

Returning to Europe and bone tool assemblages associated with later chronological periods, the paper by Vitezović deals with variability in raw material selection in bone tool assemblages from the Late Neolithic and Chalcolithic Vinča Culture in modern day Serbia. This region is very important as a kind of staging area for many cultural impulses that were to infiltrate Central and Western Europe mediated through the Central Balkans as a node of transmission of know-how and information. This paper provides ample material for comparisons with bone assemblages from neighbouring areas. Of particular interest is the treatment of antler, particularly from red deer, which is not equally abundant on all sites suggesting some settlements had some measure of control and access to this valuable raw material. Special treatment accorded cervid antler appears in many papers in this volume. Luik's paper is also concerned with bone tool assemblages from the Late Neolithic and Bronze Ages but from a very different part of Europe, the Baltic region. Here, bone was available from a rather different spectrum of species, especially wild species including seal. She finds that while seal bone is important for producing a number of different types of tools and ornaments in the Baltic Neolithic period there seems to have been a marked break in manufacturing traditions, including raw material selection, where bone from more easily available domestic species was preferred. She suggests that Neolithic belief systems and attitudes were more centred on the sea and the bones of sea mammals had special symbolic significance. Shifts in belief systems meant that later Bronze Age people living in large fortified settlements, only used seal bone on an ad hoc basis either to make tools or for ornaments.

The final paper in this section, by Colominas, deals with a small bone tool workshop from the Roman city of *Baetulo* in Spain. Roman bone tool and ornament production was commoditized and serialized within market systems across the empire. Not surprisingly, there is most often a high degree of standardization, not only in the finished pieces, but even in the waste and raw material, in this case, cattle metapodials. The acquisition of raw materials was shown to be strongly linked both to butchering practices and the consumption of meat at this Spanish site.

Social aspects of raw material selection

The next section comprises a group of eight papers in which the intellectual emphasis is on the social life of raw materials. Farbstein's paper returns to Palaeolithic material with a study of technical and material attributes of late Magdalenian portable art from two sites in south-central France, Montastruc and Courbet. She uses the notion of the *chaîne opératoire*, normally associated with the practices of technology, to dissect the symbolic world embodied in these artefacts. The paper has important methodological implications since critical examination of choice should help in understanding how far practical considerations of efficiency and coeval subjective notions of value and socio-aesthetic dictated technical and artistic choice at these two roughly contemporary sites. Moving to another early bone tool assemblage from Argentina, Cornaglia Fernández and Buc review the socio-technological aspects of a small assemblage of 14 bone tools used by Holocene hunter and gatherer populations living in Santa Fe's Pampa Lagoons at the Laguna El Doce site. The standardized form and technical style exhibited by bevelled tools in the assemblage lie at the heart of their study. The different research skill sets of the two authors bring complexity to the study and reveal that these highly standardized tools were, somewhat surprisingly, connected to well-developed lithic tool production practices not skin processing. Concerned as well with bone use in tool manufacturing among early hunter and gather populations but in a different region of Argentina, the paper by Miotti and Marchioni compares and contrasts rules of manufacturing at three cave sites on the Central Plateau of Santa Cruz, Piedra Museo, Los Toldos and La Primavera, from the Pleistocene/Holocene transition and middle Holocene periods respectively. As with the previous paper it seems clear that these early colonial populations brought with them firm traditions of bone tool use and manufacture, adhering to strict rules of raw material selection and manufacturing technique. It is only with the later material that experimentation with the use of materials from new species appears suggesting that simple availability again becomes a factor in shaping the production process, perhaps signalling changes in other parts of these small band-level societies.

Still set in the deeper past but again at a time of important subsistence changes in the Near East in Jordan, the paper by Becker deals with a particular kind of object among the 586 bone points, needles, ornamental accessories and flat "smoothing" utensils. It is this latter tool type that the author explores in order to cast light on the vexed issues of separating availability versus tradition in shaping the composition and technical style of worked bone assemblages. Becker also makes a convincing argument that these tools would have had an important function in processing large clay surfaces comprising building walls for structures in this early settlement.

The paper by Mannermaa and Rainio brings us back to Northern Europe and a very special grave goods assemblage in a burial of a woman at the Neolithic site of Ajvide on the island of Gotland in the Baltic Sea. This extraordinary assemblage of ambiguous bone tubes and seal teeth, and fish bone pendant objects again reflecting the Neolithic focus on sea beliefs discussed in Luik's paper, explores the use of bone objects to create particular soundscapes with social meanings of their own. While the authors stress that the study of these objects is just at its beginning, it is a sharp reminder that when researchers study objects made from hard osseous animal materials it is not only the symbolic, look or plasticity of such materials that should be considered but sound as well. Sight and sound as well as smell and touch, all combine together to evoke sometimes powerful emotional responses in both the user and social audience. It is food for thought that not only may the tubes be part of a complex sounding device but the click of the tooth beads – the sound of this person moving through the world in a socially ascribed fashion – must have produced special but predictable responses while she was alive as well as at her burial.

Back in continental Europe but at the very end of the Neolithic, Toth also explores the subject of rules of manufacturing in terms of raw material selection and manufacturing techniques as these present themselves at the site of Aszód–Papi földek in Central Hungary. This settlement lies on the border between the two main cultural complexes of the Late Neolithic and this cross-cultural position seems to have resulted in a blurring of manufacturing norms, at least in comparison with other settlements from the late and final Neolithic in Hungary. Interestingly, the same trend toward a greater focus on red deer antler production at some settlements found in Vitezović's material from more or less the same time period in Serbia and the Balkans also seems to be found at Aszód. The notion of the meaning of standardization and rules of manufacture has been a recurring topic in papers throughout this volume and will be a topic that needs further work in the future to understand the social implication of changes in technical choices which can be seen to tighten and loosen over time within various societies.

One area touched upon explicitly in Stone's paper as well as the paper by Meier has been the role of experimentation married to identification in understanding bone tool types. Meier looked at worked caprine astragali and phalanges found at the Middle Bronze Age sites of Zagyvapálfalva-Homokbanya and Kisterenye-Hársas in Northern Hungary. Astragali as a topic return in the archaeological literature again and again, sometimes presented as tools but more often in the guise of gambling or ritual-connected objects. As has been seen, such facetted astragali appear in Vinča material from Serbia and certainly are objects found later at many Middle Bronze Age settlement materials in the Carpathian Basin. These objects are variously described in the literature as tools or gambling objects but most often with little rigorous effort to demonstrate what these objects were in fact used for. Parenthetically, the consistent use of this bone may indeed be linked at the same time to both symbolic ideas about the animal and the skeletal element itself and their use as functional objects. Here, however, Meier has convincingly demonstrated through experiment that the flat facets on these tools can indeed be produced by burnishing curved, dry ceramic surfaces before the final firing.

Like Izeta *et al.*, the final paper in the section on social aspects of raw material selection deals with bone tool assemblages from three Formative village sites in Bolivia. Katherine Moore looks carefully at preferences for certain skeletal elements from a small number of animal species in order to understand the organization of craft production and the social and economic importance of a number of the bone types within the assemblage of 349 bone tools. Although most bone tools were made from the bones of local and mostly domesticated camelids, there were specialized tools made from dog, birds and deer antler. The use of carefully selected scapulae, the ilium part of the pelvis, and mandibles to make particular tools including a scapular tool made for reed harvesting is particularly interesting. The appearance of waste bone around structures shows there was typically household production of ornaments and tools at all three sites for use mainly in weaving as well as basket-making, leather-working and shaping ceramics.

New methods of materials identification

The final section contains three papers dealing with an array of new methods which can be employed in raw material identification. Sometimes, tools and ornaments are either so degraded or so heavily worked that it becomes virtually impossible to determine the raw materials they were made from. As evidenced in the paper by O'Connor, also co-editor of this volume, being able to identify raw materials precisely on structural criteria can add immeasurably to the story they can eventually tell about the people who made and used them. Her paper concerns some Iron Age sword handles from South Cave in East Yorkshire, UK with surprising (surprising perhaps because they are rarely properly identified) organic components including horn and antler but also cetacean bone, cetacean ivory and, amazingly, elephant ivory. Knowledge of what raw materials were selected to make these handles and in which combinations has numerous social implications connected to wealth, status and beliefs about the animals associated with the raw materials employed in the manufacture of these hilts. However, identification of the raw materials in these unique objects also has huge implications for their conservation and protection.

A new and exciting technique pioneered at the University of York permitting taxonomic identification of osseous raw materials of tools or ornaments where features of the skeletal element have been lost or removed is ZooMS (Zooarchaeology by Mass Spectrometry). By looking at certain species-specific peptides in the protein collagen from hard osseous materials, Hounslow and his co-authors show that it is possible to identify the species of worked bone objects. Although the number of collagen fingerprints or sequences is still small at this stage it is growing and, compared to the expensive and delicate DNA sequencing, holds great promise for the future by opening up doors to identification which have previously been closed for heavily worked or damaged objects with obvious implications for their analysis and conservation.

The final paper in the volume by Ashby deals with the important issue of distinguishing objects such as combs made from cervid antler. In Northern Europe, where early medieval antler combs were important practical and symbolic objects, identifying the antler type is very important to clarify aspects of their manufacture, including acquisition of raw materials and the circulation of the finished objects. Ashby assesses the accuracy of traditional diagnostic criteria employed by zooarchaeologists using macro and micro techniques. Antler is a pivotal raw material in prehistoric and proto-historic Europe as well. Although much of the worked material has eliminated obvious identifying traces the criteria tested here in a series of blind-tests show that archaeozoological identification criteria work well for larger pieces. However, the identification accuracy is less conclusive for small or extremely degraded pieces so that, where necessary, researchers will have to turn to other technical solutions for identification.

Thus, this volume demonstrates that the issue of raw material identification has numerous implications for conservation work, reproduction of objects, the physical characteristics of the tool or ornament, availability of raw materials, the materials chosen for procurement and the cultural reasons that lie behind the choice of raw materials from particular species and skeletal elements to produce planned tool and ornament types. Together, these papers emphasize the need for confident and correct materials identification and demonstrate that functionality is by no means the only, nor necessarily the most important, factor in the selection of osseous raw materials for the fabrication of tools and other cultural objects.

Bibliography

Birtalan, Á. (2003) Ritualistic use of livestock bones in the Mongolian belief system and customs. In A. Sárközi and A. Rákos (eds), *Altaica Budapestinensia MMII: proceedings of the 45th Permanent International Altaistic Conference (PIAC)*, Budapest, Hungary, June 23–28, 2002. 34–60. Budapest, Hungarian Academy of Sciences.

Bourdieu, L. (1977) *Outline of a Theory of Practice*. Cambridge, Cambridge University Press.

Lemonnier, P. (1993) *Technical Choices. transformation in material cultures since the Neolithic*. London and New York, Routledge.

CHAPTER 1

Keynote Paper

Hidden Agendas: Ancient Raw Material Choice for Worked Osseous Objects in Central Europe and Beyond

Alice M. Choyke

Hard osseous materials have many special characteristics that made them ideal for manufacturing a variety of tools used in many different activities as well as ornaments. Bone and antler tools in particular are especially good for use on skins, textiles, bark-processing and even ceramic-production. However, efficiency is not the only reason a skeletal element from a particular species might have been chosen to manufacture such tools. The first crucial step in the *chaîne d'operatoire*, raw material selection, was just as dependent on traditions of technical style which in turn is partially connected with the culturally ascribed quality of the animal in a particular place or region. Knowledge of what makes a skeletal element a culturally appropriate raw material for a particular tool or ornament would have been passed down between generations while differences in choice of raw material provided material expression of separate social identities between discrete social groups. Case studies of targeted raw material selection (species and/ or skeletal element) from the Neolithic and Bronze Ages of the Carpathian Basin and Anatolia will be presented here. Each object represents the variety of ways selection of bony raw material may take place.

Keywords
Raw materials; choice; accessibility; physical characteristics; ascribed characteristics.

Introduction

How did selection for osseous materials in manufacturing sequences take place in the past? Artisans certainly considered availability and the physical suitability of a particular raw material but there was a strong subjective element at play as well since there are 'many ways to skin a cat' to produce a bone object (hereafter, 'bone' will be used to generally denote osseous materials). Whether easily available bones from food refuse or rare, expensive imports from far-off lands, bony materials are often closely associated in the minds of artisans with the animals they derive from. For each of those animals there are collective notions held by members of particular societies about both the practical qualities of the raw materials taken from these animals and the ascribed qualities connected to culturally specific notions about the animal itself. In the following, I will aim to show that while practical qualities and limitations of raw materials were always important in raw material selection for tools and ornaments, the symbolic aspects of certain raw materials, closely connected to the culturally ascribed attributes of the animal species they came from as well as technical tradition, could also be of key significance in raw material choice. The case studies presented here, deliberately reflecting a broad range of time and geographical area, comprise very specialized objects to simple tools used in everyday activities.

With the exception of antler and various exotica, bony materials were generally selected either from debris left over from food, hide and food processing within settlements and their immediate surroundings or else were deliberately set aside and preserved for working at some stage of carcass dismemberment. Nevertheless, the reason for choosing certain osseous materials to make tools and ornaments was not only easy availability or that much abused and anachronistic word 'efficiency'. Animal-derived osseous materials have special physical characteristics of surface and durability that make it easy to produce non-splintering, smooth surfaces as well as edges and points on tools that are good for working and processing textiles (in spinning and weaving both wool and plant-based fibres), in basketry and matting, scraping and burnishing hide and leather, bark removal and processing, working soft wood and even moist clay surfaces in ceramic production (LeMoine 1997; Beugnier and Maigrot 2005; Christidou and Legrand 2005, 386).

Thus, choice of which animals and skeletal elements should be selected for making such tools must have been dictated by a shifting combination of availability, appropriateness of the shape of the skeletal element, its fracturing properties and beliefs in the qualities of certain bones and animal species. Local butchering and food processing traditions further narrowed which bones remained available for working. Potentially, many skeletal elements from a range of available species fit criteria needed to make them good raw material for making tools and ornaments. Family, local and regional beliefs and traditions could thus still play a role in what materials could and should be selected for manufacturing.

Not only were 'bone' tools parts of tool kits but osseous materials could also be shaped to make a variety of end-product objects such as projectile points, and parts for compound composite objects made in mixed materials. Further, bony materials could be shaped into beads, ornaments, amulets and decorative clothing accoutrements such as buckles, clasps and pins. Very often it seems that more considered selection for raw material, reflecting layers of social meaning, went into the production of such individual objects that, in addition to their actual function, also possessed social components related to display and/or ritual. The choice of raw materials for making such objects must have been frequently dictated by widely held beliefs in the power of the intrinsic attributes of the animal species and particular skeletal elements to increase the efficacy of the object. The ultimate expression of such selection of various parts of the animal body harnessing the ascribed power of the animal may be found in protective amulets. Skeletal elements, particularly from the head and feet, have been and continue to be used as protective amulets with the single bone representing the living animal (Choyke 2010, 201). Even today, for example, the 'lucky' rabbit's foot can be found dangling from key chains or car mirrors. Prehistoric 'bone' tools tended to be household products, made individually rather than in workshop environments, although their form

and use may have followed rather strict rules of manufacture, morphology and use. 'Bone' objects from proto-historic and historic assemblages, especially from urban contexts, are often less individual. Products of such workshops reflect customer demand, are usually made in a series and tend to be more rapidly affected by the fashion dictates of the day. These bone objects lean toward standardization, differing only in the degree of serialization, mass-production and uniformity. Standardization was related to increasing levels of industrialized production characteristically found in complex state-level societies, and particularly in urban settings. Predictability in production often dictated raw material choices on the part of artisans in more permanent workshops (Choyke 2012a, 2012b).

However, whatever the time period, individual people or defined groups still chose special materials to express various social identities and increase their efficacy. Conversely, changes in the choice of raw material could be deliberately manipulated and made visible in the face of resistance to change in local, traditional attitudes. Examples of the latter process can be found in many places in the modern world where ancient forms, originally produced from various hard osseous materials, are today made in plastic, a raw material representing 'progress and modernity'(Choyke 2008, 8–9).

Sources of raw materials

There are a variety of sources for raw materials that were available for artisans. Hard osseous materials could come from the carcasses of domestic animals. In prehistoric communities these were often animals living intimately with the population. Animals were brought to the settlements, slaughtered and their carcasses split up, together with the bones. Animal bodies were further divided in food processing. At any point in these post-mortem processes, bones could be extracted for working. Osseous materials intended for planned, standardized types would be extracted earlier in the process and ad hoc tools after food processing, including marrow extraction and consumption.

With the rise of urban, complex society domestic animals were raised at more of a distance from consumers. Bones for working often entered the manufacturing chain through the mediation of other craftspeople such as butchers and leather-workers. Large workshops either used specific bones from butcher's and leather-working ateliers, improving predictability in manufacturing, while smaller, more mobile bone-workshops would have been dependent on more variable scrap bone, largely from horse or cattle-sized animals. After the commencement of Neolithic to our own time, domestic animals remained one of the chief sources of raw material bone in Europe and the Near East.

Wild animals provided another source of bone as well as tusk and antler, albeit one that involved more energy to procure with less predictable outcomes. Prehistoric manufacturing often involved targeted use of wild bone for particular standard tool and ornament types although wild bone could also be used to make more expedient objects as well (for a discussion of expediency in bone tool manufacture see the classic study of Eileen Johnson (1982; Choyke 1997). Hunting was often the privilege of elites.

In contrast to the situation with bone, some raw materials from animals were gathered seasonally. This is the situation for shell and, more importantly, cervid antler, particularly red deer (*Cervus elaphus*). Whether in prehistoric or proto-historic and historic times, antler was always a very important source of raw material, valued for its density and resilience (MacGregor 1985, 18) and its connection to the powerful male of an important game species. Most of the antler, however, came not from hunted animals but from shed antler, gathered in the early spring when stags dropped their antlers (MacGregor 1985, 32, 35).

Gathering this highly valued raw material would always have been organized among people intimately familiar with the surrounding environs of a settlement since individual stags tend to drop their racks in the same locations. They need to be gathered quickly to avoid damage through gnawing by the deer themselves, in addition to damage from insects and rodents. Antler can be stored in cool damp places for future use over the year. Whole or segmented antler found in pits and sometimes interpreted as ritual deposits, are more likely to represent abandoned, stored antler in the absence of any other material evidence.

Antler is normally worked after soaking for a couple of weeks either in a slightly acidic solution or even simply in water (Osipowicz 2007, 2, 19; Schibler 2001) during which residual blood may be released into the water making it appear almost a living material (Adám Vecsey, per comm. 2011). Soaking makes it soft and much more malleable (MacGregor 1985, 63). The compacta, especially in the beam closest to the skull, is quite thick so it can be used to make more massive objects than bone. Antler is also more elastic and resistant to breakage from sudden shocks (MacGregor 1985, 26–28), a fact consistent with the way the stags use their antlers for fighting. Therefore, antler, especially from red deer, was often used to make ornaments as well as combs, hammer/adzes and axes in both prehistoric and historic times.

From very earliest times imported raw materials or objects made from exotic raw materials have been considered valuable. Such exotic raw materials include Spondylus shells, in circulation during the Neolithic and Chalcolithic periods across Europe. Archaeological spondylus shell has received particular scholarly attention in recent years culminating in an edited volume by Infantidis and Nickolaidou (2011). Within that same volume, the article by Siklósi and Csengeri (2011) shows the importance of spondylus artefacts in graves to gender and age differentiation in the Middle to Late Neolithic of the

Carpathian Basin as well. Finally, in addition to numerous other occurrences of shells used as beads or even utensils, cowrie shells should also be mentioned. They were frequently used as ornaments and amulets from Palaeolithic times. Cowry shells were often imitated in other materials such as stone, clay, bone, mother of pearl, metal and glass and examples of this even may be found in Migration period Hungary. They were even used as money in India and China in the ancient past, along with their imitations in a variety of other raw materials (Kovács 2008, 41–43, 44–47, 52–55).

The other notable class of finds made from imported or traded raw materials in the same region comprises objects made from elephant and hippopotamus ivory which appear in assemblages from the Chalcolithic and Early Bronze Age in the Near East and in Central Europe during the Roman period, as the ivory trade expanded and many luxury objects made from both elephant and hippo ivory (Barnett 1982, 71) appear in the archaeological record. In early medieval Northern Europe at least, walrus and whale tooth ivories also become quite important (MacGregor 1985, 38–41; Smirnova 2001; O'Connor this volume) raw materials in the production of both secular and religious elite objects such as the truly exotic (for Hungary) bishop's crosier (Fig. 1.1) found in the area of a twelfth century monastery in the Queen's palace in Vesprem, Hungary. The trade in elephant ivory increased steadily, especially during the Middle Ages and Early Modern times (Rijkelijkhuizen 2009) so that while still valuable it gradually became available to a developing middle class. The beginnings of this process can also be traced in the relatively consistent presence of 15th and 16th century single piece double-sided ivory combs found in archaeological excavations of urban settlements including Hungary (Choyke and Kováts 2010).

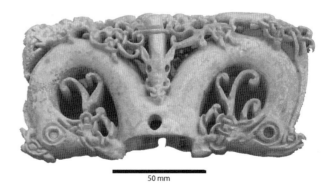

50 mm

Figure 1.1 Imported walrus ivory Bishop's crosier (early medieval) from the area of a monastery in the twelfth century queen's palace in Veszprem, Hungary. The type is typical of early medieval walrus ivory examples from Northern Europe (photograph: Alice Choyke).

Physical qualities of raw materials

Animal bone, antler, teeth (including ivory and tusk) and shell all share different properties which made them more or less appropriate to be manufactured into particular tools and ornaments used for a variety of activities. Horn, normally missing from archaeological assemblages, will not be discussed here. MacGregor (1985; MacGregor and Currey 1983) has provided the best review of the mechanical differences between these different parts of the animal body. Bone tends to be harder and break longitudinally along the diaphysis of the long bones. It is also more brittle than antler (MacGregor 1985, 25) and therefore much better for making into objects requiring sharp points or hard edges such as awls and scrapers.

Ethnographically attested ascribed characteristics of osseous raw materials

Although a great deal of work has been done to understand raw material distributions within the practical aspects of manufacturing technologies, rather less attention has been paid to more subjective but no less important reasons to explain raw material selection in the past. Here, ethnographies can be used to provide models of how such selection based on traditional ascribed belief systems may have worked. This kind of selection moves beyond the practical limitations set by availability, skeletal element morphology (size and shape restrictions) and the mechanical properties of a particular raw material all outlined above. As mentioned, there were many adequate raw material choices available to individual craftspeople and yet we see over and over again that even for simple tools artisans from a particular cultural context tend to choose from a restricted menu of species and skeletal elements.

Although 19th and early 20th century ethnographers put together long, descriptive lists of objects used by the people they studied, some of which includes valuable descriptions of types, technology and function such as the handbook of California Indians (Kroeber 1925). However, only passing mention is usually made of why a particular raw material was chosen – the practical self-evident physical traits being taken for granted as the main guiding factors in selection. Nevertheless, animal skeletal elements may also have been sometimes deliberately selected for manufacture based on the ascribed characteristics of the animal they come from. Thus, bones from one animal species may have been preferred for making particular tools used in certain activities because the finished object was seen as imbued with the attributed characteristics of the animal.

A modern, Italian example collected by the author would be special awls used to test the quality of Parma hams called '*osso di cavallo*' (Fig. 1.2). According to informants these objects must be made from horse bone because "horse is pure and will not pollute the ham and takes up the scent of the meat better than the bones from other animals." This idea is given as the reason for separating shops selling horse meat exclusively and those selling meat from pigs, cattle and caprines. Furthermore, this cortical tissue from horse long bone diaphysis is selected to be carved into something closely resembling the fibula of a horse. The awls were used mostly by men and could even be inherited. Even after 20 years of use the manufacturing wear was still visible above the tip of the awl shown in Figure 1.2. There are examples of this kind of meat processing tool, made exclusively from horse bone from Gyula in South-Eastern Hungary as well (Anna Biller, per. comm. 2011).

There is other scattered ethnographic reporting that supports the idea that different skeletal elements may also be

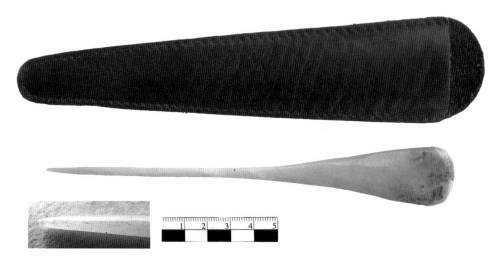

Figure 1.2 This modern tool, the osso di cavallo *for testing Parma-type hams, is made consciously with horse bone. The inset of the tip shows the remains of manufacturing striations after 20 years of continuous but gentle use (photograph: Alice Choyke).*

ascribed particular characteristics or powers. Animal scapulae, for example were often used as divination bones in the not too far distant past, the astragali of various species (bovid, cervid, beaver, canid) are also good examples of skeletal elements routinely ascribed special qualities even today in various parts of the world. Birtalan (2003, 37) actually reveals a huge range of largely apotropaic beliefs associated with different parts of the animal body in Iron Age Mongolia that may be found in ancient texts and even today canid and caprine bronze astragali are used as amulets for trucks in Mongolia. Animal teeth from a variety of species were used in multiple ways. Whether prehistoric or historic they were usually considered a special and valuable raw material, something probably related to the difficulty involved in procuring the teeth of dangerous carnivores and wild boar and a transfer of those special qualities to the human wearer. In prehistoric times, teeth often functioned as both ornament and amulet representing the whole of the animal, embodying the so-called pars pro toto principle, along with that animal's ascribed characteristics. Examples of imitation of animal claws, animal teeth and astragali in bronze and other media appear in the northern Iron Age across Europe and Asia in a zone extending from the Baltic countries into Mongolia (Luik 2010, 46).

Finally, a word should be added about the special subjective, symbolic qualities of antler. The red deer stag, with its imposing antler rack, was a frequent subject of iconographic display over time and space across Europe and Eurasia. Ethnographically, red deer was considered both an important game animal and an important totem animal in stories of clan genesis in many parts of Eurasia (Jacobsen 1993, 47). In Hungarian, a Finno-Ugric language, '*szarvas*' is the word used to refer to deer. The root of '*szarvas*' is the word for 'antler', that is, the one who has antlers – since direct naming of important totem animals was taboo. Although the meaning ascribed to this cervid certainly altered depending on the cultural context the fact remains that antler would have had a gendered, wild aspect to it as well. Furthermore, personal experience has shown that antler, even old antler, will exude blood when soaked. All these factors must have affected attitudes towards what could or should be made from antler.

The folklore literature of 19th and early 20th century Europe clearly reveals that such ideas about the power inherent to different parts of animal physiognomy were not restricted to Mongolia. Similar symbolic aspects of raw material choice have been noted in other cultural spheres as well. McGhee (1977) describes the symbolic use of certain raw materials among the Inuits of Arctic Canada and Greenland. For example, at the Thuile winter village of Debliquy (QiLe-l), the six harpoon heads (for hunting sea mammals) brought to light during excavations are made either from ivory or sea mammal bone, while all eight of the arrowheads are made from caribou antler (for hunting land game), a generalization that may be extended to other Thule groups (McGhee 1977, 142, 144). He postulates that:

"ivory was linked symbolically by the Thule craftsman with a set of mutually associated concepts: sea mammals, women, birds, and winter life on the sea ice. Antler, the most useful alternative to ivory in Thule technology, may have been linked with a set of concepts opposed to these: land mammals, particularly the caribou, men and summer life on the land" (McGhee 1977, 145).

This is consistent with the Thule view that the world was divided in a sea realm and a land realm, with land and sea animals seen in an opposition that was extended to technology (McGhee 1977, 146).

Thus, choice of raw materials can depend on availability both in terms of the species that are exploited and the ways in which their bodies are divided and broken up during food and hide-processing. Choice is also connected to the form and mechanical properties of the raw material being selected and finally selection can depend on traditions of manufacture and culturally ascribed qualities which may be closely connected to beliefs in the animal or skeletal element itself. These various aspects always work in combination with one or more taking precedence. Two archaeological examples from very different archaeological contexts will be presented here.

Specialized objects with specific raw materials

In households, villages or special contexts, there is often a strong consensus about how and why special objects should be made in very particular ways. One such example is the well-known Early Neolithic cattle metapodial bone spoons from the Carpathian Basin (Nandris 1972; Choyke 2007, 655; Selena Vitezović, poster presented at the 2011 WBRG in Salzburg; Popuşoi and Beldiman 1993–1998, 148; Makkay 1990, 24–28). Among the small, semi-permenent Starcevo-Körös-Kriş culture sites in the Carpathian Basin these rules of raw material selection and manufacture and use were very strictly enforced for around 600 years. It was John Nandris (1972) who first suggested that these special and rather beautiful objects were made exclusively from the metatarsus of wild cattle (*Bos primegenius*). A closer look shows that these spoons were made from the metatarsus of both wild and large domestic cattle (*Bos taurus* Linné 1758) alike. A complete spoon from Ecsegfalva (Choyke 2007), was made from a large domestic cattle or small aurochs while based on size, the broken handle-end could well have been carved from the distal metatarsus of a large wild cattle (Fig. 1.3). These spoons were continuously re-modelled and re-used and may have been used over long periods of a household's existence through settlement moves every few years. Their consistent presence on archaeological sites of the period in the region suggests these objects had a symbolic importance hard to comprehend today.

An example of another special purpose object where the source of particular raw material was very likely to have been entangled with the ascribed characteristics of red deer (*Cervus*

Figure 1.3 Example of Early Neolithic aurochs or domestic cattle metatarsal spoon from the site of Ecsegfalva (after Choyke 2007 [Fig. 18], photograph: Alice Choyke).

elaphus Linné 1758) and the object's use, are seals. The well-preserved object in Figure 1.4 comes from a layer in phase VII at the tell site of Arslantepe in Eastern Anatolia. Phase VII at this site represents the Late Chalcolithic Period in the region (3800–3400 BC). The first evidence of monumental, elite architecture appears in this phase at the site. Use of clay sealings (cretula), evidence a degree of administrative management of goods has been found even earlier in the Middle Chalcolithic, Ubaid, large village context at Arslantepe where the author identified small stamp seals made from ivory and wild boar tusk (Christiani *et al.* 2007, 364–365, 415).

While clay sealings are plentiful, with over 2000 examples representing 200 iconographic types discovered in special contexts in the Palace complex from the Final Chalcolithic phase at the tell, seals themselves are relatively rare, perhaps because seals would have been kept with the people with rights to use them and even buried with them (Laurito and Lemorini 2008, 414). The seal from the Late Chalcolithic (phase VII) at Arslantepe has been studied closely although unfortunately not by a trained zooarchaeologist. Much of the experimental work was carried out on the premise that the seal (Arslantepe VII, inv. no. 3994) was carved from a cattle patella (Christiani *et al.* 2007, 365; Laurito and Lemorini 2008, 416)! In fact, the seal (Fig. 1.4 a–b) is made from the rose (i.e. the burr) and lower beam of a smallish red deer antler rack. The design shows a stylised bull and a lion. The authors correctly note the presence of spongiosa at the centre of the

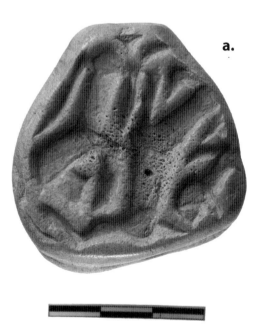 

Figure 1.4 Seal made from red deer antler rose and beam from Late Chalcolithic levels at the tell site of Arslantepe in Eastern Anatolia. a) Seal face b) side view with suspension hole (photograph: Roberto Ceccacci).

design, a feature which was noted on a number of clay sealings suggesting that it was usual to use antler as well as ivory, clay, stone and wood, to manufacture seals (Christiani *et al.* 2007, 364–365; Laurito and Lemorini 2008, 414).

Other tools can be found made from antler in the Late Chalcolithic and its final phases at the site indicating that antler was available as a raw material. The small rose and lower beam of young stags would have been an ideal size for creating the most common middle range cluster of seals (4.1–5.06 cm; Laurito and Lemorini 2008, 414). The density and malleability of antler would also have made it an appropriate raw material for seals.

The 4th millennium glyptics on sealings at Arslantepe (Frangipane and Pittman 2007) show a preference for animals with red deer and goats being the most commonly depicted animals (ibid., 251). In addition there are fantastical animals with antler racks and other designs stylising the antler rack alone as a design. Thus, the choice of antler may also be linked to the importance of red deer stags in the iconography of Arslantepe glyptics.

Special objects such as these spoons and the antler seal are often made from a very restricted range of raw materials. Perhaps, the very species and skeletal elements chosen in the manufacture of particular tools, ornaments and special purpose objects such as the stamp may have been ascribed special affective qualities that can only be guessed at today.

Simple tools, targeted raw materials over huge region over centuries

Strong selection of raw material also occurred in much simpler tools used in daily activities around the settlements. Often similarities in choice of raw materials and manufacturing methods for certain tool types appeared and spread relatively rapidly over apparently broad areas within Central and Eastern Europe. These simple tools seemingly represent the general technical ethos of an era with widespread consensus in what kinds of tools should be used in certain manufacturing processes. The question is not why such tools are produced but rather how such consensus developed in terms of raw material selection and manufacturing over extended periods and regions.

The Early Bronze Age in Europe and Eurasia is characterized by the appearance of mandible-based 'thong-smoothers' from Khazakstan (Botai culture at around 2800 BC, Olsen 2001). However, a century or so later these tools appear on Early Bronze Age sites in Slovenia, Hungary and the Czech Republic (Rene Kysely, pers. comm. 2009). These tools were made from the mandibles of cattle, horse and red deer depending on availability. The mandibles are modified distal to and around the third molar (Fig. 1.5 a–b). Appearance of these thong-smoothers may be connected to a need to produce quantities of straps associated with control of domestic horses. This was

also a period where people are on the move through actual population movements and trade. Mandible-based thong-smoothers disappear from the archaeological record in this form within 200 years.

Later a similar phenomenon occurs with a radius-based tool of unknown function from the end of the Middle Bronze

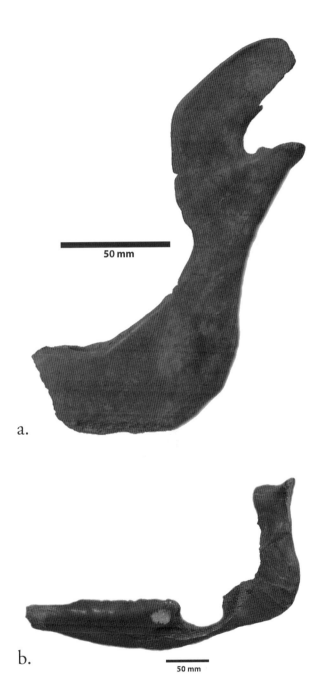

a.

b.

Figure 1.5 a) Early Bronze Age cattle mandible thong-smoother from Ljubiansko Barje in Slovenia (photograph: Alice Choyke) and b) Early Bronze Age (Bell-Beaker) cattle mandible thong-smoother from Szigetszentmiklós-Üdülösor in Budapest on a Danube River island (photograph: Alice Choyke).

Age to the beginning of the Late Bronze Age, found on sites in a huge geographical area stretching from the Black Sea (Valentin Pankovskiy, per comm. 2012) to Hungary (Choyke and Bartosiewicz 2009; Kustár and Tugya, B. 2010), to Slovakia and even Poland (at Biskupen) by the Early Iron Age (Drzewicz 2004). Although most earlier publications describe these objects as skates and the wear on them mimics wear on actual bone skates it is now clear that these were tools, used in some kind of widespread and important craft activity, perhaps leather or felt-working. The fact that they can be made on species differing in size from aurochs to roe deer or even wild pig clearly indicates that they could not be skates. They are characterized by a facet extending along the dorsal face and may sometimes be drilled in a medio-lateral direction through the distal diaphysis just above the epiphysis (Fig. 1.6 a–c).

The species selected is clearly affected by local availability. In Hungary, these tools are made mostly from cattle but in Slovakia, for example at the large early Late Middle Bronze age tell site of Nitriansky Hrádok, species used varied from

domestic cattle, horse, caprines, red deer, roe deer and wild pig. However, artisans everywhere adhered strictly to the rule that these objects should be made from radius showing that this tradition was copied from place to place and the choice of skeletal element involved rigorous selection whatever the minor local differences in the formal morphology of the tool.

Discussion

Degrees of similarity in the choices made in bone tool production reflect manufacturing traditions which were acquired from other, more experienced family members at the household level by watching and practice. However, people marry or move outside their close community for other reasons such as trade, bringing styles of object manufacture to new social contexts. That is the mechanism by which local rules of bone tool and ornament manufacture spread. These rules mark one way individuals may express various degrees of social

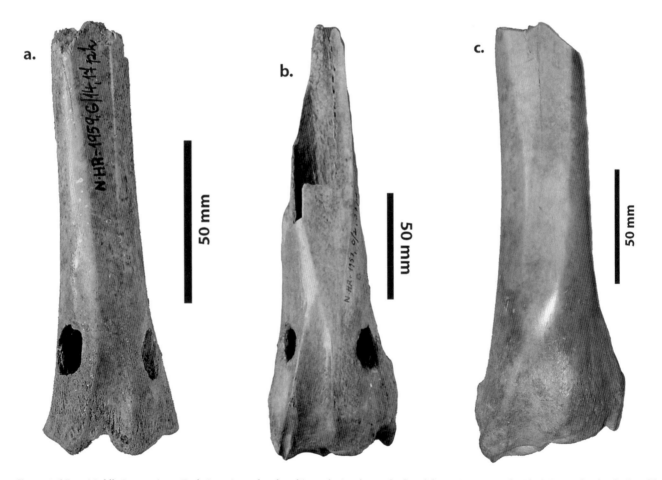

Figure 1.6 Late Middle Bronze Age – Early Iron Age radius-based 'smoother' tools may be found from Hungary to the Black Sea and Poland. a) Wild pig (Sus scrofa) radius smoother from late Middle Bronze Age levels at the tell site of Nitriansky Hrádok (Mad'arovce Culture) in southern Slovakia. b) Red deer radius thong-smoother, also from Nitriansky Hrádok. c) Cattle thong-smoother from the late Middle Bronze A levels at the tell site of Százhalombatta-Földvár over-looking the Danube River in Hungary, just 30 km south of Budapest (photograph: Alice Choyke).

consensus in a variety of groups organized around age, gender, social status, occupational and regional identities.

Bone manufacturing of everyday objects in prehistoric times would have been largely learned within the household. The form and manufacture of such objects tends to be conservative, making utilitarian objects particularly sensitive indicators of local social affiliations (Choyke 2009; Choyke *et al.* 2004). In proto-historic and historic times in urban contexts these close links between individual expressions of their place in society and styles of manufacture were greatly weakened since form and style would have been influenced by greater mobility and driven by market forces. Nevertheless, the technology of daily life exemplified in bone implements suggests shared public knowledge (Ingold 1990) and a prescribed consensus for how certain objects should be made, for instance on the immediate household, village or even wide regional level. Tools made from osseous materials are also linked to the source of the raw materials, that is, animals exploited though husbandry, hunting or trade.

In addition to questions of relative availability of particular species and the suitability of skeletal elements in manufacturing targeted objects, culture specific, symbolic or iconographic attitudes toward animals also influence which of their skeletal parts are chosen for the production of tools and ornaments. In this manner, worked osseous objects connect people to the society they live in, the people and animals around them as well as events with their own emotional associations. Objects are connected in a complex network of social and symbolic ideas even if these not always explicitly understood by the people making and using the objects. Workers of bone objects in pre-industrial periods in the Carpathian Basin and beyond, thus, made continuous, informed technical choices at most stages of production from procurement and choice of raw material to final decoration. Constrained by both conscious and, perhaps, unexpressed but understood traditions within the narrow focus of the household in traditional, conservative village and town settings, these choices were nevertheless subject to individual interpretations (Wobst 1999, 120–121). Inherent in the manufacturing of all material objects was the knowledge of manufacturing processes that are passed on from person to person through dozens of generations but always with the possibility of being modified within acceptable social limits by craftspeople (Gosselain 1992).

Thus, there is a constant pressure to maintain social-practice in traditional societies that would have been generally characteristic of prehistoric societies in Europe and the Near East. Personal connectivity in state-level society workshop contexts might have been somewhat more attenuated but even in the more complex societies of the Early States period in this region there seems to have been pressure for conformity at this manufacturing level. This social pressure for maintaining sameness has been called habitus (Bourdieu 1977). Together with a shared familiarity in the manufacturing practice and its continuous repetition, Bourdieu considered this shared technical

knowledge one way communities could maintain social stability in the face of external pressures for change. Thus, as one way of maintaining social coherence, people would have especially relied on this "habituation, familiarity, and repetition" in their daily round of activities (Stark 1999, 28). Conversely, marked and sudden changes in the way people chose to make their tools surely signal the advent of significant social change, whether in the form of new ideas or actual movement of new populations into the area. This is also reflected in the way prehistoric craftspeople worked osseous materials.

Conclusions

Like any other class of archaeological artefact, 'bone tools and ornaments' are particularly useful for answering certain kinds of questions and less useful for answering others. Studying worked osseous materials also requires specialized know-how particularly with regard to recognition of the raw material, manufacturing techniques and use wear, studies that can only be acquired through serious study and practice. Identification is only the first step albeit a critical one. Recognizable patterns of raw material choice need to be placed within their own particular cultural contexts.

Given the tendency toward conservatism in the form and function of such tools, especially in prehistoric times, changes in the manufacturing process, for example are particularly good markers of profound cultural change. Differences and changes in the way artisans selected raw materials at the level of serial workshop production can also elucidate economic organization in proto-historic and historic contexts. The study of technical style, starting with raw material choice, sheds light on the way individuals used osseous materials, to express social and spiritual identities. This field of study has shown marked growth internationally and will slowly but surely improve our understanding of how people in the past lived.

Bibliography

Barnett, R. D. (1982) *Ancient Ivories in the Middle East*. Jerusalem, Institute of Archaeology, Hebrew University.

Beugnier, V. and Maigrot, Y. (2005) La fonction des outillages en matières dures animales et en silex au Néolithique final. *Bulletin de la Société préhistorique française*, 102 (2), 335–344.

Birtalan, A. 2003 Ritualistic use of livestock bones in the Mongolian belief system and customs. *Altaica Budapestinensia* MMII, 34–62.

Bourdieu, P. (1977) *Outline of a Theory of Practice*. Cambridge, Cambridge University Press.

Choyke A. M. (1997) The manufacturing continuum. *Anthropozoologica* 25–26, 65–72.

Choyke A. M. (2007) Objects for a lifetime – tools for a season: the worked osseous material from Ecsegfalva 23. In A. Whittle (ed.), *The Early Neolithic on the Great Hungarian Plain. Investigations of the Körös Culture Site of Ecsegfalva 23, County Békés*. Vol. II, Varia Archaeologica Hungarica XXI, 641–666. Budapest, Institute of Archaeology of the Hungarian Academy of Sciences.

Choyke A. M. (2008) Shifting meaning and value through imitation in the European Late Neolithic. In P. F. Biehl and J. Rassamakin (eds), *Import and Imitation in Archaeology*, 5–22. Langenweissach, Verlag Beier & Beran (Schriften des Zentrums für Archäologie und Kulturgeschichte des Schwarzmeerraumes 11).

Choyke, A. M. (2009b) Grandmother's awl: individual and collective memory through material culture. In I. Barbiera, A. Choyke and J. Rasson (eds), *Materializing Memory, Archaeological Material Culture and the Semantics of the Past*, 21–40. Oxford, Archaeopress (British Archaeological Report S1977).

Choyke, A. (2010) The bone is the beast: animal amulets and ornaments in power and magic. In D. Campana, P. Crabtree, S. D. DeFrance, J. Lev-Tov and A. Choyke (eds), *Anthropological Approaches to Zooarchaeology: colonialism, complexity, and animal transformations*, 197–209. Oxford, Oxbow Books.

Choyke, A. M. (2012a) The bone workshop in the church of San Lorenzo in Lucina. In O.Brandt (ed.), San Lorenzo in Lucina. *The transformations of a Roman quarter*, 335–346. Stockholm, Swedish Institute in Rome (Acta Instituti Romani Regni Sueciae 4 (61)).

Choyke, A. M. (2012b) Skeletal elements from animals as raw materials. In M. Biró, A. M. Choyke, L. Vass and Á. Vecsey (eds), *Bone Objects in Aquincum*, 43–53. Budapest, History Museum, Budapest (Az Aquincum Múzeum Gyűjteménye 2/Collections of the Aquincum Museum 2).

Choyke, A. M. and Bartosiewicz, L. (2005) Skating with horses: continuity and parallelism in prehistoric Hungary. *Revue de Paléobiologie*, vol. spec. 10, Ville de Genève, Muséum d'Histoire Naturelle, 317–326.

Choyke, A. M. and Bartosiewicz, L. (2009) Telltale tools from a tell: bone and antler manufacturing at Bronze Age Jászdózsa–Kápolnahalom, Hungary. *Tiscium* XX, 357–376.

Choyke, A. and Kováts, I. (2010) Tracing the personal through generations: Late Medieval and Ottoman combs. In A. Pluskovski, G. K. Kunst M. Kucera, M Bietak and I. Hein (eds), *Bestial Mirrors: using animals to construct human identities in Medieval Europe*, 115–127. Vienna, Vienna Institute for Archaeological Science, University of Vienna (Animals as Material Culture in the Middle Ages 3).

Choyke A. M., Vretemark M. and Stens S. (2004) Levels of social identity expressed in the refuse and worked bone from the Middle Bronze Age Százhalombatta-Földvár, Vatya Culture, Hungary. In S. Jones O'Day, W. van Neer and A. Ervynck (eds), *Behaviour Behind Bones: the zooarchaeology of ritual, religion, status and identity*, 177–189. Oxford, Oxbow Books.

Christiani, E., Laurito, R. and Lemorini C. (2007) Methods of manufacture and materials used in seal production at Arslantepe. In M. Frangipane, P. Ferioli, E. Fiandra, R Laurito, and H. Pittman (eds), Arslantepe Cretulae. *An Early Centralised Administrative System before Writing*. 355–380. Rome, Università di Roma a La Sapeienza.

Christidou, R. and Legrand, A. (2005) Hide working and bone tools: experimentation design and applications. In H. Luik, A. Choyke, C. Batey and L. Lõugas (eds), *From Hooves to Horns, from Mollusc to Mammoth: manufacture and use of bone artifacts from prehistoric times to the present*. 385–396. Proceedings of the 4th meeting of the (ICAZ) Worked Bone Research Group, Tallinn, (Muiasaja Teadus 15).

Drzewicz, A. (2004) *Wyroby z kości i poroża z osiedla obronnego ludności kultury łużyckiej w Biskupinie* (Bone and Antler Implements from the Ludnosci Culture site of Biskupinie), Warsaw, Wydawn Nauk. Semper.

Frangipane, M. and Pittman, H. (2007) The fourth millenium glyptics at Arslantepe. In M. Frangipane, P. Ferioli, E. Fiandra, R Laurito, and H. Pittman (eds), Arslantepe Cretulae. *An Early Centralised Administrative System before Writing*. 175–354. Rome, Università di Roma a La Sapeienza.

Gosselain, O. (1992) Technology and style: potters and pottery among the Bafia of Cameroon. *Man* (New Series) 27, 559–586.

Ifantidis, F. and Nikolaidou, M. (eds), (2011) *Spondylus in Prehistory: new data and approaches – contributions to the archaeology of shell technologies*. Oxford, Archaeopress (British Archaeological Report S2216).

Ingold, T. (1990) Society, nature and the concept of technology. *Archaeological Review from Cambridge* 9 (1), 5–17.

Jacobsen, E. (1993) *The Deer Goddess of Ancient Siberia*. Leiden, Brill.

Johnson, E. (1982) Paleo-Indian bone expediency tools: Lubbock Lake and Bonfire Shelter. *Canadian Journal of Anthropology* 2 (2), 145–157.

Kovács, L. (2008) *Vulvae, Eyes, Snake Heads: archaeological finds of cowrie amulets*. Oxford, Archaeopress (British Archaeological Report S1846).

Kroeber, A. (1925) *The Handbook of the Indians of California*. Washington, Goverment Printing office (Smithsonian Institution, Bureau of American Ethnology Bulletin 78).

Kustár, R. and Tugya, B. (2010) "Csontkorsolyák" a késő bronzkorban ("Bone skates" in the Late Bronze Age). In J. Gömöri and A. Kőrösi (eds), *Csont és bőr: az állati eredetű nyersanyagok feldolgozásának története, régészete és néprajza* (Bone and Leather: history, archaeology and ethnography of crafts utilizing raw materials from animals), 19–30. Sopron (Hungary), Magyar Tudományos Akadémia VEAB Soproni Tudós Társasága.

Laurito, R. and Lemorini, C. (2008) Seal Impressions on Cretulae at Arslantepe: a new approach. In H. Kühne, R. M. Czichon, and F. Janoscha Kreppner (eds), *Proceedings of the 4th International Congress of the Archaeology of the Ancient Near East, 29 March–3 April 2004, Vol 1*, 413–420. Wiesbaden, Harrassowitz Verlag.

Le Moine, G. (1997) *Use Wear Analysis on Bone and Antler Tools of the Mackenzie Inuit*. Oxford, Archaeopress (British Archaeological Report S679).

Luik, H. (2010) Beaver in the economy and social communication of the inhabitants of south Estonia in the Viking Age (800–1050 AD). In A. Pluskovski, G. K. Kunst M. Kucera, M. Bietak and I. Hein (eds), *Bestial Mirrors: using animals to construct human identities in Medieval Europe*, 46–54. Vienna, Vienna Institute for Archaeological Science, University of Vienna (Animals as Material Culture in the Middle Ages 3).

MacGregor A. and Currey, J. D. (1983) Mechanical properties as conditioning factors in the bone and antler industry of the 3rd to the 13th century AD. *Journal of Archaeological Science* 10, 71–77.

MacGregor, A. (1985) *Bone, Ivory and Horn. The Technology of Skeletal Material since the Roman Period*. London, Croom Helm.

Makkay J. (1990) Knochen, Geweih und Eberzahngegenstände der frühneolithischen Körös-Kultur. *Communicationes Archaeologicae Hungariae* (1990), 23–58.

Nandris J. (1972) *Bos primigenius* and the bone spoon. *Bulletin of the Institute of Archaeology, University of London* 10, 63–82.

McGhee, R. (1977) Ivory for the Sea Woman: the symbolic attributes of a prehistoric technology. *Canadian Journal of Archaeology* 1, 141–149.

O'Connor, S. (this volume) Exotic materials used in the construction of Iron Age sword handles from South Cave, UK. In A. Choyke and S. O'Connor (eds), *From These Bare Bones: raw materials and the study of worked osseous materials*. Oxford. Oxbow Books.

Olsen, S. (2001). The importance of thong-smoothers at Botai, Khazakstan. In A. M. Choyke and L. Bartosiewicz (eds), *Crafting Bone – skeletal technologies through time and space*, 197–206. Oxford, Archaeopress (British Archaeological Report S937).

Osipowicz, G. (2007) Bone and antler: softening techniques in prehistory of the north eastern part of the Polish Highlands in the light of experimental archaeology and microtrace analysis. *euroREA* 4, 1–22.

Popușoi, E. and Beldiman, C. (1993–1998) L'industrie des matières dures animals dans le site de la cvilization Starčevo-Criş Trestiana, dép. De Vaslui. Un example d'étude: les spatules. *Acta Moldaviae Meridoalis* XV–XX (1), 82–115.

Rijkelijkhuizen, M. (2009) Whales, walruses, and elephants: artisans in ivory, baleen and other skeletal materials in seventeenth- and eighteenth-century Amsterdam. *International Journal of Historical Archaeology* 13 (4), 409–430.

Schibler, J. (2001) Experimental production of neolithic bone and antler tools. In A. Choyke and L. Bartosiewicz (eds), *Crafting Bone – Skeletal Technologies through Time and Space*, 63–5. Oxford, Archaeopress (British Archaeological Report S937).

Siklósi, Zs. and Csengeri, P. (2011) Reconsideration of Spondylus usage in the Middle and Late Neolithic of the Carpathian Basin. In F. Ifantidis and M. Nikolaidou (eds), *Spondylus in Prehistory: new data and approaches – contributions to the archaeology of shell technologies*, 47–62. Oxford, Archaeopress (British Archaeological Report S2216).

Smirnova, L. (2001) Utilization of rare bone materials in Medieval Novgorod. In A. M. Choyke and L. Bartosiewicz (eds), *Crafting Bone–Skeletal Technologies through Time and Space*, 9–18. Oxford, Archaeopress (British Archaeological Report S937).

Stark, M. (1999) Social dimensions of technical choice in Kalinga ceramic traditions. In E. S. Chilton (ed.), *Material Meanings: critical approaches to the interpretation of material culture*. 24–43. Salt Lake City, University of Utah Press.

Wobst, M. (1999) Style in archaeology or archaeologists in style. In E. S. Chilton (ed.), *Material Meanings: critical approaches to the interpretation of material culture*, 118–132. Salt Lake City, University of Utah Press.

Raw Material Selection and Curation within Tool Types

Chapter 2

Osseous Retouchers from the Final Mousterian and Uluzzian Levels at Fumane Cave (Verona, Italy): Preliminary Results

Camille Jéquier, Matteo Romandini, Marco Peresani

This contribution presents the results of a study carried out on a large sample of retouchers made from osseous materials found in the Uluzzian and Mousterian layers at Fumane Cave (Verona, northern Italy). This osseous industry has attracted the interest of many researchers in the last decades, in order to reconstruct stepwise lithic reduction sequences and site formation processes with the help of lithic technology and experimental references. The analysis of 148 pieces focused on inferring the criteria which lead the selection of the blanks, the use and discard in each separate stratigraphical unit. Middle Palaeolithic groups, in general, used long bones from ungulates, mostly cervids, due to their similar morphological characteristics: straight, flat and thick. A canine from *Ursus spelaeus*, a femur from *Ursus arctos* and two antler fragments were also used. Four different types of stigmata have been observed: punctiform impressions, linear impressions, striae and wells, whose number, concentration and morphology can vary depending on the strength, intensity of use and degree of preservation of the bone surface.

Keywords
Retouchers; technology; Mousterian; Uluzzian; Fumane.

Introduction

Bone retouchers have a long history of research mostly addressed to their function, but sometimes even their actual existence. After the first description by Henri Martin in 1906 based on the Mousterian series at La Quina (Henri Martin 1906, 1907, 1907–1910), many hypotheses about their significance have been proposed to suggest that they were probably used as retouchers in direct percussion for shaping flint artifacts (Patou-Mathis 2002; Mozota Holgueras 2007a, 2007b). Binford, in contrast, cast doubt on their existence and suggested that carnivores were the agents of the pits/cores formation (Binford 1981). Retouchers can be made of bone, antler or ivory and do not require any particular preparation, although some pieces show evidences of preliminary scraping. They present four different kinds of stigmata: punctiform impressions, linear impressions, strias and wells (Patou-Mathis and Schwab 2002; Mozota Holgueras 2007a). In Europe, they are known from the Early Palaeolithic through to the Neolithic (Schwab 2002; Giacobini and Patou-Mathis 2002; Patou-Mathis and Schwab 2002; Auguste 2002). However, many different aspects of them are yet to be studied, as for example, possible differences between the stigmata in connection with the methods used in lithic flake-production. Moreover, how these retouchers were used is still to be ascertained. Bordes (1961) explained that the stigmata could be obtained either through direct percussion or pressure. Finally, many site materials are yet to be carefully investigated from an archaeozoological point of view.

The present contribution is part of a broader study conducted on a large sample of bone retouchers found at Fumane Cave (Verona, northern Italy), a key-site for the study of the bio-cultural shift between the Middle and the Upper Palaeolithic and the replacement of *Homo neandertalensis* by Anatomically Modern Humans. The specimens come from the Mousterian layers, A5–A6 dated to 44ky cal BP, and the Uluzzian layers, A3–A4 dated somewhere in the 44–41ky cal BP range, (Higham *et al.* 2009). This preliminary study here shows how the economic choices were structured in terms of raw material choice and skeletal elements selected. Moreover, we will present a typology of the stigmates found on the bone surface after contact with the edge of a stone artefact.

Materials and methods

All of the faunal remains were examined in order to find either entire and fragmentary items bearing traces ascribable to this kind of tool. Taxonomic and anatomic identification was carried out, making use of the faunal collection stored at the University of Ferrara and at the Pigorini Museum in Rome. Taphonomic as well as technological analyses were carried out using an optical microscope (Leica S6D Green Ough, 10× to 64× magnification).

Fumane Cave

Fumane Cave lies at 350 masl in the Lessini Mountains. It was discovered in 1964 and has been systematically excavated since 1988 under the direction of teams from the Universities of Milan and Ferrara. The already mentioned importance of this site is connected to the 12m-thick late Pleistocene stratigraphic sequence which finely records the Middle–Upper Palaeolithic boundary. In the Mousterian–Uluzzian sequence, dated to the MIS3 (Higham *et al.* 2009; Peresani *et al.* 2008), huge numbers of well preserved faunal remains and stone artefacts have been found embedded in thin layers excavated by the cave entrance.

The final Mousterian layers A6, A5+A6 and A5 record human frequentation ranging from intense (A6) to ephemeral (A5), with combustion structures (A6) even surrounded by slabs (A5), flint implements and bones. The faunal assemblages are dominated by *Cervidae* (mostly *Cervus elaphus* but also *Megaloceros* sp. and *Capreolus capreolus*) (Cassoli and Tagliacozzo 1994; Peresani *et al.* 2011), whereas bovids (*Bos* sp., *Bison priscus* and, less present, *Capra ibex* and *Rupicapra rupicapra*) are less well represented. Among the few carnivores, *Ursus spelaeus, Ursus arctos* and *Vulpes vulpes* are the most common species. Flint implements were flaked from cobbles provisioned

in the close surroundings in order to extract stepwise Levallois blades and flakes that were more often formed into scrapers and points than denticulates. Cortical flakes and the very few waste flakes were also tool-shaped. Retouch ranges from marginal to moderately invasive (Peresani 2012).

Layers A4 and A3 contain Uluzzian flint and bone tools (Peresani 2008) which reflect the progressive disappearance of the Levallois technology to be replaced by increased variability in flake-production and the appearance of blade and bladelet making. Evidence of human frequentation is more sparse and ephemeral in comparison with the previous Mousterian layers. Tools in layer A4 are still Mousterian scrapers retouched in a marginally to moderately invasive manner. Tools in A3 have also been found scattered in proximity to hearths or within the fill of dump material (flakes, bones and charcoal): these items include splintered pieces, a few moderately retouched scrapers, one end-scraper and backed knives. The faunal assemblages do not differ from the Mousterian layers (Tagliacozzo *et al.* in press; Romandini 2007–2008): *Cervus elaphus* predominate and, to a lesser extent, *Bos/Bison*. Carnivores are much less well represented but there is evidence for human exploitation for *Ursus spelaeus* and *Ursus arctos* as well as *Vulpes vulpes* and *Canis lupus* (Tagliacozzo *et al.* in press).

A few centimetres above the Uluzzian layers, the onset of the Aurignacian sequence coincides in layers A2–A1 with a drastic change in the faunal association due to the predominance of bovids as suggested by the most common species, *Capra ibex* (Fiore *et al.* 2004; Cassoli and Tagliacozzo 1994) and *Bos/Bison*. Several indexes suggest that human occupation was intense and repeated (Broglio *et al.* 2006).

The retouchers

Altogether, 145 bones, one probable canine and two possibly fragmented antlers were used as retouchers. The greater part of the material comes from the final Mousterian and only a few pieces from the Uluzzian (A3: 11 pieces; A4: 10; A5+A6 complex: 46; A6: 81). This wide discrepancy has to be viewed in terms of the different way the cave was used from the Mousterian to the Uluzzian. Thus, the comparison between these two complexes is biased from a statistical point of view.

The most common raw material used for retouching flint artefacts is bone. A few pieces from antler and a possible occurrence on a single tooth are the only evidence for use of different materials from bone flakes. Some of the bone surfaces have been scraped before being used, perhaps for removing residues of meat and tendon or the periostium. Scraping is shown by long, parallel striae over a small area.

Recovery of the bones

Long bones were fractured in order to get at the bone marrow, as is attested by the high frequency of deliberately fragmented bones recovered. The fragmentation is most probably the result of random blows. However, discussions about whether the breakage of the bones was predetermined and aimed at obtaining blanks of similar size and weight (Mozota Holgueras 2009; Tartar 2009) have recently introduced a different explanation. The study showed that experimental bone breaking can calibrate length and weight, in order to produce good blanks for bone retouchers. These results need to be compared with the overall fragmented bones from Fumane Cave, with a focus on the localisation of impact spots. The analysis is still in progress.

Species

Uluzzian retouchers were mostly made from cervid bones. In A3, *Cervus elaphus* is the most common species with six occurrences (54%). Along with the three pieces attributed to the *Cervidae* genus (27%), they represent the 81% of all the pieces in this stratigraphical unit (Table 2.1). As for A4, the animal range is wider: although cervids are still the most represented species (*Cervus elaphus*: three pieces; *Cervidae*: one element), two fragments are attributed to the *Ursus* genus, one to *Ursus arctos* and a second to *Ursus spelaeus*. In four cases it was not possible to make a more accurate identification than estimating the mammal size range from large to small (Table 2.1).

Mousterian layers reveal a more complex situation than the Uluzzian, perhaps due to the different dynamics of the human occupation. However, cervids dominate the faunal spectra in both A5+A6 and A6 levels (23 in A5+A6, 51%; 54 in A6, 67%), with *Cervus elaphus, Capreolus capreolus* (only one piece in A6), and very large specimens of *Megaloceros giganteus* or *Alces alces* (Table 2.1). Bovids, represented by a single piece, are only identified as *Bos/Bison* in A5+A6 and in three cases in A6 including one *Bos/Bison* and two medium-size species: *Rupicapra rupicapra* and *Capra ibex*. The percentage of large-size mammals is high: 16% (7 pieces) for A5+A6 and 12% (10) for A6. The large number of pieces made from cervid bone is consistent with the faunal composition described by Fiore *et al.* (2004) and Tagliacozzo *et al.* (in press) for all the stratigraphical units.

Anatomical portions

Diaphyses from the limb bones are most often used as retouchers. However, two antler fragments might also have retouch stigmata on them as well as one *Ursus spelaeus* canine, which has still to be carefully examined. Among the identifiable skeletal elements from the Uluzzian (A3) sample (Table 2.2), femur is the bone most represented (3 pieces), followed by tibia and metapodial (2 pieces), metatarsal (1) and humerus (1). Two pieces are undeterminable. A4 contains the *Ursus spelaeus*

Table 2.1 Retouchers – taxonomic distribution.

Taxa retouchers	US A3 NR	US A3 %	US A4 NR	US A4 %	US A5+A6 NR	US A5+A6 %	US A6 NR	US A6 %
Ursus spelaeus			1	10.0				
Ursus arctos			1	10.0				
Cervus elaphus	6	54.5	3	30.0	16	34.9	40	49.9
cfr. *Cervus elaphus*					1	2.3	2	2.5
Capreolus capreolus							1	1.2
Cervus-Megaloceros					2	4.7	6	7.4
Megaloceros-Alces					1	2.3	1	1.2
Cervus-Alces-Megaloceros					1	2.3	2	2.5
Cervidae	3	27.3	1	10.0	2	4.7	2	2.5
Capra ibex							1	1.2
Rupicapra rupicapra							1	1.2
Bos/Bison					1	2.3	1	1.2
Megaloceros-Alces-Bos/Bison							2	2.5
Megaloceros-Bos/Bison			1	10.0	2	4.7		
Ungulata					1	2.3	4	4.9
Mamm. big size	1	9.1	1	10.0	7	16.2	10	12.2
Mamm. medium-big size					6	14.0	4	4.8
Mamm. medium size	1	9.1	1	10.0	2	2.3	1	1.2
Mamm. small size			1	10.0				
Indeterminate					4	7.0	3	3.6
TOTAL	**11**		**10**		**46**		**81**	

canine (Table 2.2). Again in this stratigraphical unit, femurs are the most common (3) skeletal element. Tibia, metacarpal, radius and rib are represented by one piece each. One of the femurs comes from *Ursus arctos*. The A5–A6 complex looks a bit different from the Uluzzian (Table 2.2): out of 46 bones, tibia fragments are the most common skeletal elements used as retouchers (11 pieces or 23%), followed by femur (5), metatarsals and radii (3), metacarpals (2) and, finally, one probable antler fragment and one humerus fragment. The high incidence of unidentifiable pieces (20: 43%) seems to be related to the intense deliberate or accidental fragmentation the bones underwent.

Finally, among the identifiable tools, A6 contains similar numbers of tools made from femurs (20 pieces or 24%) and tibias (17 pieces or 21%) (Table 2.2). Metapodials are also numerous (9 metacarpals or 11%), 3 metatarsals and one generic metapodial. Radii and humeri are present (6 pieces each or 7% each). The unique axial elements identified include 2 ribs and one antler fragment as well as part of a mandible.

Figure 2.1 shows the concentrations of the different skeletal elements for *Cervus elaphus* in both the Uluzzian (A3–A4) (Fig. 2.1 a) and the final Mousterian (A5–A6) complexes (Fig. 2.1 b). As shown previously, tibias are numerically more important in the late Mousterian complex than in the Uluzzian.

Table 2.2 Retouchers – skeletal elements.

Anatomical element	US A3 NR	US A3 %	US A4 NR	US A4 %	US A5+A6 NR	US A5+A6 %	US A6 NR	US A6 %
Antler					1	2.3	1	1.2
Tooth			1	10.0				
Mandible							1	1.2
Humerus	1	9.1			1	2.3	6	7.4
Radius			1	10.0	3	7.0	4	4.8
cfr. Radius							2	2.5
Metacarpal			1	10.0	2	4.7	9	11.1
Rib							2	2.5
cfr. Rib			1	10.0				
Femur	3	27.2	3	30.0	5	11.7	20	24.9
Tibia	2	18.2	1	10.0	11	23.2	17	21.0
Metatarsial	1	9.1			3	7.0	3	3.7
Metapodial	2	18.2					1	1.2
Indeterminate	2	18.2	2	20.0	20	41.8	15	18.5
TOTAL	**11**		**10**		**46**		**81**	

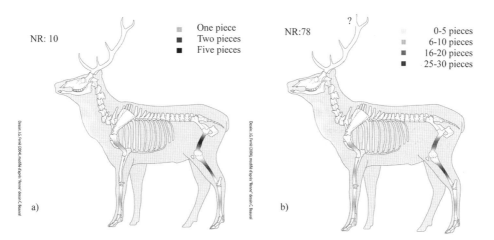

Figure 2.1 Anatomical distribution a) Uluzzian complex (A3–A4), Cervus elaphus*; b) Mousterian complex (A5+A6–A6),* Cervus elaphus*. NR = number of retouchers.*

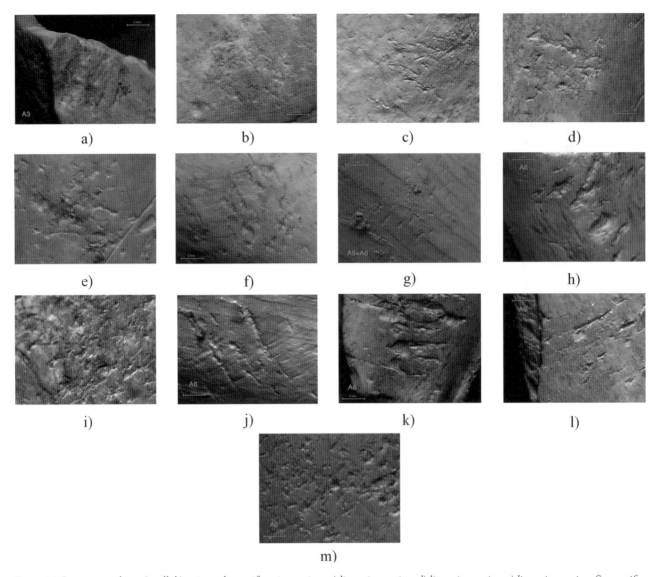

Figure 2.2 Stigmata typology. a) well; b) strias and punctiform impressions; c) linear impression; d) linear impression; e) linear impression; f) punctiform impression with scraping strias; g) linear impression; h) very concentrated punctiform impression; i) linear impression and punctiform with scraping striae; j) linear impression and wells; k) linear and punctiform impression; l) punctiform impression. Intersecting with two use zones; m) wells.

Stigmata

Four typologies of stigmata have been recognized: punctiform impressions, linear impressions, strias and wells (Fig. 2.2).

Punctiform impressions are the most common in all the stratigraphic units. They can vary in depth and are very often associated with other marks such as striae. Their concentration also can be very marked and some of the areas can be crossed by differently patterned stigmata which suggest a secondary use.

The linear impressions also can have different depths and, even if their morphology is very close to the striae, they are wider. In some cases, scraping striae are interrupted by linear impressions. They are often associated with other types of stigmata.

Striae connected to retouching are short, small and less deep than linear impressions. They are frequently associated with these latter and might represent a secondary stigmata that is linked to them.

The less common category of stigmata is represented by wells which are deep depressions resulting from repeated strikes on the bone surface. Features vary according to the strength of the blow, the number of previous hits and the type of principal stigmata.

The stigmata usually form thick, concentrated areas on the bone surfaces. On each piece we were able to identify up to three different functional zones which sometimes overlap (Fig. 2.3). However, the majority of the blanks have only one impacted zone: 72.7% in A3, 80.0% in A4, 78.3%

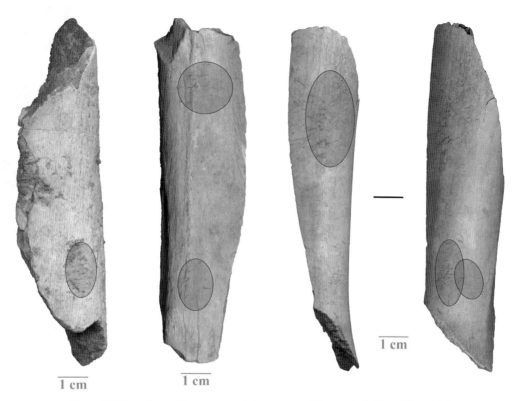

Figure 2.3 Retouchers with one, two and three use-zone(s) respectively (from left to right).

in A5+A6 and 79.0% in A6. This said, experimental work showed that retouching often does not leave marks from the blows (Armand and Delagnes 1998).

Summary

Retouchers from the Uluzzian and final Mousterian layers of Fumane cave share many common features. Choice of species and skeletal elements are usually the same, even if A6 records the use of medium-sized mammals such as *Capra ibex* and *Rupicapra rupicapra*. The *Ursus* sp. femur and probable canine in A4 are remarkable for their uniqueness which proves exclusive exploitation of the plantigrades in this level. This point of view is nevertheless skewed by the important numeric discrepancy between the two techno-cultural complexes (21 retouchers for the Uluzzian and 127 for the final Mousterian). Thus, the species of the fragmented bones used for retouching are consistent with the faunal spectra and the taphonomic analysis (Tagliacozzo *et al.* 2010).

As for the skeletal elements used to make retouchers, only level A5–A6 differentiates a little from the other units: tibias prevail over the remainder of the available skeletal elements although there is no significant gap between tibia and femur use in this layer. The study showed that the most selected skeletal elements were relatively flat, straight and thick and included fragments from femur, tibia and metapodial diaphyses. Radii and humeri are less common although they too were sometimes used. In some cases, the cortical surface of the bones were scraped beforehand to remove meat, the periostium or tendon residues (Vincent 1993) or perhaps to increase resistence in impact dynamics (Malerba and Giacobini 2002).

The four classes of stigmata include punctiform impressions, linear impressions, striae and wells resulting from a combination of different agents: strength, intensity of use, area concentration or state of the raw material (Vincent 1993; Mozota Holgueras 2007a). Punctiform impressions are the most common. The cortical surfaces connected to retouch stigmata are usually concentrated in small areas. At Fumane Cave, the blanks can have up to three zones of use, but usually have only a single zone (82.4% of all the pieces studied). Some of the zones of use were superimposed. In this case, the pattern (orientation and depth) of the marks allowed us to separate out the two different uses.

In conclusion, this contribution shows there was great similarity in terms of the choice of species, skeletal element and stigmata between the two different archaeological cultures. In the future it would be important to compare these results with the bone retouchers from the Proto-Aurignacian levels above the Uluzzian and the Discoid assemblages below the Levallois A5–A6 complex (Lemorini *et al.* 2003).

Acknowledgments
Research at Fumane is supported by the Archeological Superintendence of Veneto, Venetian Region, CA.RI. Verona Foundation, Comunità Montana della Lessinia, Fumane Municipality. This study has also been made possible with the collaboration of A. Tagliacozzo, Museo L. Pigorini di Roma (Italy), M. Romandini and Prof. B. Sala, Scienze Preistoriche ed Anthropologiche, Università degli studi di Ferrara (Italy).

Bibliography
Armand, D. and Delagnes, A. (1998) Les retouchoirs en os d'Artenac (couche 6c): perspectives archéozoologiques, taphonomiques et expérimentales. *Economie Préhistorique: les comportements de subsistance au Paléolithique, XVIIe Rencontres Internationales d'Archéologie et d'Histoire d'Antibes.* Sophia Antipolis, APDCA.

Auguste, P. (2002) Fiche éclats diaphysaires du Paléolithique moyen: Biache-Saint-Vaast (Pas-de-Calais) et Kulna (Moravie, République Tchèque). In M. Patou-Mathis (ed.), *Retouchoirs, Compresseurs, Percuteurs... os à impressions et éraillures,* 39–57. Paris, Société Préhistorique Française.

Binford, L. R. (1981) *Bones: ancient men and modern myths,* Academic Press Inc.

Bordes, F. (1961) *Typologie du Paléolithique Ancien et Moyen.* Bordeaux, Université de Bordeaux, Institut de Préhistoire.

Broglio, A., De Stefani, M., Tagliacozzo, A., Gurioli, F. and Facciolo, A. (2006) Aurignacian dwelling structures, hunting strategies and seasonality in the Fumane Cave (Lessini Mountains). In S. A. Vasil'ev, V. V. Popov, M. V. Anikovich, N. D. Praslov, A. A. Sinitsyn and J. D. Hoffecker (eds), *Kostenki & the Early Upper Paleolithic of Eurasia: general trends, local developments,* 263–268. Voronez, Platonova.

Cassoli, P. F. and Tagliacozzo, A. (1994) Considerazioni paleontologiche, paleoecologiche e archeozoologiche sui macromammiferi e gli uccelli dei livelli del Pleistocene superiore del Riparo di Fumane (VR) (scavi 1988–91). *Bullettino del Museo Civico delle Scienze Naturali di Verona* 18, 349–445.

Fiore, I., Gala, M. and Tagliacozzo, A. (2004) Ecology and subsistence strategies in the eastern Italian Alps during the Middle Palaeolithic. *International Journal of Osteoarchaeology* 14, 273–286.

Giacobini, G. and Patou-Mathis, M. (2002) Fiche rappels taphonomiques. In M. Patou-Mathis (ed.), *Retouchoirs, Compresseurs, Percuteurs... os à impressions et éraillures.* Paris, Société Préhistorique Française.

Henri Martin, L. (1906) Maillets ou enclumes en os provenant de la couche moustérienne de la Quina (Charente). *Bulletin de la Société Préhistorique Française* 3, 155–162.

Henri Martin, L. (1907) Présentation d'ossements utilisés de l'époque moustérienne. *Bulletin de la Société Préhistorique Française* 4, 8–16.

Henri Martin, L. (1907–1910) *Recherches sur l'Évolution du Moustérien dans le Gisement de la Quina I – industrie osseuse.* Paris, Schleier.

Higham, T., Brock, F., Peresani, M., Broglio, A., Wood, R. and Douka, K. (2009) Problems with radiocarbon dating the Middle to Upper Palaeolithic transition in Italy. *Quaternary Science Reviews* 28, 1257–1267.

Lemorini, C., Peresani, M., Rossetti, P., Malerba, G. and Giacobini, G. (2003) Techno-morphological and use-wear functional analysis: an integrated approach to the study of a discoid industry. In M. Peresani, (ed.), *Discoid Lithic Technology. Advances and implications,* 257–275. Oxford, Archaeopress (British Archaeological Report S1120).

Malerba, G. and Giacobini, G. (2002) Fiche éclat diaphysaires avec marques transversales d'utilisation. In M. Patou-Mathis (ed.), *Retouchoirs, Compresseurs, Percuteurs... os à impressions et éraillures,* 29–37. Paris, Société Préhistorique Française.

Mozota Holgueras, M. (2007a) *El Hueso como Materia Prima: Las industrias óseas del final del Musteriense en la Región Cantábrica. Los niveles B–C–D de Axlor (Dima, Bizkaia).* Departamento de Ciencias Históricas. Universidad de Cantabria.

Mozota Holgueras, M. (2007b) Estudio tafonómico y tecnológico de un útil doble "cincel/retocador", proveniente del nivel C (Musteriense) de Axlor-Dima, Bizkaia. *Zephyrus* 60, 207–214.

Mozota Holgueras, M. (2009) El utillaje óseo musteriense del nivel "D" de Axlor (Dima, Vizcaya): análisis de la cadena operativa. *Trabajos de Prehistoria* 66, 27–46.

Patou-Mathis, M., (ed.) (2002) *Retouchoirs, Compresseurs, Percuteurs... os à impressions et éraillures,* Paris, Société Préhistorique Française.

Patou-Mathis, M. and Schwab, C. (2002) Fiche générale. In M. Patou-Mathis (ed.), *Retouchoirs, Percuteurs, Compresseurs... os à impressions et éraillures,* 11–19. Paris, Société Préhistorique Française.

Peresani, M. (2008) A new cultural frontier for the last Neanderthals: the Uluzzian in northern Italy. *Current Anthropology* 49, 725–731.

Peresani, M. (2012) Fifty thousand years of flint knapping and tool shaping across the Mousterian and Uluzzian sequence of Fumane cave. *Quaternary International* 247, 125–150.

Peresani, M., Cremaschi, M., Ferraro, F., Falguères, Ch., Bahain, J. J., Gruppioni, G., Sibilia, E., Quarta, G., Calcagnile, L. and Dolo, J. M. (2008) Age of the final Middle Palaeolithic and Uluzzian levels at Fumane Cave, Northern Italy, using ^{14}C, ESR, ^{234}U/^{230Th} and thermoluminescence methods. *Journal of Archaeological Science* 35, 2986–2996.

Peresani, M., Chravzez, J., Danti, A., de March, M., Duches, R., Gurioli, F., Muratori, S., Romandini, M., Tagliacozzo, A. and Trombino, L. (2011) Fire-places, frequentations and the environmental setting of the final Mousterian at Grotta di Fumane. A report from the 2006–2008 research. *Quartär* 58, 131–151.

Romandini, M. (2007–2008) Sfruttamento del cervo e della volpe nei livelli uluzziani della Grotta di Fumane (Monti Lessini VR). *Scienze Preistoriche.* Ferrara, Università degli Studi di Ferrara.

Schwab, C. (2002) Fiche éclats diaphysaires du Paléolithique moyen et supérieur: la grotte d'Isturitz (Pyrénées-Atlantiques). In M. Patou-Mathis (ed.), *Retouchoirs, Compresseurs, Percuteurs... os à impressions et éraillures,* 59–73. Paris, Société Préhistorique Française.

Tagliacozzo, A., Romandini, M., Gala, M., Fiore, I., de March, M. and Peresani, M. (in press) Animal exploitation strategies during the Uluzzian at Grotta di Fumane (Verona). In, Variability in human hunting behavior during Oxygen Isotope Stages (OIS) 4/3: implications for understanding modern human origins. *Vertebrate Paleobiology and Paleoanthropology Series.*

Tartar, E. (2009) *De l'Os à l'Outil. Caractérisation technique, économique et sociale de l'os à l'Aurignacien ancient. Etude de trois sites: l'abri Castanet (secteur nord et sud), Brassempouy (grotte des Hyènes et abri Dubalen) et Gatzarria.* Vol. 1 and 2, PhD thesis. Université Paris I.

Vincent, A. (1993) *L'Outillage Osseux au Paléolithique moyen: une nouvelle approche. UPR 7537 "Débuts de la sédentarisation au Proche-Orient".* Vol. 1 and 2, PhD thesis. Université Lyon, Paris X.

CHAPTER 3

Raw Material used in the Manufacture of Osseous Artefacts during the Portuguese Upper Palaeolithic

Marina Almeida Évora

The bone tools industry in Portugal has never received much attention from researchers, probably because the sample size is so small (N=<200). However, it is important to study even this small sample so comparisons can be made with materials from other archaeological sites. In this study, the raw materials used for manufacturing of osseous tools are bone and antler; none of the artefacts reviewed was made of ivory or horn. They were collected from 12 archaeological sites in Portugal located in Estremadura, Alentejo and south-western Algarve. During the Upper Palaeolithic in Portugal, the availability of the antler may have been dependent on the season, as deer (*Cervidae*) do not have antlers all year round and its quality varies throughout its development. As to bone, its cortical tissue, which is most of the bone, was heavily exploited by these prehistoric hunter-gatherers. After extracting the bone marrow by fracturing the long bones people would modify the size and shape of these flakes until the desired tool was finished. To date, the prevalence of utensils made of bone is much higher (N=20) than for antler (N=11) in Portuguese Gravettian layers; levels with Solutrean occupations also dominate the bone utensils (N=7), there is only one object made of antler; in the levels of Magdalenian occupations, there are far fewer bone tools (N=7) compared to antler tools (N=14). Although this might be related to differential preservation.

Keywords
Upper Palaeolithic; raw material; bone industry; Portugal.

Introduction

Bone tool assemblages from Portuguese Upper Palaeolithic (UP) archaeological sites are poor compared to other collections found in similar chronological assemblages in Central and Western Europe. The low numbers may be because this class of artefactual material did not receive much attention from archaeologists or zooarchaeologists in Portugal. In this paper, the goal is to summarize the existing data on this subject in terms of osseous raw material choices.

The first published papers on Portuguese UP bone tools (Gomes *et al.* 1990; Cardoso and Gomes 1994) only presented a typological analysis of the objects known at the time. In the same year, Aubry and Moura (1994) published an article about the cave of Buraca Grande where they presented a typological and technological analysis of its bone tools. Later Zilhão (1997) in his PhD dissertation, mentioned a few bone artefacts recovered from some UP archaeological sites but without further comment or analysis. These articles only describe the finished pieces, and they did not connect the material to bone technology, manufacturing techniques or debitage by-products, with the exception of Aubry and Moura's (1994) paper. Chauviere (2002) published a paper about the Caldeirão Cave bone industry along with its technological and typological analysis. Two years later, Bicho *et al.* (2004) published a paper on shell ornaments and bone tools from the site of Vale Boi, connecting it to southern Iberian assemblages.

In 2007, all information about dispersed Portuguese Upper Palaeolithic bone industries (Évora 2007) was gathered and in 2010 the technological analysis of osseous artefacts from Vale Boi was begun (included in a wider project and until now the largest sample from a Portuguese UP site). The project is still on-going including identification of the means of acquisition of raw materials.

The location of the sites and Radiocarbon Dates

The majority of sites with a bone industry are located in Estremadura, one in Alentejo and another in south-western Algarve, near St. Vincent Cape (Fig. 3.1). The sample comes from 12 caves and rockshelter sites. The artefacts from Vale Boi (south-western Algarve) came from the terrace and the slope, not from the interior of the rockshelter. The earliest date for human occupation in the Upper Palaeolithic in Portugal, is the early Gravettian; 26,020±320 BP for Gruta do Caldeirão in Estremadura (Marreiros 2007, 29; Zilhão 1997, 187) and 27,720±370 BP for Vale Boi in Algarve (Bicho *et al.* 2010, 225; Marreiros *et al.* 2012, 12). The latest occupation begins in the terminal Magdalenian at Estremadura; 9720–11,010 cal BP for Abrigo Grande das Bocas I (Bicho *et al.* 2011).

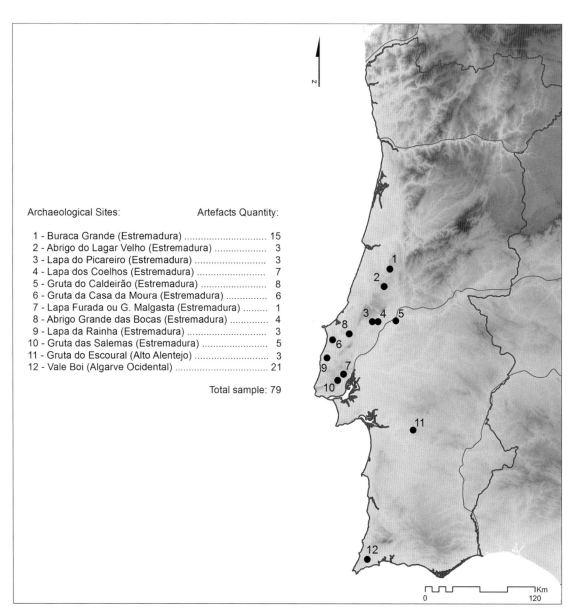

Figure 3.1 Portuguese Upper Paleolithic archaeological sites with bone tool industries.

The Sample

At Portuguese archaeological sites with Gravettian occupations, the majority of tools made from osseous materials were made from bone (N=20) with fewer made in antler (N=11). Tools made from bone (N=7) also dominant in Solutrean occupations with only a single object made from cervid antler. By contrast, in the Magdalenian levels, bone artefacts are present in lower numbers (N=9) in contrast to antler tools (N=14) (Évora 2008, 31) (Figs 3.2–4). Following Hahn's methodology (Hahn 1988,

9), the morphological analysis shows that during the Gravettian, bone was used to manufacture more spindle-shaped, followed by lanceolate and then bevel-ended tools. Antler was also chosen to make spindle-shaped objects, followed by bevel-ended and then lanceolate-shaped tools. During the Solutrean, preference was given to slender and lanceolate shapes in bone and spindle shapes in antler. The preferred morphology in Magdalenian occupations, were bevel-ended and spindle shaft shapes and bone was chosen to produce spindle-shaped tools.

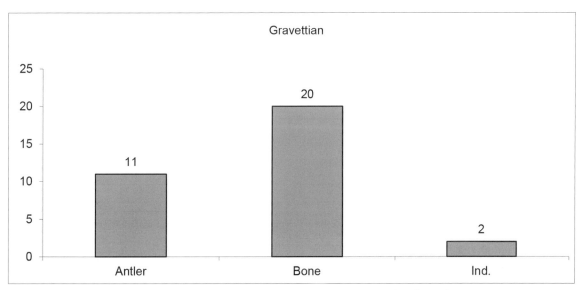

Figure 3.2 Number of bone tools in six Gravettian levels used in this study.

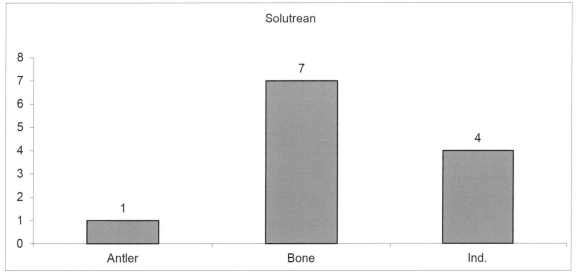

Figure 3.3 Number of bone tools in four Solutrean levels used in this study.

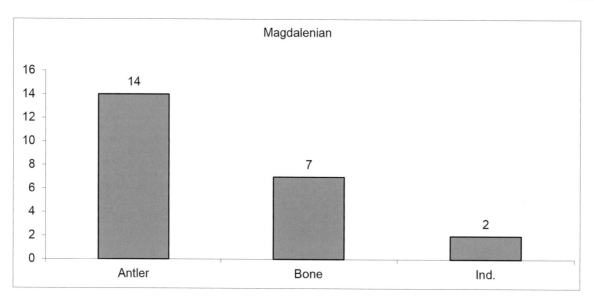

Figure 3.4 Number of bone tools in five Magdalenian levels used in this study.

Some of these implements may possibly be used in hunting and fishing activities, including some bone tips with a narrow and elongated morphology (spindle-shape) made from bone (Évora 2008, 30) found at the Lapa dos Coelhos site in association with fish vertebrae (predominantly *Salmonidae* and *Barbus barbus*) (Almeida *et al.* 2004, 165). The same type of bone points were found in Gravettian levels at Vale Boi and are possibly present in Magdalenian levels from Buraca Grande. These points were also made from bone (Évora 2008, 30) with parallels to bone points used in the fishing equipment found at Cueva de Nerja (Málaga, Spain) (Aura Tortosa and Pérez Herrero 1998, 341; Bicho *et al.* 2003, 75). To date, the sample as a whole is still small (N=<200) and the artefacts are mostly fragmented.

One reason for these small numbers may be taphonomic. Older excavation methods, housing and sorting of find materials contribute to these low numbers. Most of the fragmented remains that were studied come from recent excavations at Vale Boi, Caldeirão Cave, Buraca Grande, Lapa dos Coelhos, Abrigo do Lagar Velho sites while the number of fragments from older excavations is quite small: Casa da Moura Cave (N=4), Salemas Cave (N=1), Lapa da Rainha (N=2) and Escoural Cave (N=2) (Fig. 3.1) (Évora 2008, 31). The latter sites were excavated at the beginning and the middle of the twentieth century where the faunal assemblages suffered from collection and curation biases (Hockett and Haws 2009, 9; Manne 2010, 32). It is known that artefacts were sometimes still selected in the field and then again in the places where they were studied and deposited. Small fragments and splinters (of bone or stone) were discarded (Marks *et al.* 1994, 60).

Another reason, of course, for these low numbers may be connected to a conscious preference by the hunter-gatherer groups for using another raw material like wood (Guthrie 1983, 278), largely available, less time and energy-consuming to acquire and faster to work than bone or antler (Évora 2008, 31). Wood was readily available during the Gravettian and the Magdalenian since the climate in this territory was forest friendly. There may have been a cultural preference for stone as a raw material during the Solutrean (*ibid.*). The low frequency of such osseous artefacts during the Solutrean may be related to climate change connected to the Last Glacial Maximum that may have forced some of the wild herbivores that had previously been hunted, such as red deer (*Cervus elaphus*) and roe deer (*Capreolus capreolus*), to shift their habitats. The vegetation changed from forest to steppe-type, more condusive to other species better adapted to cold such as ibex (*Capra pyrenaica*) and chamois (*Rupicapra rupicapra*). It was for this reason that these hunter-gatherers may have prefered lithics as they lost the easy access to antler as a raw material for manufacturing their hunting equipment (Évora 2008, 31). Then, after the Polar Front regression about 17,000 BP, the cold-adapted ungulate species found in higher frequencies in the faunal assemblages in the earlier Solutrean levels (*Rupicapra rupicapra* and *Capra pyrenaica*) were again replaced by red deer, horse (*Equus* sp.) and wild boar (*Sus scrofa*) (Bicho 1994, 665). Antler as a raw material becomes more available during the Magdalenian.

After the Last Glacial Maximum, the climate improved significantly with rising temperatures and humidity. The Polar Front retreated further and further to the north encouraging expansion of the temperate forest and reduction in open spaces, making it again favourable to red deer and roe deer (Évora 2008, 31). There may be one other reason why so few bone tools seem to have been used. Not all of these sites were residential. These hunter-gatherer groups were less likely to manufacture osseous materials in temporary camps although the objects could be simply abandoned there, with the exception of Vale Boi and Caldeirão Cave, where some debitage by-products have been found. This hypothesis is supported by the fact that most of the recovered osseous artefacts comprise bone points fragments that were possibly broken during use, as attested by the fracture patterns on them (mostly oblique, tongue and saw fractures: Bertrand 1999, 113; Pétillon 2006, 90, 91, 93). These objects seem to have been left behind after the animal carcasses were butchered (Évora 2008, 27).

On the other hand, poor bone preservation is unlikely to be a reason for the low numbers because the faunal remains are very well preserved in all the UP Portuguese sites were a bone industry was found, aside from certain taphonomic marks such as fractures resulted from direct percussion, manganese oxide stains spread evenly over the surface of these artefacts, calcareous concretions, tooth imprints of small rodents and marks of roots, superficial chipping and osseous dissolution. There is even old varnish left on the surface of tools from older excavations connected with labelling inventory numbers. In this sample, only bone and antler were selected for manufacture; no artefacts were made from ivory or horn.

The Raw Materials

During the UP in Portugal, as at other locations, animal bone as a raw material for manufacturing weapons and dairy equipment is directly related to food-making activities (Goutas 2004, 55) resulting in bone fracturing for marrow extraction. Bone would be easy to acquire since hunter-gatherers could choose to collect certain kinds of bone fragments after the animal carcasses were butchered. The fractured bone flakes could be transformed into a variety of shapes and sizes, until the desired tool was produced. This sequence is corroborated within the faunal sample. This data has already been published from certain archaeological sites, like Lapa do Picareiro, Lapa dos Coelhos, Vale Boi, and Caldeirão Cave. Bones from these sites display intensive carcass fragmentation of large game animals. Most mammal bones were fractured by direct percussion to extract the bone marrow (Hockett and Haws 2009, 9; Manne and Bicho 2009, 5, 12), with the exception of the assemblage from the site of Lagar Velho because the sample is so small (Moreno-Garcia 2002). For other sites such as Casa da Moura, Lapa da Rainha, Salemas Cave and Escoural Cave the faunal analysis carried out by Cardoso (1993, 526, 528, 529, 532) indicates that these old faunal assemblages are quantitatively poor and do not permit conclusions to be drawn about means of raw material acquisition.

Bone is a raw material that combines approximately one-third of organic matter (collegen) and two-thirds of inorganic matter in its composition giving it hardness, stiffness, elasticity and resilience (Brothwell 1981, 18; Davis 1987, 48). This composition makes it a preferred raw material in the production of some osseous artefacts and the *compacta* was most exploited by hunter-gatherer groups to manufacture their hunting and fishing toolkits (Évora 2008, 15). By contrast, the availability of antler may have been dependent on seasonality, as *Cervidae* do not carry their antlers all year around and its quality also varies throughout its development (Goutas 2004, 56). Its mechanical properties vary for fresh antler (which is obtained with the hunted animal) or shed antler (which has fallen off the stag naturally) and depends also on the animal's age, on the environmental and living conditions to which the animal was exposed and the conditions the antler suffered after it was shed (Goutas 2004, 56). As stated by some researchers like Guthrie (1983, 278), Ramseyer (2004, 190), Rigaud (2004, 80) or Osipowicz (2007) and from our own experiments in working with red deer antler, it can be seen that it is relatively easy to work if we softened it in water. However when antler is dry, it is very hard and difficult to work with. Anyway, antler would still be available for collection in the wild at the end of the Winter or early Spring (Averbouh 2000, 119, 122; Ramseyer 2004, 189), but might also be easy to acquire it during hunting (Knecht 1991, 292). In the latter case, however, the antler may not have completed its growth cycle, having implications for its conservation and conditions of working it, to the extent that the degree of calcification is naturally different from shed antler (Goutas 2005, 62, 63). In the Portuguese sample, the already cited papers do not indicate how antler might have been acquired and that is one of the aims in our research project. On the other hand, analogy with Portuguese Mesolithic archaeological sites with bone industries is not yet possible because it has not yet been studied nor have any questions been addressed to this data set.

Conclusion and Perspectives

The papers published on faunal assemblages show that bone was easily available throughout the Upper Palaeolithic in the territory of Portugal making bone available for manufacture. The bone was drawn from bone fractured during food production activities where bone splinters resulting from direct percussion fractures to extract bone marrow were exploited to make tools.

Faunal analysis has not revealed how the antler was acquired although it probably derived from shed antler or during hunting, although this is yet to be determined. Anyway, artisans likely knew the mechanical properties of each raw material and which one was the best to use for the desired tool and so they knew which knapping techniques they needed to use when manufacturing a particular tool. In sites with Gravettian and Solutrean occupations, the majority of osseous tools are made from bone. On the other hand, in Magdalenian times, antler seems to have been the more preferred raw material. In Portugal, the Upper Palaeolithic bone tool industry sample is, as we have seen, still small and very fragmented but nevertheless we believe its study is important, together with zooarchaeological analysis, for helping clarify our understanding of the interactions between hunter-gatherers and the animals living in this territory at that time. The technological analysis, never carried out before tematically for these collections, is now being carry out on the Vale Boi bone industry, integrating it into a wider site sample from Southern Iberia. This analysis will help us in the future to clarify whether osseous technology and typology reflect cultural systems, that is, stylistic and territorial markers in the Southern Iberian peninsula.

Acknowledgments

To Fundação para a Ciência e a Tecnologia (SFRH / BD / 61988 / 2009) and to ICAZ 2010 Organizing Committee for their financial support. Also to N. Bicho, T. Pereira, J. Cascalheira, C. Detry and J. Marreiros for their suggestions to the text. To C. Gonçalves for providing a map in ArcGIS. To A. Choyke and S. O'Connor for their revisions and comments to the text. And I also thank the unknown reviewers for their comments.

Bibliography

Almeida, F., Angelucci, D., Gameiro, C., Correia, J. and Pereira, T. (2004) Novos dados para o Paleolítico Superior Final da Estremadura Portuguesa: resultados preliminares dos trabalhos arqueológicos de 1997–2002 na Lapa dos Coelhos (Casais Martanes, Torres Novas), *Promontoria* 2 (2), 157–192.

Aubry, T. and Moura, M. H. (1994) Paleolítico da Serra de Sicó. Actas do Iº Congresso de Arqueologia Peninsular, Porto. *Trabalhos de Sociedade Portuguesa de Antropologia e Etnologia* 34, 43–60.

Aura Tortosa, J. E. and Pérez Herrero, C. I. (1998) Micropuntas dobles o anzuelos? Una propuesta de estudio a partir de los materiales de la Cueva de Nerja (Málaga). In J. L. Sanchidrián and M. D. Simón (eds), *Las Culturas del Pleistoceno Superior en Andalucía*, 339–348. Patronato de la Cueva de Nerja.

Averbouh, A. (2000) *Technologie de la Matière Osseuse Travaillée et Implications Palethnologiques. L'exemple des chaines d'exploitation du bois de cervidé chez les Magdaléniens des Pyrénées*, Ph.D. Thesis, 2 vols, Université de Paris I, Panthéon-Sorbonne.

Bertrand, A. (1999) *Les Armatures de Sagaies Magdaléniennes en Matière Dure Animate dans les Pyrénées*. Oxford: British Archaeological Report S773.

Bicho, N. F. (1994) The end of the Paleolithic and the Mesolithic in Portugal, *Current Anthropology* 5 (5), 664–674.

Bicho, N. F., Stiner, M. and Lindly, J. (2003) Notícia preliminar das ocupações humanas do sítio de Vale Boi, Vila do Bispo, *Arqueologia e História*, 55, 9–19, Lisboa.

Bicho, N., Stiner, M. and Lindly, J. (2004) Shell ornaments, bone tools and long distance connections in the Upper Paleolithic of Southern Portugal. In M. Otte (ed.), *La Spiritualité, ERAUL* 106, 71–80, Liège.

Bicho, N., Manne, T., Cascalheira, C., Mendonça, C., Évora, M., Gibaja, J. and Pereira, T. (2010) O Paleolítico superior do sudoeste da Península Ibérica: o caso do Algarve (The Upper Palaeolithic of Southwestern Iberia: the case of Algarve), *El Paleolitico Superior Peninsular, Novedades del Siglo XXI*, 219–238, Barcelona.

Bicho, N., Haws, J. and Almeida, F. (2011) Hunter-gatherer adaptations and the Younger Dryas in central and southern Portugal, *Quaternary International* 242 (2), 336–347.

Brothwell, D. R. (1981) *Digging Up Bones. The excavations, treatment and study of human skeletal remains*. British Museum of Natural History, 3rd edition, Ithaca, New York, Cornell University Press.

Cardoso, J. L. (1993) *Contribuição para o Conhecimento dos Grandes Mamíferos do Plistocénico Superior de Portugal*. Centro de Estudos Arqueológicos do Concelho de Oeiras, Oeiras.

Cardoso, J. L. and Gomes, M. V. (1994) Zagaias do Paleolítico Superior de Portugal, *Portvgalia*, Nova Série XV, 7–31.

Chauviere, F. X. (2002) Industries et parures sur matières dures animales du Paléolithique Supérieur de la grotte de Caldeirão (Tomar, Portugal), *Revista Portuguesa de Arqueologia* 5 (1), 5–28, Lisbon.

Davis, S. J. M. (1987) *The Archaeology of Animals*. New Haven and London, Yale University Press.

Évora, M. A. (2007) *Utensílagem Óssea do Paleolítico Superior em Portugal*. Unpublished M. A. Thesis, Universidade do Algarve, Faro.

Évora, M. A. (2008) Artefactos em haste e em osso do Paleolítico Superior Português, *Promontória* 6 (6), 9–50, Faro.

Gomes, M. V., Cardoso, J. L. and Santos, M. F. (1990) Artefactos do Paleolítico superior da Gruta do Escoural (Montemor-o-Novo), *Almansor* 9, 15–36.

Goutas, N. (2004) Fiches exploitation des matières dures d'origine animale au Gravettien. In Fiches de la Commission de nomenclature sur l'industrie de l'os préhistorique, *Matières et Techniques*, Cahier XI, 53–74, Paris, Éditions Société Préhistorique Française.

Goutas, N. (2005) *Caractérisation et Evolution du Gravettien en France par l'Approche Techno-économique des Industries en Matières Dures Animales (étude de six gisements du Sud-Ouest)*, PhD Thesis, 2 vols, Université de Paris I – Panthéon – Sorbonne.

Guthrie, R. D. (1983) Osseous projectile points: biological considerations affecting raw material selection and design among Paleolithic and Paleoindian peoples. In J. Clutton-Brock and C. Grison (eds), *Animals and Archaeology 1. Hunters and their prey*, 273–294, Oxford, British Archaeological Report S163.

Hahn, J. (1988) Fiches sagaie à base simple de tradition aurignacienne. In Fiches typologiques de l'industrie osseuse prehistorique, Cahier 1: *Sagaies*, Commission de Nomenclature sur l'Industrie de l'Os Prehistorique, Université de Provence, 1–17.

Hockett, B. and Haws, J. (2009) Continuity in animal diversity in the late Pleistocene human diet of Central Portugal. *Before Farming* 2, article 2, 1–14.

Knecht, H. D. (1991) *Technological Innovation and Design during the Early Upper Paleolithic: a study of organic projectile technologies*, PhD Thesis, facsimiled edition, New York University, Michigan, USA, UMI Dissertation Services.

Manne, T. (2010) *Upper Paleolithic Foraging Decisions and Darly Economic Intensification at Vale Boi, Southwestern Portugal*, Unpublished Ph.D. Thesis, University of Arizona, USA.

Manne, T. and Bicho, N. F. (2009) Vale Boi: rendering new understandings of resource intensification and diversification in Southwestern Iberia, *Before Farming* 2, article 1, 1–21.

Marks, A. E., Bicho, N., Zilhão, J. and Ferring, C. R. (1994) Upper Pleistocene prehistory in Portuguese Estremadura: results of preliminary research, *Journal of Field Archaeology* 21 (1), 53–68.

Marreiros, J. M. F. (2007) *As primeiras comunidades do Homem moderno no Algarve Ocidental: Caracterização paleotecnológica e paleoetnográfica das comunidades gravetenses e proto-solutrenses de Vale Boi (Algarve, Portugal)*, Unpublished M. A. Thesis, Universidade do Algarve, Faro.

Marreiros, J., Cascalheira, J., Bicho, N. (2012) Flakes technology from Early Gravettian of Vale Boi (Southwestern Iberian Peninsula). In *Flakes not Blades – discussing the role of flake production at the onset of the Upper Palaeolithic*, Mettmann, Neanderthal Museum.

Moreno-Garcia, M. and Pimenta, C. (2002) *The paleofaunal context. In Portrait of the Artist as a Child, the Gravettian human skeleton from the Abrigo do Lagar Velho and its archaeological context, Trabalhos de Arqueologia* 22, 112–138, Lisboa.

Osipowicz, G. (2007) Bone and antler softening techniques in prehistory of the north eastern part of the Polish Lowlands in the light of experimental archaeology and micro trace analysis, 4/2007 *euroREA*, 1–22.

Pétillon, J.-M. (2006) *Des Magdaléniens en Armes. Technologie des armatures de projectiles en bois de Cervidé du Magdalenien supérieur de la Grotte d'Izturitz (Pyrénées Atlantiques)*, Artefacts 10, Treignes, Editions du CEDARC.

Ramseyer, D. (2004) Fiche travail du bois de cerf au Néolithique dans les habitats lacustres suisses. In Fiches de la Commission de nomenclature sur l'industrie de l'os préhistorique, *Matières et Techniques*, Cahier XI, 189–203, Paris, Éditions Société Préhistorique Française.

Rigaud, A. (2004) – Fiches débitage du bois de renne au Magdalénien. L'exemple de la Garenne (Indre, France). In Fiches de la Commission de nomenclature sur l'industrie de l'os préhistorique, *Matières et Techniques*, Cahier XI, 79–87, Paris, Éditions Société Préhistorique Française.

Zilhão, J. (1997) *O Paleolítico Superior da Estremadura Portuguesa*, Ph.D. Thesis, 2 vols, Lisboa, Edições Colibri.

CHAPTER 4

The Identification of Perishable Technologies through Usewear on Osseous Tools: Wear Patterns on Historic and Contemporary Tools as a Standard for Identifying Raw Materials Worked in the Late Upper Palaeolithic

Elisabeth A. Stone

Tools made from osseous materials have been used throughout the world in contemporary and historic communities, and constitute a major class of archaeological artefacts. Using an archaeological framework and methodology, I studied a vast collection of ethnographic and historic osseous tools used for basketry, sewing, weaving, netting, and mat-making from diverse cultural settings. These ethnographic collections provide a rich data source for identifying the material outcomes of use of bone as a raw material and complement the data obtained from experiments. Here I present a microwear analysis of osseous tools used in documented contexts, as a baseline for understanding the accumulation of usewear on bone and antler during the manufacture of textiles, baskets and nets. Data on usewear was organized through a tribological model. I then present data from the sites of Entrefoces and El Perro, two small sites from northern Spain occupied at the very end of the Late Upper Palaeolithic. The osseous collections from these sites are quite small, but relatively diverse. Usewear on these artefacts is assessed using the comparative standards created through an experimental program and a traceological analysis of ethnographic objects with well-defined usewear and clearly known use histories.

Keywords
Bone tools; perishable technologies; usewear; Late Upper Palaeolithic; ethnoarchaeology.

Introduction

The challenges of classifying and inferring wear patterns on artefacts are well known. This statement is especially true for bone tools, despite being widely documented as a significant component of ethnographic and historic tool kits in many contexts, and comprising an important, if not abundant, element of the archaeological record. Osseous materials can be worked into diverse forms and such tools serve a wide range of functions. Among the most common uses of bone tools is the production of perishable technologies – including sewn garments and structures, baskets, woven fabrics, nets, and mats – which themselves survive only rarely in the archaeological record. Analysing usewear on bone tools to identify the kinds of soft materials worked into artefacts that do not preserve in the archaeological record provides new insight into subsistence, economic, and social aspects of life in the Late Upper Palaeolithic. Nonetheless, less research has been carried out on these implements and their survival in the archaeological record is less regular than that of stone, especially in deep time. In this paper, I employ a tribological model for usewear on bone used against plant and animals fibres. I then present a summary of a functional study of ethnographic bone tools used for the manufacture of perishable materials and compare those results to a sample of bone implements from two Late Upper Palaeolithic sites in northern Spain.

Tribological Model for Attrition from Plant and Animal Derived Fibres on Worked Bone

Tribology, the multi-disciplinary study of wear and friction, provides one framework for understanding surface attrition that occurs when tools are used to manipulate different materials. Developed in the context of materials engineering and industries, tribology focuses on understanding the different factors affecting the reaction of materials to contact under varying conditions, stresses and forces (Rabinowicz 1970, 1995). The basic foundations of tribological research indicate that the physical properties of two contact materials help determine the outcome of different types of contact. By extension archaeologists can use the known properties of materials to predict some of the wear patterns that might result from contact. If we apply the principles of tribological models of wear to archaeological studies, we can determine that the different microscopic surface patterns characterizing osseous surfaces worn with hard and soft materials are a function of a few primary factors:

- hardness and resiliency of both materials
- shape and form of both surfaces
- amount of friction between the surfaces
- force exerted

While the latter two variables depend on the technique employed and the skill of the tool-user and may be extremely variable, the former two can be predicted and tested with greater ease by examining the structure of the worked materials.

Soft fibrous materials worked with bone tools fall into two major categories: plant-derived and animal-derived. To predict diagnostic differences between wear from these two kinds of fibres, I consider the fundamental physical differences in their cellular, microscopic and macroscopic structures.

Fibres constitute a major structural element in many types of plants and the same qualities inherent in their living function make these fibres useful for the production of cordage and textiles: flexibility, strength and a long, narrow physical form. Plant fibres that can be converted into threads are cellulose-based with thick, rigid cell walls, are often internally aligned and are typically used in artefact manufacture in a bundled, ordered way. Due to plant diversity, these fibres are coupled

with different substances in various forms in the living state, which affect their performance as a raw material (Cook 1968). Plant fibres often require preliminary processing and may be associated with fewer inclusions, greases, lubricants, or grits when fully processed than animal hides and tendons. The primary classes of vegetal fibres that are converted into perishable industries are:

1. BAST FIBRES: bast or stem fibres are the fibrous bundles that form the inner bark or phloem of dicotyledonous plants
2. LEAF FIBRES: leaf fibres run along the leaf of monocotyledonous plants
3. SEED HAIR FIBRES: fibres found in seeds and fruits; most seed fibres are derived from domesticated sources, such as cotton
4. COMPLETE PLANT ELEMENTS: stems, leaves, rushes, grasses, or other unmodified or minimally modified plant parts

Animal fibres, on the other hand, do not have a thick cell wall. Keratin and collagen, the main elements in hair, skin and tendon, have softer cell structures and a less orderly arrangement of cells (Bailey 2003). While the cells of sinew or tendon are somewhat aligned, the fibrils in hides are matted and disorderly, much like a felt. Fur, if attached to a skin, is arranged in an ordered way, although the cells are not rigid like those of cellulose. Additionally, internal inclusions in animal hides may be of varied size and material and should result in striations and gouges of unpredictable form. Although the kinds of soft materials of animal origin are numerous and varied, the most common are:

1. HIDE: skin is largely divided into the keratin-rich epidermis and the corium. Corium, the primary component of processed hide products, is made up of disorderly interlocking collagen fibres which are matted together without any predominant order
2. TENDON OR SINEW: long collagen sheaths are bundled to form tendons that bind muscles and bones in the body
3. HAIR AND FUR: hair is made up primarily of keratin. Hair and fur may not have been worked frequently prior to the domestication of fur-bearing animals; the hair on domesticated wool-bearing animals is markedly different from that of their non-domesticated counterparts, as it has been selected to grow longer and favouring the soft, curled, interlocking under-hair

Given the structural differences between plant and animal derived fibres, predications can be made for the differences between vegetal and animal fibre wear. Plant fibre wear, produced by strong, rigid cell walls and containing minimal non-fibrous inclusions, should cause:

- planar microtopographic attrition
- non-invasive polish
- striae may present internal order or alignment
- may result in minimal macroscopic edge rounding

Animal fibre wear, from bundled soft cells, frequently containing small non-fibrous inclusions, should result in:

- rounded microtopographic borders
- invasive polish
- striations that may vary substantially
- attrition that deforms the original surface

These tribologically derived expectations for usewear establish a model for assessing wear from a collection of tools from ethnographic contexts with known histories of use (Table 4.1).

Ethnographic Osseous Tools used in the Manufacture of Fibre Industries

Bone tools are not common in contemporary western society (although they are still used in some cases – see Griffitts 2006), but are employed in some other cultural contexts and were common in pre-colonial communities worldwide. Ethnographic museums curate large collections of worked bone, many with detailed use histories (for example, Fig.

4.1). There are many challenges to the use of such archival documentation and the correspondence between documents, objects, and object life history is not always transparent (see Stone 2011a, 2011b). Ethnographic collections are subject to varied kinds of information loss over their life history. The goals of collectors or ethnographers rarely match those of a contemporary archaeologist, so in many cases much of the requisite information for inclusion in a functional study is not available. Additionally, ethnographic collections are complicated by the presence of tradewares, unused tools, and errors in the functional attribution of some objects. The number of tools from any one area or group is generally small, so variation within populations is difficult to assess. Thus, statistical analysis by group or region may be difficult, if not impossible. However, with careful selection of samples, and comparison at the scale of the contact surface, a traceological analysis of ethnographic artefacts can reveal usewear patterns developed in dynamic contexts of use by skilled practitioners (Fig. 4.1).

I analysed 930 ethnographic bone tools used for the manufacture of perishable technologies, both for evidence of macroscopic wear and morphological variation and patterning

Figure 4.1 Pomo basket, nearly finished, and awl used to make it, demonstrating the skill of the tool user and the outcome of the manufacture process (AMNH 50/4027; Courtesy of the Division of Anthropology, American Museum of Natural History).

in bone tools used for similar tasks. Variation among bone tools is high and form does not always correspond to function, positively or negatively (Stone 2011a, 2011b). The ethnographic artefacts studied are housed in the American Museum of Natural History (AMNH), New York City; the Burke Museum of Natural History and Culture (Burke), Seattle; the Smithsonian Institution's National Museum of the American Indian (NMAI) and National Museum of Natural History (NMNM), Suitland, MD and Washington, D.C. From the large initial sample, I selected 103 tools from NMNH for microscopic traceological analysis. I coded usewear data in several ways: narrative descriptions, micrographs, attribute analysis of variation in polish, striations, volume loss, and pitting, and predictions from the tribological model. Here, I focus on the tribological data coding.

Tribological Model for Usewear Accumulation

Artefacts were coded for usewear along the variables shown in Table 4.1. Statistical tests show that many of these variables vary as predicted by the tribological model for fibre usewear. Given the small sample, simplified model and the use of two-state attributes, significance was tested at the 0.1 level. Polish is more commonly invasive and rounded on tools used against animal-derived fibres, while the presence of striations and a patterned distribution of striae are typical of tools used against plant materials (Figs 4.2 and 4.3). The presence of pitting, however, does not correlate statistically to either use material, but rather varies by tool part (tip, mesial or perforation), suggesting that this attribute may be more indicative of handling than wear from any particular worked material (see Table 4.2).

Table 4.1 Usewear expectations from plant and animal fibres on worked bone indicated by a tribological model.

Attribute	Plant Materials	Animal Materials
Polish invasiveness	**Non-invasive**	**Invasive**
Microtopography	**Flat or planar**	**Rounded**
Presence of striations	**Yes**	**Yes or No**
Striation organization	**Patterned**	**Irregular**
Striation size	Similar to each other	Varied
Presence of pitting	Yes or No	Yes
Volume loss	Variable	High

*Variables in bold were statistically significant at the α= 0.10 level in the ethnographic sample.

Table 4.2 Chi square tests of tribological model for wear on ethnographic sample.

Attributes	Chi Square Value	p value
Material – Polish invasiveness	**3.24**	**0.070**
Material – Microtopography	**8.99**	**0.003**
Material – Striation presence	**30.39**	**0.000**
Material – Striation organization	**5.16**	**0.023**
Material – Striation size	0.65	0.421
Material – Volume loss	0.77	0.379
Material – Pitting	2.06	0.152
Location – Pitting	**11.72**	**0.003**

*Variables in bold were statistically significant at the α-= 0.10 level in the ethnographic sample.

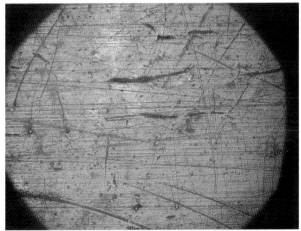

Figure 4.2 Usewear on a Winnebago needle used for sewing rushes into mats (NMNH Catalogue number E5205; Department of Anthropology, Smithsonian Institution; photograph: Elisabeth A. Stone).

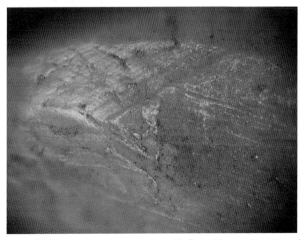

Figure 4.3 Usewear on a snowshoe needle from Ungava Bay, Canada (NMNH Catalogue number E89999; Department of Anthropology, Smithsonian Institution; photograph: Elisabeth A. Stone).

Despite the statistical significance of these variables for correlating usewear and worked material, there is no one-to-one correspondence between animal or plant derived fibres and any one specific variable identified through tribological principles. The most salient pattern of both macroscopic and microscopic variation in ethnographic tools is the wide ranges of variation in morphology and in wear patterns, despite similar use histories. The variation is sometimes, but not always, explained by differences between cultural groups, which may be due to particular technological histories and local customs of production and use of osseous tools. Some other variation may be due to personal choices in the mode of tool use, along with differences in the permitted deviation from designated tool function. All of these factors may be relevant to understanding the variation present in the archaeological record, even if they are difficult to parse out specifically.

Archaeological Collections from Northern Spain

During the Upper Palaeolithic osseous materials were worked into a range of forms, many of which are considered chronologically diagnostic in Western Europe, and in particular, northern Spain. Some of the common forms, including harpoons, hunting points, and eyed needles have relatively well-defined functions, while others, such as spatulate forms, incised rods, and fine points are less well functionally understood. Here I summarize a study of 15 worked bone and antler artefacts from two small Late Upper Palaeolithic sites from north-central Spain, La Peña del Perro and El Abrigo de Entrefoces.

La Peña del Perro (El Perro) is a small set of rockshelters on the Cantabrian coast, located near the present-day town of Santoña and close to the Bay of Santoña and marshes at the mouth of the Río Asón. The site was occupied from the Late Magdalenian (approximately 12,500–11,000 years ago) through the Azilian (11,000–10,500 years ago) and Mesolithic and contains Azilian and Mesolithic shell middens, along with representative lithic, bone, and faunal deposits from these three periods (González Morales 1990b; González Morales and Díaz Casado 1992). Although both looting and use of the rockshelters for penning livestock resulted in some stratigraphic disturbance, many of the deposits were found to be intact and excavations were carried out in five field seasons from 1985 through 1990, under the direction of Manuel R. González Morales. Level 1 was dated to the Mesolithic and will be excluded from this discussion, although the Mesolithic section of the site has been studied and published (Gutiérrez Zugasti 2005; Morales Muñiz and Moreno Nuño 1988). The lithic industry at the site is typical for the Late Magdalenian and Azilian of the Cantabrian region, with an emphasis on locally acquired raw materials and a tendency

toward microblade technologies, especially those forms with simple and abrupt retouched edges. Several stone points were recovered. Both mid-to-large sized terrestrial fauna and marine shells are abundant at the site. The shell middens document the transition from rocky tide zone species in the Azilian to estuary species in the Mesolithic. Non-figurative linear engravings were also found on the cave walls and are likely to be Upper Palaeolithic in origin, as similar engravings are common in such sites in the Cantabrian region (González Morales 1990b). The osseous industry included several temporally diagnostic pieces, including an Azilian perforated unilateral harpoon from Level 2a and a number of decorated *sagaies*, or antler points.

El Abrigo de Entrefoces (Entrefoces) is a long, narrow rock shelter located on the side of a narrow pass in the region of La Foz de Morcín, Asturias, along the Río Riosa. Excavations at the site took place from 1980–1989 and revealed a sequence of Magdalenian levels, from Early Magdalenian through the beginning of the Late Magdalenian (approximately 15,000–12,000 years ago). One carbon date from the Early Magdalenian in Level B returned a range of 14,690±200, uncalibrated (Benéitez González and Calleja Fernández 2002; González Morales 1990a). Faunal remains from the site largely consist of mid-to-large sized game typical for the Magdalenian of this area. The lithic industry is predominantly quartz, although retouched tools were preferentially made of chert. The osseous industry assemblage from Entrefoces is larger than that of El Perro, with a fairly diverse set of artefact forms represented.

Archaeological Collections Studied

El Perro

Three artefacts from El Perro were studied microscopically for traces of wear from animal or vegetal fibres. The artefacts were selected based on their availability for study at the Museo de Santander and the possibility that these items were used for processing or manipulating fibres, based on morphological characteristics. One complete eyed needle, one mesial fragment, and one point (*punzón*) were selected for analysis.

Entrefoces

Twelve artefacts were selected for analysis from the Entrefoces collection. Once again, the sampling strategy was affected by logistical constraints on the artefacts available for study at the Museo de Oviedo and narrowed down to those artefacts with morphological characteristics expected of tools for fibre industry manufacture. Three antler rods, two broken eyed needles – both retaining the base of the perforation, three mesial needle or point sections, one spatulate tool, and three partial or fragmentary *sagaies* or antler points were analysed. The collection from Entrefoces is notable for the high number of antler rods or *varillas* with perpendicular incisions, which comprise fully one quarter of the analysed sample. These objects are fairly common in the Late Upper Palaeolithic of northern Spain, but their function is unknown. Unfortunately, the analysis of usewear on antler is more difficult than on bone, as the worked surface is more porous and patterns of attrition can be difficult to identify.

Usewear Analysis of Archaeological Artefacts

El Perro

The artefacts from El Perro are suggestive of minimal maintenance or repair activities as the primary fibre-based tasks at the site. Of three artefacts studied, the eyed needle and the bi-pointed bone splinter, have identifiable wear, primarily from animal-derived sources. Given that the site is a shell midden with limited evidence of longer stays or diverse economic and subsistence activities, it is unsurprising to find little evidence for the manufacture of perishable technologies. The use of the eyed needle on hides and leathers (see Figs 4.4a and 4.4b) may have occured during repair activities, as construction of leather clothing or other structures is generally done without the aid of a needle (Amato 2010) and there is little other evidence for hide processing at the site.

Entrefoces

The Entrefoces collection varies morphologically and functionally. Generally, preservation of osseous artefacts at the site is good and usewear can be documented on many of the tools. Similar to the lithic and faunal evidence, bone and antler tools at Entrefoces indicate that a range of subsistence and economic activities took place at the site. Eight of the twelve specimens analysed have identifiable usewear, although the origin of that wear is suggested in only six of those cases. For example, A-59 is a mesial fragment of a flattened oval cross-section point or awl. The smoothed, rounded edges of all surface features indicate that this piece was probably in contact with hide or leather. The strong presence of ochre in all low points of the surface suggests that an ochre slurry may have been worked with or into the leather. Leather with ochre can be used to polish a bone surface or ochre can be worked into a hide for coloration or to discourage insects.

Wear on some of the *sagaies* may be due to their use as hunting implements, although a more comprehensive study of impact fractures would strengthen this interpretation (i.e., Petillón 2006; Letourneux and Petillón 2008). The numerous incised antler rods at the site may be implicated in the manipulation of plant fibres (Fig. 4.5a). There are three similar *varillas* from Entrefoces, which present wear that may be indicative of use with vegetal fibres. The function of these

Figure 4.4a Varillas from Entrefoces (photograph: Elizabeth A. Stone).

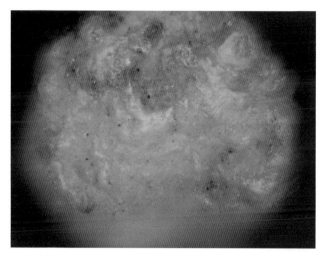

Figure 4.4b Usewear on tip of eyed needle suggestive of work against animal fibre (photograph: Elizabeth A. Stone).

rods is unknown and their general shape is not suggestive of any particular mode of use. The wear is very similar to experimental wear from weaving nettle fibres and indicates heavy use on a soft material (Fig. 4.5b). The shape of specimens like A-62 would be conducive towards use in weaving and the incisions may have facilitated the manipulation of warp threads. Although the kinds of fibre-based industries made and used in the Magdalenian are currently unknown, artefacts at Entrefoces provide evidence for the exploitation of a broad range of fibre sources at the end of the Upper Palaeolithic, including fibres of both plant and animal origin.

Discussion and Summary

The analysis presented here demonstrates both the interpretative power of usewear analysis for understanding the function of bone tools in the past and the importance of analysing both morphological and microscopic features in order to arrive at an interpretation of function. Ethnographic and experimental

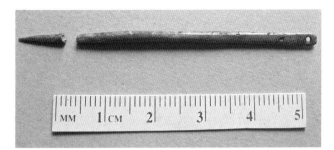

Figure 4.5a Eyed needle from El Perro (photograph: Elizabeth A. Stone).

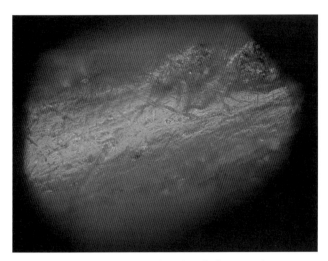

Figure 4.5b Usewear on incised surface of varilla from Entrefoces suggestive of work against plant fibre (photograph: Elizabeth A. Stone).

traceological data, organized through the analytical framework of tribology, provide comparative standards for the analysis of archaeological artefacts. The combination of these different data sources provides new insight on the use of bone as a raw material for tool production. Tribological predictions are a particularly powerful means of sorting archaeological assemblages when the extant information on use is minimal, as is the case for many osseous artefacts in the Late Upper Palaeolithic.

Microscopic attrition patterns indicate that the 103 ethnographic and 15 archaeological artefacts are characterized by high variability in wear from plant and animal fibres, highlighting the adaptability of bone tools to a range of tasks related to the manufacture of perishable artefacts. Importantly, tool form varies on a macroscopic level and microwear patterning does not correlate strongly with morphological artefact classes. There are a number of factors that could produce this strong pattern of variation, including individual variation in mode and style of tool use, the use of particular tools for numerous tasks, or the presence of worked materials that were not included in the comparative samples.

Despite significant variation, the analysis of usewear patterns is a powerful tool to identify the material of contact and suggest the roles played by bone implements. A study of the variation in morphology and attrition patterns in these assemblages helps provide information on the ways that people have used bone to meet numerous needs as they explored a changing landscape and met economic and subsistence challenges. Additionally, usewear analysis suggests a possible use of the common, but functionally enigmatic, *varilla*. Finally, microscopic analysis allows the identification of the exploitation of perishable materials that are not otherwise indicated by the archaeological record. Previously undocumented evidence for the use of several fibre classes of both plant and animal origin suggests some of the kinds of perishable materials that may have been worked with bone tools and helps elucidate the roles of osseous technology in Late Upper Palaeolithic daily life.

Acknowledgements

This research was supported by the National Science Foundation through a Graduate Research Fellowship and a Doctoral Dissertation Improvement Grant, as well as a grant from the Office of Graduate Studies at the University of New Mexico. Permission to study collections from the following institutions is greatly appreciated: American Museum of Natural History, Burke Museum, Maison Méditerranéenne des Sciences de l'Homme, Museo de Altamira, Museo de Cantabria, Museo de Oviedo, National Museum of the American Indian, National Museum of Natural History, Universidad de Cantabria. M. R. González Morales was instrumental in gaining access to archaeological collections. Thanks to Alice Choyke, Sonia O'Connor and Carole Vercoutère for inviting me to join this session. Ann F. Ramenofsky, Kari L. Schleher and anonymous reviewers provided many thoughtful and helpful comments.

Bibliography

Amato, P. (2010) Sewing with or without a needle in the Upper Palaeolithic? In A. Legrand-Pineau, I. Sidéra, N. Buc, E. David and V. Scheinsohn (eds), *Ancient and Modern Bone Artefacts from America to Russia*. 201–210. Oxford, Archaeopress (British Archaeological Report S2136).

Bailey, D. G. (2003) The preservation of hides and skins. *Journal of the American Leather Chemical Association* 98, 308–319.

Benéitez, González, C. and Calleja Fernández, S. (2002) Intervención arqueológica en el "Abrigo de Entrefoces" (La Foz, Morcín). In *Excavaciones Arqueológicas en Asturias, 1999–2002*. 215–219. Oviedo, Gobierno del Principado de Asturias.

Cook, J. G. (1968) *Handbook of Textile Fibres: vol. 1 natural fibres* (4th ed.). Watford, Merrow Publishing.

González Morales, M. R. (1990a) El abrigo de Entrefoces (1980–1983) In *Excavaciones Arqueológicas en Asturias 1983–1986*. 1, 29–36. Oveido, Gobierno del Principado de Asturias.

González Morales, M. R. (1990b) La prehistoria de las marismas, excavaciones en el abrigo de la Peña del Perro (Santoña, Cantabria), Campañas 1985–88. *Cuadernos de Trasmiera* 2, 12–28.

González Morales, M. R. and Díaz Casado, Y. (1992) Excavaciones en los abrigos de la Peña del Perro (Santoña, Cantabria). *Veleia* 8–9, 43–64.

Griffitts, J. L. (2006) *Bone Tools and Technological Choice, Change and Stability on the Northern Plains.* Unpublished Dissertation, Tucson, University of Arizona.

Gutiérrez Zugasti, F. I. (2005) *La Explotación de Moluscos en la Cuenca Baja del Rio Asón (Cantabria, España) a Inicios del Holoceno (10,000–5,000 BP) y su Importancia en las Comunidades Humanas del Aziliense y del Mesolitico.* Unpublished Dissertation, Santander, Universidad de Cantabria.

Letourneux, C. and Pétillon, J.-M. (2008) Hunting lesions caused by osseous projectile points, experimental results and archaeological implications. *Journal of Archaeological Science* 35 (10), 2849–2862.

Morales Muñiz, A. and Moreno Nuño, M. R. (1988) *El Abrigo de la Peña del Perro: el estudio óseo.* Unpublished Report, Santander.

Pétillon, J.-M. (2006) *Des Magdaléniens en Armes, Technologie des Armatures de Projectile en Bois de Dervidé du Magdalénien Supérieur de la Grotte d'Isturitz (Pyrénées-Atlantiques)* 10. Treignes, Cedarc.

Rabinowicz, E. (1970) *An Introduction to Experimentation.* Reading, Addison-Wesley.

Rabinowicz, E. (1995) *Friction and Wear of Materials* (2nd ed.). New York, Wiley.

Stone, E. A. (2011a) The role of ethnographic museum collections in understanding bone tool use. In J. Baron and B. Kufel-Diakowska (eds), *Written in Bones: studies on technological and social context of past faunal skeletal remains.* Wrocław, Instytut Archeologii Uniwersytet Wrocławski.

Stone, E. A. (2011b) *Through the Eye of the Needle: investigations of ethnographic, experimental, and archaeological bone tool use wear from perishable technologies.* Unpublished Dissertation, Albuquerque, University of New Mexico.

CHAPTER 5

Bone Material and Design Choices in Southern Patagonia

Vivian Scheinsohn

In Patagonia (southern South America) bone technology has been recorded both in the insular area (Magellanic channels and Isla Grande de Tierra del Fuego) as well as in Continental Patagonia. In the insular area it is found in association with maritime littoral adaptations and displays high variability in raw materials and design. In Continental Patagonia, bone tools are scarce but recorded in almost every site from Pleistocene/Holocene transition on, with restricted raw materials and designs. This paper concerns the results from three regions. Cerro Casa de Piedra, Pali Aike Volcanic Field and Tierra del Fuego are presented in order to test the vicariance model (Borrero 1989–1990) implications for bone technology.

Keywords
Patagonia-Tierra del Fuego; hunter gatherers; bone raw materials; bone technology.

Introduction

In Patagonia (southern South America) bone technology has been recorded both in the insular area (Magellan channels and Isla Grande de Tierra del Fuego) as well as in Continental Patagonia. In the insular area bone tools are found in association with maritime littoral adaptations (Orquera and Piana 1999). Specifically on Isla Grande (Fig. 5.1), characterized by the presence of a steppe environment in the north and forest and mountains to the south, the littoral environment acquires importance in terms of the coast/total surface ratio (Muñoz 2002). Here, bone tools are abundant and show high variability in raw materials and design (Scheinsohn 1997, 2010a). In Continental Patagonia, characterized by the predominance of a steppe environment in the east and forest and mountains in the west, bone tools are scarce although nevertheless recorded at almost every site from the Pleistocene/Holocene transition on, although the choice of raw materials is limited as are the designs.

In previous work, a model for bone raw material exploitation in Tierra del Fuego was developed and tested (Scheinsohn 1997, 2010a). This model proposed three stages in the bone raw material utilization at the island: experimental, exploitation and abandonment. The results demonstrated that between 7000–4500 BP there was no local experimental moment, given the knowledge of specific bone properties and recorded high levels of design (meaning there were distinct morphological tool groups) standardization (Scheinsohn 2010a).

Where and when did this experimental moment in bone technology take place? The first place to look, Continental Patagonia, presents an ancient bone technology, first studied at sites located in the Pali Aike Volcanic Field (PAVF). Using the information provided by those sites, Junius Bird established five cultural periods, from I to V (Bird 1938) developing the first chronological sequence for southern Patagonia. Period II was characterized by its bone points and tools. Later on, Menghin (1957) also supported the

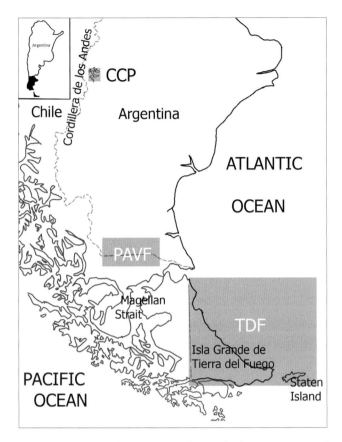

Figure 5.1 Map of southern Patagonia showing the three areas mentioned in the text (shadowed): Cerro Casa de Piedra (CCP), Pali Aike Volcanic Field (PAVF) and Tierra del Fuego (TDF). Scale 1: 1,250,000.

of the space, with specific home ranges and an increase in the variability of material culture and rapid processes of change); c) effective occupation (when all desirable space is occupied and density-dependent mechanisms appear see Borrero 1989–1990, 134). In the specific case of the Fueguian peopling, Borrero is critical of dispersion models such as those proposed by Menghin (1960) and Chapman (1986). Both suggest a cultural continuity north and south of the strait, and consider the existence of the Fueguian populations as having been pushed onto the Isla Grande by other populations. Borrero considers that the biogeographical concept of vicariance explains the situation better (Borrero 1989–1990).

Vicariance biogeography became a subdiscipline of biogeography from 1970 (see among others Croizat *et al.* 1974; Rosen 1978; Nelson and Platnick 1981; Wiley 1988). It is based on the assertion that vicariance is the predominant diversification mode, as opposed to dispersal from an origin centre, when an ancestral biota is fragmented by the appearance of a barrier. The barrier interrupts the gene flow and, consequently, this event results in allopatric speciation of many of the species constituting the ancestral biota. In accordance with this model, Borrero (1989–1990, 135) suggests that the development of the Magellan Strait produced a natural barrier that led to vicariance in an ancestrally occupied area. This division produced a rearrangement and enabled a process of independent evolution of the populations that inhabited the island. Human osteological evidence corroborates this idea, as the Fueguian populations are more similar to each other than to those of Continental Patagonia (Cocilovo and Guichón 1985–1986)

Could this vicariance model explain bone technology development in southern Continental Patagonia and Tierra del Fuego? Was bone technology also subject to vicariance? If so, bone technology should be common in southern Patagonia and Tierra del Fuego until the Magellan Strait divided them (*c.* 8000 BP) while independent evolution of that technology took place in the Isla Grande, where the bone industry followed a different path.

In this paper, I will contrast the results obtained in Tierra del Fuego (herafter TDF) and two different areas of southern Continental Patagonia: Cerro Casa de Piedra (herafter CCP) and Pali Aike Volcanic Field (hereafter PAVF; see Fig. 5.1). My main hypothesis is that bone technology was affected by vicariance and a divergence process between TDF and southern Continental Patagonia that got underway from 8000 BP and grew stronger with time. Also, I expect that bone technological divergence will be greatest between CCP and TDF given the elapsed time, geographical distance and environmental differences (Continental Patagonia precordilleran interior vs. insular Tierra del Fuego). As a result of the environmental differences between both areas, the taxa that could be utilized for bone manufacturing will be different. Also, I expect more diversity in the choice of bone raw materials on the island, given the opportunity of more diverse biomes due to the extent of coastal environment (Muñoz 2002, 2005).

importance of bone technology for this moment, defining what he called the "Riogalleguense", an industry characterized by a few lithic tools and bone awls, dated around 7000–6000 AC. He considered it to be a bone industry with a "protolithic morphology" similar to Bird's period II. Other bone artifacts found at different sites, chronologically related to the Pleistocene/Holocene transition (El Trébol, Cueva del Minero 1, Piedra Museo, Lago Sofía, Tres Arroyos, Cueva del Medio and Tagua Tagua 1; see Nami 2010) show that bone was an important raw material used by the hunter-gatherers that lived in southern Patagonia as it was first settled. After 7000 BP, bone technology lost its edge in Continental Patagonia although it was broadly developed in Tierra del Fuego, presenting new designs and use of new raw materials.

Borrero (1989–1990) has proposed that Isla Grande de Tierra del Fuego was peopled before the opening of the Magellan Strait (*c.* 8000 BP). He starts out from a general peopling model for Patagonia that presupposes three phases for the occupation of a particular area: a) exploration (the phase of initial dispersion towards an empty area); b) colonization (the phase of initial consolidation of human groups in certain parts

The vicariance model leads us to expect similarities between PAVF and CCP despite the distance between them (around 500 km) and the proximity of PAVF to the coast. This is supported by Borrero and Barberena's (2006) model where they posited that in southern Patagonia, in contrast with the Magellan channels, hunter-gatherers organizational nodes were located in the interior. This explains the absence of an intense coastal occupation and mobility reduction although the importance of marine resources in subsistence was recorded by isotopic analysis (Borrero and Barberena 2006). Coastal habitats were used in a transient manner, below the intensity of use of interior sites (Borrero and Barberena 2006). Nevertheless, given the PAVF population's access to the coast (a mean distance of *c.* 70 km), the bone technology they employed should share more preferences in bone raw materials and tool designs with CCP given its interior organizational importance.

Materials and methods

Samples and sites

The Tierra del Fuego sample comprises bone tools from different archaeological sites on the Isla Grande (shared between Chile

and Argentina, see Fig. 5.1), most of them from the Argentinean sector (with one exception see Table 5.1). All these sites have been excavated systematically and the recovered materials deposited in the Museo del Fin del Mundo (Ushuaia, Argentina), CADIC-CONICET Research Center (Ushuaia, Argentina), DIPA-IMHICIHU (Buenos Aires, Argentina) and American Museum of Natural History (AMNH, New York, USA). This sample was discussed in detail in Scheinsohn (1997 and 2010a) and its results sustain the claim that there is no bone technology older than 7000 BP on Isla Grande.

Cerro Casa de Piedra (CCP) is mainly a volcanic rhyolitic hill, located at 47°15' Lat. S and 72°10' Long. W, within Perito Moreno National Park, north-west of Santa Cruz Province, Argentina. The hill has several caves and rock shelters, among them Cerro Casa de Piedra 5 (CCP5) and Cerro Casa de Piedra 7 (CCP7). Nowadays, those sites are located in a transitional environment between *Nothofagus* forest and the shrub steppe. A series of climatic fluctuations were identified in this area, corresponding to the Neoglacial (Aschero *et al.* 2005; De Nigris 2005). As a correlate, various lakes located in the National Park (Azara, Nansen, Volcán, Belgrano, Burmeister) experienced level changes that led to a paleolake that at some time unified them all. This paleolake would have had various transgression pulses and, in this respect, it is

Table 5.1 TDF sample composition and its main characteristics (see details in Scheinsohn 2010a).

Sites	N	Radiocarbon dates (single or máximum and minimum for the whole site)*	References
Túnel I (TuI)	188	6980±110 (CSIC 310) 450±60 (BETA 4388)	Orquera and Piana (1986–1987); Orquera and Piana (1987); Piana (1984)
Valentin Bay (BV 1)	72	200 **	Vidal (1985) Scheinsohn (2011)
Rock Shelter I (RS1)	37	970±90	J. Bird. Unpublished (AMNH)
LP (Lancha Packewaia)	54	4215±305 (MC 1068) 4900±70 (CSIC 307) 1080±100 (MC 1065) 280±85 (CSIC 1064)	Orquera *et al.* (1977)
Túnel VII (TuVII)	43	100±45	Orquera and Piana (1996)
Punta María 2 (PM)	36	300±100 (AC-43) 250 or younger (GAK-10316) 720±50 (LP-237)	Borrero (1985) Borrero pers. comm.
San Pablo 4 (SP4)	5	modern ***	Borrero (1985)
Crossley Bay I -Staten Island (BCI)	13	2730±90 (BETA 25701) 1527±58 (INGEIS 0874, report 2817)	Horwitz (1990) Horwitz and Scheinsohn (1991)
Shamakush I (SHI)	4	1220±10	Orquera and Piana (1985)
Total	452		

* in years BP unless indicated
** Estimation on account of European materials presence
*** A. Figini (pers. comm. to L. Borrero). Age of the sample: between AD 1750 and 1950

interesting that the earliest dates in the area were obtained at sites located above 900 masl (Civalero and Aschero 2003). Due to the cold and dry conditions inside the cave, extraordinary preservation conditions were recorded resulting in the survival of guanaco skin/hide, sinew threads, plant fibre, bones with periosteum, and wooden artefacts. Both sites have rock art, associated with the earlier phases of human occupation in Patagonia. The studied bone tools are held at the Instituto Nacional de Antropología y Pensamiento Latinoamericano (INAPL, Argentina).

Pali Aike Volcanic Field (PAVF) is located between the northern bank of the Gallegos River and the Magellan Strait (50° and 52° Lat S. and 69° and 71° Long W), a region shared now by Chile and Argentina (Barberena 2008, see Fig. 5.1). It was one of the regions where early Patagonian archaeological research began following Junius B. Bird's excavations at Fell, Pali Aike, and Cañadon Leona in Chilean territory (Bird 1938). Fell is a small cave on the right bank of the Chico River. Bird divided the cave sequence into five periods (see above). In the lower deposits, hearths, artifacts, and bones of ground sloth, guanaco, and extinct horse were found in association with the human occupation. The artifacts include abundant projectile points of what has come to be known as the "fishtail" or Fell type. However, it was not only humans that contributed to the formation of the deposits. A recent study of the bones stored at the AMNH, not only revealed cut marks on horse bones, but also carnivore punctures on horse, *Lama* sp., and ground sloth bones (Borrero and Martin 1996). Moreover, the Fell cave deposits also included remains of hawks, falcons, and terrestrial carnivores suggesting natural deposition (Borrero 1999). Human presence can be assumed for the lower levels of Fell, as testified by cut marks on bones and abundant artifacts and hearths, but humans were not the only depositonal contributors (Borrero 1999). After this initial period, Period II was characterized by the presence of bone projectile points (and specifically, as shown in Bird 1938, fig. 26, lower right, the point we called in this paper a 'flat point') and the absence of lithic projectile points. Period III was characterized by stemless projectile points, Period IV by scrapers and stemmed projectile points, and finally, Period V by little stemmed projectile points that Bird called "ona" type attributing them to the ethnographically known Ona or Selknam people.

Pali Aike is a small cave within the caldera of an extinct volcano. Bird found the bones of seven ground sloths, american horse, and camelid (guanaco), together with human bones and artifacts. He excavated the cave completely, so that its history can be reconstructed only by studying the collections stored at the AMNH. A single radiocarbon date of 8639±450 BP (C-485) should be considered a minimum age (Bird 1988, see Table 5.2). In this case, it is difficult to determine what proportion of the bones should be attributed to human activities.

The French archaeologists, Emperaire, Laming-Emperaire, and Reichlen, also excavated Fell in the 1950s (Emperaire *et al.* 1963). Bird returned to Fell during summer 1969–1970 obtaining more materials and samples for radiocarbon datings (see Bird 1988). In the 1980s, Chilean researchers from the Instituto de la Patagonia (Punta Arenas city), continued that work (Massone 1981 and 1984). At the end of the 1980s and beginning of the 1990s Gómez Otero and Prieto developed a bi-national project in that area to study other sites (Gómez Otero 1986–1987, 1989–1990, 1991, 1994 and Prieto 1989–1990). In 2000, Hugo Nami carried out research in Rio Chico (near Fell; see Nami 1995) and finally in 2003, Borrero and others began a research project in PAVF both in Argentinean and Chilean territories (Borrero and Barberena 2006; Barberena 2008; Borrero and Charlin 2010) that still continues today. I analyzed bone tools recovered by Junius Bird from Pali Aike, Fell and Cañadón Leona sites (PAVF area), now located at the AMNH, for this work.

Since the 8000 BP date is key for testing our hypothesis I needed to establish temporal blocks to analyze the areas (see Table 5.2). The blocks were established on the basis of radiocarbon dates from the studied sites (see Tables 5.1 and 5.2). The main problem was that, given the earlier research by Bird at Fell, Pali Aike and Cañadon Leona, there are few radiocarbon dates actually available for those sites (most of them obtained in the 1969–70 fieldwork season; see Bird 1988 and Table 5.2). So, in that case, we identified pre-8000 BP layers and post 8000 BP layers while the last block conformed to the most recent findings in the upper layers following Bird's deductions (1988). The other problem that had to be considered is that the TDF sample is bigger than those from CCP and PAVF. It is known that the size of the sample determines its richness (Jones and Leonard 1989) so this is a factor that should be considered when contrasting the low diversity of PAVF and CCP with TDF, specially given this is not a problem of those sites alone but of all Continental Patagonian sites: as noted above, bone tools are scarce on every site. Here, we will compare the percentage contribution of each kind of raw material and tool design present within each sample in order to minimize this effect.

The sample is composed exclusively of bone tools, not including ornamental pieces or other kinds of artifacts. To be included in this work, bone tools must comply with the following requisites:

1. Be whole or almost so (presence of around two thirds of the estimated whole of the piece);
2. Be identifiable as a tool to the naked eye: those that, on account of their bad state or low level of elaboration were not identifiable as tools were disregarded;
3. Have a clear chronological ascription: only those tools that can be placed chronologically within one of the three blocks mentioned here were analyzed.

Table 5.2 Temporal blocks composition.

	Layers and sites	Radiocarbon datings (Layer or site)*	References
Block I (c. 10.000–8000 BP)	Cerro Casa de Piedra CCP7 layers 19–9	10530±62 9100±150	Civalero and Aschero (2003)
	Pali Aike (PA): 36–54"	8639 BP ± 450 years (C 485)	
	Fell: layer 12–17 – layer IV (1932–1937 excavation)	10720±300 (W-915) 11000±700(I-3988) Oldest occupation layer	Bird (1988) Bird (1988) Ortiz Troncoso (1980)
Block II (8000–3000 AP)	CCP5 layers 6–3 CCP7 layers 8–2	7060±105 4270±90	Civalero and Aschero (2003)
	PA 36–12"	Above level dated 8639±450 BP	Bird (1988) Ortiz Troncoso (1980)
	Fell: layer 5–11 – layer II–III (1932–1937)		
	Tierra del Fuego Sample (TDF): – inferior F and E layer from TuI – D layer from TuI	6980±110 6070±70 5630±120 6140±130	References Table 5.1
	– Dz, Xy and E layers from LP	4215±305 4900±70	
Block III (3000 to present)	CCP5: layers 2 to surface CCP7: layers 1 to surface	3480±70	De Nigris (2007)
	PA: surface to 12" Fell: surface to layer 4- S to layer I (1932–1937) CL	Presence of recent materials	Bird (1988) Ortiz Troncoso (1980)
	TDF B II BCI	2730±90 1527±58	References Table 5.1
	C layer TuI	4300±80 3530±90	
	TDF B III		
	–RS1	970±90	J.Bird Unpublished (AMNH)
	– SHI – D, A, B and C layers LP – Beta layer TU I – TU VII – SP4 – PM2 – BVS1	1220±10 1080±100 280±85 450±60 100±48 1750–1950 300±100	References Table 5.1

* in years BP unless indicated

The morphological groups were established following the criteria defined in Scheinsohn 2010a. Two criteria were used synthetically, to define the 20 different morphological groups or tool designs identified (see Table 5.3): 1) morphology of the active end, 2) raw material bone – camelid, cetacean, canid, pinniped, bird bones

The devised groups are presented in Table 5.3

Results

Raw materials

Taxa identification was made on the basis of morphological features alone. In the case of Continental Patagonia (CCP and PAVF), this implies underrepresentation of Cervidae (specifically huemul, *Hippocamelus bisulcus*,) and Rheidae

Table 5.3 Bone tools morphological groups.

Raw Material	Barbed point	Point	Blunted Point	Bevels	Surface	Tubular/ passive	Hook
Camelid (Guanaco)	**-BARBCAM** Single barbed harpoon head	**-PCAM** Camelid bone points (awls) **- PCAM Flat** Camelid bone flat points	**-BPCAM** Camelid bone blunted point (flaker)	**-BCAM** Camelid bone beveled pieces (includes foreshaft & spatulae)	**-SCAM** Camelid bone surface action tool (soft hammer percutor?)	**-TPCAM** Camelid bone tubular and passive pieces (mouth-piece and hafts)	
Cetacean	**-SB** Single barbed harpoon head **-VS** V-shaped harpoon head; **-SBMICRO** Little single barbed harpoon head; **-MB** Multibarbed harpoon head; **-PCET TANG** Broken barb harpoon head	**-PCET** Cetacean bone points		**-BCET** Cetacean bone beveled piece			
Bird		**-PBIRD** Avian bone point					
Canid		**-PCAN** Canid bone points (awls)					
Pinniped		**-PPIN** Pinniped bone pointed pieces		**-BPIN** Pinniped bone beveled pieces			
Cervid			**-BP CERVID** Cervid antler blunted point (flaker)				
ND							**HOOK** Spear-thrower hook

because it is not possible to identify morphological features allowing separation from Camelidae (guanaco) where a bone has been heavily worked. Nevertheless, these two taxa are scantly represented in the archaeofaunal record on Continental Patagonia (see de Nigris 2005, 2007)

Figures 5.2–4 present the results for each temporal block. Figure 5.2 show the results for Block I. There is no sample from TDF in this older block (see above and Table 5.1). In this graph the dominance of camelid bone in both samples (CCP and PAVF) is clear, something connected with its dominance in the archaeofaunal record (see Scheinsohn 2010b and references there). Apart from those taxa, cervid antler is utilized in CCP (the only record of antler tool use in the interior of southern Patagonia but see Cruz *et al.* 2010 for an artifact recovered on the coast) while canid and bird bone are also recorded in PAVF. The utilization of these taxa is not related to their consumption in either area. De Nigris (2007) carried out extensive faunal analysis for CCP. She identified avian bones but always in proportions lower than 2% of the sample. Actually, there were only 11 bird bone specimens (two classified as Rhea or ñandú) from 4617 bone specimens. Thus, the taxa was present but rarely exploited. Two reasons were proffered to explain this pattern. Herrera (1988) posited birds were not exploited because of seasonal

factors since layer 2 and 4 occupations took place in winter. Instead, Cruz (2000) considers that given the demographic characteristics of cordilleran birds, they would only have been occasionally exploited. Nevertheless, certain bird taxa might have been important in symbolic terms: a discarded serrated epiphysis of a condor ulna was recovered amongst the CCP material (Scheinsohn and Lucero 2006).

In Block II (Fig. 5.3), the TDF sample is clearly the most diverse of the three areas. The predominance of avian bone in the TDF sample is not connected to its predominance in the archaeofaunal record but can be attributed to the over-representation of avian bone at one site (Túnel I site; Scheinsohn 2010a). Nevertheless, there is more to the presence of bird bones (sometimes in high percentages) than the subsample from that site and the fact that it is represented in materials from all the analyzed sites (with only one exception). Avian bone must be considered one of the most important bone raw materials used by Fueguian populations. This raw material was manufactured into objects within a single morphological group, points (PBIRD see below). It is possible that, in view of its abundance, this implement group was used in more ways than has been suggested in ethnographical accounts (mostly as awls for basketry-making; see Scheinsohn *et al.* 1992 for details). I

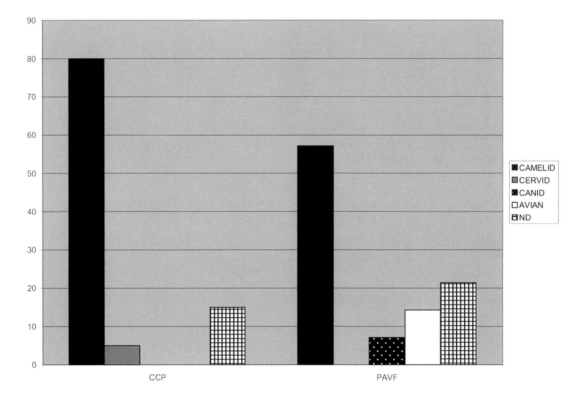

Figure 5.2 Bone raw material distribution in the three areas in Block I: CCP (Cerro Casa de Piedra), PAVF (Pali Aike Volcanic Field) TDF (Isla Grande de Tierra del Fuego) is absent in this temporal block. Y axis values are expressed in percentages.

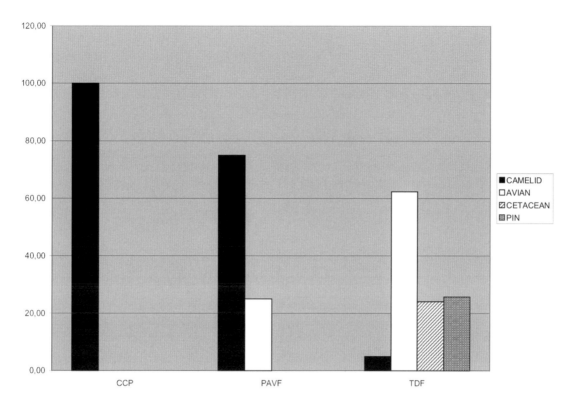

Figure 5.3 Bone raw material distribution in the three areas in Block II: CCP (Cerro Casa de Piedra), PAVF (Pali Aike Volcanic Field) and TDF (Isla Grande de Tierra del Fuego) Y axis values are expressed in percentages.

have proposed elsewhere that avian bones, beyond cormorant, which were hunted *en masse*, were scavenged from carcasses of dead birds on the beach (Scheinsohn 2010a). This was posited as part of the study of the bone tool assemblage as opposed to the avifaunal record at different Fuegian sites (Scheinsohn *et al.* 1992). Camelid bone still dominates in CCP and PAVF but is poorly represented in TDF. Cetacean and pinniped bones are only present in the TDF sample, with around 20% in each sample. Cetacean bones are usually available on the coast, as carcasses of stranded animals. It is likely that the rate of stranded whales in the past was similar to the current one (fairly often; cf. Goodall 1978; Goodall and Galeazzi 1986), so skeletons of these animals were probably available on beaches at all times as happens nowadays (cf. Borella and Favier Dubois 1994–1995, for Bahía San Sebastián). And for this reason, as Borrero (1985) points out, it is very difficult to evaluate to what extent cetaceans were part of the hunter-gatherers' diet through the analysis of their bone remains. Specifically, according to this author, the small number of cetacean bones present in the Fueguian sites might be linked to tool production

(Borrero 1985, 255). But there is no doubt that it was an important resource, since it allowed fat consumption to be increased (Borrero 1985). Pinniped bone use is as important as cetacean bone but in this case, since pinniped was the main staple in Isla Grande, it dominates the archaeofaunal record. In addition, pinniped and cetacean bone have similar mechanical properties (although the implements made from them had different purposes given their geometrical and structural properties; see Scheinsohn and Ferretti 1995 and Scheinsohn 2010a)

Finally, Figure 5.4 presents the results for Block III. This graph is similar to Figure 5.3 in terms of the raw material present in the three regions but in PAVF and TDF the proportions are different. In PAVF, although camelid bone still dominates the sample, avian bone representation increases (although note the small sample, N=8). In TDF, cetacean bone dominates, avian bone representation decreases and camelid bone representation increases so that it becomes as important as avian bone. Pinniped almost disappear from assemblages and there is only one case of canid bone being utilized.

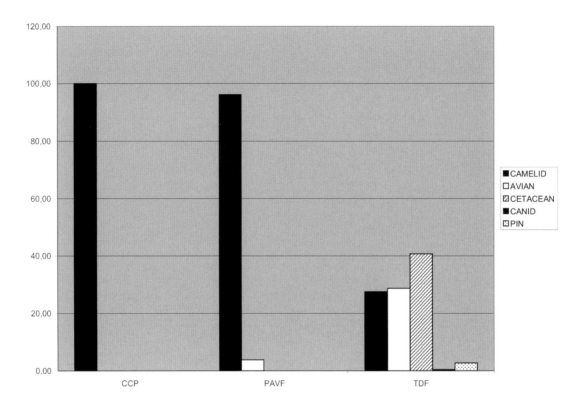

Figure 5.4 Bone raw material distribution in the three areas in Block III: CCP (Cerro Casa de Piedra), PAVF (Pali Aike Volcanic Field) and TDF (Isla Grande de Tierra del Fuego) Y axis values are expressed in percentages.

Designs or morphological groups of tools

Results with regard to design of implements can be considered in four ways: 1) tool designs found and recorded in all the areas, 2) tool designs found and recorded in PAVF and TDF, 3) tool designs found and recorded in PAVF and CCP, 3) tool designs found and recorded in one region only (see Table 5.4 for results).

1. TOOL DESIGNS RECORDED IN ALL AREAS

The only group or design which is present in all the samples in all temporal blocks is BPCAM (see Table 5.4). Functionally, this group could be considered flakers utilized for manufacturing stone tools (from their morphology and use wear marks; see Nami and Scheinsohn 1997). Leaving aside differences in stone tool-making traditions, the way flakers are used does not allow for much morphological variation. Tools like this could be found anywhere where stone tool-making occurred, and with not much variation. The only common factor worthy of consideration here is tool decoration (see below).

The other tool design which is present in most of the areas and temporal blocks is PCAM, that is only absent in the TDF BII and CCP BIII assemblages. In the first case, its absence

could be due to the huge frequencies of PBIRD, since there may have been some functional overlap. However, in the later case, the small sample size is the most likely cause. Individual piece in this group employ an epiphysis as a proximal end. As such, they could be used as awls for working hide or other soft materials. However, some of them may have been hafted and in that case they were not utilized as awls but rather as projectile points, at least in two cases from CCP BI, although this function is hard to tell from distal end morphology alone. Microwear studies need to be developed here.

The other tool design present in all the three regions is TPCAM. In this group, mouthpieces (two cases) and hafts, recorded in CCP and TDF, should be differentiated from the 33 pieces in PAVF BIII which can be considered pestles ("machacadores" *sensu* Hajduk and Lezcano 2005) given the wear marks on them. In any case, in the sample analyzed here, they are only present at the site of Cañadon Leona although they were recorded at many other early sites from southern Patagonia (see Hajduk and Lezcano 2005). The tools recorded as TPCAM in TDF were recorded only at the site of Punta María. The wear marks on them have not been extensively studied so it is not clear how they functioned although they exhibit few percussion marks.

2. Tool designs recorded in PAVF and TDF

PBIRD (absent in all the temporal blocks from CCP; see Table 5.4) is amazingly abundant in TDF whilst rare in PAVF. Another design shared between PAVF and TDF is PCANID although in different temporal blocks and with only two cases (Table 5.4). Finally, BCAM is recorded in the two regions but the two examples from PAVF are actually foreshafts (Scheinsohn 2010b) and not spatulae or beveled tools as they are in TDF. There are spatulate tools made from camelid bone (rib) from PAVF but since they were on exhibit, they could not be studied or included in the sample.

3. Tool designs recorded in PAVF and CCP

The designs shared between these two regions include SCAM, PCAM Flat and HOOK tools (see Table 5.4). Probably, SCAM tools are soft percussion tools connected to stone tool working. In CCP, they were first identified in the archaeofaunal record by De Nigris (Scheinsohn and Lucero 2006; Scheinsohn 2010b), who carried out extensive studies of the archaeofaunal record (De Nigris 2005 and 2007). This form is probably absent in the TDF sample because they were not identified as tools and separated from the archaeofaunal record.

PCAM flat, actually the bone point that Bird established as indicator of Period II, is recorded in both areas but also in many others in southern Patagonia (Scheinsohn 2010b). Their wear marks suggest they are actually devices used in pairs to attach another (stone?) tool, like hafts or oversized foreshafts. Detailed studies are still to be carried out.

HOOK is recorded only in Block I in this region. It is supposed that they are spearthrower hooks but actually the one recorded in CCP is considerably smaller than the one recorded in PAVF (Scheinsohn 2010b) so maybe the two tools had different functions or the smaller one is a toy or model.

4. Tool designs recorded in only one region

Ten out of 20 tool designs are "endemic" to TDF, i.e. these designs are only present in that region and not in the others. These implements are connected to pinniped hunting, since they are mostly harpoon heads (SB, SBmicro, MB, VS, BARBCAM although this last might be used for fishing; Scheinsohn 2010a) harpoon heads blanks (PCET) or recycled harpoon heads (PCET TANG) and woodworking tools (BCAM, BCET and BPIN). BPCERVID (manufactured in huemul antler, probably only present in the cordilleran area) was the "endemic" design for CCP while BCAM, like the two foreshafts mentioned above, represents a single case for PAVF.

Table 5.4 Morphological groups analyzed by temporal block and area.

Design*	CCP BI	PAVF BI	CCP BII	PAVF BII	TDF BII	CCP BIII	PAVF BIII	TDF BIII	Total
SCAM	2	–	5	–	–	2	2	–	11
BPCAM	6	2	2	5	4	1	13	22	55
TPCAM	1	–	6	–	–	–	33	16	56
PCAM Flat	2	1	–	–	–	–	–	–	3
PCAM	7	5	4	1	–	–	2	18	37
BARBCAM	–	–	–	–	–	–	–	6	6
BCAM	–	2 (F)	–	–	5	–	–	9	16
BPCERVID	1	–	–	–	–	–	–	–	1
PCAN	–	1	–	–	–	–	–	1	2
PBIRD	–	2	–	2	114	–	2	74	194
PCET	–	–	–	–	5	–	–	20	25
SB	–	–	–	–	16	–	–	19	35
SB MICRO	–	–	–	–	3	–	–	7	10
MB	–	–	–	–	8	–	–	10	18
VS	–	–	–	–	6	–	–	1	7
PCET TANG	–	–	–	–	–	–	–	22	22
BCET	–	–	–	–	6	–	–	26	32
BPIN/PPIN	–	–	–	–	16	–	–	7	23
HOOK	1	1	–	–	–	–	–	–	2
Total	20	14	17	8	183	3	52	258	555

*See Table 5.3 for definitions of design types.
CCP BI= Cerro Casa de Piedra Block I; PAVF BI= Pali Aike Volcanic Field Block I; CCP BII= Cerro Casa de Piedra Block II; PAVF BII= Pali Aike Volcanic Field Block II; TDF BII= Tierra del Fuego Block II; CCP BIII= Cerro Casa de Piedra Block III; PAVF BIII= Pali Aike Volcanic Field Block III; TDF BIII= Tierra del Fuego Block III; (F) = Foreshaft.

Discussion

In CCP and PAVF, guanaco (camelid) dominates as a source of bone raw material. What is interesting is that some of the tool forms made from camelid bone were utilized for weapon manufacture (foreshafts, atlatl hooks), probably to hunt guanaco. Since camelid and cervid bone are taken as prey, bone raw material exploitation is connected to animal consumption in CCP. In the case of PAVF, it is harder to tell because there has never been an extensive study of the archaeofaunal record recovered by Bird although L'Heureux has carried out archaeofaunal studies at other more recent sites in the area (3500 BP dated Orejas de Burro I site; L'Heureux 2008) where *Rodentia* dominates, although these bones probably found their way naturally into the sample. This taxa is followed by camelid, avian, molluscs and fish remains. The taxa composition of bone tools, although more ancient at the sites of Fell and Pali Aike, is coherent with this picture.

The presence of canid bone in PAVF and condor bone in CCP is worth noting (not recorded here since it is probably debris of bead or tube manufacture; Scheinsohn and Lucero 2006; Scheinsohn 2010b). The meat of these two animals was not normally consumed by human populations in Patagonia (although there is evidence of processing on fox and puma bones; see L'Heureux 2008), so it is a possibility that their bones were scavenged or, specifically in the case of the canid (fox), that this animal was exploited for its fur.

In TDF, avian followed by cetacean and pinniped bone dominates the bone tool raw material. While these taxa are represented in the archaeofaunal record, their importance differs. Avian taxa recorded in archaeofaunal evidence are not the same and do not have the same importance as in avian bone tools. Frequencies of avian bone tools are biased by the Túnel I site sample. Thus, this could be a case in which specific activities local to a particular settlement bias the sample. However, it is also possible that it was used in more varied ways than is suggested in ethnographic accounts (associated with basket-making; Scheinsohn *et al.* 1992). Cetacean bone is associated with littoral hunting gear, taking advantage of cetacean bone properties (Scheinsohn and Ferretti 1995) as well as wood-working. This last was the case for pinniped bone that had similar properties although the smaller size of their bones does not permit as much tranformation of the material. (Scheinsohn and Ferretti 1995). Clearly, here the divergence is related to the ecology of the Isla Grande (pinniped littoral hunting and wood exploitation). Thus, the sample size of the TDF sample cannot account for its variety alone.

In the case of tool forms, flakers are the only tool found in all three regions. With few endemic forms, CPP and PAVF share more tool forms in common while TDF has more diverse and endemic forms from the BII onwards.

Conclusions

In conclusion, it can be said that bone technology in CCP and PAVF in the first temporal block was somewhat varied with the suggestion that weapons were present. Following that temporal block, bone tools were limited to flakers and awls, signaling a general impoverishment in bone tool variability in Continental Patagonia. Since in the next temporal blocks there is no hunting gear manufactured in bone, the question arises if this impoverishment has to do with a change in hunting methods and technology. The evidence appears to fits the proposal that hunting in the Middle Holocene was collective and done using bola stones (Aschero 2000).

In contrast, bone tools in TDF diversified (in terms of tool morphological groups) soon after their appearance in temporal block II.

There were almost no endemic designs in CCP and PAVF but, while some TDF tool forms were shared with these areas, there were ten tool groups endemic to TDF.

Most of the results presented here support our hypothesis on TDF divergence given the quantity of endemic tool forms and diversity within tool classes. However, it must be pointed out that variability in decoration, a factor not specifically studied here, could change the picture. Recent research carried out by Fiore (2006, 2011) on decoration on bone tools from TDF made her question Borrero's vicariance model (Fiore 2006). The spread of decoration in TDF and the Magellan Channels was connected to the development of littoral marine systems (Fiore 2006). When studying the PAVF collection, I recorded bone beads made from avian bones that had a similar decoration to that recorded in TDF (Fiore 2006). Nevertheless, it should be taken into account that PAVF is close to TDF so that avian bone beads could actually be Fueguian bone beads and their presence in PAVF a consequence of exchange with Fueguian populations. The same could be true for the remainder of their shared bone tool design repertoire.

These decorative motifs are also geometric and basic, so it is difficult to say whether they really represent a shared pattern. The comparison of CCP, PAVF and TDF bone tool decoration patterns is promising and deserves more extensive study. Here, I will only suggest that there is a specific decorative pattern, present in PAVF and CCP, on flakers. This pattern consists of marks on the lateral surfaces. I have also found a similar pattern of use-wear marks on one flaker. Perhaps this is a case where a worn flaker was appreciated because it represented the dexterity of its owner and then the wear pattern was later transformed into a decorative pattern (see fig. 2 Scheinsohn 2010b comparing the two cases). These kinds of common decorative patterns was also recorded by L'Heureux (2008, figs 9 and 14) on PAVF at the Orejas de Burro I site.

In conclusion, the divergence hypothesis, maintained by Borrero could be supported by bone technology data. From a common base shared with CCP and PAVF in BI, TDF followed a separate trajectory very early on (BII) although most of its variety was connected with factors unique to TDF such as insularity, littoral hunting technology and wood exploitation.

PAVF and CCP bone tools are closer in terms of shared tool designs and the raw materials exploited, despite the 500 km that separate these areas. Those similarities point to interconnected populations. This picture is reinforced by the presence of the same tool forms at other Patagonian sites near these regions (such as the flat points from the Deseado Basin and Rio Pinturas and other sites mentioned by Nami 2010, and pestles; see Lezcano and Hajduk 2005) and fits with Borrero's peopling model expectations. In any case, PAVF was not totally isolated from TDF since they share traditions of canid and avian bone exploitation, although with different intensities, and possibly some basic decorative modifs.

Nevertheless, given the absence of the BI sample from TDF, the Continental Patagonia bone technology could be interpreted as ancestral to the Fueguian in terms of the tool forms that they share. Divergences present on the island and its independent development was led by its special ecological and cultural circumstances. The common visual code implied by the decoration is intriguing in this context and will be dealt in future publications.

Acknowledgements

Thanks to Alice Choyke, Sonia O'Connor and Carole Vercoutère for inviting me to contribute this paper to the ICAZ symposium. Also thanks to the XI ICAZ Conference organizers for the grant that allowed me to attend the meeting. Sonia O'Connor and Alice Choyke had also kindly helped me with the English translation. Carlos Aschero, Teresa Civalero, Damián Bozzuto, Antonella Di Vruno and the others members of the Cerro Casa de Piedra archaeological project helped me with their knowledge and their support. Also, I want to acknowledge the Study Collection Grant that the American Museum of Natural History gave me in order to study the bone tools from the sites of Fell, Pali Aike and Cañadón Leona. I want to thank Sumru Aricanli and Tom Amorosi for their kindness when I was working at the American Museum of Natural History. Mariana De Nigris, Pablo Fernández, Isabel Cruz and Natacha Buc contributed their taxonomic identifications and many, many comments and discussions that enriched this paper in addition to Gabriela Guraieb suggestions. Ana Fondebrider contributed the map. Sabrina Leonardt, Florencia Rizzo and Paula Serpe (students at the University of Buenos Aires) helped me to organize the data. Finally, many thanks to the anonymous reviewer who helped to improve this work. This study was carried out thanks to ANPCYT, CONICET and UBA grants.

Bibliography

Aschero, C. (2000) El poblamiento del territorio. In M. Tarragó (ed.), *Nueva Historia Argentina, Tomo I: los Pueblos originarios y la Conquista*, 17–60. Buenos Aires, Sudamericana.

Aschero, C. A., Goñi, R. A., Civalero, M. T., Molinari, R., Espinosa, S., Guraieb, A. G. and Bellelli, C. (2005) Holocenic Park: arqueologia del Parque Nacional Perito Moreno. *Anales de Parques Nacionales* 17, 71–119.

Barberena, R. (2008) *Arqueologia y Biogeografia Humana En Patagonia Meridional*. Buenos Aires, SAA.

Bird, J. (1938) Antiquity and migrations of the early inhabitants of Patagonia. *Geographical Review* 28 (2), 250–275.

Bird, J. (1988) *Travels and Archaeology in South Chile*, J. Hyslop (ed.), Iowa, University of Iowa Press.

Borella, F. and Favier Dubois, C. (1994–1995) Observaciones tafonómicas en la Bahía San Sebastián, Costa Norte de Tierra del Fuego, Argentina. *Palimpsesto* 4, 1–8.

Borrero, L. A. (1985) *La Economía Prehistórica de los Habitantes del Norte de la Isla Grande de Tierra del Fuego*. Unpublished PhD thesis, Universidad de Buenos Aires.

Borrero, L. A. (1989–1990) Evolución cultural divergente en la Patagonia Austral. *Anales del Instituto de la Patagonia* 19, 133–140.

Borrero, L. A. (1999) The prehistoric exploration and colonization of Fuego-Patagonia *Journal of World Prehistory* 13 (3), 321–355.

Borrero, L. A. and Barberena, R. (2006) Hunter-gatherer home ranges and marine resources. An archaeological case from Southern Patagonia. *Current Anthropology* 47 (5), 855–867.

Borrero, L. A. and Martin, F. M. (1996) Tafonomía de carnívoros: un enfoque regional. In J. Gómez Otero (ed.), *Arqueologia. Solo Patagonia*. 189–198. Puerto Madryn, CENPAT- CONICET.

Borrero, L. A. and Charlin, J. (2010) *Arqueología de Pali Aike y Cabo Vírgenes*. Buenos Aires, CONICET-IMHICIHU.

Chapman, A. (1986) *Los Selk'nam. La vida de los Onas*. Buenos Aires, Emecé.

Civalero, M. T. and Aschero, C. A. (2003) Early occupations at Cerro Casa de Piedra 7, Santa Cruz Province, Patagonia Argentina. In L. Miotti, M. Salemme and N. Flegenheimer (eds), *Where the South Wind Blow: ancient evidences for paleo South Americans*. 141–147. Dallas, A&M University Press.

Cocilovo, J. and Guichón, R. (1985–1986) Propuesta para el estudio de las poblaciones aborígenes del extremo austral de Patagonia. *Anales del Instituto de la Patagonia* 16, 111–123.

Croizat, L., Nelson, G. and Rosen, D. E. (1974) Centers of origin and related concepts. *Systematic Zoology* 23, 265–287.

Cruz, I. (2000) Los restos de aves de los sitios arqueológicos del Parque Nacional Perito Moreno (Santa Cruz, Argentina). *Anales del Instituto de la Patagonia* 28, 305–313.

Cruz, I., Muñoz, A. S. and Caracotche, M. S. (2010) Un artefacto en asta de huemul (*Hippocamelus bisulcus*) en depósitos arqueológicos de la costa atlántica. Implicaciones para la movilidad humana y la distribución de la especie. *Magallania* 38 (1), 287–294.

De Nigris, M. (2005) *El Consumo en Grupos Cazadores-recolectores. Un ejemplo zooarqueológico de Patagonia Meridional*. Buenos Aires, Sociedad Argentina de Antropología.

De Nigris, M. (2007) Nuevos datos, viejas colecciones: los conjuntos óseos de Cerro Casa de Piedra Cueva 5 (Parque Nacional Perito Moreno, Santa Cruz), *Intersecciones en Antropología* 8, 253–264.

Emperaire, J., Laming-Emperaire, A. and Reichlen, H. (1963) La Grotte Fell et autres sites de la region volcanique de la Patagonie Chillienne. *Journal de la Société des Américanistes* 52, 167–257.

Fiore, D. (2006) Puentes de agua para el arte mobiliar: la distribución espacio-temporal de artefactos óseos decorados en Patagonia meridional y Tierra del Fuego. *Cazadores-recolectores del Cono Sur. Revista de Arqueología* 1, 137–147.

Fiore, D. (2011) Art in time. Diachronic rates of change in the decoration of bone artefacts from the Beagle Channel region (Tierra del Fuego, southern South America). *Journal of Anthropological Archaeology* 30, 484–501.

Gómez Otero, J. (1986–1987) Investigaciones arqueológicas en el alero Potrok-aike (Prov. de Santa Cruz.) Una revisión de los períodos IV y V de Bird. *Relaciones de la Sociedad Argentina de Antropología* 18, 173–200.

Gómez Otero, J. (1989–1990) Cazadores tardíos en la zona fronteriza argentino-chilena (paralelo 52° S) El sitio Juni-aike 1. *Anales del Instituto de la Patagonia* 19, 47–71.

Gómez Otero, J. (1991) Un modelo predictivo-explicativo sobre el sistema de asentamiento de la fase Magallanes IV. *Shincal* 3 (3), 191–195.

Gómez Otero, J. (1994) The function of small rockshelters in the Magallanes IV Phase settlement system. *Latin American Antiquity* 4 (4), 325–345.

Goodall, R. N. P. (1978) Report on the small cetaceans stranded on the coasts of Tierra del Fuego. *Scientific Reports of the Whales Research Institute* 30, 197–230.

Goodall, R. N. P. and Galeazzi, A. (1986) Cetacean survey in eastern Tierra del Fuego and Isla de los Estados. *Antarctic Journal* XXI (4), 15–17.

Hajduk, A. and Lezcano, M. (2005) Un "nuevo-viejo" integrante del elenco de instrumentos óseos de Patagonia: los machacadores óseos. *Magallania* 33 (1), 63–80.

Herrera, O. (1988) Arqueofauna del sitio Cerro Casa de Piedra 5. *Resúmenes de las Ponencias Científicas Presentadas al IX Congreso Nacional de Arqueología Argentina*, Buenos Aires, Facultad de Filosofía y Letras – UBA, 67.

Horwitz, V. D. (1990) *Maritime Settlement Patterns in Southeastern Tierra del Fuego (Argentina)*. Unpublished PhD Thesis, University of Kentucky.

Horwitz, V. and Scheinsohn, V. (1996) Los instrumentos óseos del sitio Bahía Crossley I (Isla de los Estados).Comparación con otros conjuntos de la Isla Grande de Tierra del Fuego. In J. Gómez Otero (ed.), *Arqueología. Solo Patagonia*, Puerto Madryn, CENPAT-CONICET, 359–368.

Jones, G. and Leonard R. (1989) The concept of diversity: an introduction. In R. Leonard, and G. Jones (eds), *Quantifying Diversity in Archaeology*, 1–3, Cambridge, Cambridge University Press.

L'Heureux, L. (2008) La arqueofauna del Campo Volcánico Pali Aike. El sitio Orejas de Burro 1, Santa Cruz, Argentina. *Magallania* 36 (1), 65–78.

Massone, M. (1981) Arqueología de la región volcánica de Pali Aike (Patagonia meridional chilena). *Anales del Instituto de la Patagonia* 12, 95–124.

Massone, M. (1984) Los paraderos Tehuelches y Proto Tehuelches en la costa del estrecho de Magallanes. Una aproximación teórica y metodológica. *Anales del Instituto de la Patagonia* 15, 27–42.

Menghin, O. F. A. (1957) El protolítico en América. *Acta Praehistorica* I, 5–40.

Menghin, O. F. A. (1960) Urgeschichte der Kanuindianer des Sudlichsten Amerika. *Steinzeitfragen del Alten und Neuen Welt*, 343–375.

Muñoz, A. S. (2002) *La Explotación de Mamíferos por Cazadores-Recolectores Terrestres de Tierra del Fuego*. Unpublished PhD Thesis, Universidad de Buenos Aires.

Muñoz, A. S. (2005) Zooarqueología del sector atlántico de la Isla Grande de Tierra del Fuego. *Relaciones de la Sociedad Argentina de Antropología* 30, 59–77.

Nami H. G. (1995) Archaeological research in the Argentinean Rio Chico Basin. *Current Anthropology* 36 (4), 661–664.

Nami, H. (2010) Late Pleistocene technology in the New World: bone artifacts from Cueva del Medio and other sites in the Southern Cone of South America. In A. Legrand-Pineau, I. Sidéra and N. Buc, E. David, V. Scheinsohn (eds), *Ancient and Modern Bone Artefacts from America to Russia. Cultural, technological and functional signature*, 279–286, Oxford, Archaeopress (British Archaeological Report S2136).

Nami, H. and Scheinsohn, V. (1997) Use-wear patterns on bone flakers. In L. A. Hannus L. Rossum and R. P. Winham (eds), *Proceedings of the 1993 Bone Modification Conference , Hot Springs, South Dakota*. Sioux Falls, Occasional Publication 1, Augustana College 256–264.

Nelson, G. and Platnick, N. (1981) *Systematics and Biogeography: cladistics and vicariance*. New York, Columbia University Press.

Orquera, L. and Piana, E. (1985) *Octava Campaña en Tierra del Fuego: la localidad Shumakush*. Paper delivered at VIII Congreso Nacional de Arqueología Argentina, Concordia.

Orquera, L. and Piana, E. (1986–1987) Composición tipológica y datos tecnomorfológicos y tecnofuncionales de los conjuntos arqueológicos del sitio Túnel I (Tierra del Fuego, República Argentina). *Relaciones de la Sociedad Argentina de Antropología* 17, 201–239.

Orquera, L. and Piana, E. (1987) Human littoral adaptation in the Beagle Channel region: The maximum possible age. *Quaternary of South America and Antarctic Peninsula* 5, 133–62.

Orquera, L. and Piana E. (1996) Túnel VII. La cronología. In J. Estévez Escalera and A. Vila Mitjá (eds.) *Encuentros en los conchales fueguinos*, Treballs D'Etnoarquelogía 1, 105–112, Barcelona, UAB.

Orquera, L. and Piana, E. (1999) *Arqueología de la Región del Canal Beagle (Tierra del Fuego, República Argentina)*. Buenos Aires, Sociedad Argentina de Antropología.

Orquera, L., Sala, A., Piana, E. and Tapia, A. (1977) *Lancha Packewaia. Arqueología de los Canales Fueguinos*. Buenos Aires, Huemul.

Ortiz-Troncoso, O. (1980) Inventory of radiocarbon dates from southern Patagonia and Tierra del Fuego. *Journal de la Société des Américanistes* 67, 185–212.

Piana, E. (1984) Arrinconamiento o adaptación en Tierra del Fuego, In *Ensayos de Antropología Argentina (año 1984)*. Buenos Aires, Editorial de la Universidad de Belgrano, 7–110.

Prieto, A. (1989–1990) Cazadores tardíos en la zona fronteriza del paralelo 52° sur. El alero Peggy Bird. *Anales del Instituto de la Patagonia* 19, 73–85.

Rosen, D. E. (1978) Vicariant patterns and historical explanations in biogeography. *Systematic Zoology* 27, 159–188.

Scheinsohn, V. (1997) *Explotación de Materias Primas Óseas en la Isla Grande de Tierra del Fuego*. Unpublished PhD Thesis, Universidad de Buenos Aires.

Scheinsohn, V. (2010a) *Hearts and Bones: Bone raw material exploitation in Tierra del Fuego*. Oxford, Archaeopress (British Archaeological Report S2094).

Scheinsohn, V. (2010b) Down to the bone: tracking for bone technology in southern Patagonia. In A. Legrand-Pineau, I. Sidéra and N. Buc, E. David, and V. Scheinsohn (eds), *Ancient and Modern Bone Artefacts from America to Russia. Cultural, technological and functional signature*, 1–6, Oxford, Archaeopress (British Archaeological Report S2136).

Scheinsohn, V. (2011) El trabajo del hueso en el fin del mundo: tecnología ósea en Bahía Valentín. In A. Zangrando, N. Vázquez and A. Tessone (eds), *Los Cazadores-recolectores del Extremo Oriental Fueguino. Arqueología de Península Mitre e Isla de los Estados*, 271–286, Buenos Aires, Sociedad Argentina de Antropología.

Scheinsohn, V. and Ferretti, J. L. (1995) Mechanical properties of bone materials as related to design and function of prehistoric tools from Tierra del Fuego (Argentina). *Journal of Archaeological Science* 22, 711–17.

Scheinsohn, V. and Lucero, M. (2006) *Explotación de Materias Primas Óseas en el Sur del Continente: el caso de Cerro Casa de Piedra*. Available on-line in BoneCommons http://www.alexandriaarchive.org/bonecommons/items/show/465

Scheinsohn, V., Di Baja, A. Lanza, M. and Tramaglino L. (1992) El aprovechamiento de la avifauna como fuente de materia prima ósea en la Isla Grande de Tierra del Fuego: Túnel I, Lancha Packewaia y Shamakush I. *Arqueología* 2, 135–148.

Vidal, H. (1985) *Los conchales de Bahía Valentín*. Licenciatura Thesis, University of Buenos Aires.

Wiley E. O. (1988) Vicariance biogeography. *Annual Review of Ecology and Systematics* 19, 513–542.

CHAPTER 6

Changed into Tools. Camelid Bones from the Southern Calchaquíes Valleys (Formative Period, North-western Argentina)

Andrés D. Izeta, Roxana Cattáneo, M. Cristina Scattolin and Leticia I. Cortés

This paper presents the results of macro- and microscopic analysis of a sample of ten bone tools dated to the Formative Period in the southern Calchaquíes valleys, north-western Argentina. All these implements were manufactured from South American camelid metapodials following a very standardized technique. In accordance with previous models of handling and use of camelid resources, we propose that these instruments could have been employed in the processing soft materials (e.g. weaving or basketry).

Keywords
Zooarchaeology; South America; north-western Argentina; bone instruments; microscopic analysis.

Introduction

Over the last 30 years, the Formative Period (*c.* 1500 BC–AD 600) in the southern Calchaquíes valleys has been subject of extensive archaeological research, increasing both the number of excavated sites and the lines of evidence that have been explored. Household architectural patterns, archaeobotany, obsidian provenance analysis, pottery manufacture, iconographic studies, zooarchaeological and funerary analysis have been pursued in the complex task of reconstructing pre-Hispanic local history (e.g. Scattolin and Gero 1999; Gero and Scattolin 2002; Scattolin 2006a, 2006b; Izeta 2007; Palamarczuk *et al.* 2007; Bugliani 2008; Calo 200; Lazzari *et al.* 2009; Scattolin *et al.* 2009b; Pereyra Domingorena 2010; Scattolin 2010; Cortés 2011; Oliszewski 2011).

The Formative Period in the archaeology of north-western Argentina has been described as a time of segmented groups with low levels of social hierarchy, a mixed economy subsistence system based on agriculture, hunting and herding and a settlement pattern of scattered architectural units and agricultural fields (e.g. Tarragó 1992; Olivera 2001; Scattolin 2006a, 2010). Houses were usually made of stone or adobe walls and thatched roofs, arranged both in circular and square plans, isolated or combined in a variety of sizes (e.g. Scattolin 2006a, 2010). Cemetery areas and burial structures have been found in association with dwelling structures as well as beneath house floors. Although mostly self-sufficient, these villages were connected through distribution and exchange of goods on a regional scale. During the Terminal Formative Period (AD 500–600), architectural layouts diversified and residential and ceremonial places are found separated from each other. Contemporary with Tiwanaku expansion, social inequalities increased. At the same time, there was a reduction in population mobility, residential expansion, and increased stability. These changes fostered craftsmanship and popularized the use of various raw materials and manufactured goods such as pottery, basketry, textiles, metalwork, stone and bone tools, among others things. (Fig. 6.1).

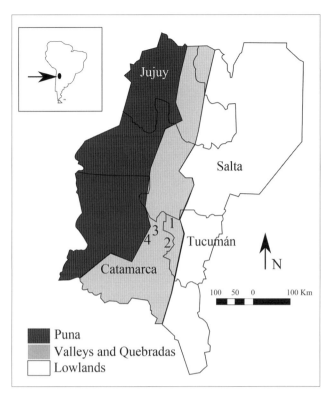

Figure 6.1 Map of the region showing the locations of sites mentioned in this paper.

The archaeological investigations in the southern part of the Calchaquíes valleys began with initial work of Scattolin on the western slopes of the Aconquija mountain range (Scattolin 1990) and the adjacent Santa María Valley (Scattolin *et al.* 2001) later expanding towards the western Cajón Valley (Scattolin and Gero 1999). The combined work of all team members has deepened our understanding of lifeways at the first agrarian villages settled in these three areas, which were otherwise mainly known from evidence of the subsequent Late Period (*c.* AD 1000–1500).

In particular, the study of faunal assemblages carried out by Izeta began to unravel the local strategies of management and use of wild and domesticated species (Izeta 2007, 2008). The ubiquity of camelid bones in the archaeological record shows that they were used and consumed in a variety of forms. The domestication of some Andean camelids (*Lama glama, Vicugna pacos*) was fundamental to the daily life of past peoples: not only were they consumed as food resources (meat, grease, marrow, bone grease and possibly even milk) but also their fibres. It may be leather and tendons were also employed for a variety of purposes. As many well studied archaeological and ethnographic contexts reveal, camelid fibers were widely used in textile manufacture throughout the Central and Meridional Andes. Although the evidence for these practices comes from indirect sources in our study area – such as spindle-whorls,

possible wool textile imprints in baked mud (Calo 2008) – or from adjacent regions – human remains dressed or wrapped in fabrics made of camelid wool from the Puna (López Campeny 2000, 2010; Agüero and Cases 2004), camelid fabrics from Ansilta, San Juan Province (Renard 1997). Thus, it is safe to assume that camelid textile manufacture was also commonly practiced in the Formative Period of the Calchaquíes valleys (Renard 1997).

Furthermore, the use of llamas as beasts of burden has been the main argument behind one of the most popular models in the cultural development of the South Central Andes area (Núñez and Dillehay 1979). Indirect evidences such as ceramic, vegetable and obsidian trade support the widespread hypothesis of camelids being used to carry goods along the caravan routes and networks that connected different areas within north-western Argentina (Núñez and Dillehay 1979; Scattolin and Lazzari 1997; Yacobaccio *et al.* 2004). Alternative models for camelid handling and use have, however, been proposed for the Puna region (Haber 1999).

Earlier considerations of the zooarchaeological record based on the analysis of faunal remains from 15 archaeological contexts dated to the Formative Period resulted in a consistent image of animal handling and use (Izeta 2007, 2008; Scattolin *et al.* 2009a). South American camelid age profiles, bone fracture and discard patterns within household activity areas indicate that mainly adult animals were consumed throughout the whole period (Izeta 2007). In particular, age profiles of domestic camelids (*Lama glama*) have shown that they were primarily exploited as cargo animals or for their secondary products (wool or fleece) rather than primary ones (meat, grease, etc.). Supporting evidence for the use of camelids as beasts of burden has been verified by palaeopathological alterations on camelid phalanges (Izeta and Cortés 2006; Cartajena *et al.* in press). In other words, domestic animals appeared to have been consumed after they reached a 'non-productive' age instead of being slaughtered while still young. Nevertheless, a different pattern has been observed in contemporary occupations in nearby areas such as the Ambato valley, Antofagasta de la Sierra in the southern Puna, and at least in one location in the Santa María Valley, where primary products appear to have been the main purpose of camelid husbandry (Belotti 2007; Dantas 2010; Grant Lett-Brown 2008; Olivera 1998).

As a result, the study of animal bones has been central to the understanding of early subsistence strategies among ancient villagers in north-western Argentina (Izeta 2008; Izeta *et al.* 2012). In this sense, zooarchaeological analysis emphasized approaches to animal bones as indicators of culinary or transport activities, rather than bones as implements.

While systematic research on the use of bone as a raw material and the associated technical strategies has been undertaken in the last few years in different regions of Argentina, it is still at its beginning for material from the

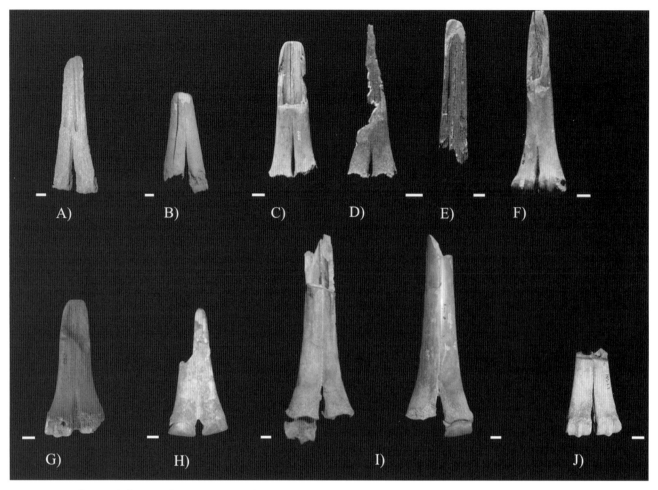

Figure 6.2 Artefacts made from South American camelid metapodials. A) C493-1, Cardonal Tomb 1; B) C493-2, Cardonal Tomb 1; C) Yu-1341, Yutopián Structure 1; D) Yu-165, Yutopián Structure 4; E) Yu-141, Yutopián Structure 4; F) Yu-54, Yutopián Structure 4; G) C58-2, Cardonal E 2; H) 469-1, Bañado Viejo; I) 404-8, Bañado Viejo; J) 105-1, Loma Alta Nucleus E. All scales represent 1 cm.

north-western region (e.g. Casiraghi 1985; Scheinsohn 1997; Núñez Regueiro 1998; Nasif and Gómez Cardozo 1999; Buc and Loponte 2007; Buc 2011). To date, little is known about the techniques used in the manufacture of personal bone adornment, needles, awls, musical instruments, figurines, among other worked osseous objects.

Therefore, although previous investigations have deepened our understanding of the different modes of acquisition, production, consumption and discard of animal remains (leather, meat, fleece, etc.), the use of bones as a raw material or the occurrence of bone tools is yet to be fully considered. The analysis of a sample of ten implements made of camelid metapodials discussed in this paper (Fig. 6.2) thus begins to fill this gap by offering a first approach to the study of bone as a raw material during the Formative Period in north-western Argentina.

Archaeological contexts and bone tools

As far as the records show, bones from different taxa were employed in the manufacturing of implements of various kinds (Table 6.1) although South American camelids appear to have been preferred over other species reflecting the extensive use of all of the South American camelid sub-products. Without exception, they are the most common and frequent animals found on all recorded archaeological sites in the north-west region of Argentina (Izeta 2008; Olivera 1998). Another reason can be related with culturally weighted preferences for particular species and skeletal elements as raw material. Miller (1979) in his ethnoarchaeological research in the Central Andes noted that modern female Aymara weavers' use a particular bone tool called *wichuña* and they prefer llama bones over alpaca, and adult camelid bones rather than bones from younger animals. Such preferences correspond to certain

Table 6.1 Bone artefacts quantification from selected southern Calchaquíes Valley Formative sites.

Taxon	Body Size	Bañado Viejo	Loma Alta	Yutopián	Cardonal T1	Total
AVES	2	1	–	–	–	1
Rodentia	2	–	1	–	–	1
CARNIVORA	2	–	–	1	–	1
Ungulata	4	1	4	6	–	11
Camelidae	4	2	2	1	2	7
Lama guanicoe	4	–	1	–	–	1
Unknown	1	–	1	–	–	1
	3–4	–	1	–	–	1
Total		4	10	8	2	24
NISP (whole site)		1527	1763	5341	2	8633
NISP % bone instruments		0.26	0.57	0.15	100.00	0.27

archaeological samples as far as choices of raw material for tool-making is concerned.

The assemblage of bone tools considered here comes from four sites located in the southern Calchaquíes valleys: Bañado Viejo, Loma Alta, Yutopián and Cardonal (Fig. 6.1). These sites have been discussed elsewhere (Scattolin 1990; Scattolin and Gero 1999; Scattolin et al. 2001; Izeta 2005, 2007; Scattolin et al. 2009a). However, a summary description of them is provided below.

Bañado Viejo

Bañado Viejo is a multi-component open-air site with no associated architectural features, located in Santa María Valley bottom, 5 km north of the modern town of El Bañado (Tucumán Province). Pottery shards, bone fragments and lithic materials were found densely dispersed all over the surface. A 4 m² test pit, reaching a depth of 3.60 m revealed five stratigraphic units (or deposits). Three radiocarbon dates are available: 1760±100 BP (LP962) Deposit VI, 1400±40 BP (LP940) Deposit III, and 1170±40 BP (LP923) Deposit II (Izeta 2007; Scattolin et al. 2001). Two bone tools were recovered (Table 6.2). Item 404-8 (Fig. 6.2H) from Deposit II is associated with the most recent date while item 469-1 (Fig. 6.2I), from Deposit IV, corresponds to an intermediate date in-between the other two layers.

Loma Alta

Loma Alta is located on the western slopes of the Aconquija mountain range at 3000 masl. The architectural layout shows a sparse concentration of domestic structures surrounded by agricultural fields. One bone instrument, item 105-1 (Fig. 6.2J), comes from the domestic compound called Nucleus E (NE) which associated with radiocarbon dates spanning a time from 1600±120 BP (GX21580) to 1560±130 BP (GX21581) (Izeta 2007; Scattolin 1990). Loma Alta NE had different

kinds of modified bone, although only the above-mentioned specimen (105-1) corresponds to a transformed metapodial.

Yutopián

Yutopián is situated in the Cajón Valley, at 3000 masl, west of the Santa María Valley. Of the several excavated domestic compounds, a total of eight worked bones were recovered from Structure 1(1777±45 BP, AA 82255), Structure 4 (1630±60 BP, Beta 95611), Structure 5 (1870±60 BP, Beta 95608) and Structure 11 (1940±90 BP, Beta 95610) (Scattolin and Gero 1999; Gero and Scattolin 2002; Izeta 2005, 2007). Of these, three from Structure 4, items YU-54 (Fig. 6.2F), YU-141 (Fig. 6.2E) and YU-165 (Fig. 6.2D), and a fourth from Structure 1, YU-1341 (Fig. 6.2C), correspond to transformed camelid metapodials.

Cardonal

Cardonal is situated in the locality of La Quebrada, only 10 km from Yutopián. The settlement of Cardonal runs along a shallow terrace at 3000 masl and occupies a privileged place along a natural route that connects the territories of Puna (highland plateau) and Yungas (humid eastern slopes of north-western Argentina). Dated to cal. AD 70–220 (Scattolin et al. 2009a), Cardonal is a remarkable example of the first sedentary agricultural communities in this region. Both domestic and funerary contexts have been the subject of recent investigations. The excavation of Structure 2 of the household compound Nucleus 1 yielded one bone instrument coded C58-2 (Fig. 6.2G).

Another two instruments with similar characteristics were found in association with human remains in a funerary context located a few minutes walk uphill from the residential area of the household structures. The sepulchre – a rounded structure formed by several concentric rows of stones – contained the body of one adult male whose head had been removed previous

Table 6.2 Qualitative and quantitative description of transformed metapodials.

CAT	SITE	PROVENIENCE	FIELD SEASON	COMPLETENESS	WEATHERING	EPIPHYSIAL FUSION	MT37	MT38	MT39	MT40	MT41	MACRO AND MICROSCOPIC TECHNOLOGICAL FEATURES	MICROSCOPIC FEATURES
C493-1	Cardonal	TOMB 1	2008	Complete	3	Fused	130,00	46,37	60,86	17,39	10,00	Altered	Altered
C493-2	Cardonal	TOMB 1	2008	Complete	2–3	Fused	101,26	55,80	17,18	10,04	18,77	Altered	Altered Polished
YU-1341	Yutopian	STR 1	1994	Complete	2	Unfused	118,00	60,14	49,12	21,04	6,90	Cutting Graving Flaking	Polished
YU-165	Yutopian	STR 4	1996	Fractured	1	Unfused	112,00	–	–	–	–	Flaking	–
YU-141	Yutopian	STR 4	1998	Fractured	1	–	126,00	–	–	17,25	18,70	Flaking Cutting	Polished
YU-54	Yutopian	STR 4	1998	Complete	1	Fused	155,00	52,38	64,89	15,14	12,67	Graving Flaking Cutting	Polished Microflaking Posdepositational alteration
C58-2	Cardonal	STR 2	2006	Complete	1	Fused	104,00	58,47	28,37	17,61	6,11	Graving Flaking	Altered
469-1	Bañado Viejo	S1 L14 Component IV	1998	Complete	3	Fused	101,00	–	–	–	–	Altered	CO3Ca Micro polished area
404-8	Bañado Viejo	S1 L4 Component II	1997	Fractured	2	Unfused	132,00	–	–	–	–	Cutting Graving Flaking	Cut marks Striations
105-1	Loma Alta	R47	1989	Fractured	1	Fused	73,00	54,19	–	–	–	Transversal cut marks	Transversal cut marks

MT37: max length (mm); MT38: Distance between distal fusion line and transversal cut (handle area); MT39: active area (from transversal cut to the tip); MT40: max width between beginning of roundedness and tip; MT41: Length of the rounded area

to inhumation. Both implements C493-1 (Fig. 6.2A) and C493-2 (Fig. 6.2B) were found around the pelvic area (Cortés 2011). Dated to 1326±43 BP (AA87286), this interment is actually several centuries later than the residential compounds.

In sum, the studied sample comprises ten worked camelid metapodial implements (Fig. 6.2) from four archaeological sites ascribed to different moments within the local Formative Period: two from Bañado Viejo; one from Loma Alta; four from Yutopián; and three from Cardonal. A discussion of the macro and micro analyses that were carried out and the results obtained follows.

Raw material, fragmentation patterns and bone tools

A relevant point made by Stahl (2007) triggered our interest in delving further into the analysis of the particular fragmentation pattern of bone observed at these archaeological sites and to consider how these patterns connected to the sub-products of implement production (Izeta 2007, 2013). A consistent trend between discarded and manufactured bones was observed: discarded elements corresponded mainly to the proximal epiphyses of the metapodials, while diaphyses and distal epiphyses are most commonly found in the form of worked implements.

A first consideration of the sample shows that no particular preference was observed with regard to the age of the animals (Table 6.2): in six cases (Cardonal Tomb 1, Cardonal Structure 2, Yutopian Structure 4, Loma Alta NE, and Bañado Viejo Deposit IV) fused epiphyses indicate that these camelids were older than 36 months and therefore came from adult animals. By contrast, bones of immature animals were used to make the other three tools (Yutopian Structure 1 and 4, and Bañado Viejo Deposit II). The remaining implement (Yutopian Structure 4) was fragmented and therefore could not be assigned to any age category. Further considerations of the preference of using mature or immature bone as raw material was hampered by the small sample size.

Measurements of a set of continuous variables were taken on each of the instruments: maximum length (MT37), maximum length between the line of fusion of the distal epiphysis and the line of the transverse cut (MT38), length of the active area from the transverse cut to the apex of the instrument (MT39), maximum length between the rounded area and the tip (MT40) and width of the active portion of the rounded area (MT41) (Fig. 6.3). Results show that the maximum length of the instruments varies between 73 mm and 155 mm, with 110–120 mm being the most common range. The distance between the line of fusion and the transverse cut shows great regularity, the difference between the lower and the higher value being no greater than 13 mm. The length of the active area is also very regular, except in one case (C58-2). Finally, both the maximum width between the rounded area and

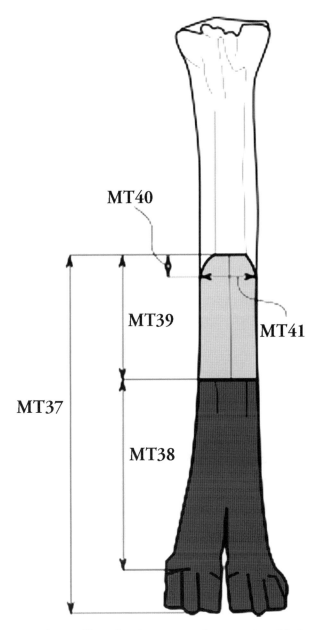

Figure 6.3 Variables used in the osteometric characterization of the bone implements. The template corresponds to a South American camelid metacarpal and is used without distinction for recording both for metacarpals and metatarsals.

the tip, and length of the active portion of the rounded area display consistent values with very little dispersion. Therefore, the overall dimensions of the bones are similar in every case, indicating a great mental regularity in the concept of this kind of implement, in other words, the ways of making and using this type of tool over time were maintained.

Implements were differentially affected by various taphonomic agents and processes. Weathering (Behrensmeyer

1978) was one of the main factors that produced obstacles to performing microscopic analyses on many of these objects.

Macroscopic analysis showed that instruments were discarded at different stages in their use-life (Choyke and Daróczi-Szabó 2010). Six of them were complete and the remaining four were fractured. Given the type of fracture pattern, two appear to have been broken in a dry state, probably as a result of taphonomic processes. The remaining two have marks consistent with fresh-bone fracture (404-8 from Bañado Viejo and 105-1 from Loma Alta (Fig. 6.2I and 2J).

Manufacturing techniques encompassed actions of flaking and cutting while re-modelling or curation was a direct consequence of use. Macroscopic traces revealed cutting, grooving and flaking marks in the remaining portion of the shaft, most of them related to manufacturing (Table 6.2). Cut marks similar to those described as processing cut marks (Fisher 1995) were distinguished on implement 404-1 (Fig. 6.4, 2b). Four implements exhibited a deep transverse section

(probably made by cutting) leaving the distal end complete and the proximal end severed on the dorsal face (Fig. 6.4, 1b and 1d). As a result, the internal face of the dorsal portion of the metapodial was exposed. In those same implements, grooving was recognized in soft textured zones in different parts of the bone. Flaking was identified on six of the instruments. It was caused by two distinct actions: reduction of the element and use, evidenced by traces of microflaking microscopically observed on one of the instruments (Fig. 6.4, 2a). The same analysis permitted polish and micropolish attributes to be distinguished as well as cut marks. A Motic SMZ168 stereomicroscope was used at 20× and 40× and a Nikon Epiphot 300 inverted metallographic microscope was used at 200× and 500× for all microscopic observations.

As far as this last point is concerned, it is likely that these implements were employed in the processing of soft materials as opposed to their use as flakers or tools for working hard materials (Fig. 6.4, 3a–c). Furthermore, according to the

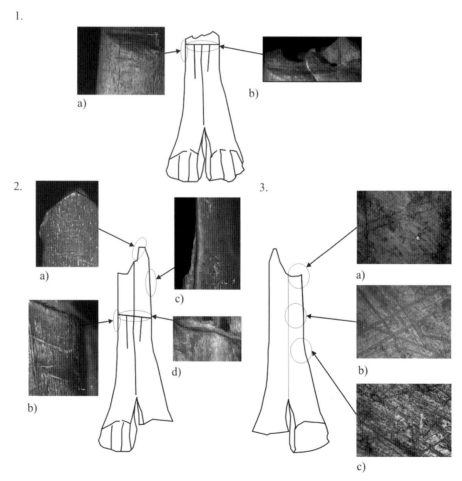

Figure 6.4 Examples of manufacture and use wear patterns. 1) Item 105.1 with a) detail of tool production cut-mark (50×) and b) detail of tool production cut-mark (20×); 2) Item 404-1 norma caudalis with a) polish over the edge and transverse striations made by use, b) polish over the edge and cut-marks probably made during transverse cutting during implement production, c) polished area along the edge and d) transverse cut detail; 3) Item 404-1, norma cranialis with a) surface showing micropolish and the later formation of striations (500×), b) surface showing micropolish and the later formation of striations (200×) and c) surface showing micropolish and the later formation of striations breaking bone fibres (200×).

microscopic features observed (Table 6.2, Fig. 6.4) there is no evidence of reworking of the active area with new flaking of the edges. In the cases described with an unaltered surface these were usually the largest tools, in other cases (Fig. 6.2G and 2H) it is not possible to asses any reworking process or curation because of the post-depositional alteration of the bone surface.

Conclusions

The archaeological record for the southern Calchaquíes valleys offer a unique opportunity to reconstruct lifeways of the pre-Hispanic societies of north-western Argentina. This article was aimed at presenting some of the technological choices related to the manufacturing of bone instruments within the study area, emphasizing several points to complement earlier approaches to animal processing and use during the Formative Period.

Results show that camelid metapodials were employed as the sole raw material for this type of implement and that their shaping was to a great degree standardized. If, as previous analyses have shown (Izeta 2004, 2007, 2008), camelid use was mainly devoted to secondary products such as transport or wool production, these instruments could be interpreted as part of the toolkit for camelid wool producing/weaving. It is likely that these blunt-ended instruments were used for working soft materials such as organic fabrics for basketry and textile manufacturing. Both practices have been inferred by indirect sources of evidences at Cardonal. Interestingly, and for a long period of time, the way these implements were made did not vary significantly.

The great majority of the instruments were found within domestic contexts although two objects were found in association with human remains. The presence of these instruments both within domestic and funerary contexts will foster further consideration of their significance in the past.

Acknowledgements

This research was supported by the National Agency of Scientific and Technological Promotion (ANPCyT) – FONCyT- Project PICT Raíces 116, and the National Council of Scientific and Technical Investigations, Project CONICET-PIP 256 directed by María Cristina Scattolin. The authors would like to thank the communities of La Quebrada and Yutopian (Catamarca, Argentina) for their hospitality and collaboration during the last twenty years of research in the area. Joan Gero, Fabiana Bugliani, Lucas Pereyra Domingorena, Marilin Calo and Marisa Lazzari helped in fieldwork and made some remarks on a previous draft of the paper.

Bibliography

Agüero, C. and Cases, B. (2004) Quillagua y los textiles formativos del Norte Grande de Chile. *Chungará* 36 (supl. espec), 599–617.

Behrensmeyer, A. K. (1978) Taphonomic and ecological information from bone weathering. *Palaeobiology* 4, 150–162.

Belotti, C. (2007) *Zooarqueología del Sitio Soria 2 (Departamento. de San José, Provincia de Catamarca) y Estudio Comparativo del Registro Zooarqueológico del sur de los Valles Calchaquíes, para los Periodos Formativo y Desarrollos Regionales (siglos I a.C. y XV d.C.)*. Licenciatura Dissertation. Facultad de Filosofía y Letras, Universidad de Buenos Aires, Argentina.

Buc, N. (2011) *Tecnología Ósea de Cazadores-recolectores del Humedal del Paraná Inferior (Bajíos Ribereños meridionales)*. Doctoral Dissertation. Facultad de Filosofía y Letras. Universidad de Buenos Aires.

Buc, N. and Loponte, D. (2007) Bone tool types and microwear patterns: some examples from the Pampa region, South America. In C. Gates Saint-Pierre and R. B. Walker (eds), *Bones as Tools: current methods and interpretations in worked bone studies*, 143–157. Oxford, Archaeopress (British Archaeological Report S1622).

Bugliani, M. F. (2008) *Consumo y Representación en el Sur de los Valles Calchaquíes (Noroeste Argentino): Los Conjuntos Cerámicos de las Aldeas del Primer Milenio A.D.* Oxford, Archaeopress (British Archaeological Report S1774).

Calo, C. M. (2008) Improntas del pasado: las canastas de Cardonal. *Revista Española de Antropología Americana*, 38 (2), 39–55.

Cartajena, I., López, O., Núñez, L. and Linares, C. (in press) Lesiones en extremidades inferiores de camélidos: una comparación entre los conjuntos del Arcaico Tardío y Formativo Temprano (vertiente occidental de la Puna de Atacama). In A. D. Izeta and G. L. Mengoni Goñalons (eds), *De la Puna a las Sierras. Avances y Perspectivas en Zooarqueología Andina*. Oxford, Archaeopress (British Archaeological Reports International Series).

Casiraghi, M. (1985) Análisis de los artefactos óseos de Huachichocana III (Provincia de Jujuy, Rep. Argentina). *Paleoetnológica* 1, 19–33. CAEA, Buenos Aires.

Choyke A. M. and Daróczi-Szabó, M. (2010) The complete and usable tool: some life histories of Prehistoric bone tools in Hungary, In A. Legrand-Pineau, I. Sidéra, N. Buc, E. David, V. Scheinsohn, D. V. Campana, A. M. Choyke, P. Crabtree and E. A. Stone (eds), *Ancient and Modern Bone Artefacts from America to Russia Cultural, technological and functional signature*, 235–248. Oxford, Archaeopress (British Archaeological Report S2136).

Cortés, L. I. (2011) *Paisaje Funerario al sur del Valle del Cajón. Cuerpos, contextos y trayectorias históricas*. Doctoral Dissertation. Facultad de Filosofía y Letras, Universidad de Buenos Aires, Argentina. Ms.

Dantas, M. (2010) *Arqueología de los Animales y Procesos de Diferenciación Social en el Valle de Ambato, Catamarca, Argentina*. Doctoral Dissertation, Facultad de Filosofía y Humanidades, Universidad Nacional de Córdoba, Argentina.

Gero, J. and Scattolin, M. C. (2002) Beyond complementarity and hierarchy: new definitions for archaeological gender relations, In S. M. Nelson and M. Rosen-Ayalon, (eds), *In Pursuit of Gender. Worldwide Archaeological Approaches*, 155–172. Walnut Creek CA, Altamira Press.

Grant Lett-Brown, J. L. (2008) *El Recurso Camelidae en Sitios de la Puna Meridional Argentina: una aproximación osteométrica*. Unpublished Licenciatura Dissertation. Facultad de Filosofía y Letras, Universidad de Buenos Aires, Argentina.

Fisher, J. W. (1995) Bone surface modifications in zooarchaeology. *Journal of Archaeological Method and Theory* 2, 7–68.

Haber, A. (1999) *Una Arqueología de los Oasis Puneños. Domesticidad, interacción e identidad en Antofalla, primer y segundo milenios d. C.* Unpublished Doctoral Dissertation, Facultad de Filosofía y Letras, Universidad de Buenos Aires. Ms.

Izeta, A. D. (2004) *Zooarqueología del Sur de los Valles Calchaquíes: estudio de conjuntos faunístico del Periodo Formativo.* Unpublished Doctoral Dissertation, Universidad Nacional de La Plata, Argentina.

Izeta, A. D. (2005) South American Camelid bone density: what are we measuring? Comments on datasets, values their interpretation and application. *Journal of Archaeological Science* 32 (8), 1159–1168.

Izeta, A. D. (2007) *Zooarqueología del Sur de los valles Calchaquíes (Provincia de Tucumán y Catamarca, República Argentina). Estudio de conjuntos faunísticos del primer milenio A.D.* Oxford, John and Erica Hedges (British Archaeological Report S1612).

Izeta, A. D. (2008) Late Holocene camelid use tendencies in two different ecological zones of northwestern Argentina. *Quaternary International* 180 (1), 135–144.

Izeta, A. D. (2013) Perfil de fragmentación ósea: una aproximación basada en el análisis de imágenes generadas por sistemas de información geográfica (SIG). In M. J. Figuerero Torres and A. D. Izeta (eds), *El uso de SIG en la Arqueología Sudamericana.* Oxford, Archaeopress (British Archaeological Reports International Series 2497) 173–184.

Izeta, A. D. and Cortés, L. I. (2006) South American Camelid palaeopathologies. Examples from Loma Alta (Catamarca, Argentina). *International Journal of Osteoarchaeology* 16 (3), 269–275.

Izeta, A. D., Srur, M. G. and Costa, T. (2012) Desechos culinarios y de formatización de instrumentos. Algunas consideraciones metodológicas. In M. P.Babot, F. Pazzarelli and M. Marschoff (eds), *Las Manos en la Masa. Arqueologías y Antropologías de la Alimentación en Suramérica.* Museo de Antropología, Córdoba, Argentina.

Lazzari, M., Pereyra Domingorena, L., Scattolin, M. C., Cecil L., Glascock, M. and Speakman, R. J. (2009) Ancient social landscapes of northwestern Argentina: preliminary results of an integrated approach to obsidian and ceramic provenance. *Journal of Archaeological Science* 36, 1955–1964.

López Campeny, S. M. L. (2000) Tecnología, Iconografía y ritual funerario. Tres dimensiones de análisis de los textiles formativos del Sitio Punta de la Peña 9. (Antofagasta de la Sierra, Argentina). *Estudios Atacameños* 20, 29–65

López Campeny, S. M. L. (2010) Tramando identidades: análisis de patrones representativos en textiles arqueológicos, Antofagasta de la Sierra, Catamarca. *Werkén* 13, 287–304

Miller, G. (1979) *An Introduction to the Ethnoarchaeology of Andean Camelids.* Unpublished PhD Dissertation. University of California.

Nasif, N. and Gómez Cardozo, C. (1999) El material olvidado: análisis de los instrumentos de hueso del sitio arqueológico del El Mollar (Tafí del Valle, Tucumán). *Actas del XII Congreso Nacional de Arqueología Argentina* 1, 102–106.

Núñez Regueiro, V. A. (1998) *Arqueología, Historia y Antropología de los Sitios de Alamito.* Tucumán, Ediciones INTERDEA.

Núñez, L. and Dillehay, T. (1979) *Movilidad Giratoria, Armonía Social y Desarrollo en los Andes Meridionales: patrones de tráfico e interacción económica (ensayo).* Edición numerada: 22. Chile, Universidad del Norte.

Oliszewski, N. (2011) Ocupaciones prehispánicas en la Quebrada de Los Corrales, El Infiernillo, Tucumán (*ca.* 2500–600 años AP). *Comechingonia* 14, 155–171.

Olivera, D. E. (1998) Cazadores y pastores tempranos de la Puna Argentina. *Etnologiska Studier* 42, 153–180.

Olivera, D. E. (2001) Sociedades agropastoriles tempranas: el Formativo Inferior del noroeste argentino. In E. Berberián, and A. Nielsen (eds), *Historia Argentina Prehispánica I,* 83–125. Córdoba, Editorial Brujas.

Palamarczuk, V., Spano, R., Magnífico, D., Weber, F., López, M. S. and Manasiewicz, M. (2007) Soria 2. Apuntes sobre un sitio Formativo en el valle de Yocavil (Catamarca, Argentina). *Intersecciones en Antropología* 8, 121–134.

Pereyra Domingorena, L. (2010) *Manufacturas Alfareras de las Sociedades Aldeanas del Primer Milenio d.C. al Sur de los Valles Calchaquíes.* Unpublished Doctoral Dissertation. Facultad de Filosofía y Letras, Universidad de Buenos Aires, Argentina. Ms.

Renard, S. (1997) Objetos textiles, pasos y caminantes trasandinos. Piezas similares y rasgos comunes entre textiles arqueológicos de Argentina y Chile. *Estudios Atacameños* 14, 291–305

Scattolin, M. C. (1990) Dos asentamientos formativos al pie del Aconquija. El sitio Loma Alta. (Catamarca, Argentina), *Gaceta Arqueológica Andina* 5 (17), 85–100.

Scattolin, M. C. (2006a) De las comunidades aldeanas a los curacazgos en el Noroeste Argentino. *Boletín de Arqueología PUCP* 10, 357–395.

Scattolin, M. C. (2006b) Contornos y confines del período Formativo en el Noroeste Argentino. El universo iconográfico precalchaquí en el Valle de Santa María. *Estudios Atacameños* 32 119–139.

Scattolin, M. C. (2010) La organización del hábitat precalchaquí (500 a.C.–1000 d.C.). In M. E. Albeck, M. C. Scattolin, and M. A. Korstanje (eds), *El Hábitat Prehispánico. Arqueología de la Arquitectura y de la Construcción del Espacio Organizado,* 13–51, Editorial de la Universidad Nacional de Jujuy (Edi UNJu), Argentina.

Scattolin, M. C. and Gero, J. M. (1999) Consideraciones sobre fechados radiocarbónicos de Yutopián (Catamarca, Argentina). *Actas del XII Congreso Nacional de Arqueología Argentina,* 3, 352–357.

Scattolin, M. C. and Lazzari, M. (1997) Tramando redes: obsidianas al oeste del Aconquija. *Estudios Atacameños* 14, 189–209.

Scattolin, M. C., Bugliani, M. F., Izeta, A. D., Lazzari, M., Pereyra Domingorena, L. and Martínez, L. A. (2001) Conjuntos materiales en dimensión temporal. El sitio Formativo "Bañado Viejo" (Valle de Santa María, Tucumán). *Relaciones de la Sociedad Argentina de Antropología.* 24, 167–192.

Scattolin, M. C., Bugliani, M. F., Cortés, L. I., Calo, C. M., Pereyra Domingorena, L. and Izeta, A. D. (2009a) Pequeños mundos: hábitat, maneras de hacer y afinidades en aldeas del valle del Cajón, Catamarca. *Relaciones de la Sociedad Argentina de Antropología* 34, 251–274.

Scattolin, M. C., Cortés, L. I., Bugliani, M. F., Calo, C. M., Pereyra Domingorena, L., Izeta, A. D. and Lazzari, M. (2009b) *Built landscapes of everyday life: a house in the early agricultural village of Cardonal (Cajón Valley, northwestern Argentina)*. *World Archaeology* 43 (1), 396–414.

Scheinsohn, V. (1997) *Explotación de Materias Primas Óseas en la Isla Grande de Tierra del Fuego.* Unpublished Doctoral Dissertation, Facultad de Filosofía y Letras, Universidad de Buenos Aires, Argentina.

Stahl, P. W. (2007) Comentario de: zooarqueología del sur de los valles Calchaquíes (Provincias de Catamarca y Tucumán, República Argentina). *Intersecciones en Antropología* 8, 369–370.

Tarragó, M. N. (1992) El Formativo y el surgimiento de la complejidad social en el Noroeste argentino. In P. Ledergerber-Crespo (ed.), *El Formativo Sudamericano, una Reevaluación. Ponencias presentadas en el Simposio Internacional de Arqueología Sudamericana. Homenaje a Alberto Rex González y Betty J. Meggers,* 302–313 ABYA-YALA, Quito.

Yacobaccio, H. D., Escola, P. S., Pereyra, F. X., Lazzari, M. and Glascock, M. D. (2004) Quest for ancient routes: obsidian research sourcing in northwestern Argentina. *Journal of Archaeological Science* 31, 193–204.

CHAPTER 7

Osseous Raw Materials in the Vinča Culture

Selena Vitezović

This paper will focus on the analysis of raw and worked osseous materials from several Vinča Culture (Late Neolithic and Chalcolithic) sites from the Central Balkans including the methods of acquiring of raw materials and managing available raw materials for certain types of objects. Variability in the presence of red deer and roe deer antlers suggest that they were probably not collected and worked on every site, raising possibilities that an exchange system for raw materials existed between clustered sites. The existence of such a system suggests differences in economic organization on Vinča Culture sites. The preferences for certain skeletal parts for manufacturing specific objects suggest a high level of technological skills, but also probable symbolic values attributed to certain raw materials.

Keywords
Vinča culture; Late Neolithic; Central Balkans; osseous raw materials.

Introduction

The first exploration of the Vinča Culture began over hundred years ago with excavations on the eponymous site of Vinča – Belo Brdo in the vicinity of Belgrade. Today, hundreds of Vinča Culture sites are known in Serbia alone. Figure 7.1 shows the sites specifically mentioned in the text. Its territory also encompassed eastern parts of modern Croatia and Bosnia on the west and the regions of Oltenia and Transylvania in the east (Garašanin 1979, Srejović 1989).

Beside the large number of sites, often with thick cultural layers and remains of burnt wattle and daub houses, the Vinča Culture is characterized by a very rich and diverse material culture. Ceramic production is especially rich and includes a variety of high quality bowls, pots and cups, anthropomorphic as well as zoomorphic figurines and altars. The flint and ground stone industry also suggest intensive production and high craft skills. There is also evidence for trade in obsidian and for copper metallurgy.

Then latest absolute dates obtained for Vinča Culture sites fall roughly into the period between 5400 and 4500/4450 cal BC. For Divostin, dates obtained at the Oxford Laboratory lie between 4750–4550 cal. BC and for Vinča-Belo Brdo they cover the period from 5300 to 4500 cal. BC (Borić 2009).

Studies of technology and the economy in general for Vinča Culture sites and materials are not numerous. Apart from the stone industry (Antonović 1992, 2003), little is known about the organization of raw material procurement, organization of production, or use of objects. So far, it has been claimed that craft specialization did not exist in the Vinča Culture as separate workshops and specialized tool-kits have not been encountered (Chapman 1981, 118). However, many questions regarding the economy in the Vinča Culture still need to be explored.

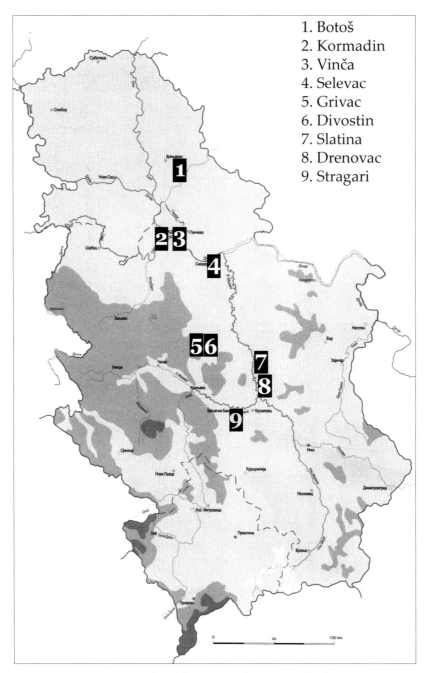

1. Botoš
2. Kormadin
3. Vinča
4. Selevac
5. Grivac
6. Divostin
7. Slatina
8. Drenovac
9. Stragari

Figure 7.1 Map of Neolithic sites in Serbia mentioned in the text.

Bone industries from Vinča sites

The bone industry of the Vinča Culture is among the least known segments of its technology. The faunal remains were not carefully collected on older excavations and assemblages of bone objects were published only as short reports or just mentioned in excavation reports; the only work that gave an overall picture on the bone industry in the Neolithic is one written by Bačkalov (1979). Faunal analyses are also rare and restricted to reports on individual sites. As a general trend in

the Vinča culture, there is to be a dominance of domestic fauna on most sites, mainly cattle (*Bos taurus*), with caprines and pigs (*Sus dom.*) in second and third place respectively. However, it seems that on some sites such as Petnica or Opovo, hunting activities were significant. Among wild species, red deer (*Cervus elaphus*) and aurochs (*Bos primigenius*) are followed by wild pigs (*Sus scrofa*), roe deer (*Capreolus capreolus*) and other small game (cf. Greenfield 1986; Bökönyi 1988; Lazić 1989; Legge 1990; Russell 1993).

In this paper data from several settlement sites and also from one of the two known cemeteries will be analyzed (Fig. 7.1). The data on bone tool assemblages from Vinča and Selevac are taken from publications while the partially published data for Divostin were supplemented with the data obtained after the revision, carried out by the author, on material kept today at the National Museum in Kragujevac. All the remaining assemblages were analyzed by the author

(some of them are still unpublished). The difference in the quality of the assemblages is mainly due to different methods of excavation, which consequently lead to uneven quality in the data. Osseous materials are taken in their widest sense (Averbouh 2000, 187; Poplin 2004, 11), thus, encompassing all the animal hard tissue used for making objects i.e. vertebrate bones and teeth, Cervidae antlers, as well as mollusc and turtle shells (Table 7.1).

Table 7.1 The use of various skeletal elements from different species as raw materials.

SITE	LONG BONES	RIBS	OTHER BONES	ANTLERS	TEETH	MOLLUSC
Jakovo – Kormadin						
Large mam.	1	3	–	–	–	–
Medium mam.	3	2	–	–	–	–
Indet. Mam.	7	2	5	–	–	–
Ovis/capra	4	–	–	–	–	–
Sus	–	–	–	–	1	–
Cervus elephus	–	–	–	54	–	–
Cattle	–	–	1	–	–	–
Total	15	7	6	54	1	0
Divostin						
Large mam.	–	1	–	–	–	–
Medium mam.	16	–	–	–	–	–
Indet. Mam.	18	10	5	–	–	–
Ovis/capra	4	–	4	–	–	–
Sus	–	–	–	–	2	–
Cervus elephus	5	–	–	54	–	–
Capreolus	–	–	–	2	–	–
Cattle			1			
Total	43	11	10	56	2	3
Grivac						
Large mam.	3	9	–	–	–	–
Medium mam.	9	3	–	–	–	–
Indet. Mam.	9	–	2	–	–	–
Ovis/capra	–	–	–	–	–	–
Sus	–	–	–	–	2	–
Cervus elephus	–	–	–	5	–	–
Capreolus	2	–	–	–	–	–
Cattle	–	–	1	–	–	–
Total	23	12	3	5	2	0
Slatina–Paraćin						
Large mam.	5	23	3	–	–	–
Medium mam.	8	10	–	–	–	–
Indet. Mam.	9	26	15	–	1	–
Ovis/capra	2	–	–	–	–	–
Sus	–	–	–	–	–	–
Cervus elephus	–	–	–	17	–	–
Capreolus	–	–	–	2	–	–
Total	24	59	18	19	1	0
Drenovac						
Large mam.	1	17	–	–	–	–
Medium mam.	28	26	–	–	–	–
Indet. Mam.	48	78	51	–	1	–
Ovis/capra	10	–	–	–	–	–
Sus	–	–	–	–	4	–
Cervus elephus	–	–	–	48	–	–
Capreolus	1	–	–	6	–	–
Cattle	2	–	–	–	–	–
Total	90	121	51	52	5	3
Stragari						
Large mam.	–	3	1	–	–	–
Medium mam.	1	4	–	–	–	–
Indet. Mam.	5	5	2	–	1	–
Ovis/capra	–	–	–	–	–	–
Sus	–	–	–	–	–	–
Cervus elephus	1	–	–	11	–	–
Capreolus	–	–	–	2	–	–
Total	7	12	3	13	1	0

Settlements

Vinča – Belo Brdo

Vinča – Belo Brdo is the eponymous site for the Vinča culture, situated in the vicinity of Belgrade, 14 km to the south-east, on the right bank of the Danube River. It was first excavated in the early 20th century, from 1908 and in the 1930s. New excavations were carried out in 1978–1981, continued in 1999 and are still in progress.

During M. Vasić's excavations, approximately 1000 objects made of different osseous materials (bone, antler, teeth and mollusc shells) came to light. However, this extraordinary collection was only partially published (Vasić 1936, 157–166; Srejović and Jovanović 1959; Bačkalov 1979). The number of objects from new excavations is unknown and so far only some shell ornaments have been published (Dimitrijević and Tripković 2002)

Among bone objects, metapodials and ribs from caprine-size animals seem to be the most numerous, used to manufacture a variety of pointed tools, mostly awls. Red deer antlers were also present in large quantities and used to produce a number of different objects – hooks, biserial, uniserial and toggle harpoons, hammers, and various intermediary pieces. Shell objects were also very numerous and the presence of at least three different species of mollusc can be confirmed – *Dentalium*, *Spondylus* and *Glycimeris* used to make beads, bracelets, buttons and other decorative items. Of the objects made from teeth, only several decorative plaques and pendants from boar's tusk can be mentioned. It is not known whether teeth were used to make tools as well.

The variety of objects and sheer number of them shows that the osseous tool and ornament industries were very important at Vinča settlement and also that this site was an important centre on trade routes as, so far, it has richest collection of shell ornaments of any Vinča Culture site known.

Jakovo – Kormadin

The site of Jakovo Kormadin is situated in Srem, in the vicinity of Belgrade near the modern village of Jakovo. The first excavations were carried out at the beginning of the 20th century, and smaller rescue excavations took place in 1956–1958, when two houses with bucrania were discovered (Jovanović and Glišić 1961). In 2006, several small trenches were excavated and during this campaign about 80 worked pieces of bone and antler were discovered.

This assemblage contained objects made from bones, antler, and one made from boar's tusk. Different skeletal elements, mainly long bones and ribs from medium-sized mammals, were used to make diverse pointed tools. Antlers were exclusively from red deer and were used to manufacture points, picks, axes, punches and intermediary pieces for inserting other tools (sleeves and hafts) (Fig. 7.2). One antler spatula and one wedge also came to light (Vitezović 2010).

Of particular interest was a find of a dozen pieces of antler with traces of working, probably waste, and also approximately two dozen antler flakes, probably waste as well. Unfortunately, traces from tools were not preserved due to depositional erosion of surfaces. They were found in a semi-subterranean feature so it seems this find represents a workshop area or place where rubbish from such an antler workshop was discarded. Although the presence of workshops or working areas was expected and they are assumed to exist at each Vinča Culture site, this was the first time that one was actually confirmed.

Selevac

The site of Selevac is situated in the valley of the Velika Morava River in central Serbia, approximately 20 km south from its confluence with the Danube. The modern village of Selevac lies between the towns of Smederevska Palanka and Smederevo and the neolithic settlement was situated about 5 km to the east, on the banks of the Vrbica stream. This settlement was one of the largest Vinča settlements ever discovered, covering an area of almost 53 ha. The cultural layer was 1.5 m thick although sometimes it exceeded 3 m. It was first registered in the 1960s and the first small excavations took place in 1968–1970 and 1973. A larger area was excavated as part of the Selevac Archaeological

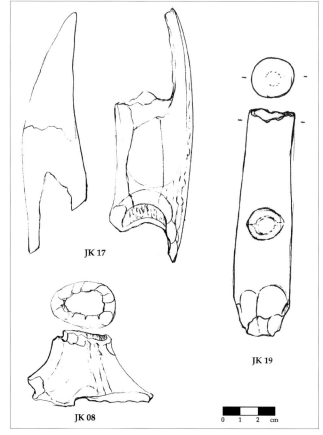

Figure 7.2 Antler artefacts from Jakovo: fragmented axe JK 17, handle JK 08 and fragmented pick JK 19.

Project during the period between1976–1981. (Tringham and Krstić 1990)

Over 1000 bone objects were recovered (1032 in total). Various points represent the dominant class of osseous find material. These points were made from ribs, metapodials, ulnas and other long bones, but also from pig's tusks. Other objects included knives, choppers, burnishers, spatulae, pressure flakers, digging, pressure flakers, decorative items, and also probable preforms and production waste. Apart from different long bones and ribs, astragali, red deer antler and pig's tusks were worked while even segments of cranium, two maxillas and four turtle shells were used. There is no mention of the use of molluscs as a raw material. The percentages of various raw materials are unknown; bone was the dominant material with a small number of worked pig tusk was found. The proportion of red deer antler is unknown. (Russell 1990)

Among the faunal remains, cattle bone (*Bos taurus*) predominates in all horizons and its importance increased over time. Sheep (*Ovis aries*), goat (*Capra hircus*) and domestic pig (*Sus domesticus*) were also present in differing percentages in different building horizons. Red deer was also present and roe deer (*Capreolus capreolus*) in small numbers; both cervid species decline throughout the Selevac sequence (Legge 1990).

Divostin

Divostin is situated near the modern town of Kragujevac in the valley of the Velika Morava River in central Serbia. It was excavated in the 1967–1969 in a joint Yugoslav-American campaign. A large area was excavated with a total of approximately 200 m². The site had layers from Vinča and Starčevo culture, with excellently preserved remains of buildings. A rich portable material culture was also discovered including pottery, figurines, stone, flint, antler and bone tools, shell ornaments and even copper objects (McPherron and Srejović 1988).

Approximately 100 bone objects were recovered from Vinča culture layers. Both flat and long bones were used to manufacture a variety of pointed objects. Several worked astragali were found. Red deer antler pieces were more numerous and were used in the production of different pointed tools, picks, hammers and chisels (Fig. 7.3). Apart from objects made from tines, there was a diversity of artefacts made from the basal and beam segments of the red deer antler rack. Several axes from very large antler racks (Bačkalov 1979), are particularly noteworthy. A number of shell ornaments were also mentioned (McPherron *et al.* 1988).

Domestic animals predominated among the faunal remains (85% domestic and 15% wild) in Vinča layers. Among domestic animals, the most numerous were remains of *Bos taurus* comprising over 70% of all remains, followed by caprine and domestic pig remains (approx. 12% respectively). Among the wild animals, remains of aurochs (*Bos primigenius*) were most numerous (almost 40% of wild fauna, 6% total) followed by wild pig (30%, 5% total) and red deer (25%, 4% total).

Roe deer was only found in small numbers (less than 3% of wild fauna). (Bökönyi 1988).

Grivac

The site of Grivac is situated 20 km from Kragujevac, on the banks of the Grivac stream. Divostin is situated nearby as well as several other neolithic sites. Grivac has been excavated since the 1950s in several campaigns. A large settlement of the Vinča Culture was discovered there, with four building horizons and also three building horizons of the Starčevo Culture. The site yielded well preserved architectural remains, large quantities of pottery and also a very rich stone industry (Bogdanović 2008). In fact, it was suggested that there had been a large workshop for stone objects at Grivac (Antonović 2003).

As opposed to the stone industry, the bone industry is relatively poor. Although not all the faunal material was collected in every campaign, and only selected objects were collected from older excavations, the total of bone objects is still very low, about 50 artefacts. These finds were made mostly from ribs, metapodials and other long bones. Only a few artefacts made from antler may be attributed to the Vinča layers, and they were, in contrast with Divostin, mainly made from tines with smaller dimensions and less elaborate shaping.

Slatina – Paraćin

The site of Slatina is situated at the very entrance to the town of Paraćin, in marshy, salty soil, on the slopes of Karđorđevo hill by the banks of the Crnica river. It was discovered in 1960s. All the excavations carried out at the site have been rescue excavations – first during the work on the Belgrade-Niš highway, in 1985–1986, and later during the building of a factory, between 1997–2003. Several small trenches were excavated, revealing a large settlement of the Vinča Culture spread over 10 ha, with at least three building horizons and possible modest remains of a Starčevo Culture settlement. (Vetnić 1974, 139–40, 149)

About 120 objects of osseous materials were recovered from these excavations; however, this number must have been larger, since bones were not carefully collected in all the trenches. Bone was the dominant raw material; 18 objects were made from red deer antler while only one object was made from tooth. The most common tool type is pointed tools – various awls, made from metapodials and ribs, needles and pins made from bone flakes and different burnishing objects, also made from long bones and ribs (Fig. 7.4). Several punches were present. Other tool types occur in small numbers – projectile points, wedges, chisels, hammers and sleeves. (Vitezović 2007)

Faunal analysis was carried out only on the material from one trench. There was a predominance of domestic animals (approx. 70% of the total faunal sample), with cattle bone being most numerous, followed by skeletal elements from sheep, goats and pigs; of the wild animals, aurochs, red deer, roe deer and wild swine were present (Cvetković 2004).

Figure 7.3 Antler artefacts from Divostin: hammer-axe Dvs 054, handle Dvs 157, manufacture debris Dvs 207 and fragmented tool, probably punch Dvs 203.

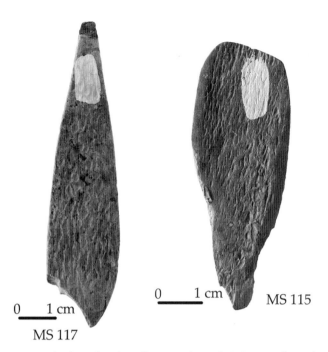

0   1 cm   MS 115

0   1 cm

MS 117

Figure 7.4 Rib artefacts from Slatina: awl-spatula MS 117 and spatula MS 115.

DRENOVAC

The site of Drenovac–Turska česma is situated 8 km south of the town of Paraćin, on the slopes above a terrace of the Velika Morava River. A large Neolithic settlement, covering about 30 ha, was discovered in the 1960s and the first excavations were carried out in 1968–1971. Fourteen trenches were excavated, revealing a multi-layer site of the Vinča Culture and a settlement of the Early Neolithic Vinča Culture with rich remains of houses and artefacts (Vetnić 1974, 125–139, 149). From 2004, new on-going excavations got underway that are still in progress. Trench no. 15 revealed at least four building horizons of the Vinča Culture and a Starčevo Culture settlement.

Almost 400 bone objects were recovered from all these excavations, most of them from the trench 15, excavated in 2004–2006, when all the bones were carefully collected. Bone represents the dominant osseous raw material. Ribs are the most numerous skeletal elements, followed by long bones. Other skeletal elements were poorly represented (several astragali and a few unidentified flat bones) (Fig. 7.5). A relatively high ratio of ribs on both Drenovac and Slatina is probably the result of careful collecting, since these artefacts are less conspicuous than those objects made from long bones. Worked antler occurs in relatively large numbers, and, beside the red deer antlers, several artefacts made from roe deer antlers should be mentioned. Teeth artefacts were not numerous, and the occurrence of shells is particularly

interesting, as the presence of shells has not been noted before in areas outside the Danube valley.

Artefacts made from osseous materials from Drenovac reveal a well developed industry, with objects of standardized shapes and mode of production. Different pointed tools dominate including awls, needles, heavy points, but also polishing tools (different types and subtypes of spatulas and scrapers, including combined awls-spatulas) and punching tools (punches, hammers and hammer-axes). Also a variety of other intermediary pieces and objects of special use were discovered – sleeves and handles, used astragali, bone rods, probably used as spindles, etc., as well as pieces of jewellery and manufacture debris. (Vitezović 2007).

STRAGARI

The site of Šljivik – Stragari is situated near the village of Stragari, in the vicinity of the town of Trstenik. The neolithic site was located on the gentle slopes surrounded by a meander of the Riljačka River which flows into the Zapadna Morava River 7 km downstream. Several trenches were excavated in the 1980s, revealing at least two horizons from the Early Vinča Culture, and there was also a layer with mixed Vinča and Starčevo Culture material.

Approximately forty objects made from osseous materials from the 1988–1989 campaigns were at my disposal for the study. Faunal remains were carefully collected and the low number of osseous artefacts is due to unfavourable preservation conditions (high soil acidity). Bone, red and roe deer antlers were represented and there was also one tooth artefact. However, there were no shell objects discovered. This small collection consisted of awls, spatulas, picks, chisels, objects with worked surfaces, as well two particularly nicely shaped objects classified into the group of objects of special use. They were perhaps used as spindles of some sort for producing spun fibres. The few fragments of antler with traces of shaping represent manufacturing waste.

Cemeteries

Grave finds from the Vinča Culture are extremely rare and the total number of graves discovered so far is very low; only one small intramural cemetery at Gomolava and one extramural cemetery at Botoš have been discovered. Botoš yielded interesting information on the use of some objects made from osseous materials.

BOTOŠ – ŽIVANIĆA DOLJA

The site Botoš near Zrenjanin (in Banat) was discovered in the 1920s and M. Grbić excavated 18 graves from an already destroyed cemetery. There was one double grave and three separate skulls as well as grouped ceramics (cenotaphs or offerings). Grave goods consisted of pottery, various stone tools as well as personal ornaments – among others *Spondylus* and *Glycimeris* bracelets and large biconical beads made from

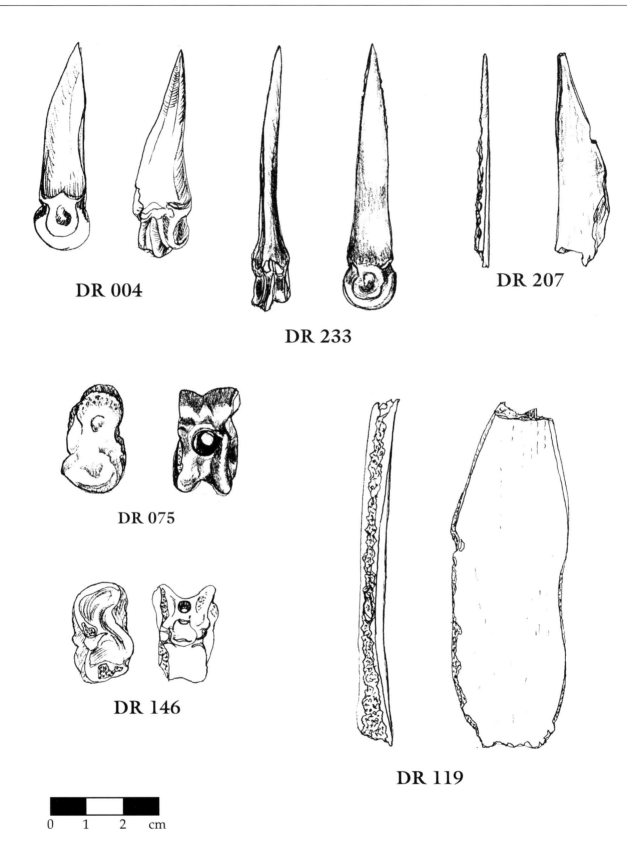

Figure 7.5 Use of bones at Drenovac: metapodial awls Dr 004 and 233, rib awl Dr 207, rib spatula Dr 119 and perforated astragals with traces of use Dr 075 and 146.

shells (at least 45 beads and nine bracelets). Based on the stylistic characteristics of the ceramic material, the cemetery is dated to the Early Vinča Culture. (Marinković 2002, 2010)

Osseous raw materials

Bones

The prevailing raw material among the bones, were metpodials and ribs. Metapodials as well as ribs from caprines or other medium size mammals were most represented. Metapodials (from cattle) or ribs from large animals are less common in this assemblage while some long bones were almost never used – ulnas or fibulas, for example. Also, other flat bones (for example, scapula) occur only rarely in a worked form (Fig. 7.6, Table 7.1).

As for other skeletal elements, astragali, exclusively cattle and caprines, were selected with, perhaps, some phalanges. Although modified astragali are known in the Neolithic of the Near East and Asia Minor (cf. Martin and Russell 1996, 211, with references), such artefacts are otherwise unknown in

the Starčevo Culture and they appear in the Balkans with the Vinča Culture (Vitezović 2011a). Vinča astragali were most likely used as burnishing tools (and perhaps had some role in the fibre-making processes – cf. Vitezović 2007, 98–100), unlike those from Near East which are supposed to be gaming pieces (Martin and Russell 1996, 211).

Some bones such as cranial bones were never worked, except for a few expedient tools from mandibles or maxillas. Some worked cranial bones are reported from Selevac (Russell 1990). Mandible tools exist on some neolithic sites in other parts of Europe (for example, Chalain in France; Maigrot 2003, 24). In the Balkans area they have been noted in the Chalcolithic Period (a few pieces were found at Bubanj; Vitezović 2011b).

Metapodials were probably carefully removed during the butchering and stored for later use. Ribs were also removed during the butchering process, while some bones, for example flakes from large long bones, probably represent kitchen waste – bones were broken to extract marrow and after that the pieces were put aside for further use. Bones were taken from freshly killed animals, and not from occasionally found carcasses, as suggested by absence of carnivore gnawing or other depositional traces beneath the marks of shaping and use.

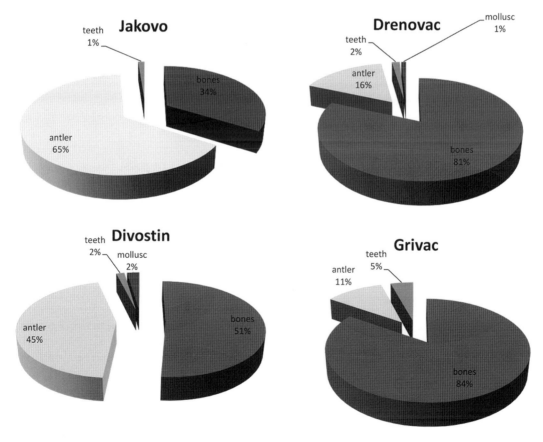

Figure 7.6 Ratio of different osseous raw materials at Jakovo, Divostin, Grivac and Drenovac.

Bone for working was also carefully selected from particular species. The dominance of bones from medium-sized animals is not consistent with the dominance of cattle in the faunal record. However, there were probably enough bones from medium-sized animals, although the bones may have been stored after killing the animal for later use. The apparent avoidance of pig bones perhaps suggests cultural other than practical reasons (pig bones are not particularly suitable because most skeletal elements possess a torque). It should be noted that, pig bones are present in faunal record, so this is not related to butchering and depositional practices. Pig's bones were also absent in Starčevo Culture assemblages, but a few pieces were noted in Chalcolithic Period assemblages (on Bubanj; cf. Vitezović 2011b).

In comparison with assemblages of the Early and Middle Neolithic Starčevo Culture there is a decline in the use of cattle and bones from other large mammals and the greater ratio of caprine and bones from other small and medium-sized animals in the Vinča Culture material. Several tool types were made from cattle metapodials on Starčevo Culture sites and were preferred or even the exclusive choice for some culturally very specific artefact types – spatulas-spoons with elongated handles and recipient and projectile points (Vitezović 2011a). Large mammal bones (from cattle, red deer) were also used for different tools, for example, rib scrapers and decorative items from long bone diaphysis segments. It is noteworthy that the ratio of cattle rose from the Early to Late Neolithic although the use of its bones as raw materials declined. In addition, Starčevo items made from these bones fall into the category of highly valued, long used and often repaired objects (Class 1 in the manufacturing continuum; cf. Choyke 1997).

The mode of using bones is more or less uniform on different Vinča sites. Only the Drenovac and Slatina assemblages have a higher ratio of objects made from ribs (as a result of the carefully collected fauna) and Selevac is the only site with greater diversity in skeletal elements (including scapulae, cranial bones and higher ratio of teeth used in a variety of ways) (see also Table 7.1).

Bones were mainly used for a variety of tools and weapons, but could also be used for decorative objects such as amulets, plaques or belt hooks. Lots of diverse objects were made from bones – from awls, needles and spatulae, wedges, as well as hooks and objects with a special use. Often, the advantage of natural traits was used completely – the rounded half of the distal epiphysis of the metapodial was used as a handle; the abrasive surface of the spongiosa was used for rib spatulas and scrapers, the prominent surfaces of astragali were used for polishing.

Antlers

The antlers that were used were predominantly from red deer. Judging by those antlers where the basal part was preserved, mostly shed, gathered antlers were used. As for the other antler fragments, the calcified inner structure suggests that they were shed as well while traces of rodent teeth and other depositional traces, found on some specimens, suggest that they were collected. Only a few worked pieces of antlers from Divostin were unshed. Therefore, the method of acquiring antlers was completely different than the method of acquiring bones – while bones were secondary products obtained during the butchering of a killed animal, antlers were collected in the woods, perhaps along with some other raw materials, for example, wood (consequently, red deer *were not* killed for their antlers). On Neolithic lake-dwelling sites in Switzerland, it was possible to correlate the use of antlers with the practice of hunting red deer – antlers decreased in size due to over-hunting in periods when hunting was more important (Schibler 2001). However, on Vinča sites, it was possible only to note that at the site where antler use dominates, Divostin, cattle comprised about 80% of the total faunal assemblage, and red deer only 4% (cf. Bökönyi 1988). Lack of data did not permit any diachronic patterns to be established.

Antlers were probably stored for later use after being collected. Such a cache has not yet been discovered on these sites, however, we may assume that all the antler pieces found in a site were either meant to be worked or were production waste (antlers without traces of use were noted at Drenovac, Slatina and Jakovo). Bones occur on most of the sites in higher proportions, however, there are no indications that antlers were rare. On the contrary, flakes from antler recovered at Jakovo and at Drenovac and the very technique of whittling, not an economic way to deal with this material, suggest that they were abundant.

The difference in antler ratios between sites is particularly interesting – certain Vinča Culture sites have a very rich and varied antler industry, whilst on other sites antlers occur in small numbers and consist of simple, not particularly elaborated tools. Certain differences in percentages of antlers between sites may be explained in two ways – one is that they were not present in the part of the site that was excavated and the other is that they were not present in equal proportions on every site. Pairs of sites with large and poor proportions of antlers can be mentioned, for instance Grivac *vs.* Divostin (Fig. 7.6) or, to a certain extent, Slatina *vs.* Drenovac (see also Table 7.1). The difference between these two pairs of sites is not only in terms of the total number of pieces recovered but Divostin and Drenovac have clearly elaborate bone industries. Here are found certain "standard" shapes including masterpieces, in terms of the labour invested, and also flakes from production waste, which suggests that the objects were made at the site. Jakovo and Vinča do not represent such a pair, although they lie relatively close to each other, as their territories did not overlap. Several other Vinča Culture sites on the territory of Belgrade (i.e. Banjica and Žarkovo, to mention the excavated ones), unfortunately do not have bone industries that are sufficiently well preserved to suggest patterns of production of antler objects in this area.

Close clustering of Vinča Culture sites already suggested the possibility of economic specialization within sites in individual regions and the distribution of osseous raw materials confirmed this suggestion. It may be assumed that not all, but only one or more sites within one region, were specialized in the collection and working of antlers, and perhaps also specialized in tasks related to antler tools (such as wood-working).

In the Mesolithic Period, antler was the dominant raw material (cf. bone industry from Vlasac in the Iron Gates; Bačkalov 1979). If we compare materials from Vinča sites with Starčevo sites, a similar pattern of sites with richer and poorer antler industries emerges. In the Starčevo Culture, although the richest antler industry was discovered in the Iron Gates region in eastern Serbia, other sites with large proportions of objects made from domestic animals also had significant antler industries – for example the eponymous site of Starčevo-Grad and Divostin, where continuity in exploitation of antlers in both the Starčevo and Vinča Culture horizons may be observed (Vitezović 2011a).

All parts of the antlers were used – the basal part, the beam and all the tines (Fig. 7.3). Antlers may be used in their natural form or this form may be slightly worked or curated, or an antler can be considerably reworked. As with bones, the natural characteristics of the antler were clearly known to prehistoric craftspeople and exploited well – antlers were mainly used as punching or large cutting tools such as punches or axes, and their natural shape was exploited to produce T-shaped sleeves and other types of intermediary pieces for inserting other parts of various tools. This is consistent with their natural properties for absorbing shock. Also, the spongiosa of antlers was used for its abrasive qualities in a similar manner to the spongiosa in ribs. In addition to these, several carefully made, unusual objects may be mentioned, such as the toggle harpoon from Divostin.

Worked roe deer antlers reveal a completely different picture. They occur rarely and, when it was possible to determine, they came from killed animals. They were mainly used as *ad hoc*, expedient tools, although there are a few carefully made pieces (e.g. Dr 023; Vitezović 2007, table xxxvi). Roe deer antlers are smaller in dimensions and less resilient than those of red deer (for physical and mechanical properties of antler, cf. Suter 1981, Christensen 2004) but roe deer is also not represented in large numbers in the faunal remains (cf. Bökönyi 1988; Legge 1990). Minimal use of their antlers was, therefore, the consequence of both their inadequate qualities, and their relative scarcity, i.e. this was more a technological than cultural choice.

Teeth

Teeth were used only occasionally for making objects (Fig. 7.6, Table 7.1). Except for several scrapers made from boar's tusk and one needle made from non-identified tooth found at Drenovac, all the other teeth objects were non utilitarian.

Only boar's tusks were regularly used for making tools but occur in relatively small numbers. Boar's tusks represent a much more common raw material in the Mesolithic Period (Bačkalov 1979). Their use declined from the time of the Starčevo Culture (Vitezović 2011a).

More common are various decorative objects made from diverse teeth, although they also occur in relatively low numbers. Carnivore and red deer canines seem to have been preferred, although even perforated cattle molars may be found. Perhaps the most interesting discovery is a stray find from the vicinity of the site of Pločnik, near Prokuplje, in south-eastern Serbia, which consists of 33 perforated red deer canines, with traces of a green colour, probably from contact with malachite. These objects were found with several hundred *Spondylus* beads and may represent grave goods from a disturbed Vinča cemetery (or perhaps a hoard). These finds may be attributed to the Vinča Culture with certainty on the basis of their technological features (the shape and method of perforating teeth, compared to the techniques used on other Vinča Culture sites).

The limited number of these decorative items does not permit broader comparison with neighbouring sites. This low number is probably linked to the fact that the cemeteries are almost completely unknown. These objects were generally used for a long time, often repaired and the finds from the settlements are mainly just broken, discarded pieces (cf. also Choyke 2009).

Mollusc shells

At least three mollusc species have been identified so far – *Dentalium*, *Spondylus* and *Glycimeris* shells. Judging from the drawing, even *Cardium* shell may have been present at Vinča – Belo Brdo (Srejović and Jovanović 1959, fig. 17: 35). They were used for production of a variety of objects including beads, bracelets, pendants, decorative plaques and buttons. Often they are found broken while some of the *Spondylus* bracelets seem to have been repaired – after breaking, one or more perforations were added and the objects were turned into a pendant or clothing ornament. All this suggests that they were worn for a long time and not lightly discarded. The grave finds from Botoš suggest that shell ornaments were worn as personal and highly treasured decorative ornaments and perhaps also seen as symbols of rank.

The richest collection of shell objects, as mentioned above, was discovered at Vinča – Belo Brdo. However, one must keep in mind that this site also has the largest excavated area. Shell objects may have been equally important on other sites as well. In fact, the recent discovery of *Spondylus* ornaments at the site of Drenovac in the Morava valley (Vitezović 2007), shows that the distribution of shells is not restricted to the Danube valley. With careful collection of material and sieving, future excavations will probably yield even more shell pieces. This shows that the routes for trading and exchange were far more complex than previously thought and this also challenges the over simplistic view of the centre and periphery in Vinča culture, with the eponymous site as the only or the largest centre. *Spondylus* trade and exchange within Vinča culture is only a part of a large network spread throughout prehistoric Europe (cf. Séfèriadès 1995), and careful mapping of sites with such findings may help in reconstructing the trade routes.

Osseous and other raw materials in Vinča culture

Very often bone industries are regarded as *ad hoc* use of kitchen waste, something unimportant in the daily life of the community, something that was easily made, easily discarded and not as valued as, for example, carefully made polished stone tools. Closer examination of the bone industry in Vinča culture, however, reveals a planned, well developed bone technology. Mechanisms of acquiring and managing osseous raw materials provide significant insight into the ways raw materials in general were managed as well as some of the cultural connections between humans and animals.

The main skeletal elements used were metapodials, ribs and red deer antler, followed by other long bones and in much lower percentages other flat and short bones, teeth, roe deer antlers and mollusc shells. Caprines and other medium-sized ungulates are dominant in tool assemblages, followed by cattle and other large ungulates, while bones from pigs and other animal species seem to have been avoided.

Used osseous materials reflect the situation encountered in the faunal material only up to certain extent. Skeletal elements found in the faunal remains in large quantities, however, are not the most commonly used for tool or ornament manufacture. It appears that caprine bones were often chosen, although cattle prevail in the faunal samples on most sites. Also, although pigs were relatively numerous, and probably some of the unidentified ribs and long bone flakes may be from domestic or wild pig, the use of their skeletal elements is not confirmed with certainty, except for the tusks.

A general model for the acquisition and use of osseous materials may be proposed here. Osseous materials in the Vinča Culture were obtained as products from husbandry and hunting, through selective collecting and through exchange.

Bones were the most common and easiest to obtain; they were also used in large quantities on all sites, although careful choice of the most appropriate and/or most desired skeletal elements may be observed (the preference for bones from ungulates, especially of smaller size). Antlers were acquired in the vicinity of the settlement, probably collected with some other raw materials, and exchanged on a small scale as raw materials or finished products. Probably within certain area there was some sort of settlement specialization in antler collection and working.

Teeth worked for decorative purposes were obtained through hunting (or slaughter of large domestic boars) while shells were obtained through some kind of exchange network whose mechanisms are not known (starting with whatever other goods were in circulation).

Contemporary sites in surrounding areas reveal similar patterns of raw material use with a dominance of bone followed by antler. This situation is, for example, evident on Early Vinča sites in Romania (Beldiman 2007). In the osseous industry from Late Neolithic/Chalcolithic period from Karanovo (Bulgaria), metapodials were the most common skeletal element used, although there is a somewhat greater variety in use of long bones (ulnae, tibiae, etc.), followed by ribs, antlers and the occasional use of scapulas, mandibles and other bones (Lang 2005).

In the central Balkans, antlers occur in greater percentages than in the southern Balkans (BYR Macedonia, Greece), where the ratio of worked antler is lower (cf. Smoor 1976; Stratouli 1998). However, they were not as important as, for example, in the Mesolithic period (Bačkalov 1979) or on contemporary sites elsewhere in Central Europe (Schibler 1980).

Osseous materials were mainly used for everyday tools – from small household tools such as awls, needles, perforators, spatulae, burnishers and scrapers, to large tools for activities in the field such as hammers, axes, picks. They were also used for making weapons, mainly fishing and hunting equipment. A variety of fish hooks and harpoons are known, although these do not occur in large quantities. All these osseous materials were used in such a manner that their natural physical and mechanical properties, i.e. their shapes, as well as their resistance to shocks, etc., were well exploited. The preferred choice of metapodials and ribs is mainly due to the characteristics of bones themselves. A nice, but thin and sharply pointed, tool can be most easily obtained from smaller bones and the distal or proximal epiphysis can be used conveniently as a handle. Judging from intensive traces of use visible on most of the rib artefacts, the spongiosa was utilised for scraping and burnishing processes.

Finally, osseous raw materials, mainly shells and teeth, were also valued for making decorative objects, although bones and antler could be used as well. Their main qualities were most likely their white colour (cf. Luik 2007; Vitezović, 2012) and the specific animal species from which they originated. Personal ornaments were made almost exclusively from osseous materials, stone and copper, and most often they were white or green in colour. Stone beads were made from various white rocks (such as marble and limestone, cf. McPherron *et al.* 1988) and resemble or imitate shell beads. However, these raw materials were not considered adequate for making human and animal figurative representations. Figurative representations made from osseous materials are completely absent, which is all the more striking when one considers the rich and diverse clay figurative representations found on Vinča Culture sites.

Such a choice of raw materials for personal ornaments must have been cultural. The colour must have been important and also the origin of certain raw materials – teeth came mainly from wild, hunted animals, shells came from exotic, distant places and stones and copper came from some place outside the settlement – it is, therefore, the outer sphere (beyond the confines of the settlement, the wild habitat – *sensu* Hodder 1990) that gave them certain value or meaning. As figurines were mainly linked with the domestic sphere, this may also explain the avoidance of bones or stone in the manufacture of figurines.

Conclusion

The osseous materials industry in the Vinča Culture was based on the use of bones from domestic animals and there were strict rules for the choice of both species and skeletal element. The natural properties of bone were well exploited and uniform techniques of manufacture reveal a well developed industry. The use of antlers, and especially differences in the antler-bone ratios between some of the sites, suggest the possibility of specialization on a regional level. Teeth, especially those from wild animals, as well as shells obtained through exchange, were valued raw materials, used for decorative items. The particular cultural value of different osseous raw materials may be observed in the patterns of their use – cattle bones were less important than in previous periods, although their significance in the everyday economy was growing. Pig bones were generally not chosen for manufacturing, and osseous materials in general were considered inappropriate for producing figurative representations but not only appropriate, but preferred for making personal ornaments.

Acknowledgments

This research was conducted while I held a fellowship from the Ministry of Science and Technological Development of the Republic of Serbia, who also financed my travel to the ICAZ Paris conference. I would also like to thank the session organizers for giving me the opportunity to participate and to colleagues from Serbian museums who entrusted me with the study of these materials from the National Museum of Kragujevac, the City Museum of Belgrade, the Regional Museum of Jagodina, the Regional Museum of Paraćin and Centre for Archaeological Research at the Faculty of Philososphy, Belgrade University. Drawings were made by Željko Utvar (Drenovac) and Aleksandar Kapuran (Jakovo), whom I would once again like to thank here.

Bibliography

Antonović, D. (1992) *Predmeti od glačanog kamena iz Vinče. (The Ground Stone Industry from Vinča)*. Beograd, Univerzitet u Beogradu, Filozofski fakultet, Centar za arheološka istraživanja.

Antonović, D. (2003) *Neolitska industrija glačanog kamena (Neolithic Ground Stone Industry in Serbia)*. Beograd, Arheološki Institut.

Averbouh, A. (2000) *Technologie de la Matière Osseuse Travaillée et Implications Palethnologiques*. Unpublished doctoral thesis, Université de Paris I.

Bačkalov, A. (1979) *Predmeti od kosti i roga u predneolitu i neolitu Srbije. (Bone and Antler Objects in the Pre-Neolithic and Neolithic of Serbia)*. Beograd, Savez arheoloških društava Jugoslavije.

Beldiman, C. (2007) *Industria Materiilor Dure Animale în Preistoria României. Resurse naturale, comunităţi umane şi tehnologie din paleoliticul superior până în neoliticul timpuriu*. Bucureşti, Asociaţia Română de Arheologie, Studii dePreistorie, Supplementum 2, Editura Pro Universitaria.

Bogdanović, M. (2008) *Grivac. Settlements of Starčevo and Vinča Culture*. Kragujevac, Center for Scientific Research of Serbian Academy of Sciences.

Bökönyi, S. (1988) Neolithic fauna of Divostin. In A. McPherron, and D. Srejović, (eds), *Divostin and the Neolithic of Central Serbia*, 419–445. Pittsburgh, University of Pittsburgh.

Borić, D. (2009) Absolute dating of metallurgical innovations in the Vinča Culture of the Balkans. In T. K. Kienlin and B. W. Roberts (eds), *Metals and Societies. Studies in honour of Barbara S. Ottaway*, 191–245. Universitätsforschungen zur prähistorischen Archäologie. Bonn, Habelt.

Chapman, J. (1981) *The Vinča Culture of South-East Europe. Studies in chronology, economy and society*. Oxford, British Archaeological Report S117.

Choyke, A. (1997) The bone manufacturing continuum. *Anthropozoologica* 25–26, 65–72.

Choyke, A. (2009) Grandmother's awl: individual and collective memory through material culture. In I. Barbiera, A. Choyke and J. Rasson (eds), *Materializing Memory: archaeological material culture and the semantics of the past*, 21–40. Oxford, Archaeopress (British Archaeological Report S1977).

Christensen, M. (2004) Fiches caractères morphologiques, histologiques et mécaniques des matières dures d´origine animale. In D. Ramseyer (ed.), *Matières et Techniques. Fiches de la commission de nomenclature sur l'industrie de l'os préhistorique* XI, 17–27. Paris, CNRS.

Dimitrijević, V. and Tripković, B. (2002) New *Spondylus* findings at Vinča-Belo Brdo 1998–2001 campaigns and the regional approach to problem. *Starinar* LII, 48–62.

Garašanin, M. (1979) *Praistorija na tlu SR Srbije*. Beograd, Srpska književna zadruga.

Greenfield, H. (1986) *Paleoeconomy of the Central Balkans (Serbia): a zooarchaeological perspective on the Late Neolithic and Bronze Age (c. 4500–1000 B.C.)*. Oxford, British Archaeological Report S304.

Hodder, I. (1990) *The Domestication of Europe*. Oxford, Basil Blackwell.

Jovanović, B. and Glišić, J. (1961) Eneolitsko naselje na Kormadinu kod Jakova (Station énéolithique dans la localité de Kormadin près de Jakovo). *Starinar n. s.* II, 113–139.

Lang. F. (2005) Knochen- und Geweihobjekte. In S. Hiller und V. Nikolov (eds), *Karanovo, Die Ausgrabungen im Nordsüd–Schnitt, 1993–1999, Band IV.1*, 263–374. Wien, Phoibos Verlag, Archäologisches Institut der Universität Salzburg und Archäologisches Institut mit Museum der Bulgarischen Akademie der Wissenschaften, Sofia.

Lazić, M. (1989) Fauna of mammals from the Neolithic settlements in Serbia. In D. Srejović, (ed.) *The Neolithic of Serbia. Archaeological research 1948–1988*. Belgrade, University of Belgrade, Faculty of Philosophy, Centre for Archaeological Research.

Legge, A J. (1990) Animals, economy, environment. In R. Tringham, and D. Krstić, (eds), *Selevac: a Neolithic village in Yugoslavia*, 215–242. Los Angeles, Institute of Archaeology, University of Los Angeles (Monumenta Archaeologica 15).

Marinković, S. (2002) *Vinčanska Kultura na području Srednjeg Banata*. Zrenjanin, Narodni muzej Zrenjanin.

Marinković, S (2010) Arheološki materijal sa lokaliteta Živanićeva Dolja iz zbirke Narodnog muzeja u Zrenjaninu – vinčanska kultura (The archaeological finds of the site Živanićeva Dolja from the collection of the National Museum of Zrenjanin – Vinča culture), *Rad Muzeja Vojvodine* 52, 21–36.

Maigrot, Y. (2003) *Étude Technologique et Fonctionnelle de l'Outillage en Matières Dures Animales. La station 4 de Chalain (Néolithique final, Jura, France)*. Unpublished doctoral thesis. Université de Paris I

Martin, L. and Russell, N. (1996) Surface material: animal bone and worked bone. In I. Hodder (ed.), *On the Surface: Çatalhöyük 1993–95*, 199–214. Cambridge and London, McDonald Institute for Archaeological Research and British Insitute of Archaeology at Ankara.

McPherron, A., Rasson, J. and Galdikas, B. (1988) Other artifact categories. In A. McPherron and D. Srejović, (eds), *Divostin and the Neolithic of Central Serbia*, 325–343. Pittsburgh, University of Pittsburgh.

McPherron, A. and Srejović, D. (eds) (1998) *Divostin and the Neolithic of Central Serbia*. Pittsburgh, University of Pittsburgh.

Poplin, F. (2004) Fiche éléments de nomenclature anatomique relative aux matères dures d'origine animale. In D. Ramseyer (ed.), *Matières et Techniques. Fiches de la commission de nomenclature sur l'industrie de l'os préhistorique* XI, 11–15. Paris: CNRS.

Russell, N. (1990) The bone tools. In R. Tringham, and D. Krstić, (eds), *Selevac: A Neolithic village in Yugoslavia*, 521–548. Los Angeles, Institute of Archaeology, University of Los Angeles (Monumenta Archaeologica 15).

Russell, N. (1993) *Hunting, Herding and Feasting: human use of animals in Neolithic southeast Europe*. Unpublished PhD thesis, University of California, Berkley.

Schibler, J. (1980) *Typologische Untersuchungen der Cortaillodzeitlichen Knochenartefakte. Die Neolithischen. Ufersiedlungen von Twann*. 17. Bern, Staatlicher Lerhmittelverlag

Schibler, J. (2001) Red deer antler: exploitation and raw material management in neolithic lake dwelling sites from Zürich, Switzerland. In H. Buitenhuis and W. Prummel (eds), *Animals and Man in the Past.*

Essays in honour of Dr. A. T. Clason Emeritus Professor of Archaeozoology, 82–94. Groningen, ARC-Publicatie 41, Rijksuniversiteit Groningen.

Séfèriadès, M. L. (1995) 1995b *Spondylus Gaederopus*: The earliest European long distance exchange system – A symbolic and structural archaeological approach to Neolithic societies. *Poročilo o Raziskovanju Paleolitika, Neolitika in Eneolitika v Sloveniji* 22, 238–46.

Smoor, B. (1976) Bone tools. In M. Gimbutas (ed.), *Neolithic Macedonia. As reflected by excavation at Anza, Southeast Yugoslavia*, 189–197. Los Angeles, University of Los Angeles.

Srejović, D. (ed.) (1989) *The Neolithic of Serbia. Archaeological Research 1948–1988*. Beograd, University of Belgrade, Faculty of Philosophy, Centre for Archaeological Research.

Srejović, D. and Jovanović, B. 1959. Oruđe i oružje od kosti i nakit iz Vinče. (Ustensiles et armes en os et parures de Vinča). *Starinar* n. s. IX–X, 181–190.

Stratouli G. (1988) *Knochenartefakte aus dem Neolithikum und Chalkolithikum Nordgriechenlands*. Bonn, Rudolf Habelt.

Suter, P. (1981) *Die Hirschgeweihartefakte der Coraillod-Schichten. Die Neolitischen Ufersiedlungen von Twann* 15. Bern, Staatlicher Lerhmittelverlag.

Tringham, R. and Krstić, D. 1990. Introduction: the Selevac Archaeological Project. In R. Tringham, and D. Krstić, (eds), *Selevac: A Neolithic village in Yugoslavia*, 1–12. Los Angeles, Institute of Archaeology, University of Los Angeles (Monumenta Archaeologica 15).

Vasić, M. (1936) *Preistoriska Vinča IV*. Državna štamparija, Beograd.

Vetnić, S. (1974) Počeci rada na ispitivanju kulture prvih zemljoradnika u srednjem Pomoravlju. *Počeci Ranih Zemljoradničkih Kultura u Vojvodini i Srpskom Podunavlju. Materijali X, Simpozijum praistorijske sekcije SADJ*, 123–163. Beograd, Savez arheoloških društava Jugoslavije.

Vitezović, S. (2007) *Koštana industrija u neolitu srednjeg Pomoravlja*. Unpublished masters (magistar) thesis, Faculty of Philosophy. University of Belgrade.

Vitezović, S. (2010) Neolitska koštana industrija sa lokaliteta Kormadin u Jakovu (iskopavanja 2008. godine). *Godišnjak Muzeja Grada Beograda* LVII.

Vitezović, S. (2011a) *Koštana industrija u starijem i srednjem Neolitu centralnog Balkana (Bone industry in the Early and Middle Neolithic in the Central Balkans)*. Unpublished PhD thesis, Faculty of Philosophy, University of Belgrade.

Vitezović, S. (2011b) Koštana industrija sa Bubnja – preliminarni rezultati (The bone industry from Bubnja). *Paper Abstracts. XXXIV Annual meeting of the Serbian Archaeological Society, held in Kraljevo, 26–28. 05.2011.*

Vitezović, S. (2012) The White Beauty – Starčevo culture jewellery. *Documenta Praehistorica XXXI*, 91–203

CHAPTER 8

Seals, Seal Hunting and Worked Seal Bones in the Estonian Coastal Region in the Neolithic and Bronze Age

Heidi Luik

Seal bones constitute a large share of faunal remains in both Neolithic and Bronze Age coastal settlements on Saaremaa Island (Estonia). Seal-hunting played an important role in both periods. Seal bones prevail among animal bones from the Neolithic settlements of Naakamäe, Loona and Kõnnu. Seal bones are also quite numerous among the faunal remains of the fortified Bronze Age settlements of Asva and Ridala although most of the animal bones from these settlements come from domestic animals. Seal bones were used for making artefacts only in the Neolithic, the products being mainly awls from seal limb bones and tooth pendants. Seal bones were not used apparently to make bone objects at the Bronze Age settlements. The article seeks an answer to the reason behind these differences in raw material choices in bone manufacturing between the two periods. The wider background to seal-hunting and the range of bone tools are shortly discussed as well as the way seals were used from archaeological and ethnographic data.

Keywords
Estonia; the Baltic Sea; Neolithic; Bronze Age; pinnipeds; worked seal bones.

Introduction

The aim of the paper is to provide an overview of seal exploitation based on finds from Neolithic and Bronze Age sites in Estonia. In Estonian archaeology the periods of the Neolithic and the Bronze Age are divided as follows: the Early Neolithic 4900–4200/4100 BC, the Middle Neolithic 4200/4100–3200/3000 BC, the Late Neolithic 3200/3000–1800 BC, the Early Bronze Age 1800–1100 BC and, the Late Bronze Age 1100–500 BC (Lang and Kriiska 2001). Sites used in the following analysis belong mostly to the Late Neolithic and Late Bronze Age.

First, the contribution of seal bones to several faunal assemblages both from the Neolithic and the Bronze Age will be presented together with an overview of hunted seal species. The main emphasis of the article is the use of seal

bone as raw material for making artefacts. Although seal bones have been found on both Neolithic and Bronze Age sites, they were used for making artefacts only in the Neolithic. The paper seeks an answer to explain the difference in raw material preferences between the two periods. Was the cultural attitude towards seal as species different? Or were the raw materials obtained from seals used in ways that made it possible or impossible to make artefacts from their bones? Or were bones of domestic animals simply preferred for making artefacts at these Bronze Age settlements? In the following, I will discuss the broader background to seal-hunting and the bone implements used in it as well as review the way seals appear in both archaeological and ethnographic data.

The article concentrates mainly on the sites on Saaremaa Island, although seal bones have also been found on Neolithic and Bronze Age sites on Hiiumaa Island and along coastal areas of north and west Estonia (Fig. 8.1). Seal bones found at settlement sites in Estonia have mainly been identified and analysed by the archaeozoologist, Lembi Lõugas (1994, 1997a, 1997b, 1998; Storå and Lõugas 2005; Lõugas and Tomek 2013). To date, no special attention has been paid to artefacts made from seal bones, although pendants made from seal canines have been mentioned (e.g. Jaanits *et al.* 1982, 99, fig. 71; Lõugas 1997a, appendix II: B). Artefacts from seal bones attracted my attention in connection with a project dealing with Bronze Age bone artefacts from the Baltic countries (ESF grant 6898). Differences and similarities in bone artefacts from Saaremaa, at the transition from the Neolithic to the Bronze Age (Luik *et al.* 2011), were also analyzed in the framework of this project. During the course of this research, it appeared that finds from the Neolithic settlements of Saaremaa (Naakamäe (2680±210 cal BC) and Loona (2725±375 cal BC). Jussila and Kriiska 2004, table 2: 50, 57) include artefacts made from seal bones, while the find material of the Bronze Age settlements studied (Asva and Ridala (900–500 BC), and Kaali (760–210 BC). Lang 2007, 60–65, 75–77, fig. 21) did not contain seal bone artefacts, although faunal remains of these sites contain quite a large number of seal bones. What could be the explanation?

Besides the above-mentioned Bronze Age settlements and finds from the Late Neolithic sites of Naakamäe and Loona I studied the material from some more sites (Kõnnu on

Saaremaa, Kõpu settlement sites on Hiiumaa) for this article. Finds from Kõpu (settlements from different phases of the Mesolithic and Neolithic) did not include bone artefacts probably due to poor preservation of bone material in the soil there (Lõugas *et al.* 1996a; Kriiska and Lõugas 1999). The finds from the Kõnnu Early Neolithic settlement site also consisted mainly of stone artefacts and bone artefacts were few. Seal bone artefacts in Kõnnu were represented by tooth pendants connected to Late Neolithic burials on the site (Lõugas 1997a, 16, appendix II: B). A small number of bone artefacts, including a couple of seal tooth pendants, also came to light at the Late Neolithic settlement site excavated recently on Vabaduse Square in Tallinn (3200–2800 BC; Kadakas 2010, 27, 68–70, pl. 14, 15; Lõugas and Tomek 2013).

Seal bones in the Neolithic and Bronze Age sites

As Lembi Lõugas has already published the data about seal bones and seal exploitation from different time periods at Estonian archaeological sites quite thoroughly (e.g. Lõugas 1994, 1997a, 1997b, 1998; Storå and Lõugas 2005; Lõugas and Tomek 2013), only a short overview of these data is given here. According to Lõugas, the seal bones are most numerous at the settlement site of Naakamäe, where the number of seal bones is over 7000 (Table 8.1). The Neolithic settlement sites

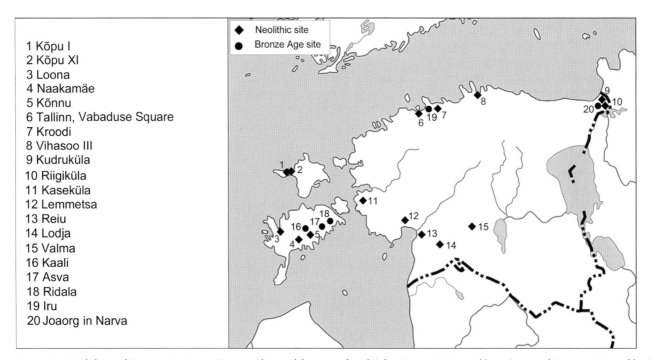

1 Kõpu I
2 Kõpu XI
3 Loona
4 Naakamäe
5 Kõnnu
6 Tallinn, Vabaduse Square
7 Kroodi
8 Vihasoo III
9 Kudruküla
10 Riigiküla
11 Kaseküla
12 Lemmetsa
13 Reiu
14 Lodja
15 Valma
16 Kaali
17 Asva
18 Ridala
19 Iru
20 Joaorg in Narva

Figure 8.1 Neolithic and Bronze Age sites in Estonia where seal bones are found (after Lõugas 1997a, table 3; Storå and Lõugas 2005, table 1). (Figure by K. Siitan and H. Luik).

Table 8.1 Number of seal bones found at Neolithic and Bronze Age sites (compiled after Paaver 1965, appendix I: 2; Lõugas 1997a, table 3, Storå and Lõugas 2005, table 1, Lõugas and Tomek 2013, table 1).

	SITE	NO. SEAL BONE FRAGS
Neolithic sites	Kõpu I	532
	Kõpu XI	141
	Loona	933
	Naakamäe	7029
	Kõnnu	242
	Tallinn, Vabaduse Sq.	353
	Kroodi	3
	Vihasoo III	2
	Kudruküla	67
	Riigiküla	986
	Kaseküla	29
	Lemmetsa	13
	Reiu	47
	Lodja	2
	Valma	3
Bronze Age sites	Kaali	39
	Asva	665
	Ridala	377
	Iru	110
	Joaorg in Narva IV	5

of Riigiküla, Kõpu, Loona, Kõnnu and Vabaduse Square in Tallinn also contained a large number of seal bones (from a couple of hundred to about a thousand finds). Some other sites (Kroodi, Kudruküla, Kaseküla, Reiu, Vihasoo, Lemmetsa, Lodja, Valma) contained a small number (from some single bones to one hundred) seal bones. Only single bones have been found on inland sites (Fig. 8.1, Table 8.1; Paaver 1965, appendix I: 2; Lõugas 1997a, table 3, 1997b, 1998; Kadakas 2010, 26; Kadakas *et al.* 2010, 40; Lõugas and Tomek 2013, table 1). Seal bones have also been found in low numbers (from a couple to a hundred) from Mesolithic sites (Lõugas 1997a, table 3). Seal bones have been most numerous at Asva among the Bronze Age sites and they have been found also at Ridala, Iru and Kaali; a few fragments come as well from Joaorg in Narva (Fig. 8.1, Table 8.1; Lõugas 1997a, table 3; Storå and Lõugas 2005, table 1).

The species mainly represented are harp seal (*Phoca groenlandica*), ringed seal (*Phoca hispida*) and grey seal (*Halichoerus grypus*); bones of harbour seal (*Phoca vitulina*) are less numerous; besides these main species, the Neolithic finds also include bones of porpoise (*Phocaena phocaena*) (Table 2; Lõugas 1997a, table 3, 1997b, table 1; Storå and Lõugas 2005, 98–99, table 1; Kadakas *et al.* 2010, 40; Lõugas and Tomek 2013, table 1).

Settlement sites with a large number of seal bones among the finds are also found on other parts of the Baltic coast and islands, on the coasts of Finland, Lithuania, Latvia and Sweden, on Gotland and Åland (Forsten 1977; Forsten and Blomqvist 1977; Gustavsson 1997; Storå 2000, 2001, 2002; Daugnora 2000; Zagorska 2000; Edgren 2000; Ukkonen 2002; Eriksson 2004; Storå and Lõugas 2005; Mannermaa 2008; Martinsson-Wallin 2008; Fornander *et al.* 2008; Stančikaitė *et al.* 2009).

In the following, a more detailed review is provided of faunal remains from the sites where I studied the finds to discover artefacts made from seal bones. The largest proportion of animal bones from Naakamäe come from seal (91%). Most numerous are bones of harp seal, but ringed seal and grey seal are also represented; bones of porpoise were also relatively numerous (Table 8.2; Paaver 1965, appendix I: 2; Lõugas 1997a, table 3, 1997b, table 1). Wild boar (*Sus scrofa ferus*) bones are most numerous among the remains of terrestrial animals. At Loona, seal and wild boar bones are also numerous although the number of fish bones (mostly cod – *Gadus morhua*) is also remarkable (7893 identified bone fragments). Seal bones constitute 72% of all mammal bones and here too, bones of harp seal were most numerous (Table 8.2; Lõugas 1997a, tables 2, 3, 1997b, table 1). At both sites, other mammal species are represented by single bones, e.g. fox (*Vulpes vulpes*), marten (*Martes martes*), elk (*Alces alces*), bear (*Ursus arctos*), hare (*Lepus timidus*), beaver (*Castor fiber*) (Paaver 1965, appendix I: 2; Lõugas 1997a; Kriiska 2002, 48). At Kõnnu, which is earlier than Naakamäe and Loona and dates to the Early Neolithic, seal bones, mostly ringed seal although bones of grey seal also occur, constitute 87% of all mammal bones (N=277) (Table 8.2; Paaver 1965, appendix I: 2; Lõugas 1997a, table 3). About 45% of identified mammal bones (N=804) at the settlement site on Vabaduse Square settlement site in Tallinn come from seal while porpoise bones are also numerous (Table 8.2; Lõugas and Tomek 2013, table 1).

Seal bones are also numerous at Late Bronze Age sites in Saaremaa, accounting for 38% in Asva (N=665) and 19% in Ridala (N=377), whilst terrestrial wild animals are represented by a few bones, about 2–3% on each site, including elk, wild boar, bear, fox, marten, hare and beaver. At Asva and Ridala, the majority of faunal remains come from domestic animals, accounting for 60% in Asva (N=1061) and even 78% in Ridala (N=1587). Caprine bones are most numerous, followed by bones from cattle, pig and horse (Paaver 1965; Lõugas 1994; Maldre 1999, 2008; Lang 2007, 110–111; Maldre and Luik 2009). At Asva, most of identifiable marine mammal bones come from harp seal, followed by grey seal; bones of ringed seal and harbour seal occur in small numbers; in Ridala all four of the above-mentioned species are represented, but bones of harp seal and grey seal prevail. In Kaali, where the number of faunal remains is quite modest, seal bones constitute 28% of identified mammal bones. Most of the identifiable seal bones come from grey seal (Table 8.2; Lõugas 1994, 85–89, tables 12–14; Storå and Lõugas 2005, table 2; Maldre 2008, 271).

Seal bone as raw material for artefacts

Bone artefacts can be generally divided into two groups: (1) *ad hoc* artefacts for which a bone was chosen having as suitable a shape as possible; (2) carefully thought out and worked artefacts which were often made from the compact diaphysis of long bones. Seal bones are not particularly suitable for making artefacts in the second group, since seals do not have large bones with thick straight diaphysis. However, fibulae of seals have an appropriate shape for making awls and seal canines can easily be used for pendants. Comparing the proportion of seal bones among the faunal remains and the proportion of artefacts made from seal bones among all bone and antler artefacts, the latter is much smaller (Fig. 8.2).

Table 8.2 Numbers of mammal and seal bones at Neolithic and Bronze Age sites in Saaremaa and Tallinn, Vabaduse Square (compiled after Paaver 1965, appendix I: 2; Lõugas 1997a, table 3, appendix II: A; Storå and Lõugas 2005, table 1; Maldre 2008, table 1; Lõugas and Tomek 2013).

	NEOLITHIC SITE				BRONZE AGE SITE		
	Naakamäe	Loona	Kõnnu	Vabaduse Sq.	Asva	Ridala	Kaali
Terrestrial and marine mammals	7676	1290	277	804	1754	2020	136
Seals:	7029	933	242	353	665	377	39
Ringed seal (*Phoca hispida*)	12	5	76	20	8	2	–
Grey seal (*Halichoerus grypus*)	51	2	25	–	32	22	14
Harp seal (*Phoca groenlandica*)	1083	110	–	46	44	28	2
Harbour seal (*Phoca vitulina*)	–	–	–	–	12	6	–
Indeterminate seal (*Phocidae*)	5883	816	141	287	569	321	23
Porpoise (*Phocaena phocaena*)	470	2	–	132	–	–	–

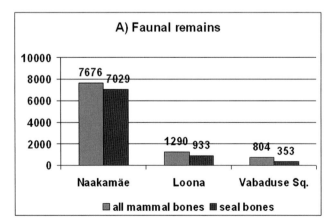 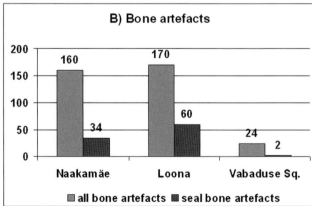

Figure 8.2 A) The number of seal bones compared with the number of total mammal bones and B) the number of seal bone artefacts compared with all bone and antler artefacts at the Neolithic sites of Naakamäe, Loona and Tallinn, Vabaduse Square.

Tools

The known artefacts made from seal bones are mostly awls made from their fibulae (Table 8.3). Altogether 26 awls of seal bones have been found at Naakamäe, 25 of them from fibulae and one from a metatarsal bone (Fig. 8.3: 1–4, 7). An artefact with a chisel-shaped end made from a seal tibia, was also found at Naakamäe, as well as the fragment of an artefact, made from a fibula, which might have been the tip of a fishing spear (Fig. 8.3: 6, 8). Loona produced 12 seal bone awls; besides awls made from fibulae, one specimen was made from a tibia (Fig. 8.3: 5). Although awls could be made from the bones of other animals (e.g. elk, wild boar) and birds as well, seal bone awls are particularly characteristic of the settlement sites of Naakamäe and Loona (Luik *et al.* 2011, 247, fig. 6).

Besides the sites of Saaremaa, seal bone awls have been found from Middle Neolithic sites on Gotland where seal bones occur in large numbers in the faunal assemblage. For example at Ire in the northern part of Gotland, one awl was found that was made of a harbour seal's tibia, one from a fibula probably from harp seal and one from a fibula of an unidentified seal species (Janzon 1974, 58, 131, table 21, pls 11, 13). In the Neolithic in Gotland, awls, as well as harpoons were more frequently made from wild boar bones (Janzon 1974, 59, 131, table 21, pls 15, 26; Martinsson-Wallin 2008, 179). A seal bone awl has been also found from the Neolithic settlement of Šventoji in Lithuania (Rimantienė 1996b, 129, fig. 49: 4) in addition to some scrapers made from seal tibia (Rimantienė 1996a, 51, fig. 38: 9; 1996b, 131, 169, fig. 49: 1, 2).

It is remarkable that although seal bones are numerous among the faunal remains from the Late Bronze Age fortified sites of Asva and Ridala, they have not been used for making artefacts. Among the nearly 700 bone artefacts from Asva there is only one fragment which can be assumed to be the point of an awl made from a seal fibula. However, this artefact is very fragmentary and the raw material information cannot be verified (Fig. 8.4: 1; Table 8.3). It seems that in the Bronze Age (Fig. 8.4: 2–6; Luik 2009) caprine metapodial bones were preferred for making awls of about the same size as the Neolithic seal bone specimens. One seal rib fragment has use wear on the tip of its broken end, but probably it is not a planned bone tool, but an *ad hoc* point which someone has used briefly for some task.

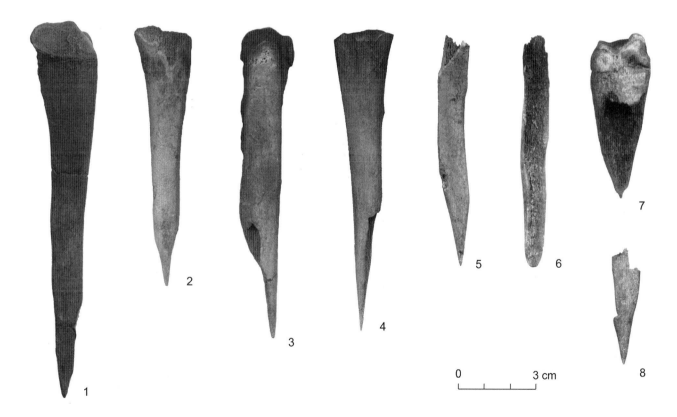

Figure 8.3 Tools from seal bones from the Neolithic sites of Naakamäe (1–4, 6–8) and Loona (5). (1–4) awls from seal fibula, (5) awl from seal tibia, (6) bevel-ended tool from seal tibia, (7) awl from seal metatarsus, (8) probable tips of a fishing spear from seal fibula (AI (Archaeological collections of the Institute of History, Tallinn University) 4211: 1328, 1534, 1430, 1438; 4210: 848; 4211: 263, 307, 242) (photograph: Heidi Luik).

Table 8.3 Numbers of all bone and antler artefacts compared with the number of artefacats made from seal bones at Neolithic and Bronze Age sites in Saaremaa and Tallinn, Vabaduse Square.

	NEOLITHIC SITE				BRONZE AGE SITE		
	Naakamäe	Loona	Kõnnu (burial)	Vabaduse Sq.	Asva	Ridala	Kaali
All bone and antler artefacts	160	170	69	24	700	120	17
Artefacts made from seal bones:	34	60	14	2	2	–	–
awls	26	12	–	–	2	–	–
other tools	2	–	–	–	–	–	–
tooth pendants	6	48	14	2	–	–	–

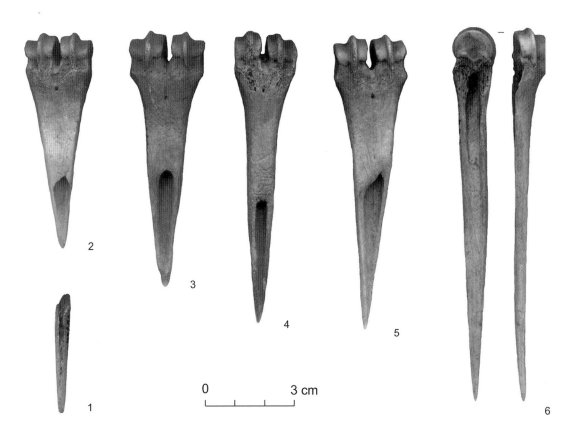

Figure 8.4 An awl fragment probably made from seal bone (1) and awls from caprine metapodials (2–6) from the Late Bronze Age fortified site of Asva (AI 4366: 1503, 1169, 1777, 1558, 1435, 823) (photograph: Heidi Luik).

Pointed implements were mainly used as awls to make holes in various materials – e.g. hides and furs, where holes had to be made along the edges, for stretching them on a frame or staking on the ground (Christidou and Legrand 2005). In the settlements of Saaremaa, the processing of seal skins must also be considered. For example, Kenneth Gustavsson (1997, 92–93, 99) has suggested that sealskin bags may have been used for transporting seal-oil. The seal bone scrapers of Šventoji have been also regarded as leather-working tools (Rimantienė 1996b, 169; Zagorska 2000, 281).

Awls are a very widespread type of bone artefacts in many regions and in many periods. There may have been a variety of reasons behind the selection of animals whose bones were used for making awls. Practical reasons would have been important. One reason for a choice was certainly the suitability of a certain bone for making an awl. Another important reason was the availability of bones, something that could differ e.g. seasonally (Russell 2001, 244). But were the choices based on practicalities only, or were they also influenced by other factors? In various times and places people understood the nature of materials differently; their understanding of materials depends on their boarder knowledge of the world (Conneller 2011, 5–13). As Tim Ingold puts it, the properties of materials are not fixed, but processual and relational (Ingold 2007). Probably traditions also existed concerning the suitability of a bone from certain species or of certain skeletal part for making a particular tool or artefact (Choyke 1997, 66–67; Choyke et al. 2004, 178). According to Pierre Lemonnier (1993, 3), the choice of a certain technique, raw material or tool may sometimes depend on some symbolic value attributed to them by the society rather than on their real physical properties. Thus, the use of a certain material or technique may have been considered imperative in certain cases, regardless of the fact that the artefact could have been made in a different way or from different material, or, on the contrary, some raw materials were rejected completely notwithstanding the excellent potential suitability of the material. Members of a society have "ideas" about raw materials, tools, actors, right time and place (Lemonnier 1993, 3–4). Beliefs about how certain skeletal parts should be used may be influenced by the mythical qualities of particular animals (Choyke and Daróczi-Szabó 2010, 238). For example, Robert McGhee, who has analysed the choices of bone, antler and walrus ivory in bone working of the Arctic peoples of North America, has suggested that besides the functional properties of materials, the symbolic meanings attributed to them were also important. He supposes that walrus ivory was symbolically linked with concepts associated with the sea (e.g., seal mammals, birds, and winter life on the sea ice) and antler with the land (land mammals, particularly the caribou, and summer life on the land). From ethnographic data it is known that the Inuit concept of environment was centred around the dichotomy between the land and the sea, e.g. the meat of caribou and sea mammals could not be cooked in the same pot or eaten on the same day, caribou skins could not be sewn on the sea ice etc. (McGhee 1977). But the choice may be also contrary-wise. For example, Christer Westerdahl has analysed the dichotomy of land and sea in northern Europe. In the case of Bothnian coastal sites, elk antlers from inland were chosen for making seal harpoons. In Westerdahl's opinion it is possible that the reason for choosing elk antler for making tools used at sea was not the excellent properties of antler, but the fact that antlers were acquired from inland areas. Later ethnographic sources contain beliefs that on board a boat at sea one should use only things received from the land and not use or eat anything that was produced by or lived in the sea (Westerdahl 2005, 7).

The harpoons used in seal-hunting in the Neolithic and Bronze Age in Estonia as well as in neighbouring regions were made mostly from elk antler or elk bone (Luik 2011, 41; Luik et al. 2011, 247, figs. 3, 4; see below). Helene Martinsson-Wallin has suggested that on different sites of the Pitted Ware Culture on Gotland, animal species chosen for food as well as for making bone artefacts expressed the identity and beliefs of the group; e.g. in the northern part of Gotland (Ire) people preferred seal and avoided the use of wild boar, but in the western part (Hemmor and Västerbjers) it was just the opposite (Martinsson-Wallin 2008, 179 and references there). Both seal and wild boar were also important game animals in Saaremaa in the Neolithic but it is not possible to observe such different preferences in different sites at the present stage of investigation

Although bones of some marine mammals are less dense than bones of terrestrial mammals, some marine mammals, including seals have very dense limb bones (e.g. Wall 1983; Maas 2008, 125–126) so this material is quite well suited for making awls. In Estonia, at the Neolithic settlements of Naakamäe and Loona, seal bones were evidently among the most easily available materials and, since seal fibulae were suitable for making awls, they were used for that. In the Late Bronze Age settlements, bones of domestic animals, which also dominate the faunal remains, were mostly used for making artefacts. Elk antler was mostly used of wild animal skeletal elements. It was preferred for making artefacts, which, owing to their size or shape, could be only made from antler (e.g. large harpoons, ard blades or hoe blades, e.g. Luik 2011; Luik 2013, 393, 396, figs 7, 11). An artefact about the size of an awl from seal fibula could be made from a caprine metacarpal or metatarsal bone. Caprine bones are most numerous among the bones of domestic animals from the Late Bronze Age fortified settlements of Saaremaa. Awls made from caprine metapodials are a type of artefact found in many regions and in different periods, probably because of their functionality; examples can be found from all over Europe, from the Neolithic as well as from the Bronze Age. Such awls are very uniform and their manufacturing technique was also standardized (Fig. 8.4: 2–6; Luik 2009, and references there). Although it would have been also possible to use seal bones, in view of their large percentual contribution to the faunal remains, the practice of making such awls from caprine bones evidently represents a cultural choice. The metapodials of caprines were probably also easier to use since these bones have little meat on them. Seal bones in the Bronze Age settlements of Saaremaa are very fragmented (Storå and Lõugas 2005, 99–100) – perhaps seals were utilised in a way that made it impossible to make tools from their bones. However, to date it is still unclear why these bones are so fragmentary and if it is connected, for example, with prolonged cooking or boiling. It is also possible that there were traditions or taboos making it inadvisable to manufacture tools from seal bones.

Pendants

Besides fibula, used for making awls, seal canines were also used to make pendants (Table 8.3). These pendants were mostly pierced although the root end of the tooth could sometimes be grooved for suspension (Fig. 8.5: 11, 12). Tooth pendants are more numerous among the finds from Loona – 48 specimens (Fig. 8.5: 1–12); only 6 pendants of seal canines were found at Naakamäe (Fig. 8.5: 13–14). In additon to seal canines, perforated teeth and canines of other species are known from Naakamäe and Loona, mostly from elk, but also wild boar, fox, auroch (*Bos primigenius*) and bear (Luik *et al.* 2011, 251–253, fig. 21). Seal canine pendants were also found at Kõnnu, where one grave contained three skeletons – two adults and a child. The grave contained a total of 69 tooth pendants, 14 canines of grey seal (Fig. 8.5: 15–18); the other species whose teeth appear in the grave as pendants include elk, wild boar, auroch, dog (*Canis familiaris*), wolf (*Canis lupus*) and fox (Lõugas 1997a, 16, appendix II: B). A couple of tooth pendants were found at the Neolithic settlement site on Vabaduse Square in Tallinn (Kadakas 2010, 70, pl. 15: 6, 7; Kadakas *et al.* 2010, 39, fig. 9: 6; Lõugas and Tomek 2013, 470). Single seal canine pendants were found in each of two male burials; one from Kõljala, together with some wild cat (*Felis silvestris*) canine pendants (Jaanits *et al.* 1982, 99, fig. 71; Lõugas *et al.* 1996b, 417), and the other from the site of Kaseküla (Kriiska *et al.* 1997, fig. 7: 1).

Animal tooth pendants are characteristic finds of the Mesolithic and Neolithic in Estonia (e.g. Tamula burials, Jaanits 1954, figs 12, 13; Lõhmus 2007, figs 3, 5, Kriiska

et al. 2007, fig. 8; Jonuks 2009, 90–97, fig. 2) as well as in Latvia (e.g. from the Zvejnieki cemetery, Zagorska and Lõugas 2000; Larsson 2006; Lõugas 2006). It is noteworthy that in the Zvejnieki cemetery, located inland, seal canine pendants occur in quite large numbers; in addition, a perforated seal phalange pendant was found in an Early Neolithic burial (Zagorska 2000, 282; Larsson 2006, 279; Lõugas 2006, 88, figs. 7, 8, 11). Seal canine pendants and a perforated seal radius, probably worn as an amulet, have been also found at the Neolithic settlements of Šventoji in Lithuania (Rimantienė 1996a, 54, 76, fig. 40; 1996b, 135, 169, figs. 51: 7–9; 56; Zagorska 2000, 282, fig. 5: 3–10), as well as in Neolithic burials on Gotland (Janzon 1974, 132, pl. 13; Burenhult 1991, figs 109, 112: 11; Eriksson 2004, 136; Martinsson-Wallin 2008, 176, 178).

It has been suggested that both the species and age of animals represented by animal bones and teeth placed in burials of the Pitted Ware Culture may have had a meaning possibly connected with the status of the deceased or represent a defined group or clan membership. According to Helene Martinsson-Wallin, differences in animal bones from different sites may reflect the tenets of the community, related to animals as symbols and exponents of group identity (Martinsson-Wallin 2008, 179; compare e.g. Choyke 2001). The large number of tooth pendants in some graves of the Zvejnieki cemetery in Latvia, especially head-dresses adorned with tooth pendants, have also been interpreted as marking the special status or social affiliation of the deceased. In different times, teeth of different species were favoured (Zagorska and Lõugas 2000;

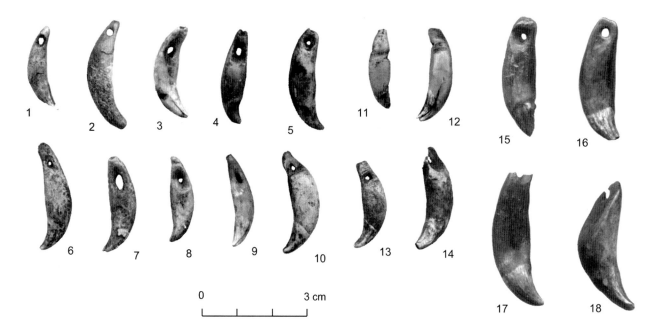

Figure 8.5 Seal canine pendants from the Neolithic sites of Loona (1–12), Naakamäe (13–14) and the Neolithic burial at Kõnnu (15–18) (AI 4210: 185, 6, 1285, 615, 756, 478, 572, 998, 1172, 793, 620, 641; 4211: 267, 1524; 4951: 362, 353, 359, 358) (photograph: Heidi Luik).

Larsson 2006, 274; Lõugas 2006, fig. 8). Both in the Zvejnieki and Tamula (south Estonia) cemeteries pendants made from the teeth of several species are usually represented in a single grave, although in most graves one species dominated (Larsson 2006, 274–281; Lõugas 2006, fig. 7; Jonuks 2009, 116). As seal canine pendants are still known only from a couple of burials in Estonia – from the triple burial of Kõnnu and a male burial at Kõljala – it is not possible to draw conclusions about their connection with the sex, age or status of the deceased persons.

The finds from the Bronze Age fortified settlements of Estonia do not include seal canine pendants or canine pendants from any species. Hence, there is no reason to suggest that attitudes toward seals changed but rather changes occurred in attitudes towards the use of tooth pendants in general. Canine pendants, numerous in the Neolithic, do not occur in the Bronze Age material, a circumstance probably connected with changes in beliefs (Jonuks 2009, 146). In the beliefs of the Neolithic Period, which in this region based mainly on hunting and fishing economy (see e.g. Kriiska 2001), the importance of hunting magic has been assumed, in parallel with totemist and shamanist notions reflected in the use of canine and tooth pendants (Jonuks 2009, 111–136 and references there). With the transition to farming, natural phenomena (the sun and rain) gained in significance leading to changes in the beliefs and burial customs (*ibid.*, 136–158). In Estonia, tooth pendants came into use again in the Viking Age, mainly of terrestrial carnivores' canines as well as pig (*Sus scrofa*) and wild boar tusks and teeth (Luik 2003, 2005; Jonuks 2009, 291–294). Tooth pendants likely had different meanings in different cultural contexts, for example in the way they connected to protective magic, represent shamanistic equipment, symbolize a special kind of group identity, ancestors, the role of animal species in mythology etc. (e.g. Zagorska and Lõugas 2000; Choyke 2001, 2009, 33–36; Choyke and Daróczi-Szabó 2010, 245; Asplund 2005; Larsson 2006; Jonuks 2009, 119).

Seal hunting and use of seals: archaeological and ethnographic record

Seals were also hunted in the Baltic Sea in historical times. Ethnographic data has been collected about seal hunting as well as the use of seals (Manninen 1931, 70–91; Gustavsson 1997, 111–121; Viires *et al.* 2000, 42; Zagorska 2000, 281; Luts 2008, 126–128). In the folklore of many nations – Estonians among them – there are legends in which seals are really people, Pharaoh's army, which, according to the Old Testament, drowned in the Red Sea (Loorits 1935; Puhvel 1963; Westerdahl 2005, 9). Martin Puhvel considers such legends as later narrative stratifications upon earlier lore which regarded seals as descendants of drowned people (Puhvel 1963, 326, 330–331); nevertheless, it is not known how far back in time such tenets go.

Bone and antler artefacts connected with seal hunting

Various seal species farrow at different times and also exhibit different behaviours. Metric analyses of bones have been carried out at many sites to establish at which time of year seals were hunted there (Forsten 1977; Forsten and Blomqvist 1977; Lõugas 1997a, 1997b, 1998; Gustavsson 1997, 111; Zagorska 2000; Storå 2001, 2002; Storå and Lõugas 2005). From historical times, various hunting methods have been recorded depending on whether seals were killed on ice or in water. Clubs, nets and harpoons, and in historical times also firearms, were used (Manninen 1931, 70–91; Gustavsson 1997, 111–112; Luts 2008, 126–128).

Archaeological finds from both the Neolithic and the Bronze Age include harpoons used for seal hunting made from antler or bone. Direct evidence for this has been found, for instance, in Finland, where in some places (Kristiinankaupungi, Närpiö, Oulunjoki, Hammarland) seal skeleton or bones have been found together with a harpoon head (Edgren 2000, 51–55; Storå 2002, 61). A harpoon head also was found near seal bones in Sārnate, Latvia (Zagorska 2000, 281). All these sites belong to the Neolithic Period.

Bone and antler artefacts connected to seal hunting have been found in the settlements of Saaremaa, already discussed in this article. Neolithic harpoon fragments from Naakamäe and Loona are made from bone (Fig. 8.6: 1–3; Jaanits *et al.* 1982, fig. 63: 1; Luik *et al.* 2011, fig. 3: 11–13) and they are smaller than the later Bronze Age harpoons. A few bone harpoon heads have been found in the settlements of Kõnnu (Fig. 8.6: 4; Jaanits 1979, 365, fig. 2: 2), Riigiküla (Kriiska *et al.* 1997, fig. 8) and Vabaduse Square, Tallinn (Kadakas 2010, 69, pl. 14: 5, 6; Kadakas *et al.* 2010, fig. 9: 1, 2). The identifiable harpoon heads are made from elk long bones (Luik *et al.* 2011, 247, fig. 3; Lõugas and Tomek 2013, fig. 4: 1, 2). Harpoons have been also found on other coasts and Baltic islands, e.g. from Gotland, Lithuania, Latvia, Finland (Janzon 1974, pls 8, 15, 28, 48, 51; Burenhult 1991, fig. 112: 5–8; Rimantienė 1996a, 30, 75, fig. 20: 1, 3; Zagorska 2000, 281, fig. 3; Edgren 2000, figs. 2–4).

The Estonian Late Bronze Age material contains two types of harpoons. Large curved specimens with semi-cylindrical sockets made from elk antler; most of them found at the fortified site of Asva (Fig. 8.6: 5–9), one came from Iru and one fragment from Ridala (Vassar 1955, fig. 35: 1–3; Lang 1996, pl. viii: 1; Luik 2013, 396, fig. 10). Besides these large specimens, a few small straight bone harpoon heads have been found (Fig. 8.6: 10; Vassar 1955, fig. 35: 6; Luik 2013, fig. 11); specimens similar to the latter have been found at inland settlements in Latvia as well (e.g. from Mūkukalns and Ķivutkalns: Graudonis 1967, pl. xiii; 1989, pl. xviii: 1–7) and Lithuania (e.g. from Narkūnai and Vosgėliai, Volkaitė-Kulikauskienė 1986, fig. 36; Grigalavičienė 1995, 269, fig. 64: 1–3). Harpoons from the coastal settlements of Estonia

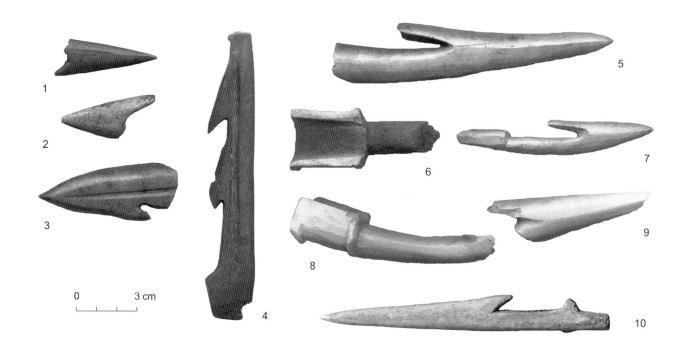

Figure 8.6 Bone and antler harpoon heads from the Neolithic sites of Naakamäe (1, 3), Loona (2) and Kõnnu (4), and the Late Bronze Age site of Asva (5–10) (AI 4211: 1344; 4210: 666; 4211: 187; 4951: 284; 4012: 113; 4366: 642; 3307: 298; 4366: 1863, 1942; 3994: 580) (photograph: Heidi Luik).

are most likely connected with seal-hunting. In the inland settlements, the small harpoons may have been used to hunt beavers or for fishing. The bones of beaver occur in large numbers in Ķivutkalns and Mūkukalns (Graudonis 1967, 123, 1989, table 10; Grigalavičienė 1995, 269).

Besides harpoons, elk antler points with spiral use-wear, occurring among Bronze Age finds, can presumably be also connected with seal-hunting (Luik 2010; Maldre and Luik 2009). To date, these points have been mostly found at Asva with a total of twelve specimens and fragments (Fig. 8.7). One fragment came to light at Ridala. Since the spiral lines are deeply grooved into the antler surface, they must have been made from some material containing or consisting of strong fibres. This hypothesis is supported also by the experimental and high power microscope studies made by Kristiina Paavel recently. Her experiments showed that most probable fibres were horsehair and sinew (Paavel 2012). Probably, there must have been more than one thread or fibre which ran around the tip of the antler artefact in the course of work – which probably was meant to make them more taut – after which these threads or fibres pulled together and were twined into a thicker cord which could be used in fishing or seal-hunting. The ethnographic record contains information about the use of horsehair cord for making fishing line as well as for attaching harpoon heads to the haft (Manninen 1931, 75; Viires *et al.* 2000, 42; Maldre and Luik 2009, 43, fig. 7).

Use of seals

In terms of the general use of seals, meat, blubber and fur represent the main products. Seal bones as raw material for tools was relatively modest.

Stable isotope analyses indicate that seal meat played an important role in the diet of the inhabitants at Neolithic coastal settlements (Eriksson 2004, 153–154, 158; Fornander *et al.* 2008, 282, 293). Dogs at Neolithic Västerbjers on the Baltic island of Gotland also mainly fed on fish and seal meat, based on stable isotope analysis (Eriksson 2004, 156). The results of stable isotope analyses from some human bones from the sites of Saaremaa have different signatures. Neolithic human bone from Naakamäe (2916 (2880)–2698 cal. BC) displays a typical marine signature value, but human bone from the Kõljala Neolithic burial (this bone fragment did not contain enough collagen to be radiocarbon dated) has an isotope signature which is mainly terrestrial; Bronze Age human bone from Loona (909 (830)–802 cal. BC) has an intermediate value, slightly more terrestrial than marine (Lõugas *et al.* 1996b, 406–409, 411–417). Based on the contents of dogs coprolites found at the Late Bronze Age fortified settlement of Asva, dogs probably did not eat much seal meat (only one seal phalanx and a couple of presumably seal bone fragments were discovered and no dog gnawing has been observed on seal bones), coprolite contents show they must have eaten lots of fish (Maldre 2003, 144–145, table 1).

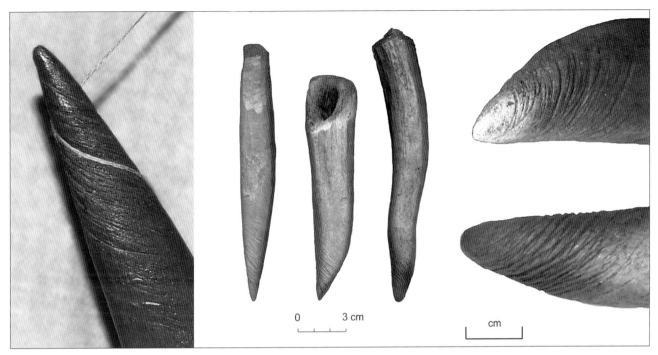

Figure 8.7 Antler points with spiral use-wear from the Late Bronze Age fortified site of Asva (AI 4366: 1883, 1772, 1823) (photograph: Heidi Luik).

From ethnographic records it is known that in later times in Estonia seal meat was not eaten often except by seal-hunters; usually meat of young seals was used, salted and smoked (Luts 2008, 126). The meat of newborn seals was preferred on the coastal regions of Finland and Sweden; only certain parts of adult seals such as their flippers, heart, liver, kidneys and head were regularly consumed for food. In Norway, salted blubber or train-oil was also used for food, usually with dry fish or meat, as a substitute for butter or other fat. On long seal-hunting trips, however, seal meat was the main food (Gustavsson 1997, 112–113, and references there).

In additon to seal meat, blubber, or train oil, was important. It has been suggested that blubber was burned in low oval earthenware dishes to light rooms in the Neolithic (Rimantiene 1996b, 170, fig. 71; Zagorska 2000, 281). In Ostrobothnia, Finland, there are cooking pits, probably dating to the Bronze Age and Pre-Roman Iron Age. Although the function of the cooking pits is not certain it has been suggested they were connected to seal-hunting and the production of train-oil (Kuusela *et al.* 2010, 26–32, and references there). Train-oil was probably very important in the Bronze Age. Based on pottery typical of the Lusatian Culture, Kenneth Gustavsson has postulated that the site of Otterböte in the Kökar archipelago of Åland was used by seal-hunters from the southern shores of the Baltic Sea (Gustavsson 1997, 122–124) whose object was train-oil. Although it has been assumed that large earthenware vessels were used for storing and transporting train-oil (Meinander 1954, 142; Forsten 1977, 59), Gustavsson's opinion is that the pottery of that period was too porous and fragile to hold train-oil. A large pot full of train-oil would have been inconvenient to transport and earthenware vessels were still too small to allow transport of large quantities. Sealskin bags could have been suited for transporting blubber (Gustavsson 1997, 92–93, 99; see also Zagorska 2000, 281). However, according to Jan Storå and Lembi Lõugas, the metric analysis of seal bones from Otterböte indicates that it was mainly young seals that were hunted there, and therefore the object of the hunt were meat and hides rather than train-oil (Storå and Lõugas 2005, 103–104; see also Forsten 1977, 59). From the ethnographic record we know that sealskin was used for making footwear, since it is waterproof to some extent, as well as for making cords and straps, valued for their strength (Gustavsson 1997, 113–114). Certainly seal hides and fur must also have been important for making footwear, clothing, bags etc in prehistory.

On the basis of the presence of seal canine pendants, seals must have had meaning for Neolithic people beyond their practical value. It has been suggested that seal occupied an important place not only in the diet but also in the identity of the Pitted Ware Culture people. For instance, Jan Storå has observed the different treatment given to seal skulls and the rest of their carcasses in the settlements of Jettböle on Åland as well as at Ajvide on Gotland (e.g. skulls were stored only in certain locations in the settlement). Some of the zoomorphic figurines of the Pitted Ware Culture on Åland may also depict seals. Although the relation between man and seal was primarily economic and utilitarian, Storå suggests that it may also have had many levels. The different treatment of skulls may be connected with some concept of soul – the living soul of a killed seal must be treated in a dignified manner (Storå 2001, 48–51; see also Eriksson 2004, 158; Fornander *et al.* 2008, 281, 295).

Concerning Estonian Neolithic animal figurines, Mirja Ots has recently expressed an opinion that an amber figurine from the Neolithic double burial at Valma could be interpreted as a seal (Fig. 8.8). This, however, is not the only possible interpretation – it has variously been identified as a wild boar or a beaver (Ots 2010, 14–15, fig. 2, and references there). Although Valma is located far from the coast, some seal bones were also found there (Paaver 1965, 438; Lõugas 1997a, table 3; Ots 2010, 15). Here, mention should be made of the numerous seal tooth pendants from the cemetery of Zvejnieki, Latvia, which is also not located on the coast; it is possible that they were obtained by contacts with coast dwellers – clothes or head-dresses adorned with tooth pendants could have been valuable trade items (e.g. Choyke 2001, 252), or perhaps inland dwellers also travelled to the coast and islands for seasonal hunting (Zagorska 2000, 282; Lõugas 2006, 88). A pine-bark seal figurine has been found at the Siliņupe settlement in Latvia while another seal figurine, carved from bone and ornamented, was found on the southern shore of Lake Ladoga (Gurina 1961, fig. 19: 13; Zagorska 2000, 281–282, fig. 5: 1).

Tooth pendants and animal figurines are generally typical of the Neolithic in the region. In this respect seal is not exceptional; there are animals (e.g. elk), whose teeth are even more frequently found drilled as pendants and whose figures are also represented more often (cf. Jonuks 2009, 103–112 and references there; Kashina and Zhulnikov 2011). Still, the occurrence of seal canine pendants and seal figurines indicates that seal possessed some importance and meaning for the people of that period which resulted in this kind of symbolic expression.

Figure 8.8 Amber animal figurine from the Neolithic double burial of Valma. It has been suggested that the depicted animal could be a seal (AI 4022: 5727) (photograph: Mirja Ots).

Conclusions

Although seal hunting was of signal importance for the inhabitants of Saaremaa in both the Neolithic and Bronze Age, clear differences can be observed in the use of seal bones for making artefacts in the two periods. Although seal bones were not used as raw material very frequently in the Neolithic either, seal bone artefacts do exist – some of them tools, mainly awls, and others ornaments/amulets, being seal canine pendants. Bronze Age worked bone, as a rule, does not include seal bone artefacts. The reasons for the absence of the two artefact types found in the previous period are probably different. As concerns the seal bone awls, the reason was most likely practical – bones of domestic animals were preferred for making tools because of their greater availability. An artefact about the size of an awl from seal fibula could easily be made from a caprine metacarpal or metatarsal. Caprine bones are most numerous among the bones of domestic animals at the Bronze Age fortified settlements of Saaremaa. The absence of the other artefact type, seal canine pendants in the Late Bronze Age finds is probably connected with changes in the belief system reflecting other important changes in the society of the period, e.g. the emergence of fortified settlements, the development of specialized crafts and exchange, the growing importance of agriculture, and changes in social structure which became more complex and hierarchical.

Acknowledgements

This research was supported by the Estonian Ministry of Education and Research (SF0130012s08) and Estonian Science Foundation (grant no 6898). The author also thanks Lembi Lõugas and Liina Maldre for their help with bone material, Kersti Siitan and Mirja Ots for help with illustrations, and Liis Soon for translating the text.

Bibliography

Asplund, H. (2005) The bear and the female. Bear-tooth pendants in Late Iron Age Finland. In S. Mäntylä (ed.), *Rituals and Relations. Studies on the material culture of the Baltic Finns*, 13–30. Helsinki, Academia Scientiarum Fennica.

Burenhult, G. (1991) *Arkeologi i Sverige, 1. Fångstfolk och herdar.* Höganäs, Förlags AB Wiken.

Choyke, A. M. (1997) The bone tool manufacturing continuum. *Anthropozoologica* 25–26, 65–72.

Choyke, A. M. (2001) Late Neolithic red deer canine beads and their imitations. In A. M. Choyke and L. Bartosiewicz (eds), *Crafting Bone: skeletal technologies through time and space. Proceedings of the 2nd Meeting of the (ICAZ) Worked Bone Research Group, Budapest, 31 August–5 September 1999*, 251–266. Oxford, Archaeopress (British Archaeological Report S937).

Choyke, A. M. (2009) Grandmother's awl: individual and collective memory through material culture. In I. Barbiera, A. Choyke and J.

Rasson (eds), *Materializing Memory: archaeological material culture and the semantics of the past*, 21–40. Oxford, Archeopress (British Archaeological Report S1977).

Choyke, A. M. and Daróczi-Szabó, M. (2010) The complete and usable tool: some life histories of prehistoric bone tools in Hungary. In A. Legrand-Pineau, I. Sidéra, N. Buc, E. David and V. Scheinsohn (eds), *Ancient and Modern Bone Artefacts from America to Russia. Cultural, technological and functional signature*, 235–248. Oxford, Archaeopress (British Archaeological Report S2136).

Choyke, A. M., Vretemark, M. and Sten, S. (2004) Levels of social identity expressed in the refuse and worked bone from the Middle Bronze Age Százhalombatta-Földvár, Vatya culture, Hungary. In S. Jones O'Day, W. van Neer and A. Ervynck (eds), *Behavior Behind Bones. The Zooarchaeology of Ritual, Religion, Status and Identity. Proceedings of the ICAZ 9th Conference, Durham, August 2002*, 177–189. Oxford, Oxbow Books.

Christidou, R. and Legrand, A. (2005) Hide working and bone tools: experimentation design and applications. In H. Luik, A. M. Choyke, C. E. Batey and L. Lõugas (eds), *From Hooves to Horns, from Mollusc to Mammoth. Manufacture and use of bone artefacts from prehistoric times to the present. Proceedings of the 4th Meeting of the ICAZ Worked Bone Research Group at Tallinn, 26th–31st of August 2003. Muinasaja teadus* 15, 385–396. Tallinn, Institute of History.

Conneller, C. 2011. *An Archaeology of Materials. Substantial Transformations in Early Prehistoric Europe*. New York, Routledge.

Daugnora, L. (2000) Fish and seal osteological data at Šventoji sites. *Lietuvos Archeologija*, 19, 85–101.

Edgren, T. (2000) A harpoon head from the depths of the sea. In V. Lang and A. Kriiska (eds), *De Temporibus Antiquissimus ad Honorem Lembit Jaanits. Muinasaja teadus* 8, 49–56. Tallinn, Institute of History.

Eriksson, G. (2004) Part-time farmers or hard-core sealers? Västerbjers studied by means of stable isotope analysis. *Journal of Anthropological Archaeology* 23, 135–162.

Fornander, E., Eriksson, G. and Lidén, K. (2008) Wild at heart: approaching pitted ware identity, economy and cosmology through stable isotopes in skeletal material from the Neolithic site Korsnäs in Eastern Central Sweden. *Journal of Anthropological Archaeology* 27, 281–297.

Forsten, A. (1977) A Bronze Age refuse fauna from Kökar, Åland. *Finskt Museum 1974*, 81, 56–60.

Forsten, A. and Blomqvist, L. (1977) Refuse faunas of the Vantaa Mesolithic and Neolithic periods. *Finskt Museum 1974*, 81, 50–55.

Graudonis, J. (1967) *Latvia v Epokhu Pozdnei Bronzy i Pannego Zheleza. Nachalo pazlozhenia pervobytno-obshchinnogo stroia.* Riga, Zinatne.

Graudonis, J. (1989) *Nocietinātās Apmetnes Daugavas Letecē.* Rīga, Zinātne.

Grigalavičienė, E. (1995) *Žalvario ir Ankstyvasis Geležies Amžius Lietuvoje.* Vilnius, Mokslo ir Enciklopedijų Leidykla.

Gurina, N. N. (1961) *Drevniaia Istoria Severo-Zapada Evropeiskoi chasti SSSR. Materialy i Issledovania po Arkheologii SSSR 87. Moskva, Leningrad, Izdatel'stvo Akademii Nauk SSSR.*

Gustavsson, K. (1997) *Otterböte. New light on a Bronze Age site in the Baltic.* Stockholm, Stockholm University Theses and Papers in Archaeology, B: 4.

Ingold, T. (2007) Materials against materiality. *Archaeological Dialogues* 14 (1), 1–16.

Jaanits, L. (1954) Novye dannye po neolitu Pribaltiki. *Sovetskaia Arheologia* XIX, 159–204.

Jaanits, L. (1979) Die neolitische Siedlung Kõnnu auf der Insel Saaremaa. *Proceedings of the Academy of Sciences of the Estonian SSR* 28 (4), 363–367.

Jaanits, L., Laul, S., Lõugas, V. and Tõnisson, E. (1982) *Eesti Esiajalugu.* Tallinn, Eesti Raamat.

Janzon, G. (1974) *Gotlands Mellanneolitiska Gravar. Acta Universitatis Stockholmiensis, 6.* Stockholm, Almqvist and Wiksell.

Jonuks, T. (2009) *Eesti Muinasusund. Dissertationes archaeologiae Universitatis Tartuensis 2.* Tartu, Tartu University Press.

Jussila, T. and Kriiska, A. (2004) Shore displacement chronology of the Estonian Stone Age. *Estonian Journal of Archaeology* 8 (1), 3–32.

Kadakas, U. (2010) *Tallinna Vabaduse Väljaku Neoliitiline Asulakoht Eesti Samaaegsete Rannikuasulate Kontekstis.* Unpublished MA thesis, University of Tartu.

Kadakas, U., Vedru, G., Lõugas, L., Hiie, S., Kihno, K., Kadakas, V., Püüa, G. and Toos, G. (2010) Rescue excavations of the Neolithic settlement site in Vabaduse Square, Tallinn. In E. Oras and E. Russow (eds), *Archaeological Fieldwork in Estonia 2009*, 27–48. Tallinn, National Heritage Board.

Kashina, E. and Zhulnikov, A. (2011) Rods with elk heads: symbol in ritual context. *Estonian Journal of Archaeology* 15 (1), 18–31.

Kriiska, A. (2001) *Stone Age Settlement and Economic Processes in the Estonian Coastal Area and Islands.* Academic Dissertation. Helsinki, University of Helsinki. http://ethesis.helsinki.fi/julkaisut/hum/kultt/vk/kriiska/

Kriiska, A. (2002) Lääne-Eesti saarte asustamine ja püsielanikkonna kujunemine. In V. Lang (ed.), *Keskus–tagamaa–ääreala. Uurimusi Asustushierarhia ja Võimukeskuste Kujunemisest Eestis. Muinasaja teadus* 11, 29–60. Tallinn, Tartu, Institute of History.

Kriiska, A. and Lõugas, L. (1999) Late Mesolithic and Early Neolithic seasonal settlement at Kõpu, Hiiumaa island, Estonia. In U. Miller, T. Hackens, V. Lang, A. Raukas and S. Hicks (eds), *Environmental and Cultural History of the Eastern Baltic Region. PACT 57*, 157–172. Rixensart.

Kriiska, A., Lõugas, L. and Saluäär, U. (1997) Archaeological excavations of the Stone Age settlement site and ruin of the stone cist grave of the Early Metal Age in Kaseküla. In Ü. Tamla (ed.), *Archaeological Field Works in Estonia 1997*, 30–43. Tallinn, National Heritage Board.

Kriiska, A., Lõugas, L., Lõhmus, M., Mannermaa, K. and Johanson, K. (2007) New AMS dates from Estonian Stone Age burial sites. *Estonian Journal of Archaeology* 11 (2), 83–121.

Kuusela, J.-M., Vaneeckhout, S. and Okkonen, J. (2010) Places of importance and social communication: studying the Pre-Roman cairn field of Viirikallio in Laihia, Finland. *Estonian Journal of Archaeology* 14 (1), 22–39.

Lang, V. (1996) *Muistne Rävala. Muistised, kronoloogia ja maaviljelusliku asustuse kujunemine Loode-Eestis, eriti Pirita jõe alamjooksu piirkonnas. Muinasaja teadus* 4. Tallinn, Institute of History.

Lang, V. (2007) *The Bronze and Early Iron Ages in Estonia.* Tartu, Tartu University Press, Estonian Archaeology 3.

Lang, V. and Kriiska, A. (2001) Eesti esiaja periodiseering ja kronoloogia. *Journal of Estonian Archaeology* 5 (2), 83–109.

Larsson, L. (2006). A tooth for a tooth. Tooth ornaments from the graves at the cemeteries of Zvejnieki. In L. Larsson and I. Zagorska (eds), *Back to the Origin. New Research in the Mesolithic-Neolithic Zvejnieki Cemetery and Environment, Northern Latvia*. 52, 253–287. Lund, Acta Archaeologica Lundensia Series in 8°.

Lemonnier, P. (1993) Introduction. In P. Lemonnier (ed.), *Technological Choices. Transformation in Material Cultures since the Neolithic*, 1–35. London, New York, Routledge.

Loorits, O. (1935) *Pharaos Heer in der Volksüberlieferung, 1. Eesti Rahvaluule Arhiivi Toimetused/Commentationes Archivi Traditionum Polarium Estoniae, 3.* Tartu.

Lõhmus, M. (2007) Mortuary practices during the Comb Ware Cultures in Estonia and the problems of their interpretation. In A. Merkevičius (ed.), *Colours of Archaeology. Material Culture and Society. Papers from the Second Theoretical Seminar of the Baltic archaeologists (BASE) held at the University of Vilnius, Lithuania, October 21–22, 2005. Interarchaeologia* 2, 33–48. Vilnius, Helsinki, Riga, Tartu.

Lõugas, L. (1994) Subfossil vertebrate fauna of Asva site, Saaremaa. Mammals. In V. Lang (ed.), *Stilus, 5. Eesti Arheoloogiaseltsi Teated,* 71–93. Tallinn, Eesti Arheoloogiaselts.

Lõugas, L. (1997a) *Post-Glacial Development of Vertebrate Fauna in Estonian Water Bodies. A Palaeozoological Study.* Tartu, Tartu University Press, Dissertationes Biologicae Universitatis Tartuensis 32.

Lõugas, L. (1997b) Subfossil seal finds from archaeological coastal sites in Estonia, east part of the Baltic Sea. *Anthropozoologica* 25–26, 699–706.

Lõugas, L. (1998) Postglacial invasions of the Harp Seal (*Pagophilus groenlandicus* Erxl. 1777) into the Baltic Sea. *Proceedings of the Latvian Academy of Sciences, B. Natural, Exact and Applied Sciences* 52 (1–2), 63–69.

Lõugas, L. (2006) Animals as subsistence and bone as raw material for settlers of prehistoric Zvejnieki. In L. Larsson and I. Zagorska (eds), *Back to the Origin. New Research in the Mesolithic-Neolithic Zvejnieki Cemetery and Environment, Northern Latvia.* 52, 75–89. Lund, Acta Archaeologica Lundensia Series in 8°.

Lõugas, L., Kriiska, A. and Moora, H. (1996a) Coastal adaption and marine exploitation of the island Hiiumaa, Estonia, during the Stone Age with special emphasis on the Kõpu I site. In A.-M. Robertson, S. Hicks, A. Åkerlund, J. Risberg and T. Hackens (eds), *Landscape and Life. Studies in honour of Urve Miller. PACT* 50, 197–211. Rixensart.

Lõugas, L., Lidén, K. and Nelson, E. (1996b) Resource utilisation along the Estonian coast during the Stone Age. In T. Hackens, S. Hicks, V. Lang, U. Miller and L. Saarse (eds), *Coastal Estonia: recent advances in environmental and cultural history. PACT* 51, 399–420. Rixensart.

Lõugas, L. and Tomek, T. (2013) Marginal effect at the coastal area of Tallinn Bay: the marine, terrestrial and avian fauna as a source of subsistence during the Late Neolithic. In K. Johanson and M. Tõrv (eds), *Man, his Time, Artefacts and Places. Muinasaja teadus* 19, 463–485. Tartu, University of Tartu.

Luik, H. (2003) Luuesemed hauapanustena rauaaja Eestis. In V. Lang and Ü. Tamla (eds), *Arheoloogiaga Läänemeremaades. Uurimusi Jüri Seliranna auks. Muinasaja teadus* 13, 153–172. Tallinn, Tartu, Institute of History and University of Tartu.

Luik, H. (2005) *Luu- ja sarvesemed Eesti arheoloogilises leiumaterjalis viikingiajast keskajani / Bone and Antler Artefacts among Estonian Archaeological Finds from the Viking Age until the Middle Ages.* Tartu, Tartu University Press, Dissertationes archaeologiae Universitatis Tartuensis 1.

Luik, H. (2009) Skill, knowledge and memory. How to make a bone awl properly? In A. Šne and A. Vasks (eds), *Memory, Society and Material Culture. Papers from the Third Theorethical Seminar of the Baltic Archaeologists (BASE), Held at the University of Latvia, October 5–6. 2007. Interarchaeologia* 3, 45–58. Riga, Helsinki, Tartu, Vilnius.

Luik, H. (2010) Tracing the function of the antler "points" from the Late Bronze Age fortified settlement of Asva in Estonia. In A. Legrand-Pineau, I. Sidéra, N. Buc, E. David and V. Scheinsohn (eds), *Ancient and Modern Bone Artefacts from America to Russia. Cultural, technological and functional signature,* 255–261. Oxford, Archaeopress (British Archaeological Report S2136).

Luik, H. (2011) Material, technology and meaning: antler artefacts and antler working on the eastern shore of the Baltic in the Late Bronze Age. *Estonian Journal of Archaeology* 15 (1), 32–55.

Luik, H. (2013) Luu- ja sarvetöötlemisest Läänemere idakaldal nooremal pronksiajal: sarnasused ja erinevused Eesti, Läti ja Leedu leiuaineses. In K. Johanson and M. Tõrv (eds), *Man, his Time, Artefacts and Places. Muinasaja teadus* 19, 381–426. Tartu, University of Tartu.

Luik, H., Ots, M. and Maldre, L. (2011) From the Neolithic to the Bronze Age: continuity and changes in bone artefacts in Saaremaa, Estonia. In J. Baron and B. Kufel-Diakowska (eds), *Written in Bones. Studies on technological and social context of past faunal skeletal remains,* 243–261. Wrocław, Instytut Archeologii Uniwersytet Wrocławski.

Luts, A. (2008) Loodusvarud majandamises. In A. Viires and E. Vunder (eds), *Eesti Rahvakultuur. Teine, täiendatud trükk,* 107–135. Tallinn, Eesti Entsüklopeediakirjastus.

Maas, M. G. (2008) Histology of bones and teeth, In W. F. Perrin, B. Würsig and J. G. M. Thewissen (eds), *Encyclopedia of Marine Mammals,* 124–128. 2nd edition. London, Elsevier.

Maldre, L. (1999) Osteological evidence for the introduction of farming in Estonia. In U. Miller, T. Hackens, V. Lang, A. Raukas and S. Hicks (eds), *Environmental and Cultural History of the Eastern Baltic Region PACT* 57, 319–323. Rixensart.

Maldre, L. (2003) Asva koerte koproliitide arheozooloogiline analüüs. *Journal of Estonian Archaeology* 7 (2), 140–149.

Maldre, L. (2008) Karjakasvatusest Ridala pronksiaja asulas. In L. Jaanits, V. Lang and J. Peets (eds), *Loodus, inimene ja tehnoloogia, 2. Interdistsiplinaarseid uurimusi arheoloogias. Muinasaja teadus* 17, 263–276. Tallinn, Institute of History.

Maldre, L. and Luik, H. (2009) Horse in Estonia in the Late Bronze Age: archaeozoological and archaeological data. In A. Bliujienė (ed.), *The Horse and Man in European Antiquity (Worldview, Burial Rites, and Military and Everyday Life). Archaeologia Baltica* 11, 37–47. Klaipėda, Klaipėda University Press.

Mannermaa, K. (2008) *The Archaeology of Wings. Birds and People in the Baltic Sea Region during Stone Age. Academic dissertation.* Helsinki, University of Helsinki. https://helda.helsinki.fi/handle/10138/19459

Manninen, I. (1931) *Die Sachkultur Estlands, I. Sonderbehandlungen der Gelehrten Estnischen Gesellschaft, I.* Tartu, Õpetatud Eesti Selts.

Martinsson-Wallin, H. (2008) Land and sea animal remains from Middle Neolithic Pitted Ware sites on Gotland Island in the Baltic Sea, Sweden. In G. Clark, F. Leach and S. O'Connor (eds), *Islands of Inquiry. Colonisation, seafaring and the archaeology of maritime landscapes. Terra Australis* 29, 171–183. Australian National University Press.

McGhee, R. (1977) Ivory for the Sea Woman: The symbolic attributes of a prehistoric technology. *Canadian Journal of Archaeology* 1, 141–149.

Meinander, C. F. (1954) *Die Bronzezeit in Finnland. Suomen Muinasmuistoyhdistyksen Aikakauskirja* 54. Helsinki, Suomen muinaismuistoyhdistys.

Ots, M. (2010) Loomakujukesed Valma keskneoliitilises kaksikmatuses. In Ü. Tamla (ed.), *Ilusad Asjad: tähelepanuväärseid leide Eesti arheoloogiakogudest. Muinasaja teadus* 21, 11–22. Tallinn, Institute of History.

Paavel, K. (2012) *Kasutuskulumise Uurimine: metoodika ja selle rakendamine pronksiaegsete sarvteravike näitel.* Unpublished BA thesis. University of Tartu, Tartu.

Paaver, K. (1965) *Formirovanie Teriofauny i Izmenchivost' Mlekopitaiushchikh Pribaltiki v Golotsene.* Tartu, Akademia Nauk Estonskoi SSR, Institut zoologii i botaniki.

Puhvel, M. (1963) The seal in the folklore of Northern Europe. *Folklore* 74 (1), 326–333.

Rimantienė, R. (1996a) Šventosios 4-oji radimvietė. *Lietuvos Archeologija* 14, 5–79.

Rimantienė, R. (1996b) Šventosios 6-oji gyvenvietė. *Lietuvos Archeologija* 14, 83–173.

Russell, N. (2001) The social life of bone: A preliminary assessment of bone tool manufacture and discard at Çatalhöyük. In A. M. Choyke and L. Bartosiewicz (eds), *Crafting Bone: skeletal technologies through time and space. Proceedings of the 2nd Meeting of the (ICAZ) Worked Bone Research Group, Budapest, 31 August–5 September 1999*, 241–248. Oxford, Archaeopress (British Archaeological Report S937).

Stančikaitė, M., Daugnora, L., Hjelle, K. and Hufthammer, A. K. (2009) The environment of the Neolithic archaeological sites in Šventoji, Western Lithuania. *Quaternary International* 207, 117–129.

Storå, J. (2000) Sealing and animal husbandry in the Ålandic Middle and Late Neolithic. *Fennoscandia archaeologica* XVI (I), 57–81.

Storå, J. (2001) *Reading Bones. Stone Age Hunters and Seals in the Baltic.* Stockholm, Stockholm University, Stockholm Studies in Archaeology 21.

Storå, J. (2002) Neolithic Seal Exploitation on the Åland Islands in the Baltic Sea on the Basis of Epiphyseal Fusion Data and Metric Studies. *International Journal of Osteoarchaeology* 12, 49–64.

Storå, J. and Lõugas, L. (2005) Human exploitation and history of seals in the Baltic during the Late Holocene. In G. G. Monks (ed.), *The Exploitation and Cultural Importance of Sea Mammals. Proceedings of the 9th ICAZ Conference, Durham 2002*, 95–106. Oxford, Oxbow Books.

Ukkonen, P. (2002) The early history of seals in the northern Baltic. *Annales Zoologici Fennici* 39, 187–207.

Vassar, A. (1955) Ukreplennoe poselenie Asva na ostrove Saaremaa. In H. Moora and L. Jaanits (eds), *Muistsed asulad ja linnused. Arheoloogiline kogumik* 1, 113–137. Tallinn, Eesti Riiklik Kirjastus.

Viires, A., Troska, G., Karu, E., Vahtre, L. and Tõnurist, I. (2000) *Eesti rahvakultuuri leksikon. 2., täiendatud ja parandatud trükk.* Tallinn, Eesti Entsüklopeediakirjastus.

Volkaitė-Kulikauskienė, R. (1986) Narkunų didžiojo piliakalnio tyrinėjimų rezultatai (Apatinis kultūrinis šluoksnis). *Lietuvos Archeologija* 5, 5–49.

Wall, W. P. (1983) The correlation between high limb-bone density and aquatic habits in Recent mammals. *Journal of Paleontology* 57 (2), 197–207.

Westerdahl, C. (2005) Seal on land, elk at sea: notes on and applications of the ritual landscape at the seaboard. *International Journal of Nautical Archaeology* 34 (1), 2–23.

Zagorska, I. (2000) Seal mammal hunting strategy in the Eastern Baltic. *Lietuvos Archeologija* 19, 275–285.

Zagorska, I. and Lõugas, L. (2000) The tooth pendant head-dresses of Zvejnieki cemetery. In V. Lang and A. Kriiska (eds), *De temporibus antiquissimus ad honorem Lembit Jaanits. Muinasaja teadus* 8, 223–244. Tallinn, Institute of History.

CHAPTER 9

Specialization or Re-utilization? Study of the Selection Documented in a Bone-Working Refuse Assemblage from Roman *Baetulo* (Badalona, Spain)

Lídia Colominas

An assemblage of faunal remains and worked osseous materials was recovered from a closed abandonment level from the Roman city of *Baetulo* (Badalona, Spain). The study of these materials has allowed us to characterize this assemblage as remains of raw and discarded bone material mainly comprising cattle metapodials. Metapodials have good physical characteristics for producing bone objects and tools. However, this anatomical element is actually discarded during primary butchery practices so that secondary utilization may also explain its use. The comparison of this assemblage with another assemblage recovered from the same abandonment level and composed of faunal remains interpreted as culinary and butchery refuse will allow us to evaluate which criteria determined the composition of this homogeneous assemblage and what economic purpose this composition reflects.

Keywords
Bone tools; cattle metapodials; Roman towns; *Hispania Tarraconensis*.

Introduction

Bone continued to be an important material for making objects during Roman times. Such implements could be used for personal grooming, gaming, furniture ornamentation or textile activities. Although Roman bone objects have been comprehensively studied and typologies have even been established, the raw material from which these goods were produced, how this raw material was obtained and fundamentally how the selection process was integrated into the economy of the towns, are questions that have rarely been investigated.

Different studies that have been carried out propose that bone-working was an activity that would have been integrated into the framework of urban crafts. It would have been characterized as a small scale activity with workshops in each city where the raw material and the clientele would have been found (Beal 1983; MacGregor 1985; Bertrand 2008; Choyke 2012a). On the other hand, it has also been shown that this production was integrated in the general trade routes within cities or countries, with the import and export of worked bone objects (Deschler-Erb 1997, 98).

Taking these considerations into account, the objective pursued by this study is aimed at understanding the degree of specialization of the manufacture of bone objects and whether or not this activity complements other craft activities in the Roman city of *Baetulo*. The composition of an assemblage of faunal remains consisting of raw and discarded bone materials as well as broken and half-finished bone objects will be compared with an assemblage of faunal remains consisting of butchery processing residues and culinary refuse. These two assemblages were recovered in the same layer of levelled ground formed during the first half of the 2nd century AD. The differences in the frequency of representation between these two assemblages at taxonomical, anatomical, as well as age and sex should permit us to determine whether the manufacture of bone objects in this city implied a selection of the most suitable bones for this production or whether those parts of animals that were not used for other purposes were reutilised.

The Roman city of *Baetulo*

The Roman city of *Baetulo,* in the north-east of the Iberian Peninsula, was situated on the coast of *Hispania Tarraconensis* (Fig. 9.1). It was constructed in the early decades of the 1st century BC. From the second half of that century the production and commercialization of wine led to the integration of *Baetulo* into Mediterranean trade routes, thus, transforming it into an important port of entry and promoting the great economic development that took place there in the last quarter of the 1st century BC (Comas *et al.* 1994). The city continued to be inhabited until the end of the 4th century AD.

Based on the archaeological excavations carried out every year since the 1970s, the topography of the city is currently known with considerable accuracy. The urban plan has an orthogonal layout, oriented from south-east to north-west with a system of terraces to stabilize the slopes of land on which the city was established. As a result of these differences in height, the city was divided into two different zones. Residences have been documented in the upper part of the city whilst in the lower part there were both public and commercial buildings. This latter area is where the buildings linked to craft activities would have been situated (Fig. 9.1).

This urban structure began to undergo a series of changes from the 2nd century AD onwards. Canalizations falling into disuse and amortizations of a number of houses in the upper part of the city have been documented as a result of a transformation and redistribution of different parts of the city and its territory (Comas *et al.* 1994). The assemblages that are presented in this article were localized in a thick layer of levelled ground formed during the first half of the 2nd century AD as a result of these transformations.

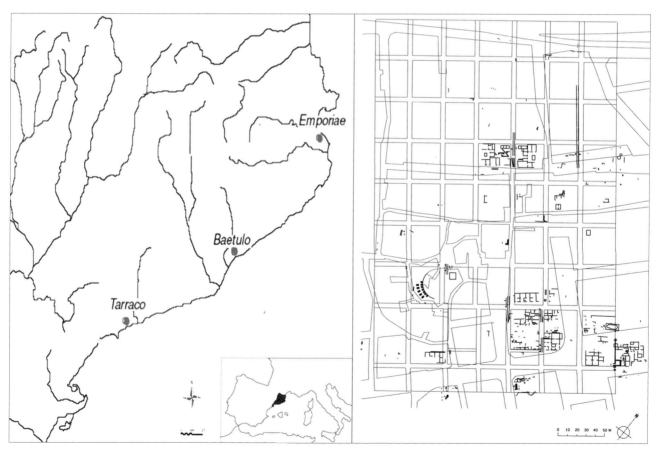

Figure 9.1 Location and plan of the Roman city of Baetulo *(Museu de Badalona).*

Results

The bone-working refuse assemblage

The bone-working refuse assemblage comprises 50 faunal remains and 35 fragments of objects made from bone. The bone objects range from pins, spatulas, punches, hinges, small spoons, tokens and sewing needles to pendants. Most of these objects are finished, some are also half-finished and others are broken (Fig. 9.2). The faunal assemblage consists of 32 cattle remains, 16 of pig, 1 of sheep and 1 of horse.

The 32 cattle bones principally correspond to the distal part of the limbs and to the trunk (Fig. 9.3) and include 12 rib fragments, 8 whole metacarpals, 1 sawn metacarpal, 4 whole metatarsals and 5 more sawn metatarsals. One fragment of a cattle mandible as well as a humerus diaphysis have also been documented.

The 16 domestic pig remains come from the head and from the proximal part of the fore-limbs (Fig. 9.3). The remains of the head include 5 left canines (2 superior and 3 inferior), 1 maxillary fragment, 1 occipital fragment and 2 mandible fragments. The remains of the proximal part of the fore-limbs comprise 5 scapula fragments and 2 fragments of humerus diaphyses. In addition to the cattle and pig remains, 1 sawn tibia from a sheep and 1 horse metacarpal have been documented (Fig. 9.3).

The information obtained from the fusion stage of the bones (according to Barone 1976) shows that all the bones in this assemblage were fully formed. All the metapodials, both of cattle and horse, display fused epiphyses that can be ascribed to individuals with ages above two years old. The five pig scapular fragments are also fully formed, corresponding to individuals of more than 12 months. The wear reported on the five permanent canines corroborates this age attribution.

The data obtained from what can be ascertained about the sexual composition of the different taxa population are not so homogeneous. Comparison of the greatest length (GL) and maximum width of the distal epiphysis (Bd) measurements of the eight cattle metacarpals with current measurements taken from three cows and one oxen from the Camargue and three bulls from Madrid (Tekkouk and Guintard 2007), those being the geographically closest available measurements where the sex is known with certainty, show that although some males and even one castrated individual are present, these metapodials principally belong to females (Fig. 9.4). In contrast, the five pig canines, the element that has been used to determine the sex of pig remains given its morphological characteristics, come from males.

The predominance or almost exclusive presence of cattle metapodials in this bone-working refuse assemblage may have been due to the physical characteristics of this element, which because of its density, straightness and its potentially usable length is particularly suitable for manufacturing objects. The metapodials have a large regular area with a dense bone cortex that enables the extraction of thin rods to fashion pins and sewing needles, punches, spatulas or cylindrical parts for the manufacture of hinges for chests, cupboards or dice. Other fragments may have been used for producing counters. This particular species-skeletal element representation may thus have been the result of a selection of those elements with physical properties conducive for such production.

However, the use of this skeletal element may also be related to the fact that it is a part that is separated in the initial phase of animal processing, as it is an element with a very low content of meat and is often separated with the skin when the slaughtered animal is flayed. This element is not as susceptible to fracture during the processing as other

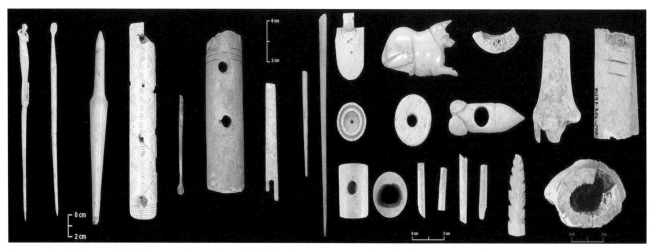

Figure 9.2 A selection of the bone artefacts and modified faunal remains recovered in the bone-working refuse assemblage (Museu de Badalona) (photograph: Lídia Colominas).

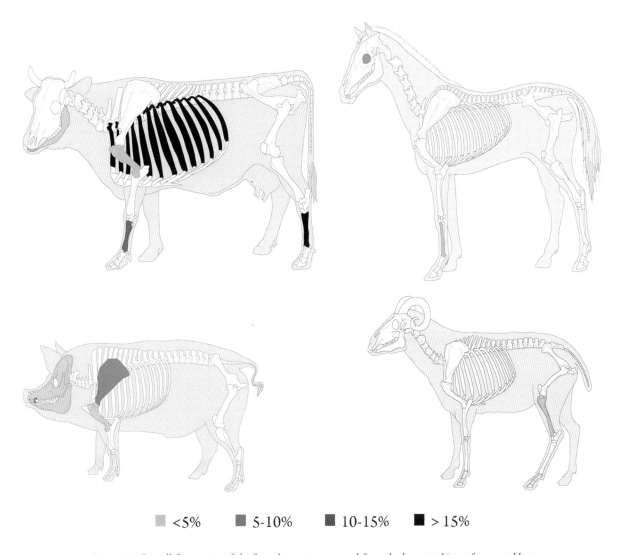

Figure 9.3 Overall frequencies of the faunal remains recovered from the bone-working refuse assemblage.

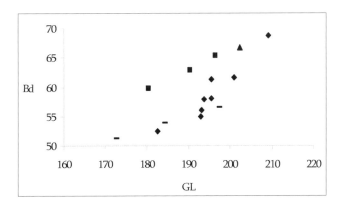

Figure 9.4 Scatter diagram of GL and Bd measurements of cattle metacarpals recovered in the bone-working refuse assemblage (rhombus) and GL and Bd measurements of cows (lines), oxen (triangles) and bulls (squares) (after Tekkouk and Guintard (2007)).

long bones, such as the tibia or the radius, that also exhibit a regular surface and thick cortical bone suitable for fashioning artefacts, but carry large amounts of meat. In this sense, the metapodials may also have been the skeletal elements that were most used for object production in *Baetulo* because they would have been separated from the animal before the intensive, secondary butchering as they would have been of little value as food.

On the other hand, there is an exclusive presence of fused elements. This may indicate a positive selection for those anatomical parts that are fully formed. Fused bones from adult animals have reached their maximum possible length and are denser than unfused bones from juvenile individuals and thus more suitable for manufacturing production (MacGregor 1985). An exclusive presence of male pigs has also been documented in this assemblage. This composition may be due to the fact that bones of male individuals are generally more robust than bones of female individuals (MacGregor 1985). This preference for males does not hold true for cattle remains, as female, male and even castrated individuals have been documented.

So which criteria determined the composition of this assemblage? The selection of good raw material for producing bone objects or the use of those available elements from the available animals? Comparison of this sample with a domestic refuse assemblage recovered in the same abandonment level will allow us to elucidate this question.

The domestic refuse assemblage

The assemblage of processing and culinary refuse comprises 572 faunal remains. Cattle (NISP= 270) and pig (NISP= 212) are by far the most common species in the assemblage, followed by sheep and goat (NISP= 85) and rabbit (NISP= 5).

Taking into account that the material displays a high degree of fragmentation, the Minimum Number of Elements (MNE) was also calculated for each taxa. The MNE was calculated on the basis of the lateral part of the skeletal element that has the highest frequency of representation. This quantification unit displays a slight change in the frequency of taxonomic representation, where the most commonly represented animal becomes pig (MNE= 83), followed by cattle (MNE= 73), sheep and goat (MNE= 35) and rabbit (MNE= 5).

The body part representation displays a very high variability of skeletal elements (Fig. 9.5). Almost all parts of the skeleton of all domestic taxa have been documented including elements from the head and trunk, as well as the extremities. Despite this variability, there is a predominance of those elements belonging to the proximal part of the limbs, and in particular the scapula, which together with the femur, show the highest frequency of representation for both cattle and pigs. The presence of metapodials is low for all taxa.

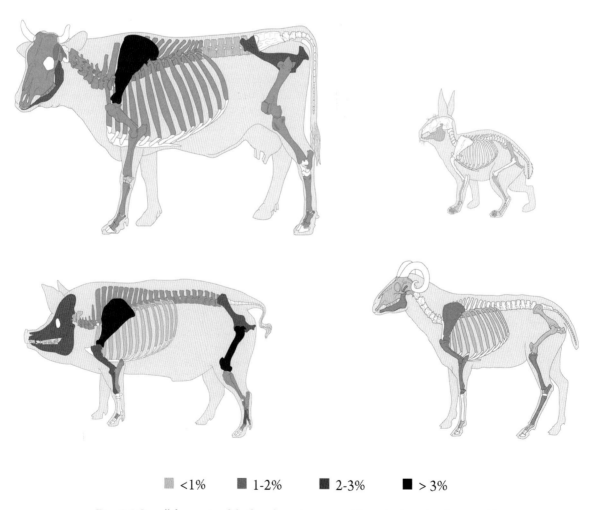

■ <1%   ■ 1-2%   ■ 2-3%   ■ > 3%

Figre 9.5 Overall frequencies of the faunal remains recovered from the domestic refuse assemblage.

The information about the fusion state of the bones displays some very different results between taxa. The results obtained for pig remains show a predominance of those anatomical parts that fuse before 30 months old. The presence of bones that fuse after this age tends towards zero (Fig. 9.6). Therefore, these animals were basically slaughtered before the age of 30 months. The ageing evidence for sheep and goat remains displays similar results. Anatomical elements that fuse before 36 months predominate and the presence of bones that fuse after this age tends towards zero (Fig. 9.6). Therefore, these animals were basically slaughtered before 36 months of age. This pattern is not documented for cattle remains. Despite the fact that unfused bones start to be documented from 30 months, bones that fuse after 48 months are also observed (Fig. 9.6). This representation shows that cattle were slaughtered at many different ages.

The data available about the sexual composition of the different taxa population are very scarce. It has been only possible to ascertain the sex distribution of pigs due to the presence of the sexually diagnostic canines, showing the presence of 2 females and 6 males. It has not been possible to determine the sex of either cattle or caprines no skeletal elements diagnostic of the animals sex were documented nor was there sufficient data to permit an osteometric approximation (Colominas 2009).

The archaeozoological analysis of the domestic refuse assemblage indicates that the main meat consumed in the city of *Baetulo* during the second half of the 2nd century AD came from pigs and cattle. In addition, there is evidence that the meat from sheep, goats and rabbits was eaten, but much more sporadically. The kill-off patterns of pigs, sheep and goats show that these animals were slaughtered at the economically most opportune time to exploit their meat. In contrast, the cattle age distribution shows that these animals were not only exploited for their meat but also and, perhaps primarily, for traction.

Discussion

The archaeozoological analysis of the faunal remains recovered in the bone-working refuse assemblage has allowed us to document the particular composition of the material with regard to the species, the anatomical parts, and the age of the faunal remains that composed this assemblage. It is likely that the choice of species and skeletal element may be connected to the physical properties of each bone. The bones were selected to obtain suitable supports for fashioning objects and tools. However, at the same time, this composition may have been dependent on what meat was being consumed in the city. The butcher discarded or gave away those parts of the animals that he did not use, but, in contrast, could be useful or indispensable to the producers of bone objects, such as the distal part of the limbs. These parts with low meat content were normally taken away with the hides of the slaughtered animals during the first phase of animal processing.

In that sense, the comparison of the frequency of representation of the bone-working refuse assemblage with the representation documented in the domestic refuse assemblage recovered in the same archaeological level shows that the taxonomic, anatomic and age representation documented in the bone-working refuse assemblage is the result of deliberate selection. This selection, however, is contingent on the availability of animal bones in the town.

Although pig bones were equally as abundant as cattle bones in the refuse assemblages from the city, a selection in favour of cattle has been recorded in the worked bone assemblage. In addition, this selection of cattle bone over pig bone was influenced by the age at which these animals were slaughtered, since the availability of adult pig bones from the butchery waste was limited whilst the availability of fully formed cattle bones was much greater.

This selection from the available raw material can also be deduced from the frequency of representation of horse remains. They are not present at all in the processing and culinary refuse

Pig	Sc.	H.d	R.p	Pel.	Ph.II	T.d	Mt.d	Ph.I	Calc.	U.p	F.p	H.p	R.d	F.d	T.p
nº elements fused	18	4	5	6	0	1	5	1	0	0	0	0	0	0	0
nº elements unfused	1	0	0	0	0	0	3	1	0	2	1	0	1	3	1
Cattle	Sc.	Pel.	R.p	Ph.II	H.d	Ph.I	T.d	Mt.d	Calc.	F.p	H.p	R.d	U.p	F.d	T.p
nº elements fused	18	12	1	3	1	6	3	9	0	0	1	0	0	1	0
nº elements unfused	0	0	0	0	0	0	0	1	2	1	0	2	0	0	2
Sheep/Goat	H.d	R.p	Sc.	Pel.	Ph.II	Ph.I	T.d	Mt.d	Calc.	F.p	H.p	R.d	U.p	F.d	T.p
nº elements fused	0	0	2	0	0	0	1	4	1	0	0	0	0	0	0
nº elements unfused	1	0	0	0	0	0	0	0	2	0	1	2	0	0	1

Figure 9.6 Number of fused bones and non-fused bones in order of age of fusion for pigs, cattle and sheep/goats in the domestic refuse assemblage (Sc: Scapula, H: Humerus, R: Radius, Pel: Pelvis, Ph: Phalanx, T: Tibia, Mt: Metapodial, Calc: Calcaneus, U: Ulna, F: Femur, d: distal, p: proximal).

assemblage and only one metacarpal has been documented in the bone-working refuse assemblage. The fact that it was not usual to consume the meat of horses in this city would explain the low utilization of bones from this animal to make objects. It should be pointed out, however, that this pattern is not documented in other cities where equid meat was not consumed but equid bones appear in bone-working refuse assemblages (Choyke 2012a), suggesting that this source of bone-working material was valued when available.

The heterogeneous, but principally female, representation of sex in the cattle remains of the worked bone assemblage may also be the result of having to choose from the material that was available. The worked pig remains, however, show a selection for male pig bones. It is possible to extract bone plaques to make small boxes, dice and tokens from the mandible of either sex (Arbogast 2006) but the male pigs have the added advantage that their large canines can be used to produce pendants, earrings and small decorative objects (Gostencnik 2001).

Taking into account the data presented up to now, we consider the production of bone objects in the city of *Baetulo* to be an activity that would have been linked to the consumption of meat in the city, as this is where the workshops would obtain the raw material.

Despite this link, we consider that it would have been an activity practiced by specialists. This specialization is documented in the supply of the raw material, in the production steps that were followed and in the sophisticated, serial nature of the final products.

The choice of particular raw material from all the bone material available was documented, with cattle metapodials being the principal skeletal element. Skeletal elements from adult and mature individuals were also preferred even if the most abundant bones generally available were those that were not fused. These selections indicate that the mechanical properties of each skeletal element were known.

The studies carried out on bone objects recovered in various cities of the Roman Empire have revealed the entire sequence of events that was involved in the production of these objects. This *chain d'operatoire* began with the preparation of the raw material and proceeded through sawing, cutting, smoothing, polishing, turning, drilling, scribing, rouletting, gauging, clamping, riveting, softening and moulding and even colouring (MacGregor1985; Beal 1983; Rascón *et al.* 1995; Deschler-Erb 1998; Choyke 2012a). Thus, a complex series of working steps within a particular processing sequence was followed in order to obtain the desired objects. The fact that finished objects and half-finished items, some having been broken during the manufacturing process, have been documented in the bone-working refuse assemblage indicates that the entire process, from the preparation of the raw material to the final finishing of the product, was possibly carried out at *Baetulo* in the same place or, at least, the different refuse materials of this working chain were discarded together.

These final products are mainly luxury or semi-luxury articles, such as hinges, intended for the decoration of furniture, for personal adornment such as hairpins or pendants, or were objects associated with games such as dice and tokens. Therefore, the production of the workshop was not geared towards primary domestic needs which could be made at home despite the presence of certain objects such as sewing needles or spatulas. This variety of objects may also demonstrate that the workshop where all these products were made was not specialized in one type of product, differing from other workshops documented in other cities of the Roman Empire (Bertrand 2008).

We consider that the fact that the bone-working refuse assemblage was documented as an individual discard, separate from the domestic refuse assemblage, underpins the idea that this work, despite its relationship with the work carried out by butchers, would have been a differentiated economic craft performed in places dedicated to this activity.

Conclusions

Bone-working can be recognized by the refuse it leaves behind, as it usually consists of the epiphyses of sawn metapodials and other long bones and antlers (MacGregor 1985; Beal 1994; Deschler-Erb 1997; Bertrand 2008; Choyke 2012b). Needles, spatulas, dice, tokens and hinges could all be made from these elements. There are also fragments of flat bones such as scapulae, ribs and mandibles from which plaques could be produced. The most common skeletal elements are cattle metapodials, although horse metapodials, caprine tibias and ulna, fibula and tusks of pigs were also used.

The refuse is usually accompanied by finished and half-finished artefacts (MacGregor 1985; Beal 1994; Deschler-Erb 1997; Bertrand 2008; Choyke 2012b). Such a composition has been documented in the bone-working refuse assemblage presented here along with broken objects and raw material supports and discarded bone waste. Therefore, the presence of a workshop dedicated to the manufacture of bone objects has been documented in the roman city of *Baetulo*. Other possible workshops for the production of bone objects in *Hispania* are those located in the city of *Complutum* (Pedreira *et al.* 1995/96), in Herrera de Pisuerga (Perez 1995), at the church of Santa Maria de Beja (Rascón *et al.* 1995) or in *Asturica Augusta* and *Lucus Augusti* (Fernández 2003).

Comparison of the bone-working refuse assemblage with the representation documented in the butchery and culinary refuse assemblage shows that bone object production in *Baetulo* would have been an economic activity that was linked to the consumption of meat carried out in the city. However, a selection in the supply of this raw material has been observed that, together with the complexity of the working processes, the stages of production and the fact that the objects formed were not for everyday use, allows us to propose that in this city bone working was a specialized activity complemented or linked with other economic activities, such as the work carried out in the butcheries.

More archaeozoological studies and more data are needed to address the complex question of the importance of bone object production within the general economic system of Roman cities. Interdisciplinary approaches to correlate the information derived from different archaeological disciplines may be the most interesting way to achieve this goal.

Bibliography

Arbogast, R.-M. (2006) L'utilisation des matières premières et de l'energie animales. In M.-P. Horard-Herbin, J.-D. Vigne (eds), *Animaux, environnements et sociétés*, 93–129. Paris, Éditions Errance.

Barone, R. (1976) *Anatomie Comparée des Mammifères Domestiques. Tome I Ostéologie*. Paris, Vigot Frères Éditeurs.

Beal, J.-C. (1983) Les ateliers gallo-romains de tabletterie à Lyon et à Vienne. *Latomus* 42, 607–618.

Beal, J.-C. (1994) Tabletterie and tabletiers d'os en Gaule romaine. In M. J. Roulière-Lambert, L. Bailly and A. S. de Cohën (eds), *Aurochs, le Retour: aurochs, vaches et autres bovins de la préhistoire à nos jours*, 120–130. Lons-le-Saunier (France), Centre Jurassien du Patrimoine.

Bertrand, I. (2008) Le travail de l'os et du bois de cerf à l'époque romaine: bilan et perspectives de la recherche sur un artisanat "mineur". In I. Bertrand (ed.) *Le Travail de l'os, du Bois de Cerf et de la Corne à l'époque Romaine: un artisanat en marge?* 3–13. Monographies Instrumentum 34. Montagnac, Monique Mergoil et Association des Publications Chauvinoises.

Choyke, A. M. (2012a) The bone workshop in the church of San Lorenzo in Lucina. In O. Brandt (ed.), *San Lorenzo in Lucina. The transformations of a Roman quarter*, 335–346. Stockholm, Swedish Institute in Rome (Acta Instituti Romani Regni Sueciae 4 (61)).

Choyke, A. M. (2012b) Skeletal elements from animals as raw materials. In M. Biró, A. M. Choyke, L. Vass and Á. Vecsey (eds), *Bone Objects in Aquincum*, 43–53. Budapest, History Museum, Budapest (Az Aquincum Múzeum Gyűjteménye 2/Collections of the Aquincum Museum 2).

Colominas, L. (2009) *La Gestió dels Animals al Nord-est de la Península Ibérica entre els Segles V ane-V dne. Proposta metodològica d'integració de les anàlisis arqueozoològiques als estudis de cronologies històriques.* PhD Dissertation. Universitat Autònoma de Barcelona, Bellaterra.

Comas, M., Llobet, C., Padrós, P., Puerta, C. and Rodríguez, M. (1994) Un espai d'ús públic a l'àrea central de Baetulo (Hispania Tarraconensis). Evolució històrica i transformacions urbanístiques. In X. D. i Raventós (ed.) *La Ciudad en el Mundo Romano, XIV Congreso Internacional de Arqueología Clásica (14. 1993. Tarragona)* 2, 110–112. Madrid, Consejo Superior de Investigaciones Científicas.

Deschler-Erb, S. (1997) Bone antler, tooth and ivory: raw materials from Roman artifacts. *Anthropozoologica* 25–26, 73–77.

Deschler-Erb, S. (1998) *Römische Beinartefakte aus Augusta Raurica. Rohmaterial, Technologie, Typologie und Chronologie.* Augst, Römermuseum (Forschungen in Augst 27/1).

Fernández, C. (2003) Ganadería, caza y animales de compañía en la Galicia Romana: estudio arqueozoológico. *Brigantium* 15, 1–238. Museo Arqueolóxico e Histórico. Castelo de San Antón. A Coruña.

Gostencnik, K (2001) Pre- and Early Roman bone and antler manufacturing in Kärnten, Austria. In A. Choyke, L. Bartosiewicz (eds) *Crafting Bone: skeletal technologies through time and space* – Proceedings of the 2nd meeting of the (ICAZ) Worked Bone Research Group Budapest, 31 August–5 September 1999, 383–397. Oxford, Archaeopress (British Archaeological Report S937).

MacGregor, A. (1985) *Bone, Antler, Ivory and Horn. The technology of skeletal materials since the Roman period.* Barnes and Noble Books, New Jersey.

Pedreira, G., Polo, J., Román, P. and Rascón, S. (1995–1996) Un nuevo conjunto de útiles realizados en hueso procedentes de la ciudad hispanorromana de Complutum: las "acus" o "ajugas de coser". *Estudios de Prehistória y Arqueología Madrileños* 10, 101–110.

Perez, C. (1995) *Herrera de Pisuerga. Un taller de útiles óseos de la legión IV Macedónica.* Universidad S.E.K. Santiago de Chile.

Rascón, S., Polo, J., Pedreira, G. and Román, P. (1995) Contribución al conocimiento de algunas producciones en hueso de la ciudad hispanorromana de *Complutum*: el caso de las *acus crinales. Espacio, Tiempo y Forma*, Serie I. Prehistoria y Arqueología 8, 295–340.

Tekkouk, F. and Guintard, G. (2007) Approche osteometrique de la variabilité des métacarpes de bovins et recherche de modèles applicables pour l'archéozoologie: cas de races rustiques françaises, algériennes et espagnoles. *Revue de Médicine Vétérinaire* 158 (7), 388–396.

Social Aspects of Raw Material Selection

CHAPTER 10

The Materiality of Production: Exploring Variability and Choice in the Production of Palaeolithic Portable Art made in Antler and Bone

Rebecca Farbstein

This paper focuses on the technical and material attributes of an assemblage of late Magdalenian portable art from two sites in south-central France, Montastruc and Courbet. A methodology called *chaîne opératoire*, which has traditionally been used to study so-called "functional", rather than symbolic material culture, is employed to study the materials Palaeolithic artists chose and the ways that they modified them. Using this methodology facilitates new analysis of antiquarian assemblages that pose analytical challenges because of the lack of contextual information that survives about the portable art. This analysis reveals how craftspeople attributed value and socio-aesthetic meaning to these materials through their modification of animal bones into both figurative and non-figurative art, and contributes to a better understanding of the similarities and differences between the artistic and technical traditions at these two roughly contemporaneous and adjacent sites.

Keywords
Palaeolithic; Magdalenian; portable art; organic materials; *chaîne opératoire*.

Introduction

Much Palaeolithic portable art was discovered in the 19th Century, when excavation methodologies were less refined than they are today. Because many archaeological sites were excavated without regard to stratigraphy, it can be difficult to build detailed chrono-stratigraphic contexts for the artefacts found in the 1800s. Despite these challenges, Palaeolithic portable art offers clear evidence that Pleistocene hunter-gatherers were technical and creative innovators. They produced both figurative and non-figurative art in a range of animal raw materials, including antler, bone and ivory. This paper focuses on these technical and material attributes of an assemblage of late Magdalenian portable art from two sites in south-central France, Montastruc and Courbet. While the limited contextual information that was recorded during initial excavations at these sites remains a challenge when studying these assemblages, a new approach to this art will be advanced in this paper. It focuses on the materials Palaeolithic artists chose, and the ways craftspeople attributed value and socio-aesthetic meaning to these materials through their modification of animal bones into both figurative and non-figurative art. This approach may reveal new insight into these challenging assemblages of late Palaeolithic art, with the potential to better distinguish between the artistic and technical traditions at these two roughly contemporaneous and adjacent sites.

Aims and scope of the paper

To date, "technical" research on late Palaeolithic art has focused extensively on the "hardware" of production (Brühl 2005; de Beaune 1999; Klíma 1997); that is, techniques have been studied *sensu stricto* and without explicit or comprehensive consideration of their social and aesthetic contexts and consequences. Some archaeologists have also implemented microscopic analysis of artefacts to recover the techniques and tools associated with the production of portable art (d'Errico 1992; Fritz 1999; White 1997). This paper advances the study of Palaeolithic organic technologies in two significant ways. Like the aforementioned approaches, this research applies a technical methodology that supplements the conventional, stylistic approaches to Upper Palaeolithic art that focus on its appearance and subject matter. However, this paper also explicitly situates these technologies within their social contexts by using a socialised *chaîne opératoire* methodology (after Leroi-Gourhan (1964), later reconsidered by Dobres (2000, 2010) and Farbstein (2010, 2011). Drawing upon the theoretical foundations of "object biographies" and "life histories" (Gosden and Marshall 1999), this paper aims to consider Palaeolithic technological choices, including raw material selection and material modification, as meaningful social practices (see Choyke (2010) for another view on how animal materials can gain social and symbolic meaning). By socialising prehistoric technology, following Dobres (2000), new insight into the complex socio-technical decisions enacted by Palaeolithic craftspeople working in different social contexts can be gained.

This paper focuses on two major considerations related to the modification of animal bone to make art. The first analysis compares bone selection strategies and overall modification choices at Montastruc and Courbet, offering insight into social variability and diversity between sites purported to be culturally contiguous. The second analysis, which focuses on a small sub-assemblage of unusual bone and antler art, offers insight into the complex social and material life history of bone and antler and the objects made in these materials.

Beyond aesthetics and iconography

This research moves beyond the persistent interest in the superficial qualities of Palaeolithic art including iconography or apparent "style" as discussed by Farbstein (2010). Although research into the appearance and style of Palaeolithic art has been fruitful (Bosinski 1991; Cohen 2003; Gvozdover 1989; Svoboda 1997), it often explicitly or implicitly isolates symbolic material culture from the overall archaeological assemblage and leads to artificial divisions between artefacts that may have been made and used alongside each other. These divisions are particularly problematic when studying assemblages such as the late Magdalenian ones that are the focus of this paper,

because much of the "art" was made on weaponry such as spear-throwers or harpoons; the "functional," "artistic" and "symbolic" significance of these objects were likely intertwined and may not be distinguishable. For the purposes of this paper, "art" was identified when a representational (human or animal) or decorative (geometric or patterned) motif or image was identified on an object. In some instances, these images were made on objects that may also have held a purpose as a weapon or other tool. In other cases, the artefact may have no discernable "function." Re-conceptualizing artists as skilled technicians, and acknowledging that the individuals who made Palaeolithic art probably also contributed to the production of non-symbolic artefacts, is one productive step towards bridging the artificial divide between "symbolic" and "functional" material culture that often exists in Palaeolithic scholarship.

Material culture, including art, gains meaning in myriad possible ways, many of which may not be immediately apparent. Art is "constitutive of or expressive of the identity of a group" (Myers 2005, 91), and this social identity may not be expressed exclusively in appearance. Both the anthropology of technology (Lechtman 1977; Lemonnier 1993; Schiffer 2001) and materiality theory (Miller 2005) assert that the *production* of artefacts, including art, is socially meaningful. Individuals and societies may attribute meaning to things by making objects in certain ways and by selecting certain materials. Similarly, Latour (1991) and Gell (1999) highlight the social significance of material objects, including their physicality and how they are embedded in daily routines. The "object biography" approach also acknowledges how material culture gains meaning, and how its meaning is transformed throughout its "life history" (Gosden and Marshall 1999) from material acquisition to production, use and, ultimately, discard. This research aims to integrate these important theoretical concepts with quantitatively rigorous *chaîne opératoire* methodology, following Leroi-Gourhan (1964), to build a comprehensive technological, and material, approach for studying Palaeolithic art. Importantly, this process demands that scholars move beyond analysis of isolated, individually striking artefacts to instead study comprehensive assemblages of Palaeolithic art.

Chaîne Opératoire in Action

The physical *chaîne opératoire* is initiated when a material is acquired and/or transported from its find spot to the location of its modification (Fig. 10.1). This initial stage of the *chaîne opératoire* immediately implicates one or more human agents into the life history of a material. Although an individual or a group may plan the acquisition and/or transportation of a material far in advance, the tangible remnants of most *chaînes opératoires* are perceptible in the physical and material qualities of an artefact. Thus, materials and choices associated

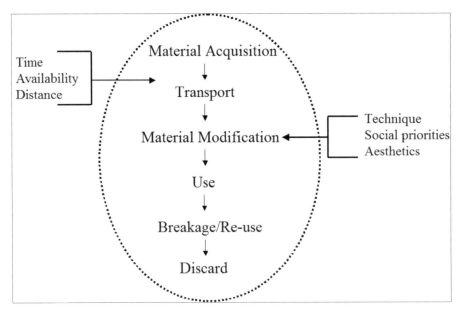

Figure 10.1 Schematic chaîne opératoire, *highlighting the way social considerations influence the physical and material choices made by artisans at work.*

with their acquisition and modification are of fundamental importance within this methodology. These initial steps in the *chaîne opératoire* are also an important part of an object's life history or biography, and these stages of production are one focus of this paper.

Chaîne opératoire has most frequently been used to study lithic assemblages and other "functional" material culture, e.g. by Pigeot (1990) and Sellet (1993). However, some archaeologists have adapted this methodology to study symbolic Palaeolithic material culture. Marcia-Anne Dobres (2000, 2010), in particular, has worked to expand archaeological conceptions of technology and develop the potential of *chaîne opératoire* methodology. Dobres' work highlights the link between tangible, visible technological *variances* and the social *choices* that underlie the actions that give rise to the production of material culture. Archaeologists who adopt an "object biography" approach raise similar considerations (Gosden and Marshall 1999). The *chaîne opératoire* is one component of an artefact's biography or life history, and both approaches acknowledge the interlinked physical, social, and symbolic transformations that an artefact endures throughout its use.

This paper employs the *chaîne opératoire* to distinguish socio-technical variability between purportedly related sites. This aim of the paper is contextualised within a long history of Palaeolithic archaeology that has studied variances between sites and the related diverse material culture. For instance, Sieveking (1987a, 49) notes the difference between the widespread Magdalenian IV tradition of three-dimensional carving compared to the distinct preference in the later

Magdalenian V for complex surface engraving. Sieveking couches these differences as typological categories, although they are fundamentally technical and relate to production sequences and socio-technical practice. Because of persistent attention to either the appearance or typology of material culture, or to the exclusively "physical" components of technology, the socio-technical characteristics of much Upper Palaeolithic material culture, particularly portable art, has not yet been rigorously assessed. Changes in material culture production and technique imply cultural changes that may have taken place over both short and long time-spans. Variability identified in symbolic or artistic assemblages can relate not just to the aesthetics and overall appearance of art but can also be fundamentally linked to the production of art and artists' engagement with raw materials.

Once specific technical traditions and *chaînes opératoires* have been identified, it can remain difficult to distinguish the *causes* of variability observed in assemblages from two or more distinct time periods, or two or more distinct regions (Crémades 1994). Environmental factors, temporal changes, or regional variances may each contribute to this variability, and it can be difficult to distinguish between these variables. This paper therefore attempts to advance the scope of the *chaîne opératoire* approach by comparing art assemblages on a much smaller scale. Focusing closely on a single, circumscribed region of occupation and comparing technological traditions between nearby, contemporaneous sites may increase our chances of distinguishing the stimuli, be they material, social, aesthetic or technological, behind the various art traditions and the emergence of distinct *chaînes opératoires* in each context.

This research incorporates both micro and macroscopic analyses, which facilitates a detailed understanding of the physical and social transformations that occurred during the life history of each object. Macroscopic analysis of organic materials such as bone and antler allows overall assessment of how the artist either preserved and worked within the confines of the natural material, or modified it to change its overall shape, size and appearance. Assessing these foundational means of material *engagement* offers insight into the priorities of the artist, the way they conceived of the raw material (in the same way as other raw materials or as a unique material chosen for its particular physical properties), and the extent to which they (or their society) valued the imposition of a new form onto a material. A microscope with up to 20× magnification facilitates more detailed evaluation of engraved marks made on the surface of various materials and helps discern the number of strokes made across the surface to embellish it. These microscopic observations can reveal the tool type or the way the material was held in the artist's hand, and can provide information about whether two or more pieces appear to have been *modified* in the same way, or possibly by the same artist. Comprehensive analysis of an assemblage of art with an aim to understand material *engagement* and *modification* can identify meaningful, widely adopted social practices as well as individual preferences enacted on a single occasion or for a specific purpose or type of artefact. These preferences in production offer insight into the cultural biography of Palaeolithic art.

Introduction to the study area

This paper applies this social *chaîne opératoire* approach to art assemblages excavated from two caves on the banks of the Aveyron river, in the Ariège region of south-central France: Courbet and Montastruc (Fig. 10.2). Both sites were excavated in the 1800s, Courbet beginning in 1864, and Montastruc in 1866 (Sieveking 1987a); consequently, the spatial and stratigraphic resolution in these contexts is poor and it remains unclear where many artefacts were found at each site. Sieveking (1987a) argues for Magdalenian IV and V attributions for much of the *couche noir* at Courbet, which is a 1.5 m context from which most of the material culture, including the art studied here, was excavated. Gambier *et al.* (2000) confirm this mid- to late Magdalenian attribution with two AMS radiocarbon dates from layers 7 and 10 at Courbet, which date to 13,490±260 BP (Gif-A 90170) and 13,400±260 BP (Gif-A 90169). Sieveking (1987a, 63) notes that the art from Montastruc lacks any stratigraphic context, making it even more difficult to identify temporally distinct techno-complexes. Nevertheless, on the basis of the absence of antler half-rods at Montastruc, which are typical in Magdalenian V contexts, she argues that Magdalenian V is more poorly represented here than at Courbet. Instead, she interprets the bone and antler assemblages as more characteristic of slightly earlier Magdalenian IV. In particular, the lack of naturalistic decorations on utilised tools at Montastruc suggests this earlier date, as the association of naturalistic figures with

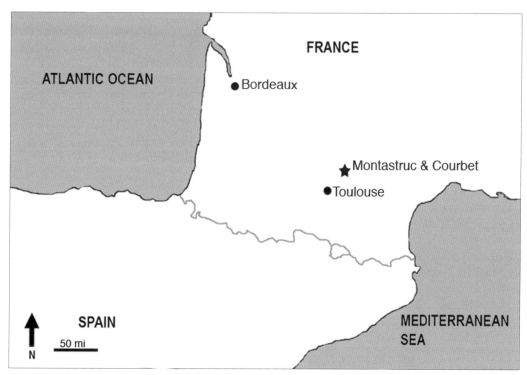

Figure 10.2 Map of southern France and northern Spain, showing the location of Montastruc and Courbet.

tools becomes more prevalent later in the Magdalenian. Thus, some of the material culture from Montastruc may, broadly, suggest a slightly older occupation period than at Courbet. However, there are also Magdalenian VI pieces at Montastruc, including double-barbed harpoons, *bâtons de commandement*, and bone points similar to those found in more securely dated Magdalenian VI contexts at La Madeleine in the Dordogne. Although radiocarbon dates from Courbet and Montastruc are limited, Magdalenian IV, V, and VI assemblages from other sites in southern France support the typo-chronological attribution for the finds from these sites. For instance, Magdalenian IV horizons at Duruthy have been radiocarbon dated to between 13,840–14,500 BP (Bertrand 1999), and at Labastide (Haute-Pyrenees), assemblages attributed to the Magdalenian IV date to 14,260 BP (Omnès 1983). Radiocarbon dates associated with Magdalenian V assemblages in southern France cluster *c.* 13,000 BP (Bertrand 1999).

Unquestionably, both sites suggest a complicated occupation history not exclusively associated with a single Magdalenian techno-complex. The poor stratigraphic resolution at both Courbet and Montastruc as well as the mixed material culture suggesting occupation ranging from Magdalenian IV to VI justify reconsideration of these assemblages using new criteria for distinguishing and grouping the artefacts. Rather than perpetuating traditional typological considerations, this research uses social *chaîne opératoire* methodologies to expose important socio-technical traits that have previously been overlooked. This process may make it possible to distinguish cultural transformations or shared traditions at the two sites and offer insight into the micro-cultures that may have developed in this area. The complexity of the late Magdalenian sequences in this region of France (Cook and Welté 1995; Gambier *et al.* 2000; Griggo 1997; Ladier 2004; Mons 1986–1987; Saint-Perier 1930; Sauvet *et al.* 2008; Welté 2000), and general agreement that many sites from the Ariège and Pyrénées do not directly link into a classic Perigordian Magdalenian sequence (Sieveking 1987a, 64) demand that new methodologies be developed to clarify these relationships.

Courbet and Montastruc yielded both symbolic and non-symbolic material culture that is broadly similar to other mid- and late Magdalenian cave and rock shelter sites in the Pyrénées, including La Vache, Enlène, Mas d'Azil, Gourdan, and Isturitz (Begouen *et al.* 1982; Buisson *et al.* 1989; Clottes 1996; Delporte 1993; Fritz 1999; Garrod 1955; Sieveking 1987b; Sieveking 1991) and therefore provide a reasonable pilot study for applying this methodology to art in this region. These broadly contemporary and nearby sites produced large corpuses of portable art that has been compared previously on stylistic grounds (Sieveking 1987a). The results presented here are a preliminary assessment of the potential of applying this technological approach to study late Magdalenian portable art in this region; additional comparative research is essential to confirm these preliminary results.

The objects discussed in this paper are curated at the British Museum and are only part of the overall assemblages from these sites. A total of 108 artefacts from Montastruc and 64 from Courbet were studied. It is acknowledged that the data presented in this paper is only a sample of the overall assemblages, and the author hopes to expand this preliminary research in the future.

Material choices

Material choices are the initial steps in any *chaîne opératoire*. Situating material choices within their social and physical contexts is especially important when studying organic materials such as bone and antler because each material choice implicates the life history of the animal from which the material came. In this way, the life history of organic materials precedes their adoption by humans. Furthermore, choosing and acquiring material also involves the interaction of one or more humans with this animal. Hunters, scavengers, butchers, and consumers might all have engaged directly with the animal from which raw materials were sourced.

As a material category, bone is often discussed as a homogeneous material class, yet it is more heterogeneous and diverse than both antler and ivory. Bones were sourced from a variety of animals, some of which might have been procured for subsistence purposes, whereas others might have been valuable for reasons unrelated to food procurement. Furthermore, the size of different animals would have been significant to craftspeople working with their bones. Each skeletal element has its own unique morphology and physical characteristics, and modifying a long bone would have been vastly different from working with a scapula. The artificial homogeneity that results from discussing all bone as a single material class clearly limits the socio-technological observations than can be contributed by using a *chaîne opératoire* approach. Furthermore, discussing all bones in the same way disregards their diverse object biographies and unique *chaînes opératoires*. Thus, this paper specifically addresses bone in more detail and considers the diverse types of bone that Magdalenian artists selected, engaged with, and modified at Montastruc and Courbet.

Socio-technical bone choices at Montastruc

Comparing the selection and modification of bone at two nearby sites can help clarify potential relationships and socio-technical similarities and differences in a circumscribed region. Bone was one of the four raw materials (bone, antler, soft stone, and ivory) selected to make art at both Montastruc and Courbet. At Montastruc, 41 of the 108 artefacts studied were made in bone, marking it as a significant and frequently used material. Various species were identifiable in this assemblage of modified bone, with reindeer and other mid-sized herbivores the most abundant species. There is no discernable preference in species that suggests deviation from the unmodified faunal assemblages typically found at middle and late Magdalenian sites in the Ariège, which includes herbivores such as reindeer, ibex, horse, mountain hare, and chamois, birds such as grouse, and moderate numbers of carnivores such as wolf (Pailhaugue 1996; Straus 1987).

Although artists at Montastruc did not demonstrate a preference for working with certain species when making art, they did seem particularly interested in skeletal elements that are naturally flat, especially ribs and scapulae. Twenty-two of the 41 bone artefacts in this assemblage came from skeletal elements that were naturally flat and were not heavily modified so the original skeletal element is often identifiable (Fig. 10.3). The preservation of the natural morphology of the bone in these instances may suggest an interest in and sensitive engagement with the natural constraints of raw materials in line with observations from other Palaeolithic art assemblages in Farbstein (2008, 2010, 2011). Ten additional bone artefacts were more intensively modified in a way that emphasised the flat surface of the bone, which was subsequently engraved. In all these instances, decorations imposed on these pieces correspond to the flat surfaces, whether they are natural or imposed. Thus, 78% of the decorated bone assemblage indicates an interest in working with flat bones or highlighting or imposing a flattened morphology. The persistent interest in flat bones is reinforced by the observation that no three-dimensionally sculpted bone exists in this assemblage; that is, all human modifications to bone led to the production of a flat object.

One potential reason craftspeople at Montastruc might have chosen flatter bones may have been the correspondence of this flat shape with a socially and aesthetically preferred mode of bone decoration and embellishment. These two traditions or preferences (material selection and embellishment) might have emerged simultaneously, or one may have influenced the other, although the sequence of their development is difficult to pinpoint. Regardless of which interest initiated these priorities, the predominant mode of art-production here was engraving either figurative or non-figurative motifs on one flat surface of a bone.

Most of the heavily modified bone art from Montastruc comprises a series of bone discs that were probably made from scapulae (Fig. 10.4). The other intensively sculpted bone object is a *contour découpée* depicting a horse's head (Fig. 10.5). *Contour découpée*, typically found in late Magdalenian contexts, are portable art objects that usually depict horse, ibex, or other animal heads by carving the silhouette and engraving facial features. The horse hyoid bone was commonly used to make these artefacts at Magdalenian sites in the Dordogne region (Clottes 1996), perhaps because of its natural morphology which is evocative of a horse's head. However, at Montastruc, the hyoid bone was not selected. Instead, artists here used a bone that was not naturally evocative of the horse head's

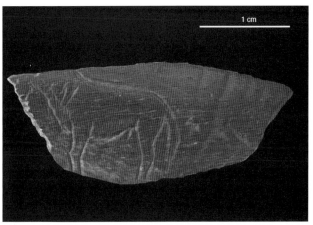

Figure 10.3 Flat piece of bone from Montastruc, engraved on one surface with depiction of a horse (Object #628 in Sieveking 1987a). Image published with permission from the British Museum (photograph: Reecca Farbstein).

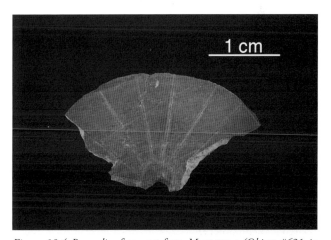

Figure 10.4 Bone disc fragment from Montastruc (Object #621 in Sieveking 1987a). Image published with permission from the British Museum (photograph: Reecca Farbstein).

Figure 10.5 Bone contour découpée from Montastruc (Object #617 in Sieveking 1987a). Image published with permission from the British Museum (photograph: Reecca Farbstein).

silhouette, possibly a scapula, and sculpted and carved it to create the desired contours. This tradition of bone carving, rather than the appropriation of the hyoid bone, more closely corresponds with the Pyrénéan technique for making *contour découpée* (Clottes 1996), possibly suggesting a socio-technical connection to this region.

Overall, there seems to be a tradition at Montastruc of working in a flat plane when making bone art. This tradition reflects the selection of flat skeletal elements like ribs and scapula. Artists at Montastruc produced bone art that both preserves the natural morphology of these chosen bones while also making more heavily modified bone art with an imposed morphology, such as the bone discs and *contour découpée*. Importantly, this interest in flatness does not apparently extend to other organic materials, including antler, which was sculpted three-dimensionally to make spear-throwers with fully rounded sculpted zoomorphic heads as well as engraved objects where the naturally round morphology of a complete antler beam was preserved. Thus, this socio-technical tradition seems restricted to the bone material choices apparent at Montastruc.

Socio-technical bone choices at Courbet

There are fewer bone objects (11 of 64 artefacts) in the assemblage from Courbet at the British Museum. This smaller assemblage size may not reflect differences in material preference at the two sites, but may rather reflect the excavation techniques or the means by which the art assemblages from Montastruc and Courbet were divided between museum collections. More research on the entire assemblage of art from these sites is necessary to confirm whether distinct material preferences are apparent between these sites.

Although fewer bone objects were available for analysis, there seem to be differences in the bone art assemblages from these two sites. At Courbet, there was an apparent interest in decorating bird bones, which were not prevalent in the decorative bone assemblage at Montastruc. Artists at Courbet consistently chose bird long bones and preserved the hollow lumen of their natural morphology (Fig. 10.6). Furthermore, craftspeople at Courbet showed less preference for flat bone art. Although bones that were naturally flat, like ribs, were sometimes used and their natural morphology was preserved, there are fewer examples of bone modification that preserves or highlights a bone's flat morphology.

Surface engraving was the primary mode of embellishing bone to make art at Courbet. The few bones from Courbet that were more heavily sculpted were made into perforated pendants (Fig. 10.7). This tradition departs from the prevalent interest in bone discs at Montastruc, and it may suggest divergent art traditions associated with the technology of bone sculpting. *Contour découpée* were also not identified in the assemblage from Courbet. Interestingly, as at Montastruc, other materials, notably antler and soft stones, were modified in vastly different ways from the bone art at Courbet. Antler was three-dimensionally sculpted to make spear-throwers and stones were minimally modified to emphasise their natural shapes that evoke a female profile. Comparison between these objects and raw materials reinforces the interpretation that the technologies and material engagement apparent in the decorative bone assemblage were unique and distinct from those employed when working with other organic and inorganic materials,

Thus, there are some clear differences in bone manufacture at Montastruc and Courbet. Artists at the two sites clearly preferred working with different species. Bone art at Montastruc was primarily made from reindeer bones or the bones of other herbivores, whereas artists at Courbet repeatedly chose to work with bird bones. Moreover, flat bones, like scapula and ribs, were preferred at Montastruc, whereas rounded and hollow long bones were often selected at Courbet. These differences in material choice are echoed in material modification as well, since bone sculpting lead to different types of art at the two sites. This initial assessment of material choices and modification sequences suggests socially, aesthetically, and technically meaningful differences in how artists engaged with bone at the neighbouring sites of Montastruc and

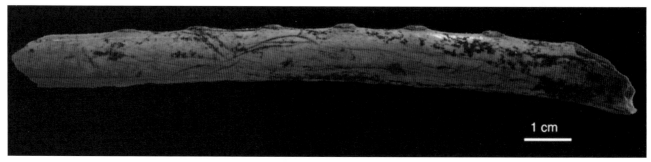

Figure 10.6 Bird bone with distinctive feather attachment protuberances in low-relief and engravings, from Courbet (Object #507 in Sieveking 1987a). Image published with permission from the British Museum (photograph: Reecca Farbstein).

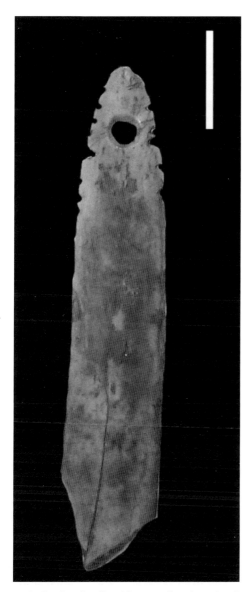

Figure 10.7 Sculpted and scalloped bone pendant from Courbet (Object #509 in Sieveking 1987a). Image published with permission from the British Museum (photograph: Reecca Farbstein).

Figure 10.8 Splintered long bone from Montastruc that was engraved to depict a horse's head, in accordance with the existing morphology of the broken bone (Object #629 in Sieveking 1987a). Image published with permission from the British Museum (photograph: Reecca Farbstein).

Courbet. In the absence of more fine-grained chrono-stratigraphic data that would help determine if the sites were occupied contemporaneously, this new technological and material analysis suggests important but previously undetected differences between the two sites.

Broken, then chosen: the life history of bone splinters at Montastruc

The observations above regarding material selection within the bone assemblages help distinguish socio-technical preferences at two nearby sites. A closer examination of specific sub-assemblages addresses the second main concern of this paper, which is to offer insight into the complex life histories of bone and some of the artefacts made in this material. A sub-group of bone artefacts from Montastruc crafted exclusively from long-bones forms a material series. These objects are united not only in material but also in subject matter, as all feature depictions of animals. They are technologically united as well, as all were decorated with surface engravings that were probably executed using a burin. Stylistically, the pieces also exhibit similarities, particularly in the means of depicting the horses' beards and in the schematic, almost caricatured means of depiction.

One of the most compelling characteristics uniting these pieces is the use of broken bones as the foundation for the engraving. From a theoretical standpoint, these pieces embody issues of material *engagement* that are fundamental to any *chaîne opératoire*. The bones used to make these pieces were already broken before they were adopted to make the art. In all instances, the shape of the broken bone was integrated into the design of the piece, such that the fractures were used to suggest the backlines, jaw lines, or heads of the animals depicted (Fig. 10.8). Furthermore, features of these splinters suggest that the bones may have been intentionally broken for marrow extraction. For instance, one object features a flake scar on its decorated surface, indicating the mode by which the bone was shattered, perhaps to access the marrow. If marrow extraction was a primary objective, the bone may have been cooked or boiled before it was engraved and transformed into art, thus adding another step in its *chaîne opératoire* and life history.

Such splintered bones had a complex life history related to subsistence and nutrition before they were decorated. The bone splinter may have been discarded as waste after the marrow was extracted. The craftsman who eventually decorated the piece of bone may not have been the person who splintered it to extract marrow. More directly, the bone was probably not collected specifically for the purpose of making art. The bones might first have been selected and valued for their nutritious marrow. The hunter who killed the animal may not have been the same individual who extracted the marrow from the bone. After the bones were splintered and marrow was extracted, the craftsperson who originally engaged with the material might have discarded them. Subsequently, they were re-appropriated and transformed into art. These objects are an important example of the complex *chaînes opératoires* and life histories of Palaeolithic artefacts. A single material or object could acquire multiple attributed meanings within a single cultural context. While a bone may have been originally valued as food, it was later valued as a foundation for art.

An antler artefact from Courbet attests to a similarly complex but inverse life history. While the antler was initially decorated with a non-figurative motif of two parallel lines of short incisions, it was subsequently splintered, a process that bisected and interrupted this motif. The groove-and-splinter scar may be evidence of the transformation of this piece of antler into a point (possibly used for hunting). What remains of this artefact is the debitage from this transformative process (Fig. 10.9). In this instance, antler was initially valued as art, and subsequently as a raw material from which a tool could be made. During the second part of this object's life history, the aesthetic or visual significance of the decoration was clearly no longer of paramount importance, as the motif was bisected as the material was transformed. In both examples, the fluidity of material meaning and material engagement is apparent.

From technological, material and stylistic standpoints, the splintered long-bone artefacts represent a unique class of art not evident in the rest of the assemblage at Montastruc. This technique of incorporating the morphologies of broken fragments was not noted in either ivory nor antler art at Montastruc. These material differences are significant and indicate that artists at Montastruc ascribed meaningful social and technical differences to bone, antler and ivory when choosing these materials to make art. Additionally, no broken bones, antler, or ivory were appropriated in a similar way at the neighbouring site of Courbet. The "object biography" perspective reinforces the distinction between the bone techniques and traditions at Courbet and Montastruc. While some bone art at Montastruc may have been made on materials that were previously exploited for subsistence purposes (e.g. marrow extraction), the series of decorated bird

art at Courbet were clearly not selected for marrow extraction purposes. Different priorities and interests motivated the collection of certain species and types of bones at these two sites. These site-specific distinctions offer additional evidence that the individuals and groups occupying these two sites may be distinguished through analysis of their material engagement and art production technologies.

Theoretical and social implications

The anthropology of technology (Lechtman 1977; Lemonnier 1993; Schiffer 2001) argues that technological actions and technological choices are evidence of socially significant and, often, socially variable behaviours in the past. Focusing on small-scale techniques and innovations can help distinguish between sites or archaeological cultures that are typically grouped together as culturally contiguous. Studying technology within specific social and archaeological contexts can lead to a consideration of "social boundaries" (Stark 1998) and cultural continuities. This understanding builds upon the notion that any technique or gesture is a "physical rendering of mental schemas learned through tradition ..." (Lemonnier 1993, 3). Evidence of shared technological traditions, or more specifically, unusual innovations, may indicate not just cultural contact but also shared knowledge between two seemingly discrete cultures. This potential sharing of knowledge applies Mauss' assertion that techniques as varied as assembling cars, baking a cake, or walking vary from one society to another (Mauss 1935). It seems unlikely that culturally discrete groups would independently develop or adopt similar small-scale, "non-functional" techniques at approximately the same time without shared knowledge and sustained contact. Consequently, the sharing of this knowledge may be a more robust indicator of cultural contact than the presence of art that looks the same in two or more places. In a previous analysis of Central European Gravettian portable art, this author demonstrated the presence of distinct preferences in

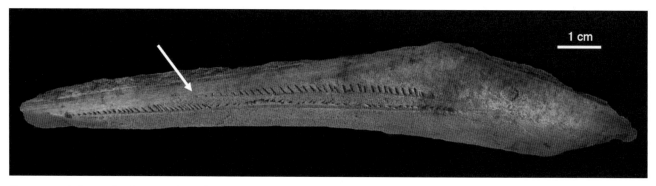

Figure 10.9 Antler artefact from Courbet (Object #504 in Sieveking 1987a). The arrow highlights the point where the manufacturing scar intersects with the engraved motif. Image published with permission from the British Museum (photograph: Reecca Farbstein).

how craftspeople engaged with ivory and modified it to made art (Farbstein 2011). These site-specific differences suggest considerable diversity in cultural and technical traditions of art production between sites located less than 500 metres from each other. While much additional research in necessary to assess if similar socio-technical preferences are apparent in this Magdalenian art assemblage, the author's previous analysis of Gravettian art confirms the validity and potential of this approach. Studying technologies, particularly those embedded in the production of symbolic material culture or "art", has the potential to reveal intricacies of Palaeolithic social life and distinguish between related sub-cultures on the basis of their preferred technological practices.

Conclusions and considerations

The observations presented in this study suggest technological diversity and differences in the modification of materials for art at Montastruc and Courbet. Artists at the two sites did not appear to be working within the same socio-technical traditions. Bones used to make art suggest different material acquisition strategies and preferences. The selection of certain types of bones also contributed to the production of two distinct aesthetics in bone art at Montastruc and Courbet. In particular, small-scale techno-aesthetic innovations like the creation of zoomorphic depictions from broken bones emerged in one location but were not evident at the other, suggesting the groups occupying the neighbouring sites did not share the same traditions and may not have been culturally contiguous.

Technological and material choices apparent at Courbet and Montastruc also indicate that much of the art endured complex "life histories" and "object biographies" at the two sites. The broken bones used at Montastruc suggest an engagement with materials that were valued for different characteristics throughout their lives. Other materials, such as antler used at Courbet, reinforce that complex object biographies developed in the production of art in this region. Artists did not appear to adhere to strictly imposed notions of how a material should be used. Bone, in particular, seemed to have had a fluid social "value" that was changeable depending on the way it was adopted and how it was modified.

Of course, the observations and interpretations advanced here are preliminary. Results from the author's previous research on Central European Gravettian art illustrate the potential of this approach when studying comprehensive assemblages. In order to elaborate upon these considerations, it will be necessary to study more complete assemblages of art from these two sites. Comparison of these techniques and material traditions to those at other sites in the region would also improve understanding of social networking throughout the Pyrénées during the middle and late Magdalenian. In particular, art from La Vache, Enlène, Mas d'Azil and Isturitz warrants close consideration.

Acknowledgements

This research was supported by the Caroline Villers Research Fellowship, which the author held at the Courtauld Institute of Art during 2009–2010. The author is grateful to Jill Cook at the British Museum, who facilitated this research and who has been of great assistance throughout this project. The author is also grateful to the anonymous reviewer and the editors of this volume for their helpful suggestions for improving the paper. Of course, all shortcomings or errors in this paper are the sole responsibility of the author. All photographs reproduced in this paper were taken by the author and are published with permission from the British Museum.

Bibliography

Begouen, R., Clottes, J., Giraud, J.-P. and Rouzaud, F. (1982) Plaquette gravée d'Enlène, Montesquieu-Avantès (Ariège). *Bulletin de la Société Préhistorique Française* 79, 103–109.

Bertrand, A. (1999) *Les Armatures de Sagaies Magdaléniennes en Matière Dure Animale dans les Pyrénées.* Oxford, Archaeopress (British Archaeological Report S773).

Bosinski, G. (1991) The representation of female figurines in the Rhineland Magdalenian. *Proceedings of the Prehistoric Society* 51, 51–64.

Brühl, E. (2005) The bone, antler, and ivory tools. In J. Svoboda (ed.), *Pavlov I Southwest: a window into the Gravettian lifestyles. Volume 2*, 252–293. Brno, Academy of Sciences of the Czech Republic, Institute of Archaeology at Brno, Polish Academy of Sciences, Institute of Systematics and Evolution of Animals.

Buisson, D., Menu, M., Pinçon, G. and Walter, P. (1989) Les objets colorés du Paléolithique supérieur cas de la grotte de La Vache (Ariège). *Bulletin de la Société Prehistorique Française* 86, 183–191.

Choyke, A. (2010) The bone is the beast: animal amulets and ornaments in power and magic. In D. Campana, P. Crabtree, S. D. DeFrance, J. Lev-Tov, and A. Choyke (eds), *Anthropological approaches to zooarchaeology: colonialism, complexity, and animal transformations*, 197–209. Oxford, Oxbow Books.

Clottes, J. (1996) Un groupe culturel homogène. In M.-H. Thiault and J.-B. Roy (eds), *L'art préhistorique des Pyrénées*, 36–59. Paris, Réunion des musées nationaux.

Cohen, C. (2003) *La femme des Origines: images de la femme dans la préhistoire occidentale.* Berlin, Herscher.

Cook, J. and Welté, A.-C. (1995) La Grotte du Courbet (Tarn): sa contribution dans l'histoire de l'homme fossile et de l'art paléolithique. *Préhistoire Ariégeoise (Bulletin de la sociéte préhistorique Ariège-Pyrénées)* 50, 85–96.

Crémades, M. (1994) L'art mobilier paléolithique: analyse des procédés technologiques. *Complutum* 5, 369–384.

D'Errico, F. (1992) Technology, motion, and the meaning of Epipaleolithic art. *Current Anthropology* 33, 94–109.

De Beune, S. (1999) De la pierre à l'os: ou comment reconstituer des *chaînes opératoires* techniques impliquant l'os et la pierre. In H. Camps-Fabrer (ed.), *Prehistoire d'Os*, 151–158. Aix-en-Provence, Publications de l'Université de Provence.

Delporte, H. (1993) L'art mobilier de la Grotte de la Vache: premier essai du vue générale. *Bulletin de la Société Préhistorique Française* 90, 131–136.

Dobres, M.-A. (2000) *Technology and Social Agency.* Oxford, Blackwell Publishers.

Dobres, M.-A. (2010) The phenomenal promise of chaîne opératoire: mindfully engaged bodies and the manufacture of personhood in a regional perspective. In R. Barndon, A. Engevik, and I. Øye (eds), *The Archaeology of Regional Technologies: case studies from the Palaeolithic to the age of the Vikings*, 51–67. Lampeter, Mellen Press.

Farbstein, R. (2008) *Pavlovian Portable Art: socio-technical process, aesthetic context*. Unpublished PhD thesis. Cambridge, UK, Department of Archaeology, University of Cambridge.

Farbstein, R. (2010) The significance of social gestures and technologies of embellishment in Paleolithic portable art. *Journal of Archaeological Method and Theory* 18 (2),125–146.

Farbstein, R. (2011) Technologies of art: a critical reassessment of Pavlovian art and society using *Chaîne Opératoire* method and theory. *Current Anthropology* 52 (3), 401–432.

Fritz, C. (1999) Towards the reconstruction of Magdalenian artistic techniques: the contribution of microscopic analysis of mobiliary art. *Cambridge Archaeological Journal* 9, 189–208.

Gambier, D., Valladas, H., Tisnérat-Labourde, N., Arnold, M. and Bresson F. (2000) Datation des vestiges humains présumés du Paléolithique supérieur par la méthode du carbone 14 en spectrométrie de masse par accélérateur. *Paléo* 12, 201–212.

Garrod, D. (1955) Palaeolithic spear-throwers. *Proceedings of the Prehistoric Society* 21, 21–35.

Gell, A. (1999) The technology of enchantment and the enchantment of technology. In E. Hirsch (ed.), *The Art of Anthropology: essay and diagrams*, 159–186. London, The Athlone Press.

Gosden, C. and Marshall, Y. (1999) The cultural biography of objects. *World Archaeology* 31, 16–178.

Griggo, C. (1997) La faune magdalénienne de l'abri Gandil Bruniquel (Tarn-et-Garonne): etudes paléontologique, taphonomique et archéozoologique. *Paléo* 9, 279–294.

Gvozdover, M. (1989) The typology of female figurines of the Kostenki Paleolithic culture. *Soviet Anthropology and Archaeology* 27, 32–94.

Klíma, B. (1997) Die knochenindustrie, zier- und kunstgegenstände (Bone industry, decorative objects, and art). In J. Svoboda (ed.), *Pavlov I--Northwest: the Upper Paleolithic burial and settlement context*, 227–286. Brno, Academy of Sciences of the Czech Republic.

Ladier, E. (2004) L'Art mobilier sur pierre de l'abri Gandil à Bruniquel (Tarn-et-Garonne, France): etude synthétique. In M. Lejeune and A.-C. Welté (eds), *L'Art du Paléolithique Supérieur: actes du XIV ème congrès UISPP*, 159–166. Liège, Université de Liège.

Latour, B. (1991) Technology is society made durable. In J. Law (ed.), *A Sociology of Monsters*, 103–131. London, Routledge, Sociological Review Monograph 38

Lechtman, H. (1977) Style and technology: some early thoughts. In H. Lechtman and R. S. Merrill (eds), *Material Culture: styles, organization and dynamics of technology*, 3–20. St Paul (MN), West Publishing.

Lemonnier, P. (1993) Introduction. In P. Lemonnier (ed.), *Technological choices: transformation in material cultures since the Neolithic*, 1–35. London, Routledge.

Leroi-Gourhan, A. (1964) *Le Geste et la Parole I--techniques et langage*. Paris, Albin Michel.

Mauss, M. (1935) Les techniques du corps. *Journal de pscyhologie* 32, 271–293.

Miller, D. (ed.) (2005) *Materiality*. Durham, Duke University Press.

Mons, L. (1986–1987) Les figurations de bison dans l'art mobilier de la grotte d'Isturitz (Pyrénées-Atlantiques). *Antiquités Nationales* 18–19, 91–99.

Myers, F. (2005) Some properties of art and culture: ontologies of the image and economies of exchange. In D. Miller (ed.), *Materiality*, 88–117. Durham, Duke University Press.

Omnès, J. (1983) The Magdalenian sanctuary of the cave of Labastide (Hautes-Pyrénées, France). *Oxford Journal of Archaeology* 2, 253–263.

Pailhaugue, N. (1996) Faune et saisons de chasse de La Salle Monique Grotte de La Vache (Alliat, Ariège). In H. Delporte and J. Clottes (eds), *Pyrénées Préhistoriques: arts et sociétés*, 173–191. Paris, Comité des Travaux historiques et scientifiques.

Pigeot, N. (1990) Technical and social actors. Flintknapping specialists at Magdalenian Etiolles. *Archaeological Review from Cambridge* 9, 126–141.

Saint-Perier, R. D. (1930) *La Grotte d'Isturitz: Le Magdalénien de la Salle de Saint-Martin*. Paris, Masson et Cie Éditions.

Sauvet, G., Fortea Pérez, J., Fritz, C. and Tosello, G. (2008) Crónica de los intercambios entre los grupos humanos Paleoliticos. La contributión del arte para el periodo 20000–12000 años BP. *Zephyrus* 61, 33–59.

Schiffer, M. (ed.) (2001) *Anthropological Perspectives on Technology*. Albuquerque, University of New Mexico Press.

Sellet, F. (1993) *Chaîne opératoire*: the concept and its applications. *Lithic Technology* 18, 106–112.

Sieveking, A. (1987a). *A Catalogue of Palaeolithic Art in the British Museum*. London, British Museum Publications.

Sieveking, A. (1987b) *Engraved Magdalenian Plaquettes*. Oxford, British Archaeological Report S369.

Sieveking, A. (1991) Palaeolithic art and archaeology: the mobiliary evidence. *Proceedings of the Prehistoric Society* 57, 33–50.

Stark, M. (ed.) (1998) *The archaeology of social boundaries*. Washington, DC, Smithsonian Institution Press.

Straus, L. G. (1987) Upper Paleolithic ibex hunting in southwest Europe. *Journal of Archaeological Science* 14, 163–178.

Svoboda, J. (1997) Symbolisme gravettien en Moravie. Espace, temps et formes. *Bulletin de la société préhistorique Ariège-Pyrénées* 52, 87–107.

Welté, A.-C. (2000) Le Magdalénien supérieur et les propulseurs dans la vallée de l'Aveyron: révision chronologique. *Memoires de la Société Préhistorique Française* 28, 201–212.

White, R. (1997) Substantial acts: from materials to meaning in Upper Paleolithic representation. In M. Conkey, O. Soffer, D. Stratmann and N. Jablonski (eds), *Beyond art: Pleistocene Image and Symbol*, 93–121. San Francisco, California Academy of Sciences.

CHAPTER 11

Evidence of Bone Technology on the Santa Fe Pampa Lagoons. The Laguna El Doce site (Santa Fe Province, Argentina)

Jimena Cornaglia Fernández and Natacha Buc

In this paper we present the first results obtained from the analysis of 14 artifacts recovered from a surface survey in the Laguna El Doce site. The settlement is located in the Pampa lagoon area of Santa Fe province (Argentina). We identified the morpho-functional groups, determined their physical structure (bone as the raw material and taxa) and carried out use-wear analysis using a microscope under high magnification. This study represents the first characterization of the bone technology employed by the hunter-gatherer societies that inhabited the area during the Holocene period.

Keywords
Bone technology; bone raw material; use-wear analysis; hunter-gatherers; Pampa Lagoon area.

Introduction

Animals exploited by hunter-gatherers not only constitute an important food resource but their bones can also be used in the manufacture of tools. Although bone tools are traditionally important for the archaeology of nearby regions from the east (Berberián 1984; González 1943), north (Larguía de Crouzeilles 1939; Pérez Jimeno 2007) and west (Bonomo *et al.* 2009; Buc in press), no similar analysis have yet been carried out on material from the Pampa Lagoon area of Santa Fe province in Argentina.

This paper represents, therefore, the first study of bone tools recovered from the Laguna El Doce (to be called LED) archaeological site. It is located in the lagoon of the same name, in the Pampa lagoon area of Santa Fe province at 33° 54' 20" W and 62° 08' 43" S, in the north-western sector of the Pampean Region (Figs 11.1 and 11.2) and represents very early human occupation of this region.

This paper concerns surface surveys carried out in the LED site, where high quantities of faunal remains (mainly *Lama guanicoe*), human bones, pottery fragments, lithic materials and bone tools were found (Avila 2006, 2011). The site is located in a deflation basin in a dune environment (Fig. 11.2), formed by the action of wind. A guanaco skeletal element with evidence of anthropic activity on its service and a human bone were dated through AMS in 7026±58 BP (AA89914) and 8274±68 BP (AA89915) (Avila 2011), respectively. Both dates place the site within an early phase of the Holocene period. However, two pottery fragments found at this site date to the Late Holocene at 1555±85 BP (AA89918) and 2350±180 BP (AA89919) (Avila 2011) showing the complex depositional history of the site which would have involved a long formation process.

In 2010 and 2011, systematic excavations were carried out at the site. Dates on newly recovered materials are currently under analysis. The excavation material recovered was very similar to what was found during surface surveys.

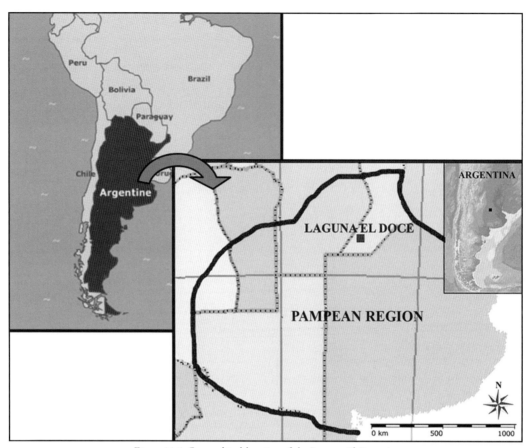

Figure 11.1 Geographical location of the Laguna El Doce site.

Figure 11.2 The Laguna El Doce archaeological site (photograph: Yanina Vranković).

Material and methodology

We analysed the morphological, physical, metric (*sensu* Scheinsohn 2010) and microscopic structure (Buc in press) of the 14 archaeological bone tools recovered from the LED site.

Firstly, artefacts were classified into morpho-functional groups based on examples from both international scholarship (mainly Camps-Fabrer 1966) and the shape of the distal or apical ends (Scheinsohn 2010). The physical structure (anatomical and taxonomical identification of units used as raw material) was determined using actual databases. The metric structure was established based on standard criteria on bone tools analysis (Scheinsohn 2010). Finally, for the analysis of the microscopic structure we followed criteria initially proposed by Semenov (1964) and developed by Le Moine (1991) and Legrand (2007; see also Averbouh 2000; Legrand and Sidéra 2007; Le Moine 1991; Sidéra and Legrand 2006), among other authors (synthezised in Buc in press, 2011). In this respect we considered: 1) volume alterations (rounding, flaking and flattening); 2) micro-topography (descriptions of the high and low points of the surface at 100×); 3) micro-relief (a detailed description of topography at 200×); and 4) striations. Since the latter are the most conspicuous traits, they were classified according to their distribution (seen at 50–100×) and morphology (seen at 200×; following Legrand 2007).

Striations can be: transversal, longitudinal or random in distribution relative to the tool's axis (Averbouh 2000); and parallel, crossed or irregular in arrangement. Based on their morphology, striations can be narrow, wide or variable in width; deep or shallow; long or short; straight or sinuous; coarse or smooth (*sensu* Le Moine 1991); closed 'V'-shaped or open 'V'-shaped (see Buc in press, 2011).

For the functional interpretation we used a previous experimental database (Buc 2011) comparing images with information published by other authors as well. An inverted metallographic microscope (Olympus MPE3) working at 50×, 100× and 200× was used to examine all pieces.

Results of archaeological analysis

Following criteria found in Camps-Fabrer (1966) and Scheinsohn (2010), the sample included the following morpho-functional groups: flakers, points, spatulas and bevelled tools (Figs 11.3, 4, 5a and 6; Table 11.1). Some culturally modified fragments could not be assigned to any morpho-functional group based on what can be found in the scholarly literature and are referred to here as "undetermined". Finally, we also recovered bones (n=4) with sawing at their perimeters or other marks that suggest they may be manufacturing by-products or only slightly modified artefacts (Table 11.1).

As seen in Table 11.1, bevelled tools comprise the most abundant morpho-functional group. They display strong selectivity in terms of the raw material since all tools are made from *Lama guanicoe* metapodials (Fig. 11.5b). In the metric structure, these artefacts display strong homogeneity in those variables not affected by artefactual re shaping, such as maximum width and thickness, and apical thickness (Fig. 11.6).

Given the importance of post-depositional processes in microscopic analysis, it is necessary to stress that the sample comes from a surface recovery in a lagoon environment. Some bone tools show taphonomic damage produced by non-human agents such as weathering, root etching, rodents' marks, and manganese and calcium concretions. Some of these damages represent a problem for microscopic analysis because they modify, erase or obscure use-wear (D'Errico and Vila 1997; Lyman 1994; Shipman 1989). For that reason, we only considered microscopic patterns and not isolated marks assuming that natural alterations, when these are not macroscopically evident (like rodent marks or root etching) either completely covers the surface of bone or just the high points (Lyman 1994; Runnings *et al.* 1989; Shipman 1989). Some pieces could not be analyzed at all because of the presence of heavy calcium carbonate concretions.

Microscopic analysis of spatulate tools and points only showed rounded and homogeneous surfaces or post-

Table 11.1 Morphological groups and support taxa represented in the bone tool sample.

Morpho-functional Groups	*n*	Taxa	Bone
Point	4	*Lama guanicoe-* Artiodactyla	radioulna-femora-splinter-metapodial
Flaker	1	*Lama guanicoe*	metacarpal
Bevelled Tool	5	*Lama guanicoe*-Artiodactyla	metapodial-splinter
Spatulate Tool	2	*Lama guanicoe*-Artiodactyla	scapula-splinter
Manufacturing by-products	4	*Lama guanicoe*	metacarpal-splinter
Undetermined	2	*Lama guanicoe*-Artiodacyla	metapodial-splinter

Figure 11.3 Flaker made on metacarpal of Lama guanicoe *(photograph: Yanina Vranković).*

Figure 11.4 Points made on radioulna and femora of Lama guanicoe *(photograph: Yanina Vranković).*

depositional alterations. Therefore, no identification of the way such tools were used could be carried out.

Use-wear was only recorded on three specimens. The flaker (LED 550) displays transversal, parallel, short and deep striations (Fig. 11.7a) similar to those recorded on all flakers

(Fig. 11.7b) recovered from another archaeological site, Saco Viejo (Borella and Buc 2010).

On the other hand, two bevelled tools (LED 630, LED 1961) display the same macro and microscopic trait patterns. Use-wear is located exclusively at the apical ends: it is formed

Figure 11.5 Bevelled tools made on metapodials of Lama guanicoe *(photograph: Yanina Vranković).*

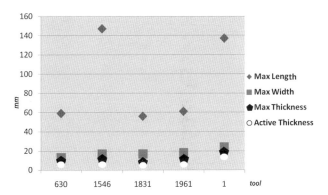

Figure 11.6 Bevelled tools. Comparison between length, width, and thickness.

by parallel, straight, wide and 'V'-shaped, longitudinal striations (Fig. 11.8a). These coarse, straight and 'V'-shaped striations are similar to those made by angular grain abrasives (Fig. 11.8b) (Buc 2011; see also Averbouh and Provenzano 1998–1999; Legrand 2007; Le Moine 1991) so these cases can be identified, with great

reliability, with longitudinal work on abrasive materials such as lithics. Although comparison with traces of manufacture on experimental tools images was carried out, the traces recorded on the archaeological specimens seem to be use the result of use as they are restricted to the apical end of the tools.

Discussion and conclusions

The above-mentioned results show that this small assemblage is dominated by tools made exclusively from the bones of guanaco (*Lama guanicoe*). In effect, despite the presence of other species in the zooarchaeological record, this taxa formed the subsistence base of these hunter-gatherer societies (Cornaglia Fernández 2009). In contrast to the distribution of guanaco skeletal elements in the archaeofaunal assemblage, metapodials predominate as the raw material used for making tools. Therefore, from a zooarchaeological point of view, this paper provides a wider understanding of the exploitation of guanaco which not only comprised an important food resource

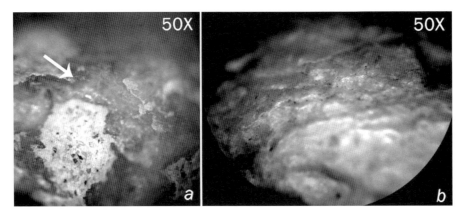

Figure 11.7 a) LED 550. Arrow shows transversal, parallel, deep, short striation, 50×; b) SV 22. Showing microscopic pattern of transversal, parallel, deep and short striations recorded in all archaeological flakers of Saco Viejo archaeological site (Borella and Buc 2010), 50× (photograph: Yanina Vranković).

Figure 11.8 a) LED 630. Longitudinal, 'V'-shaped striations, 120×; b) Experimental traces after abrading bone with sandpaper, 100× (photograph: Yanina Vranković).

but was also a key source of raw material in the manufacture of bone tools.

Morpho-functional variability on the site is low with a few artefacts representing points, spatulate tools and flakers. In contrast, there are more bevelled tools and these are high standardized in their metric, physical and microscopic structures. Within this morpho-functional group, not only were guanaco metapodials selected, but, as their metric structure indicates, a certain size range was preferred, thus, maintaining the original geometry of bones after manufacture (Fig. 11.5b). As Scheinsohn and Ferretti (1995) have shown these skeletal elements have good geometric and structural properties which are ideal for activities involving pressure without excessive deformation. This quality in the raw material must be considered along with the functional interpretation.

These two bevelled tools, as well as the flaker, display lithic use-wear patterns which indicate they were used on stony material. Despite the absence of local stone quarries, natural flakes as well as scrapers, projectile points and waste

from lithic manufacture were recovered in the surface finds made at the archaeological site, suggesting local manufacture of lithic tools (Avila 2006). In this context, the bone tool assemblage seems to be oriented to lithic technology as no other material (plants, skin, etc.) could be identified through microwear analysis. However, post-depositional alterations were important enough to make examination of much of the sample impossible, obscuring the microwear distribution.

In conclusion, bevelled tools seem to have been manufactured in a standardised manner involving strict selection of raw material (guanaco metapodials) and metrical parameters according to their use, probably in lithic activities. Maintaining the original geometry of metapodials, the geometrical properties were exploited, thus, using a material that is ideal for use in activities involving pressure for lithic production. Based on models on bone material exploitation (Buc in press; Scheinsohn 2010) such strategies suggest good management of osseous raw materials which, if early dates prove to be correct, could be the earliest evidence of well-developed bone technology in the Pampean Region.

Acknowledgments

We would like to thank the Physics Institute of Rosario, especially Dr. Martina Avalos, PhD for permitting access to the metallographic microscope. We also thank Alice M. Choyke and Sonia O'Connor for inviting us to participate in the volume and the reviewer for their valuable comments. Yanina Vranković took the photographs for us. The interpretations and errors are the sole responsibility of the authors.

Bibliography

Averbouh, A. (2000) *Technologie de la Matière Osseuse Travaillée et Implications Peleothnologiques. L'exemple des chaînes d'exploitation du bois de cervidé chez les Magdaléniens des Pyrénées.* Unpublished PhD thesis, Université de Paris I.

Averbouh, A. and Provenzano, N. (1998–1999) Proposition pour une terminologie du travail préhistorique des matières osseuses: I. Les techniques. *Préhistoire Anthropologie Méditerranées* 7–8, 5–25.

Avila, J. D. (2006) Estudio de artefactos de molienda localizados en el Sitio 1 Laguna El Doce de la localidad de San Eduardo, Departamento General López, Provincia de Santa Fe. *Programa Final y Resúmenes V Jornadas Arqueológicas Regionales*, 32. Buenos Aires.

Avila, J. D. (2011) Resultados de los fechados radiocarbónicos del sitio LED, Departamento General López, Provincia de Santa Fe. *Relaciones de la Sociedad Argentina de Antropología* 36, 337–343.

Berberián, E. (1984) Potrero de Garay: una entidad sociocultural tardía de la Región Serrana de la provincia de Córdoba (República Argentina). *Comechingonia* 4, 71–138.

Bonomo, M., Capdepont, I. and Matarrese, A. (2009) Alcances en el estudio de colecciones. Los materiales arqueológicos del delta del río Paraná depositados en el museo de La Plata (Argentina). *Arqueología Suramericana* 5 (1), 68–101.

Borella, F. and Buc, N. (2010) Ópticas y ópticos. Una aproximación a la tecnología ósea en la Bahía de San Antonio (Río Negro), Argentina. In M. Salemme, F. Santiago, M. Alvarez, E., Piana, M., Vazquez and M. E. Mansur (eds), *Arqueología de Patagonia: una mirada desde el último confín*, 421–432. Ushuaia, Editorial Utopías.

Buc, N. (in press) *Tecnología Ósea de los Cazadores-recolectores del Humedal del Paraná Inferior (Bajíos ribereños meridionales), Series Monográficas, Arqueología de la Cuenca del Plata.* Buenos Aires, Instituto Nacional de Antropología y Pensamiento Latinoamericano.

Buc, N. (2011) Experimental series and use-wear in bone tools. *Journal of Archaeological Science* 38, 546–557.

Camps-Fabrer, H. (1966) *Matière et Art Mobilier dans la Préhistoire Nord-Africaine et Saharienne. Mémoires du CEDARC* 5. Paris.

Cornaglia Fernández, J. (2009) *Zooarqueología del Holoceno Tardío en el Sur de Santa Fe. El Sitio Laguna El Doce.* Unpublished Grade thesis, Universidad Nacional de Rosario.

D'Errico, F. and Villa, P. (1997) Holes and grooves: the contribution of microscopy and taphonomy to the problem of art origins. *Journal of Human Evolution* 33, 1–31.

Larguía de Crouzeilles, A. (1939) Correlaciones entre la alfarería indígena encontrada en la región de Santa Fe y la de la provincia de Santiago del Estero. *Anales de la Sociedad Científica Argentina* IV (CXXVIII), 196–210.

Le Moine, G. (1991) *Experimental Analysis of the Manufacture and Use of Bone and Antler Tools among the Mackenzie Inuit.* Unpublished PhD thesis, University of Calgary.

Legrand, A. (2007) *Fabrication et Utilisation de l'Outillage en Matières Osseuses du Néolithique de Chypre: Khirokitia et Cap Andreas-Kastros.* Oxford, Archaeopress (British Archaeological Report S1678).

Legrand A. and Sidéra, I. (2007) Methods, means, and results when studying European bone industry. In C. Gates St-Pierre and R. Walker (eds), *Bones as Tools: current methods and interpretations in worked bone studies*, 291–304. Oxford, Archaeopress (British Archaeological Report S1622).

Lyman, L. (1994) *Vertebrate Taphonomy.* Cambridge University Press, Cambridge.

Pérez Jimeno, L. (2007) *Investigaciones Arqueológicas en el Sector Septentrional de la Llanura Aluvial del Paraná – margen santafesina –: la variabilidad del registro arqueológico.* Unpublished PhD thesis, Universidad Nacional de La Plata.

Runnings, A., Gustafson, C. and Bentely, D. (1989) Use-wear on bone tools: a technique for study under the scanning electron microscope. In R. Bonnischen and M. Sorg (eds), *Bone Modification*. 259–266. Orono, Peopling of the Americas Publication Centre for the Study of the First Americans, Institute for the Quaternary Studies, University of Maine.

Scheinsohn, V. (2010) *Hearts and Bones: bone raw material exploitation in Tierra del Fuego.* Oxford, Archaeopress (British Archaeological Report S2094).

Scheinsohn, V. and Ferretti, J. L. (1995) Mechanical properties of bone materials as related to design and function of prehistoric tools from Tierra del Fuego (Argentina). *Journal of Archaeological Science* 22, 711–717.

Semenov, S. (1964) *Prehistoric Technology.* Wiltshire, Moonraker Press.

Shipman, P. (1989) Altered bones from Olduvai Gorge, Tanzania: techniques, problems and implications of their recognition. In R. Bonnichsen and M. Sorg (eds), *Bone Modification,* 317–334. Orono, Peopling of the Americas Publications, Center for the Study of the First Americans, Institute for Quaternary Studies, University of Maine.

Sidéra, I. and Legrand, A. (2006) Tracéologie fonctionnelle des matières osseuses: une méthode. *Bulletin de la Société. Préhistorique Française* 103 (2), 291–304.

CHAPTER 12

Beyond Stones: Bone as Raw Material for Tools in the Central Plateau of Santa Cruz, Argentinean Patagonia

Laura Miotti and Laura Marchionni

Archaeofaunistic studies in Patagonia have focused on the osseous materials to make taphonomic, paleoenvironmental and economic inferences. Until twenty years ago, however, bone was rarely taken into account as a raw material for tool manufacturing. Archaeological excavations on the Central Plateau in the province of Santa Cruz allow us to formulate interpretations about use, decision-making, and the role of bone as a raw material in technological chains of tool/ornament manufacturing. This paper presents the variability within tool types from three localities with human occupation on the Central Plateau of Santa Cruz, the archaeological sites of AEP-1 at Piedra Museo, caves 3 and 13 at Los Toldos, and Maripe Cave at La Primavera, at two moments: the Pleistocene/Holocene Transition and Middle Holocene. Results indicate a high degree of bone tool design for both chronological blocks. The standardization of forms and high degree of transformation found in some of these tools allow us to infer the presence of a curation strategy. This high degree of transformation was registered in other contexts within this region and for the same moments in time. Toward the middle Holocene, a wider spectrum of taxa was observed in the bones used as raw material for tools and ornaments.

Keywords
Bone technology; Argentina; Patagonia; Central Plateau; Pleistocene/Holocene.

Introduction and goals

Although the movement and use of rocks and mineral pigments was and continues to be the reason for initiating several archaeological projects in the Patagonian region (Aschero 1975, 1983; Mansur-Franchomme 1983; Franco and Borrero 1996; Aguerre 1997; Nami 2000; Cattáneo 2002; Hermo 2008, among others), in southern Patagonia and the Mesopotamian area of the La Plata river basin there has also been an increasing number of studies of bone technology, producing reconsiderations about the technology and circulation of bone tools among hunter-gatherers. In addition to lithic objects, the presence of bone artefacts on archaeological sites on the Central Plateau of Santa Cruz province is very common although little is known about this class of artefact. In this paper, we will add to what is known about the faunal materials, not only as food waste, but also as important technological pieces in tool production chains. Likewise, it appears that bones were used as exchange goods and as items in social communication (Binford 1978; Hayden 1998). When these artefacts appear as curated (Binford 1978) or as formal tools (Andrefsky 1991, 1994), they begin to look like a material with specific economic and technological qualities generating within these objects technological, social and symbolic implications (Jackson 1989–90; Scheinsohn 1997; Miotti and Marchionni 2008; Borella and Buc 2009; Borrero and Borella 2010; Buc and Pérez Jimeno 2010; Marani and Cardillo 2010; Paunero *et al.* 2010; Pérez Jimeno *et al.* 2010).

The goal of this paper is to provide new information on the use of bone as a raw material for tools and ornaments and on the technological changes that may have occurred since the initial peopling of the Central Plateau region in Santa Cruz. The proportion of stone artefacts in the area is always higher than that of bone artefacts; stones of excellent quality used in the production of lithic artefacts are abundant, supporting the use of this raw material for the entire human occupation of *c.* 11,000 years. We believe that bone must have been more important among hunter-gatherer societies than archaeologists imagine at present. The indifference or lack of interest displayed towards this class of artefacts during previous decades may be connected to the great archaeological visibility of lithic materials in Patagonia on the ground surface as well as in stratigraphic position. The poor preservation of bone has led to low archaeological visibility.

In order to explain the artefact variability found at sites on the Central Plateau during the human hunter-gatherer occupation, the theoretical model formulated by Vivian Scheinsohn (1997) was applied (Table 12.1). Scheinsohn developed this model for bone tools from archaeological sites in the Beagle Channel region, in Tierra del Fuego. In this paper, the bone tools come from stratigraphic sites in three different archaeological localities: Alero el Puesto (AEP-1) at Piedra Museo, Maripe Cave at La Primavera, and Caves 3 and 13, both in Los Toldos. These archaeological sites are located on the Deseado Massif, Santa Cruz, Argentina (Fig. 12.1). The goal is to provide new information about the use of bones as raw material to make artefacts and the possible technological changes that occurred in their manufacture after the initial settlement of the Central Plateau of Santa Cruz, by comparing contemporaneous artefacts from these three localities.

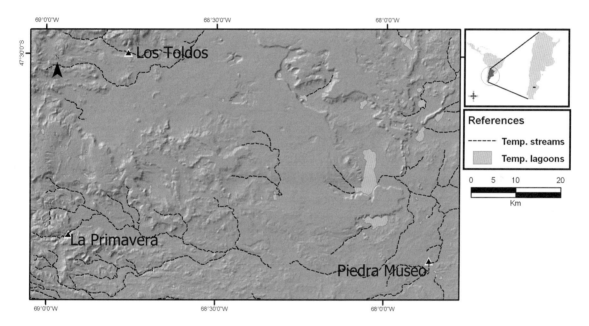

Figure 12.1 Study area, Central Plateau region of Santa Cruz province, showing the location of the archaeological sites.

Table 12.1 Synthesis of the evolutionary state model based on characteristics of the raw material (after Scheinsohn 1997).

CHARACTERISTICS	EVOLUTIONARY STATES OF RAW MATERIAL USE		
	Experimentation	*Exploitation*	*Abandonment*
Design diversity	high	low	this raw material falls into disuse
Standard basic design	low standardisation & high morphological & metrical variability	high standardisation & low morphological & metrical variability	possible causes: replacement of raw material with better ones
Raw material diversity	high	low	Incorporation of new raw material but lack of adjustment with new technologies
Diversity of techniques	high competition among techniques	low without techniques competition	extinction of human population

Material and methods

The samples are divided into two temporal blocks: Pleistocene/Holocene Transition and Early Holocene (13–8 ka BP) coinciding with the human exploration and colonization phase and the Middle Holocene (7.9–3.5 ka BP) as the moment in which Patagonian societies consolidated their territories (Borrero 1990; Miotti 1998; Miotti and Salemme 1999). The sample comprises 27 tools: four of them correspond to the first temporal block, while 23 come from mid Holocene layers (Table 12.2). All of them come from specific stratigraphic locations at each site. In all cases, they were recorded with 3-D coordinates.

Here we will present only formal tools although in Piedra Museo and La Primavera there are many informal artefacts which are not used in this study because they are part of Laura Marchionni's on-going PhD thesis. The artefacts were examined by eye and at low magnifications (10–30×).

The most abundant tools are made from camelid bone with the most common species at the sites being guanaco (*Lama guanicoe*) (N=7) as well as a single piece assigned to a camelid indet. There are ten tools manufactured from mammalian long bones. Some may correspond to skeletal elements from camelids but do not display diagnostic features to identify them to the level of genus or species. Two tools were made from canid bones and seven from the bones of medium-sized birds (i.e. wild geese, swans, Anatidae). There are no tools recorded that were made from the bones of flightless birds. This point is important because the long bones of Rheidae have good characteristics for the manufacture of tools, and skeletal elements of these flightless birds were found in archaeological sites as remains of food. However, their bones were never transformed into tools in any of the analyzed contexts (Table 12.3).

Environment and archaeological localities

Patagonia, which seems to be a homogeneous environment, actually comprises a wide spectrum of environments and resources with two main biomes: woodland in the Andean region, and steppe in the Extra-Andean region. It is assumed that there were also significant regional ecological differences in the past in this region. The studied area (Fig. 12.1) lies in the major and continuous stretch of steppes. However, the Central Plateau of Santa Cruz province is an independent geologic block with a particular environment. This geophysical structure is a volcanic plate known as the Nesocratón Del Deseado or the Deseado Massif (Di Giusto *et al.* 1980; Panza 1994).

Toward the west, the basaltic plateau is crosscut by deep ravines, which toward the east dwindle into ephemeral shallow creeks; interior drainage basins (bajos) and lagoons are very common; volcanic cones and tuff formations produce a hilly landscape rather than a monotonous plateau, more typical of the Patagonian steppe.

The sites

Los Toldos

Las Cuevas ravine, close to the Los Toldos ranch, stretches south from the middle course of the Deseado River (Fig. 12.1). The landscape in this locality is composed of volcanic plateaus which are cut by temporary river courses that determine levels from 450 masl to 600 masl in the highest plateaus and hills. This place is very rich in archaeological remains, many of which were found in the numerous caves and rock-shelters. The two caves considered here are located in Las Cuevas ravine which contains twelve additional caves and some rock-shelters.

Cave 3 is located on the southern margin of the stream. It is 20 m wide and 22 m deep. Its height decreases from 6 m at the entrance to 1.5 m in the deepest part of the two-chambered cave. The cave structure and the archaeological remains suggest that the settlement must have featured multiple activities, with a long occupational sequence (12 layers) dated between 12.6 ka BP and 4.5 ka BP. The walls and roof of the cave are covered with painted rock art (Cardich 1987). A detailed quantitative faunal analysis has been carried out for this site (Miotti 1998, chapter 7). The rock art mainly takes the form of hand stencils, constituting the oldest "Hand Stencil Style" in the region (Cardich 1987; Carden 2009).

Despite the fact that the guanaco remains predominant in the Pleistocene/Holocene Transition as well as in the Holocene faunal materials, *Lama gracilis*, *Hippidion saldiasi* and bird

Table 12.2 Distribution of tools analyzed and expressed on chronological and geographical scales.

Chronological blocks	Piedra Museo AEP-1 rock-shelter	La Primavera Maripe Cave	Los Toldos		Total Tools
			Cave 3	Cave 13	
13–7.8 Ka BP	1	–	3	–	4
7. 7–3.2 Ka BP	4	12	5	2	23
Total	5	12	8	2	27

Table 12.3 Morphological and technological attributes of the analyzed artefacts and their analogous names in other classifications.

			CHARACTERISTICS OF BONE TOOLS			MORPHOLOGICAL GROUPS		OTHERS CLASSIFICATIONS			
Temporal block	*Site*	*Locality*	*taxa*	*element*	*portion*	*Scheinson 1997*	*Fano Martinez et al. 2005; Chauviere et Rigaud 2005*	*Binford 1978*	*Andrefsky 1991; 1994*	*Hayden 1998*	*N° figure*
Pleistocene/ Holocene transition and Early Holocene	AEP-1	PM	Camelidae	metapodial	back-medial diaphysis	PUNCAM	awl	curated	formal	practice	3
	C3	LT	Mammalia	Long bone	diaphysis	PUNMAM?	awl	curated	formal	practice	4a
	C3	LT	Mammalia	Long bone	diaphysis	PUNMAM?	awl	curated	formal	practice	4b
	C3	LT	*L. guanicoe*	Tibia	distal	PUNCAM	awl	curated	formal	practice	4c
Middle Holocene	AEP-1	PM	*L. guanicoe*	Metapodial	front-back diaphysis	without correlate	burin	curated	formal	practice	6
	AEP-1	PM	*L. guanicoe*	Radio-ulna	front diaphysis	PUNCAM	bipoint	curated	formal	practice	5a
	AEP-1	PM	*Cannis* sp.	Tibia	distal	PUNCAN	awl	curated	formal	practice	10c
	AEP-1	PM	Mammalia	Long bone	diaphysis	indet.	indet.	indet.	indet.	indet.	without figure
	C13	LT	Birds	Long bone	diaphysis	without group	tube/mouthpiece	curated	formal	prestige	8
	C13	LT	*Cannis (P.) culpaeus*	Femur	proximal	without correlate	preform ornament	curated	formal	prestige	9
	C3	LT	Birds	Long bone	diaphysis	without correlate	tube/mouthpiece	curated	formal	prestige	without figure
	C3	LT	Birds	Long bone	diaphysis	without correlate	tube/mouthpiece	curated	formal	prestige	without figure
	C3	LT	Birds	Long bone	diaphysis	without correlate	tube/mouthpiece	curated	formal	prestige	without figure
	C3	LT	Birds	Long bone	diaphysis	without correlate	tube/mouthpiece	curated	formal	prestige	without figure
	C3	LT	Birds	Long bone	diaphysis	without correlate	tube/mouthpiece	curated	formal	prestige	without figure
	CM	LP	Mammalia	Long bone	diaphysis	PUNMAMROM?	rome point	curated	formal	practice/ prestige?	5b
	CM	LP	Mammalia	Long bone	diaphysis	without correlate	engraving fragment	curated	formal	prestige	7a
	CM	LP	Mammalia	Long bone	diaphysis	without correlate	engraving fragment	curated	formal	prestige	7c
	CM	LP	Mammalia	Long bone	diaphysis	without correlate	engraving fragment	curated	formal	prestige	7d
	CM	LP	Mammalia	Long bone	diaphysis	without correlate	engraving fragment	curated	formal	prestige	7e
	CM	LP	Birds	Long bone	diaphysis	without correlate	tube/mouthpiece	curated	formal	prestige	7b
	CM	LP	Mammalia	Long bone	diaphysis	PUNMAM?	awl	curated	formal	practice	10a
	CM	LP	Mammalia	Long bone	diaphysis	PUNMAM?	awl	curated	formal	practice	10b
	CM	LP	*L. guanicoe*	Radio-ulna	front-back diaphysis	without correlate	retoucher	expedient	informal	practice	11a
	CM	LP	*L. guanicoe*	Metapodial	front diaphysis	without correlate	retoucher	expedient	informal	practice	11b
	CM	LP	*L. guanicoe*	Metapodial	px. front diaphysis	without correlate	retoucher	expedient	informal	practice	11c
	CM	LP	*L. guanicoe*	Tibia	diaphysis	without correlate	retoucher	expedient	informal	practice	11d

Abbreviations: AEP-1= Alero el Puesto 1; C3= Cave 3; C13= Cave 13; CM= Maripe Cave; PM= Piedra Museo; LT= Los Toldos and LP= La Primavera remains were also identified. The high percentage of guanaco (*Lama guanicoe*) in the Casapedrense and Patagoniense occupations, both the middle and late Holocene respectively, shows an increasing tendency towards the specialization in the hunting of this animal (Miotti 1998). Here, it is not necessary to illustrate the connections between the rock art and the archaeofauna found in this cave since it is an extreme case in which the representation of animals or their parts is completely lacking in the paintings, whereas the total NISP for all the identified species and genera includes 3523 specimens.

Cave 13 is located on the left margin of Las Cuevas Canyon. The excavated area in the cave is relatively small (12.37 m²) compared to the total surface which is quite large (100 m wide and 7 m front to back). Some anthropomorphic figures and a hand stencils have been noted in addition to the excavations. Remains of red paint can be found elsewhere in the cave although no patterns could be distinguished because of the poor preservation of the paintings.

The human occupations belong to the Middle Holocene. In both components, the Casapedrense and Patagoniense, the guanaco was the species selected as a basic resource by the hunters although towards the end of the occupation small birds (Passeriformes; *Phalacrocorax* sp.), armadillo (*Zaedyus pichyi*) and red fox (nowadays *Lycalopex culpaeus* but termed *Canis (Pseudalopex) culpaeus* in previous works, Miotti 1998, 2008) may have been used as complementary resources (Table 12.3). The analysis of these remains, together with the lithic materials, the presence of a post hole and several hearth remains suggest that secondary processing of prey animals took place here where they were consumed. Lithic and bone implements were also manufactured on-site. Thus, this settlement must have functioned as a *locus* of multiple activities.

Piedra Museo

Piedra Museo is located 120 km south-east of Los Toldos (Fig. 12.1). Several open-air sites and rock-shelters have been found in this locality, situated on the Central Plateau, across the Zanjón Elornia stream which flows into the Laguna Grande. Excavations were carried out at the AEP-1 rock-shelter, which lies in an enclosed basin and acts as a topographic trap for hunting animals by ambush (Miotti 1995; Miotti *et al.* 1999).

AEP-1 features two main archaeological contexts, the oldest one dates to between 12.8–9.2 ka BP and the most recent settlement to *c.* 7.6 ka BP, on average. The excavated area is about 47 m², representing 80% of the surface under the rock-shelter.

Six stratigraphic units were defined based on the sedimentological characteristics (texture, colour, soil structures, granulometry, and layer limits). The preservation of bones, the spatial distribution, and bone modifications in each layer also contributed to the division of this deposit into discreet units. The site has an edaphic profile where there is a noticeable

unconformity between Units 1 and 2 but the other stratigraphic boundaries are transitional and gradual (Zárate *et al.* 2000).

AEP-1 is the first site in the Extra-Andean Patagonian region of Argentina where fluted lithic points, referred to as fishtail points (FTP), were found in the oldest major component, associated with a high resolution faunal assemblage (extinct and living species) and bone tools. AMS radiocarbon analyses date the earliest human occupations of the site to between 13 and 11 ka BP.

At 0.70 m above the oldest archaeological component of AEP-1, another context was recorded with a hearth, remains of living autochthonous fauna and lithic artefacts similar to those from Fell III representing a late Toldense Industry and, on a regional level, Rio Pinturas I; all horizons dating to the Early Holocene (Miotti 1995; Miotti *et al.* 1999; Cattáneo 2002).

The paintings and carvings in the rock-shelters of the Piedra Museo outcrop have been detailed in several previous works (see Carden 2009). There are many animal footprints engraved over the horizontal surface of some of the boulders within the rock-shelters. Among these, the bird tracks are the most abundant, followed by footprints of guanaco, felid and horse. The main protein resources from the Pleistocene to the Middle Holocene, however, was the guanaco (*Lama guanicoe*) with rheids (ostrich), birds, and small/medium sized mammals as complementary sources of meat.

La Primavera

Maripe Cave is located at the base of a cliff in La Primavera valley, where one of the stream tributaries of Zanjones Blanco and Rojo Basin flows. Several rock-shelters open onto both sides of the valley along this wetland area (10 km in length). La Primavera integrates the same fluvial basin where Piedra Museo is located but is 70 km to the west and at an altitude of *c.* 500 masl (Fig. 12.1).

Maripe is a big cave (*c.* 22 × 26 m). Excavations began here in 2003 (Miotti *et al.* 2007). There were several human occupations in this cave throughout the Pleistocene/Holocene Transition to the Middle Holocene 9.5 ka BP to 3.2 ka BP (Miotti *et al.* 2007). Guanaco seems to have been the main faunal resource exploited at this site, just as in the previous localities.

Assumptions

The main characteristics and variables involved in the theoretical model used here have been summarized in Table 12.1. Based on the theoretical expectations, we intend to answer when and where the technological changes could have occurred regarding the use of bone as a raw material in the region. Given that excellent lithic raw materials are abundant and varied in the Central Plateau of Santa Cruz (Miotti 1995;

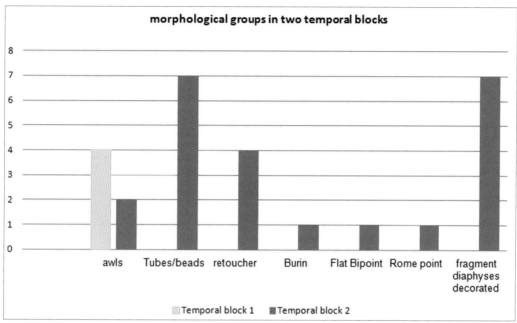

Figure 12.2 Bone tools from the Late Pleistocene (temporal block 1) and Middle Holocene (temporal block 2) from the sites at Los Toldos, Piedra Museo, and La Primavera.

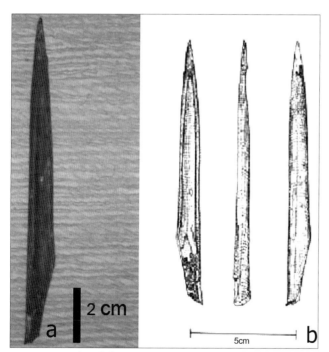

Figure 12.3 Awl made from a camelid metapodial from stratigraphic unit (SU) 5 at AEP-1, Piedra Museo (c. 11 ka BP); a) photo, b) drawing.

Cattáneo 2002; Hermo 2008; Miotti 2008; Hermo and Miotti 2011), the location of archaeological sites on this massif suggests that acquiring raw materials for the manufacturing of artefacts was not a problem for these hunter-gatherer societies.

Thus, the use of bone tools would not be connected to a lack of good stone in the region (Binford 1993). More likely the use of bone is related to it being a better raw material to work leathers, skins, and fibres (Musters 1979), as bone has more plasticity than stone and therefore is less likely to cause damage. Bone modifications connected to butchering are not considered here as they have been presented in previous papers (Miotti and Salemme 2005; Miotti and Marchionni 2009, 2011; Marchionni *et al.* 2010).

Archaeological tools on the Patagonian Central Plateau

Based on the intensity of modification (design and planning) needed to achieve a specific shape or size of tool a manufacturing continuum has been identified, classified by others as formal to informal worked osseous materials (Andrefsky 1994; Choyke 2001; Choyke and Bartosiewicz 2001), practical to prestige tools (Hayden 1998), or expeditive to curated tools (Binford 1978). The analyzed sample of bone tools is summarized in Table 12.3 and Figure 12.2.

Bone Tools from the Pleistocene/Holocene Transition and Early Holocene

Four bone tools were recorded (Table 12.3) in the first temporal block, corresponding to human occupations between 11.5–8.5 Ka BP. The tools belong to the morphological group of awls (Chauviere and Rigaud 2005; Fano Martínez *et al.* 2005) and

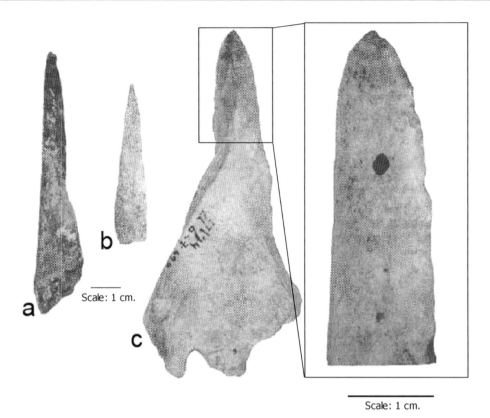

*Figure 12.4 Awls from Cave 3, Los Toldos; a) and b) made from mammalian long bone and c) made from the distal tibia of guanaco (*Lama guanicoe*) from the Toldense component, c. 10–9 ka BP (from Miotti 1998, 123).*

come from the lowest stratigraphic levels of the AEP-1 rock-shelter at Piedra Museo and Cave 3 at Los Toldos. The awls were made from the cortical tissue of long bones from mammals and, more specifically, camelids (Figs 12.3 and 12.4). These tools are not decorated but the skeletal elements display high degrees of modification by abrasion and polish, in this sense having a design corresponding to the technological category of a formal tool. According to Scheinsohn's categorisation (1997) these would be artefacts corresponding to her PUNCAM (point on camelid bone). The awl from Piedra Museo was most probably made on the long bone from a camelid species, although it might be better to say large-sized mammal.

Bone tools from the Middle Holocene

During the second temporal block (7.7–3.2 ka BP), morphological groups and artefactual intra-group variability increased (Table 12.3). Variability in the osseous raw material rises with the incorporation of bones from canids and birds in tool manufacture. However, guanaco bones remain most important for the production of tools and ornaments (Figs 12.5–12.11).

Discussion and conclusion

Since the beginning of human occupations in the late Pleistocene of the Central Plateau, bone as a raw material was exploited to make formal tools suitable for many uses. Examples of such planned tools are the awls from Los Toldos and Piedra Museo. This high standardization continues in the Middle Holocene contexts at Los Toldos, La Primavera and Piedra Museo.

Decorative design adds value to the tools as it implies longer production times on the part of craftspeople. Although such additional effort would not have a direct bearing on the efficiency of such tools, it can be interpreted as a social phenomenon that would bring craftspeople and their tools together in a sort of familial relationship of belonging and/or prestige (Hayden 1998). Examples of such decorative pieces include the tubes and fragments of mammal and bird bone diaphyses with a pattern of parallel engraved lines on them (Figs 12.7 and 12.8).

On the basis of the evidence from these three archaeological sites, it is clear that there was no stage of experimentation in the osseous raw materials at these Central Plateau contexts, as had been expected based on the evolutionary model employed

Figure 12.5 a) Drawing and b) photo, of a formal spear point from SU 2 at AEP-1, Piedra Museo; c) a double bevel spear point with decorative engraving, made from mammalian long bone, from Maripe Cave, La Primavera (c. 8.3–7.5 ka BP).

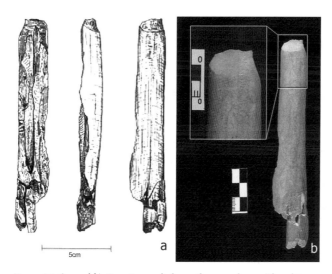

Figure 12.6 a and b) Drawing and photo of a retoucher or "détachée par ruptura après entaillage au flanc du burin" (Chauvier and Rigaud 2005, 237), made from a Lama guanicoe *metapodial, from SU 2 at AEP-1, Piedra Museo (c. 7.5 ka BP).*

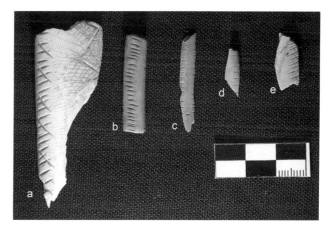

Figure 12.7 a, c, d, and e) Fragments decorated with engravings of parallel lines on mammalian diaphyses and b) tube/bead or mouthpiece decorated with a pattern of parallel lines engraved on a bird diaphysis, from Maripe Cave, La Primavera.

in the analysis. Therefore, considering the formal and technical similarities of the design of bone fragments and tubes from long bone diaphyses found at diverse paleoindian contexts in the Americas (c. 11.6–10 Ka BP) (Jackson 1989–90; Danise and Jerrems 2005; Johnson *et al.* 2000; Johnson 2005;

Paunero *et al.* 2010), the presence of decorated bones on these Patagonian sites suggests that humans arrived here with an extended knowledge of the use of bone as a raw material. This idea is also supported by the widespread presence of formal tools, where the epiphyses are retained, from archaeological

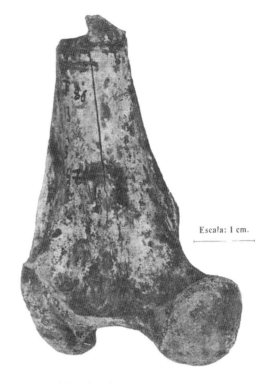

Figure 12.9 Tool (core from beads?) made on the proximal epiphysis femur of Canis *(P.)* culpaeus *(red fox) from the Casapedrense component, Cave 13, Los Toldos (Miotti 1998, 155).*

Figure 12.8 Fragment of decorated tube made from bird diaphysis, from Casapedrense component, Cave 13, Los Toldos (Miotti 1998, 155).

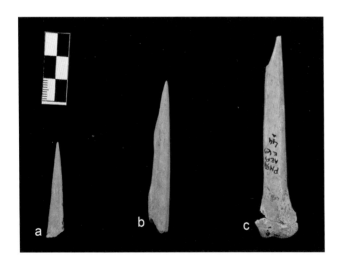

Figure 12.10 a and b) Awls made from mammalian long bones from Maripe Cave, La Primavera, and c) awl made on Canis *(P.)* culpaeus *(red fox) from AEP-1, Piedra Museo (c. 7.5 ka BP).*

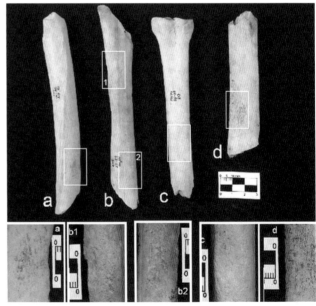

Figure 12.11 Retouchers made from a) guanaco radius- ulna, b) and c) metapodials, and d) tibia, from Maripe Cave La Primavera.

contexts in the Americas during Late Pleistocene (*c.* 12–11.6 ka BP). Hence, we can infer that the sophisticated knowledge of bones as raw materials (stage of exploitation in Scheinsohn 1997) was already in place among Old and New World hunter-gatherers of the Pleistocene.

Conclusions

The experimentation stage (Scheinsohn 1997) is not present for the bone tools found at early archaeological sites in the Central Plateau region of Santa Cruz, in terms of the technologically defined characteristics, in the evolutionary model formulated for the southern Patagonia sub-region. All the osseous raw materials from archaeological contexts on the Central Plateau display a detailed knowledge of faunal resources as subsistence items, in technology and as symbolic exchange goods. Technological use of bone was efficient and showed planned design from the time of the first human occupations in the area.

We found a pattern of standardized techniques, designs and use of certain bones to produce tools during the Pleistocene/Holocene Transition and Early Holocene, as well as in the Middle Holocene occupations. This discovery is a good indicator that these hunting and gathering societies fully exploited the bones available to them for the production of bone tools from the beginning of Patagonian settlement.

Bone was used for its intrinsic qualities and for specific aims and not as a substitute or alternative to another raw material such as stone.

Acknowledgements

A poster version of this paper was presented at the ICAZ Conference, Raw Material session, París, 2010. Funds from Consejo Nacional de Investigaciones Científicas y Tecnológicas (CONICET), Agencia Nacional de Promoción Científica y Tecnológica, and University of La Plata (UNLP): PICT 1552 ANPCyT, PIP 5885- CONICET, PI 550 FCNyM-UNLP supported different aspects of this research. Pico Truncado government authorities contributed logistically during fieldwork. We are grateful for the valuable suggestions made by Luis Orquera and Vivian Scheinsohn, and to Alice Choyke and Sonia O'Connor for improving the paper.

Bibliography

Aguerre, A. M. (1997) *Replanteo de la Industria Toldense. Arqueología de Patagonia Centro-Meridional.* Unpublished doctoral thesis, Universidad de Buenos Aires.

Andrefsky, W. (1991) Inferring trends in prehistoric settlement behavior from lithic production technology in the southern plains. *North American Archaeology* 12 (2), 129–144.

Andrefsky, W. (1994) Raw-material availability and the organization of the technology. *American Antiquity* 59 (1), 21–34.

Aschero, C. (1975) Ensayo para una clasificación morfológica de artefactos líticos aplicada a estudios tipológicos comparados. *Informe al CONICET.* Buenos Aires, ms.

Aschero, C. (1983) Ensayo para una clasificación morfológica de artefactos líticos aplicada a estudios tipológicos comparativos. Apéndices A–C. *Revisión. Cátedra de Ergología y Tecnología* (FFyL-UBA). Buenos Aires, ms.

Binford, L. (1978) *Nunamiut Ethnoarchaeology.* Albuquerque, University of New Mexico, Academic Press.

Binford, L. (1993) Bones for stones. Considerations of analogues for features found on the Central Russian Plain. In O. Soffer and N. Praslov (eds), *From Kostenki to Clovis. Upper Paleolithic-Paleo-indian adaptations,* 101–124. New York and London, Plenum Press.

Borella, F. and Buc, N. (2009) Ópticas y ópticos. Una aproximación a la tecnología ósea en la Bahía de San Antonio (Río Negro, Argentina). In M. Salemme, F. Santiago, M. Alvarez, E. Piana, M. Vázquez and E. Mansur (eds), *Arqueología de la Patagonia. Una mirada desde el último confín,* Tomo 1, 421–432. Ushuaia, Editorial Utopías.

Borrero, L. (1990) Fuego-Patagonian bone assemblages and the problem of communal guanaco hunting. In L. B. Davis and B. O. K. Reeves (eds), *Hunters of the Past,* 373–399. London, Unwin Hyman.

Borrero, L. A. and Borella, F. (2010) Harpoons and travellers: Fuegian ethnographic collections and the recent archaeological record. *Before Farming* 1, article 3, 1–14.

Buc, N. and Pérez Jimeno, L. (2010) Puntas para la comparación de la tecnología ósea en el Paraná inferior y medio. In M. Gutiérrez, M. De Nigris, P. Fernández, M. Giardina, A. Gil, A. Izeta, G. Neme, and H. Yacobaccio (eds), *Zooarqueología a Principios del Siglo XXI. Aportes Teóricos, Metodológicos y Casos de Estudio,* 439–451. Buenos Aires, Ediciones del Espinillo.

Carden, N. (2009) *Imágenes a Través del Tiempo. Arte Rupestre y Construcción Ssocial del Paisaje en la Meseta Central de Santa Cruz.* Buenos Aires, Sociedad Argentina de Antropología.

Cardich, A. (1987) Arqueología de Los Toldos y El Ceibo (provincia de Santa Cruz, Argentina). In L. Núñez and B. Meggers (eds), *Investigaciones Saleoindias al sur de la Iínea Ecuatorial,* Estudios Atacameños, 8, 98–117. Chile.

Cattáneo, G. (2002) *Una Aproximación a la Organización de la Tecnología Lítica entre los Cazadores-Recolectores de Fines del Pleistoceno en la Patagonia Argentina.* Unpublished doctoral thesis, Universidad Nacional de La Plata.

Chauviere, F. and Rigaud, A. (2005) Les "sagaies" à "base raccourcie" ou les avatars de la typologie: du technique au "non- fonctionnel" Dans le Magadalénien à navettes de la Garenne (Saint- Marcel, Indre). In V. Dujardin (ed.), *Industrie Osseuse et Parares du Solutréen au Magdalénien en Europe,* Mémoire XXXIX, 233–242. Société Préhistorique Française.

Choyke, A. M. (2001) Late Neolithic red deer canine beads and their imitations. In Choyke, A. and Bartosiewicz, L. (eds), *Crafting Bone – Skeletal Technologies Through Time and Space,* 251–266. Oxford, Archaeopress (British Archaeological Report S937).

Choyke, A. and Bartosiewicz, L. (eds) (2001) *Crafting Bone – Skeletal Technologies Through Time and Space.* Oxford, Archaeopress (British Archaeological Report S937).

Danise, A. and Jerrems, J. (2005) More bits and pieces: a new look at Lahontan chronology and human occupations. In R. Bonnichsen, B. Lepper, D. Stanford and M. Waters (eds), *Paleoamerican Origins: beyond Clovis,* 51–81. Center for the Study of the First Americans, Texas A&M University.

Di Giusto, J. M., Di Persia, C. A. and Pezzi, E. (1980) Nesocratón del Deseado. *Geología Regional Argentina* II, 1389–1430. Córdoba, Academia Nacional de Ciencias.

Fano Martínez, M. A., d'Errico, F. and Vanhaeren, M. (2005) Magdalenian bone industry from El Horno cave (Ramales, Cantabria, Spain). In V. Dujardin (ed.), *Industrie Osseuse et Parares du Solutréen au Magdalénien en Europe. Mémoire* XXXIX, 177–196. France, Société Préhistorique Française.

Franco, N. and Borrero, L. (1996) El stress temporal y los artefactos líticos. La cuenca superior del río Santa Cruz. In J. Gómez Otero, (ed.), *Arqueología, Sólo Patagonia*, III Jornadas de Arqueología de la Patagonia, 341–348. Puerto Madryn, Argentina, Centro Nacional Patagónico, CONICET.

Hayden, B. (1998) Practical and Prestige Technologies: the evolution of material system. *Journal of Archaeological Method and Theory* 5 (1), 1–55.

Hermo, D. (2008) *Los Cambios en la Circulación de las Materias Primas Líticas en Ambientes Mesetarios de Patagonia. Una Aproximación para la Construcción de los Paisajes Arqueológicos de las Sociedades Cazadoras-recolectoras.* Unpublished doctoral thesis, Universidad Nacional de La Plata.

Hermo, D. and Miotti, L. (2011) La obsidiana en el Nesocratón del Deseado (Santa Cruz, Argentina): extractos de una oscura biografía. In D. Hermo and L. Miotti (eds), *Biografías de Paisajes y Seres: visiones desde la arqueología Sudamericana,* 111–131. Córdoba, Argentina, Colección Contextos Humanos, Encuentro Grupo Editor.

Jackson, D. (1989–90) Retocadores extremos-laterales en contextos paleo-indios. *Anales del Instituto de la Patagonia* 19, 121–124.

Johnson, E. (2005) Late-Wisconsian mammoth procurement in the North American grassland. In R. Bonnichsen, B. Lepper, D. Stanford and M. Waters (eds), *Paleoamerican Origins: beyond Clovis,* 161–182. USA, Center for the Study of the First Americans, Texas A&M University.

Johnson, E., Politis, G., and Gutiérrez, M. (2000) Early Holocene bone technology at the La Olla 1 site, Atlantic coast of the Argentine Pampas. *Journal of Archaeological Science* 27 (6), 463–477.

Mansur-Franchomme, M. E. (1983) *Traces d'Utilisation et Technologie Lithique: examples de Patagonie.* Unpublished doctoral thesis. France, Bordeaux I Universite.

Marani, H. and Cardillo, M. (2010) Retocadores óseos de Saco Viejo (Río Negro, Argentina). Un enfoque morfogeométrico. In M. Gutiérrez, M. De Nigris, P. Fernández, M. Giardina, A. Gil, A. Izeta, G. Neme and H. Yacobaccio (eds), *Zooarqueología a Principios del Siglo XXI. Aportes Teóricos, Metodológicos y Casos de Estudio,* 453–458. Buenos Aires, Ediciones del Espinillo.

Marchionni, L. Miotti, L. and Mosquera, B. (2010) El uso de la fauna entre el Pleistoceno final y el Holoceno medio en la Patagonia extra-andina. In M. Gutiérrez, M. De Nigris, P. Fernández, M. Giardina, A. Gil, A. Izeta, G. Neme and H. Yacobaccio (eds), *Zooarqueología a Principios del Siglo XXI: aportes teóricos, metodológicos y casos de estudio*, 250–271. Buenos Aires, Ediciones del Espinillo.

Miotti, L. (1995) Piedra Museo Locality: a Special Place in the New World. *Current Research in the Pleistocene* 12, 37–40.

Miotti, L. (1998) *Zooarqueologia de la Meseta Central y Costa de la Provincia de Santa Cruz: en enfoque de las estrategias adaptativas aborígenes y los paleoambientes.* Mendoza [1989], Museo de Historia Natural de San Rafael.

Miotti, L. (2008) Household and sacred landscapes among Holocene hunter-gatherers of Patagonia's Central Plateau. *Before Farming* 3, article 1, 5–44.

Miotti, L. and Marchionni, L. (2008) El uso de una materia prima no tradicional en la meseta: instrumentos más allá de las piedras. In M. Gutiérrez, M. De Nigris, P. Fernández, M. Giardina, A. Gil, A. Izeta, G. Neme and H. Yacobaccio (eds), *Book of Abstracts I Congreso Nacional de Zooarqueología Argentina,* 24–25. Malargüe, Mendoza.

Miotti L. and Marchionni, L. (2009) Procesando huesos: entre la etnografía y la arqueología. In M. Salemme, F. Santiago, M. Álvarez, E. Piana, M. Vázquez and E. Mansur (eds), *Arqueología de la Patagonia. Una mirada desde el último confín vomo II,* 787–798. Ushuaia, Tierra del Fuego, Utopías.

Miotti, L. and Marchionni, L. (2011) Archaeofauna at Middle Holocene in AEP-1 Rockshelter, Santa Cruz, Argentina. Taphonomic implications. *Quaternary International* 245, 148–158.

Miotti, L. and Salemme, M. (1999) Biodiversity, taxonomic richness and specialists-generalista during Late Pleistocene/Early Holocene times in Pampa and Patagonia (Argentina, Southern South America). *Quaternary International* 53/54, 53–68.

Miotti, L. and Salemme, M. (2005) Hunting and butchering events at late Pleistocene and early Holocene in Piedra Museo (Patagonia, Southernmost South America). In R. Bonnichsen (ed.), *Paleoamerican Prehistory: colonization models, biological populations, and human adaptations,* 141–151. Center for the Study of the First Americans, University of Texas A&M.

Miotti, L., Vázquez, M. and Hermo, D. (1999) Piedra Museo un Yamnagoo Pleistocénico en la colonización de la meseta de Santa Cruz. El estudio de la arqueofauna. In R. Goñi (ed.), *Soplando en el Viento,* 113–136. Neunquén- Buenos Aires, Universidad Nacional del Comahue y Facultad de Humanidades.

Miotti, L., Hermo, D., Magnin, L. Carden, N., Marchionni, L., Terranova, E., Mosquera, B., and Salemme, M. (2007) Resolución arqueológica en la Cueva Maripe (Santa Cruz, Argentina). In F. Morello, M. Martinic, A. Prieto and G. Bahamonde (eds), *Arqueología de Fuego-Patagonia: levantando piedras, desenterrando huesos…y develando arcanos,* 555–569. Punta Arenas, Chile, Ediciones CEQUA.

Musters, G. (1979) *Vida Entre los Patagones.* Buenos Aires, Solar Hachette.

Nami, H. (2000*) Tecnología y Secuencias de Reducción Paleoindias de Norte y Sudamérica: un estudio comparativo y experimental.* Unpublished doctoral thesis, Facultad de Filosofía y Letras, Universidad de Buenos Aires.

Panza, J. L. (1994) Hoja Geológica 4969-II. Tres Cerros. Provincia de Santa Cruz. *Boletin* 213. Argentina, Dirección Nacional del Servicio Geológico, Secretaría de Minería de la Nación.

Paunero, R., Paunero, M. and Ramos, D. (2010) Artefactos óseos en componentes del Pleistoceno Final de las localidades La María y Cerro Tres Tetas, Santa Cruz, Argentina. In M. Gutiérrez, M. De Nigris, P. Fernández, M. Giardina, A. Gil, A. Izeta, G. Neme and H. Yacobaccio (eds), *Zooarqueología a Principios del Siglo XXI. Aportes Teóricos, Metodológicos y Casos de Estudio,* 459–466. Buenos Aires, Ediciones del Espinillo.

Pérez Jimeno, L., Feulliet Terzaghi, M., and Escudero, S. (2010) Evidencias de tecnología ósea en la llanura aluvial del río Paraná Medio e inferior –margen santafecina. In M. Gutiérrez, M. De Nigris, P. Fernández, M. Giardina, A. Gil, A. Izeta, G. Neme and H. Yacobaccio (eds), *Zooarqueología a Principios del Siglo XXI. Aportes Teóricos, Metodológicos y Casos de Estudio,* 467–476. Buenos Aires, Ediciones del Espinillo.

Scheinsohn, V. G. (1997) *Explotación de Materias Primas Óseas en la Isla Grande de Tierra del Fuego.* Unpublished doctoral thesis, Facultad de Filosofía y Letras, Universidad de Buenos Aires.

Zárate, M., Blasi, A., and Rabassa, J. (2000) Geoarqueología de la localidad Piedra Museo. In Miotti, L., Paunero, R., Salemme, M. and Cattáneo, G. (eds), *Guía de Campo de la Visita a las Localidades Arqueológicas, INQUA,* 56–64. La Plata, Argentina, UNLP.

CHAPTER 13

The Meaning of "Smoothing" Implements from the Levantine PPNB, seen from the Basta Perspective

Cornelia Becker

Basta, one of the large PPNB-sites in the Southern Levant/Jordan, has yielded a total of 586 worked bones, mostly points, needles, ornamental accessories and flat "smoothing" utensils. The latter comprise a variety of types as far as the raw material, the kind of processing and the use wear are concerned. It is discussed whether the availability of particular skeletal material, manufacturing traditions and/or purely technical aspects dictated choice and processing. Another question touches their particular function: From their dating (7500–6700 cal. BC) the use of these tools in ceramic production can be excluded. Many interpretations of their function are possible but a connection with the construction of special archaeological features at Basta, such as the plastered walls, seems quite plausible.

Keywords
Basta; Jordan; Late PPNB; bone artefacts; smoothing implements; typology and function.

Introduction

Despite many valuable attempts to research bone manufacture in the Near East, substantial evidence about the bone technology in the Levant still is rather patchy, especially for the PPNB (Pre-Pottery Neolithic B; Kirkbride 1966a, 1966b; Stordeur 1981b, 1999; Marshall 1982; De Contenson 2000; Olsen 2000). Either relevant data are not yet published or artefacts are described only partially. In other cases, stratigraphical or contextual information is missing or at some large sites the PPNB is poorly represented among all periods (see also Le Dosseur 2006, 2008). However, relevant data for a diachronic comparison do exist, e.g. from Neolithic Çatal Höyük (N=565; Martin and Russell 1996; Russell 2001a, 2001b, 2005), from Jarmo (N=746; Watson 1983), Cyprus (Legrand 2007) and from Natufian sites in Israel (among others Bar-Yosef and Tchernov 1970; Stordeur 1981a; Campana 1989).

Bearing all this in mind, the artefactual material from Basta (N=586 implements), coming exclusively from the Late PPNB, is of major importance (Becker and Karasneh in press). But this assemblage, too, is not without its stumbling-blocks, as will be described later. A particular category of finds, the flat implements, will be the focus of the present paper. Although such artefacts are also evidenced at many other coeval sites, their function still is poorly understood, which is why they shall be presented here in greater detail.

The site and its history

Basta is located 20 km south of the famous Nabatean site of Petra in Jordan. It is set in the lower foothills east of the southern highlands' mountain ridge, at about 1460–1420 masl (Fig. 13.1). Between 1986 and 1992, five excavation

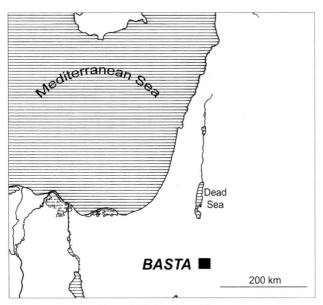

Figure 13.1 Location of Basta.

from the distant Southern Highlands. Marine molluscs and corals were imported from the Red Sea and the Mediterranean Sea for the manufacture of decorative items as were ostrich egg-shells from the Syrian steppes. One export from the region was high-quality flint, processed into bi-facial blade blanks (Gebel 2004, 10).

One explanation for the increase in the movement of goods might be that there was an increase in population as well as an exaggerated demand for particular materials and objects. Contacts over large distances must have existed and were most probably even intensified over decades. Quite naturally this must have led to an accumulation of knowledge. At the end of the PPNB, however, people abandoned their large farming communities, as they did in Basta as well. There is not yet enough information to completely answer whether or not an environmental crises, cf. the over-exploitation of resources and/or an increased aridity, or an internal systemic reason was responsible for this (cf. Kuijt 2000a, 2000b).

campaigns took place (A joint venture of Irbid University/ Jordan and the Free University/Berlin, Germany). Our aim was to reveal the structure of the settlement and collect information about habitation patterns, lithic technology, subsistence strategies and environmental considerations. Basta was a permanently inhabited site with an estimated size of 10–14 ha. It was part of the mega-site phenomenon that occurred in the Southern Levant during the Late PPNB – one of many reasons making this a rather unique period. The results from Basta support this view very well indeed (Gebel 2004). The aim of the analyses of tens of thousands of artefacts and ecofacts coming from the excavations at Basta, was to more properly understand how life was shaped in this community that existed over 600 years (Nissen *et al.* 1987, 1988, 1991; Gebel *et al.* 1988, 2004; Gebel 2004).

The population of Basta was highly advanced as far as domestic architecture was concerned and stood at the verge of experimenting with new techniques. In terms of economy, their production was half way between food gathering and food production: Hunting animals and collecting plants and fruits from a variety of biotopes still represented an important part of their diet. At the same time, domestic cereals and livestock-keeping provided, more or less, half of all food supplies (Neef 1997, 2004, 2005; Becker 1998, 2000a, 2000b, 2002, 2004, 2005). During this period, the inhabitants obviously tried to integrate new elements within their economic strategies: Domestic sheep were imported from the southern Taurus and domestic cattle from the Middle Euphrates via sites along the Levantine corridor. Additionally, linseed and flax, respectively, were most probably brought in from northern Palestine and Syria in addition to oak trees

The artefact material *in toto*

The final publication of the bone artefacts was initiated and completed (Becker and Karasneh in press) 18 years after the last campaign at Basta. On the one hand, the report was based on the MA thesis of Wajeeh Karasneh (1989) and, on the other, on a re-examination of all finds, including subsequently excavated material from later campaigns. Unfortunately, only 189 items out of 586 were available for this subsequent analysis. Over the years, the material had been stored in different places, put on exhibitions, etc. Thus, the whereabouts of some of the finds remained a mystery. Furthermore, only part of the artefacts had been copied to scale by draughts people at the excavation while others were only photographed. However, some additional information about the "vanished" items could be gathered from this photograph archive.

As a general impression, it could be said that bone processing at Basta was mostly connected to every day life and to the domestic sphere. Items with an individual decorative character such as paillettes, beads, rings and pendants, only occurred in lower frequencies and have already been discussed in the literature by B. D. Hermansen (1991, 1997, 2004). Another category of decorative artefacts were made from molluscs. They have been written about elsewhere as well (Nissen *et al.* 1987, 113f.; Hermansen 1991, 26ff.; Hermansen 2004, 95ff.; Reese forthcoming).

The entire worked bone assemblage comprises pointed implements (N=232), flat implements (N=41) and ornamental accessories (N=78). Twenty-eight items such as scoops, toggles, pressure flakers, spatulae and knives were classed together under "varia". Eleven items were characterised as unspecific *débitage* and 196 as "worked bones". The latter were not identifiable more precisely for reasons already mentioned.

Dating and context

The Basta artefacts are treated as coming from Late PPNB units without any stratigraphic differentiation. They are generally placed within a period running from 7500 to 6700 cal BC. More precise provenience is still not available. The greater part of the material stems from surface deposits and rubble layers. Consequently, nothing can be said neither of where these objects were manufactured nor of how they were used in particular spheres of living. A smaller quantity came to light in room fills or substructures within the inhabited area. Their place of recovery might reflect an activity at a particular spot or at least tells us where they were discarded or lost. The final interpretation has to be put aside as long as the function of the architectural units still is a matter for discussion.

The flat implements from Basta

This category of artefacts is quite plentiful (N=41). They comprise objects with a flat and elongated design. They differ in length and breadth, in the shaping of the ends (rounded, pointed, roof-like) and in the form of the edges (sharp, rectangular or rounded, sometimes in combination with denticulation and/or a perforation) as well as the use wear that can be observed on them. Seven types were distinguished here.

Type 1

The first category comprises very elongated slender implements with highly polished surfaces, sharply worn edges especially at the finished end sections of the artefacts (N=16; Fig. 13.2, 1). Only two of these objects were not made from (caprinae) ribs, but instead from a (caprinae) scapula and a long bone diaphysis respectively. It was not possible to identify any of these implements to species or genus. Those made from ribs were split along their length. No item in this category is preserved completely so it remains obscure how long they originally were. The longest, although still fragmented, implement of this type measures 202.5 mm. As far as preservation allows, the end parts of these implements are round in shape, almost spatula-ended. The bone compacta was cut away, most probably from a repeated and distinct use. The edges at all sides are sharpened like a knife blade. There are a number of scratches mostly running along the long axis of the bone (cf. Fig. 13.3, 3) as well as on the spongiosa and on the compacta.

Type 2

Flat implements with an almost rectangular cross-section, angular edges and a, more or less, acute-angled, roof-like or almost round tip comprise a total of fourteen items (Fig. 13.2, 2 and 7). Only one implement is preserved completely (length 166 mm). The breadth of Type 2 implements varies between 20.5–12.7 mm. They were processed from sections of ribs, split lengthwise. The front sides of these implements are covered with both fine and deep scratches running along the long axis of the rib. The back sides show either the spongiosa untouched or only slightly smoothed.

Type 3

Flat implements with completely rounded edges and a round final section are only rarely found (N=2; Fig. 13.2, 6). Both objects were made from sections of ribs from large-sized species that had been split lengthwise. Their surfaces are highly polished, displaying tiny scratches reflecting repeated utilisation and contact with a rather soft material (Fig. 13.3, 1).

Type 4

This type comprises a massive, palm-of the-hand sized oval implement. Only one object of this kind was found at Basta (Fig. 13.2, 8). It has a sharp circular edge and traces of utilisation can be detected on both sides. Most remarkably, the wear differ considerably: On one side, the traces comprise very rough, deep incisions, oriented obliquely and running in one direction (Fig. 13.3, 2). The other side displays a highly polished surface and many crosswise-orientated, fine striations. At one end of the artefact there is an outstandingly highly polished area with an extremely sharp edge, indicating that this was the main working end. The end of the artefact that was held probably lay at the opposite end of the artefact (Fig. 13.3, 2). This object was manufactured from a massive diaphysis of a long bone, perhaps a metapodium of *Bos primigenius*.

Type 5

Two denticulated flat implements are preserved along their total length (77 mm and 56 mm). The first object (Fig. 13.2, 3) can be judged only from a drawing and a black-and-white photograph. It may have been cut from a large rib of a large sized species. The object displays a regular oval shape and is relatively flat with seven or maybe eight incisions down one long side. These incisions are a few millimeters deep. The other equally well-preserved object (Fig. 13.2, 4) was, however, at hand for a re-examination. It was cut from the lateral edge of a scapula large sized ungulate, perhaps from cattle. It has a drop shape with a straight cut edge carved with a flint knife-like tool. The object is generally very flat although it is slightly convex in the middle. Only three or four intentionally carved *dentes* occur on one of the long sides as well as many traces of horizontally incised fine "cuts" (?). These fine cuts are visible on both sides of the object.

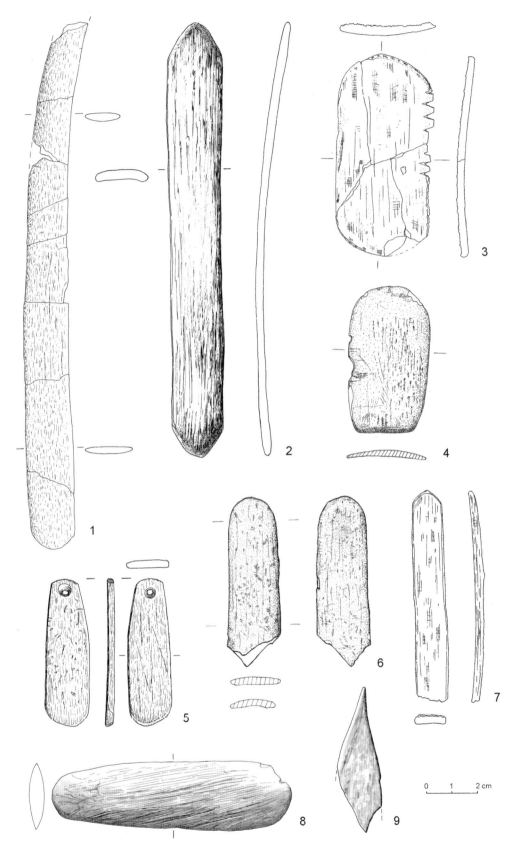

Figure 13.2 Basta. Flat implements of Type 1 (1), Type 2 (2, 7), Type 3 (6), Type 4 (8), Type 5 (3, 4), Type 6 (5), Type 7 (9). Scale as indicated (drawings: I. Raidt, P. Kunz).

Type 6

Five flat implements are perforated and could also have been worn as pendants. Four are documented as drawings (Fig. 13.2, 5) and only one was actually available for re-examination. It was cut from a diaphysis fragment of a metapodium from a large mammal. The back side is flat and the front side is slightly vaulted. The edges are slightly rounded (in contrast to the other items of Type 6 which displayed more angular rims). The end part is heavily worn and highly polished. The perforation on

this implement is perfectly round with a diameter of 2.0 mm on the front and 3.9 mm on the back. Most interestingly, there is a second, incomplete drilling mark immediately adjacent to the completed one (Fig. 13.3, 4). Based on their identical size, the holes must have been made with the same instrument. The borer has left a very fine striations running around the circumference of the hole. It remains a question whether the decorative or functional character dominates on this object. From the repertory of accessories found at Basta

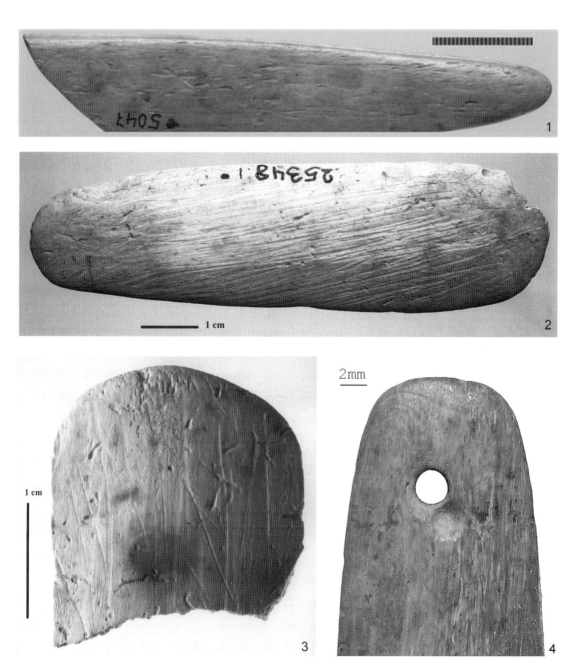

Figure 13.3 Basta. Flat implements in detail. Type 3 (1), polish and fine scratches; Type 4 (2), traces of wear; Type 1 (3), magnified final part with traces of wear; Type 6 (4), magnified proximal part with a finished and an incomplete perforation. Scales as indicated (photographs: H.-J. Nüsse).

and their highly decorative and aesthetic character – especially for the items made from molluscs – I would doubt that the Type 6 implements were truly used as a personal ornament.

Type 7

A flat implement with an extremely pointed working-end, unfortunately only recognizable from one of the black-and-white-photographs (Fig. 13.2, 9), stands out from the other flat implements. It has been re-drawn in order to present it here. The object was most probably made from a rib of a large sized species.

Issues of availability – choice of raw material

A large proportion of the flat implements (n=32; 78%) are processed from length-wise split ribs, selected from medium- and large-sized ungulates. Both the specific pattern of the spongiosa as well as the general size and shape of the items offer some clues for the identification of taxa. Ribs from large-sized ungulates, most probably cattle, were the preferred choice (65%). Ribs of middle-sized ungulates (e.g. Ovis/Capra/Gazella) were used less often (35%). The largest proportion of these implements, however, was too fragmentary and therefore could not be affiliated to either a species or genus level. The minority of the implements discussed here were processed from other skeletal elements: scapulae (2×) and diaphyses of metapodia or long bones (3×). In four cases, the skeletal element could not be identified.

To find suitable raw material for the processing of flat implements was rather easy. The regular refuse from slaughter and consumption yielded ribs in great quantities (see the analysis of the distribution of body parts in Becker 2004, 280; Becker 2002, 116). At least middle-sized animals such as goats, sheep and gazelles were butchered on site while larger mammals such as cattle and equids most probably were transported in parts to areas near the settlement. However, the number of ribs available must have met all demands. Altogether 2452 ribs from goats and sheep and 94 from cattle were identified to species/genus level, not to mention some 4000 unidentifiable rib fragments (Becker and Karasneh in press, fig. 16). To summarise, a large variety of raw material in almost inexhaustible quantities were at the disposal of the Basta inhabitants for bone manufacturing. A purposeful choice of specific raw material is indicated for the flat implements. Since the raw material and the finished end-product are quite similar in appearance, no complicated production of supports, blanks or pre-blanks was necessary. One can imagine people just chose suitable ribs or rib-sections from the garbage to translate their idea of a flat implement into reality.

Steps of processing

The simple nature of the final "flat implement" product and the fact that skilful manufacturing techniques were not necessary, reduced the number of observable steps in the *chaîne opératoire*. In the Basta material, neither specific blanks nor half-finished items occur in large quantities. The processing can be described as follows: the caudal and cranial ends of the ribs were removed; the ribs were split along their length in order to acquire two similar blanks; the spongiosa was, more or less, intensively smoothed (if at all); the end part of the prepared rib-section was given a triangular or rounded shape; the surface may have then been polished to some extent; if required, the object was finally perforated to enable suspension. These perforations were made with flint borers; most of the holes are biconical and from their slightly irregular shape were produced by hand rotation.

However, it is difficult to determine how much of the shape of these objects was due to the initial processing and how much of it was produced during final use. The same is true for the shaping of the edges which, without doubt, result from the angle or the way in which the tool was held in relation to the surface being worked. Much of the polish is clearly a result of repeated use of these non-hafted objects, the polish being produced by the grease and sweat of the palm and the fingers.

How to interpret the flat implements – some general aspects

We have seen that the flat implements from Basta display a certain variability in shape, size and wear. The critical point for any interpretation is how to evaluate each of these features. An easy solution would be to head everything under the umbrella of "multi-functional flat tools". In a more risky interpretation one would try to attribute different functions to these artefacts. A glance in the literature on flat implements from other archaeological sites might be helpful in arriving at a plausible solution. However, this might also lead to major confusion, as can be demonstrated below.

As a starting point, the best preserved Type 1 implement shall be chosen (Fig. 13.2, 1). A flat rib object that would fit rather nicely here comes from 'Ain Ghazal, Jordan (Becker 2005, 63 fig. 3.19). Unfortunately, a precise analysis for the 'Ain Ghazal implements is still awaited. There is also a "twin" piece from the PPNB levels at Jericho, Jordan (Marshall 1982, fig. 250.8). Found under the heading of "flat tools made from ribs, type II" (Marshall 1982, 572) this is interpreted as a weaving "shuttle". There is another nearly identical piece from Ghoraifé II that is described as *objects tranchant … un outil coupant, couteau ou spatula de 28cm de longeur …*" (Stordeur 1982, 18, fig. 6.1). Along with this object, similar implements are mentioned, not only from Ghoraifé but also from other sites (Stordeur 1982). In Jarmo, north-eastern Iraq, 43 implements with a similar character have been brought to light which display some parallels to the Basta assemblage (cf. fig. 144.23–25 in Watson 1983). Watson (1983, 354) calls them "burnisher (*lissoirs*)" or "hide smoothers", most of them being produced from ribs. Flat implements are also found in greater quantities in the Neolithic levels at Abu Hureyra 2, (Olsen 2000). Because a high proportion of the objects at Abu Hureyra are charred (50%), they have been placed within the context of cooking activities (Olsen 2000, 159). Unfortunately, they are only very vaguely described, there is no species allocation and neither photos nor drawings were provided. Flat implements, made from ribs and with traces of fire, are evidenced in prehistoric Olynth, Greece, where they have been found *in situ* in a Bronze Age house near a flat oven and were obviously used as sweepers for roasting legumes (Becker and Kroll 2008, 149 fig. 67.1, 2). In this case, the interpretation of the rib implement as a "cooking utensil" is plausible. Similar flat objects, but without traces of fire, are evidenced from the Neolithic levels at Çatal Höyük in Turkey (Russell 2005, 347). Here they are differentiated into two categories: "pottery polisher" (N=4) and "burnishers" (N=4). The characters distinguishing the two categories do not seem to be very clear and no supporting drawings or photos of any of these implements are provided for verification (Russell 2005). They do differ, however, in the choice of raw materials used: Pottery polishers at Çatal Höyük are exclusively made from ribs and the burnishers from scapulae (2×) and long bone splinters (2×) (Russell 2005). Unfortunately Russell does not give any information relating to the species used.

From this short list it can be seen that a variety of alternative functional suggestions exists. How can this be applied to the Basta material?

Type 1 and Type 3 implements: leather work?

The Type 1 Basta implements display sharp edges and have a relatively high polish. The character and direction of the fine scratches indicate that the operator pushed the implement forward along its axis, sometimes turning the movement a bit to the left or right. The kind of abrasion seems to be indicative for an intensive and often repeated pressure on the worked material. The worked material must have had a, more or less, soft surface such as leather or skin. As a consequence, I assume the Basta objects to have been skin-scrapers and/or skin burnishers. The flat implements of Type 1 have a morphology that seems to be very practical for performing such a function. The flat implements of Type 3, with their rounded edges and high polish, seem to fit such a function, too.

Transforming pelts or skins into soft usable leather needs several different kinds of manipulation, the first being the removal of hair, fat and connective tissue. The sharp edge

on this utensil type would be helpful or even necessary for such an undertaking. Rubbing the surface of skins with some energy is an essential treatment, not only to clean them, but also to compress the hide. Even today, most half-dressed hides undergo intense rubbing after greasing and colouring (Semenov 1964, 178).

Quite similar traces of wear have been reported for hide scrapers from the Early Neolithic in France and these have been experimentally confirmed (Legrand and Sidéra 2007, 71; see also Christidou and Legrand 2005, 386f. in particular fig. 1 right). Bone tools for burnishing skin are described by Semenov (1964, 175) for a much older period: the Upper Palaeolithic. These tools were made from deer and mammoth ribs which were split lengthwise (*sic*!). Semenov's description (1964) matches Basta Type 1 objects exactly:

> "In profile the burnisher is slightly bent, the working and spongy side forming the external part of the bend. The actual working end, curved with the spongy mass cut away, is often not only rubbed and polished but even ground down by use and sharpened like a knife blade".

In the literature, hide-burnishers are among the most common utensils mentioned for bone tool assemblages from the Late PPNB and older periods. What seems surprising is the almost complete absence of such tools from PPNB levels in Jericho. Only two artefacts of this kind are recorded at Jericho, in contrast to the large number of hide-working tools from PPNA layers and older sequences from that site (N=123; Marshall 1982, 572). Marshall proclaims this difference in numbers to mark a significant difference between the PPNA and PPNB; she even places hide-burnishers in the category of highly prized goods of remarkable quality (Marshall 1982). Considering the easy access to this raw material (ribs from bone refuse) and the simplicity of the processing, I would doubt that. However, judging from the drawings and cross-sections (Marshall 1982, figs 239–245), the hide-burnishers from Jericho do not seem to have sharp edges and have a rather irregular shape. This interpretation perhaps needs to be given new consideration.

An alternative interpretation for the Basta implements Type 1 might be that they were utensils for processing fibres. In my opinion, this suggestion should be taken with a large pinch of salt, as will be discussed later. However, there is a strong argument *pro* hide-scraper or hide-burnisher. If the Type 1 implements from Basta were all weaving utensils (probably a less plausible interpretation), no other candidates for hide-utensils can be offered and thus, one of the most important activities in a PPNB community, the processing of hides, would not be reflected in the worked bone inventory at all. Needless to say, products from leather and hides must have been very important for PPNB people and many utensils would have been needed for the manufacture of clothing, capes, footgear, hats, containers for cooking and holding liquids, for ropes and sieves and even door curtains or tents.

Type 2 implements: processing of coarse vessels and tubs?

The interpretation of Type 2 implements is based on their coarser design and the less carefully smoothed back side. The interpretation is in a way connected to pottery production. During pottery production, bone tools, in particular those that are rib-based, were among the most important utensils for millennia in this region. Used for shaping freshly made vessels, such rib-implements typically display strong polish (cf. Becker and Kroll 2008, 162). Other kinds of artefacts with denticulated edges were used, for example, for roughening the surface of storage amphorae. This measure serves to increase the surface area augmenting evaporation and, thus, increasing cooling of the amphorae's contents. Other bone implements, sharply pointed, could be used for applying decoration (Becker and Kroll 2008). These ideas are now supported through experimental work (Legrand 2007, 42).

If we turn back to the Near East and the Early Ceramic Neolithic phase, for example at Çatal Höyük, pottery polishers indeed are evidenced. Russell (2005, 347) points out that "All are made on split ribs of various sizes. None are particularly heavily used ... [but they] show striations typical for use on fine- or untempered ceramics ...". The working-edges of these pottery polishers are flat, with striations, but not really bevelled. They appear to be only occasionally used (Russell 2005, 347). What has been suggested for Çatal Höyük, encourages me to assume a similar function for the Type 2 Basta objects, although in the Pre-Pottery Neolithic, clay firing had not yet been invented of course.

What was found at Basta are some coarse vessels (Fig. 13.4, 2), bins as well as a cookery basin. These "containers" were made from *samagah* ("white earth"), a type of lime marl, most likely used with a clay admixture, chaff and a mineral temper (Gebel *et al.* 2004, 88). *Samagah* was available in limited quantities near the site and could be used without major manipulation or firing (This material still is employed over the region even today). The vessel-like containers from unfired material were naturally rather unstable. Because of that, people placed them in sub-floor channels or in corners to support them. The walls of these bins were up to 50 mm thick and their outer surfaces relatively smooth and well-finished (Gebel *et al.* 2004, 89). They seem to have been shaped by hand. It is easy to imagine Type 2 implements being used, not only for refining the shape and removing unnecessary material, but to give the containers a certain trimming and denser consistency. Less pressure would have been required than for hide-processing as a more superficial slicing movement would have been quite adequate. Unfortunately, the surface of these bins are so badly preserved that any grooves, facets or grit drag-marks that might have been produced by the smoothers are not visible.

The most striking "container" is the so-called cookery basin from Basta. It came to light during the 1987 excavation season in a corner of an open courtyard in area B, enclosed by a complex of rooms (see also Nissen *et al.* 1987; Becker 2005). Dozens of shards of various sizes (Fig. 13.4, 3a), four large scapulae (three from large cattle (domesticated/wild?) and one from an equid, possibly onager or wild ass) with traces of burning and a radius scoop were found *in-situ* along with some other items. The basin itself was about 0.80–1.00 m long and was made from *samagah*, tempered with plant fibres and coarse grit. Some shards displayed secondary burning.

We believe that the basin was placed upside down on the scapulae-platform and served as a tabun-like oven for the preparation of some kind of food (Fig. 13.4, 3b). Hints of this come from the scapulae which were burnt in an outer circle, but not touched by greater heat in their middle or by the joints. The most decisive evidence, however, came from the scoop. Processed from a *Bos primigenius* radius, it displayed traces of fire contact and some kind of abrasive action at the distal end which, in addition, was shaped like a scoop. This utensil quite obviously functioned as a large spoon for sweeping embers over the basin and removing them after the cooking process ended.

It should be stressed that these bins and basins do not represent some preceding, experimental phase in pottery production. Instead, they must be regarded as independent inventions. Some of the flat implements could, in fact, have been used in their making. However, another possible explanation is that these coarse implements could have been used to coat the walls and floors of the houses with plaster.

Type 4 (and Type 2) implements: Smoothing plaster?

In Basta, many houses were covered with a coating made from burned lime mixed with small and some of the walls even were decorated with splodges of white and red paint (Fig. 13.4, 1; Gebel *et al.* 2004, 90). This decoration would demand a relatively plain background. Coating and smoothing could easily be performed using both Type 2 and Type 4 flat implements (Fig. 13.2, 8) in particular. Massive in nature and covered with many deep striations (see Fig. 13.3, 2), the latter implement would have been suitable for applying the plaster coating onto a wall or a floor. To give the background a final smooth surface, the workers might have used the back side of this utensil. The different kinds of wear found on the two sides support this view.

Comparable "plaster tools" have been found at Çatal Höyük (Russell 2005), where they were made from large scapula-fragments (N=10).

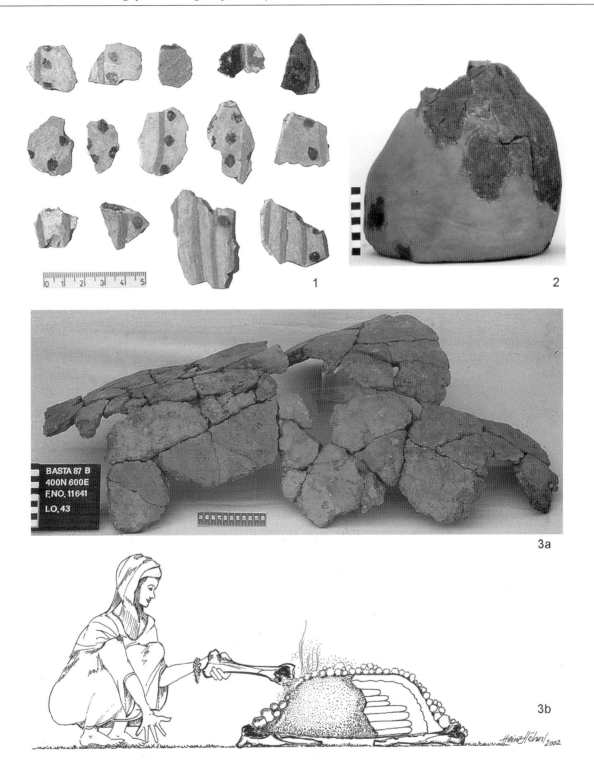

Figure 13.4 Basta. Wall-paintings (1), coarse vessel (2), fragments of cooking basin (3a) and its reconstructed function (3b). Scales as indicated. (1–3a) Courtesy of the Basta Project and H. G. K. Gebel (drawing: (3b) H. Hähnl).

Type 5 implements: processing sinews/tendons or weaving?

Type 5 implements stand out with their denticulated edges. One proposal to explain their function is that both items might have been used to stretch and smooth sinews or even to disentangle them. This procedure might have left these characteristic traces as described above. That sinews or tendons were extremely useful for many activities connected to daily life such as sewing, making strong ropes etc., goes without saying. At Basta, the removal of sinews in the joints of the fore- and hindleg is rarely evidenced. Only 0.4% of all the bone refuse from Basta bore traces of cutting with sharp flint tools (Becker 2004, 237, 264).

An alternative hypothesis would be that these objects might have served as weaving tools to push down the weft. The denticulation is much too shallow for combing flax fibres when these objects are compared to proper flax heckles. There are two additional finds from Basta, reproduced in Karasneh's thesis (1989, pl. 25) which might also belong within this category. These are modified ribs with a long line of notches along the long sides. These tools had no find numbers and therefore could not be integrated here.

Another comb-like implement has been published for Tell Ramad, (De Contenson 2000, planche xix 4a: "*peigne à carder*"). A comparable item with denticulation connected with "tissage" is known from the PPNA horizon at Mureybet, (Stordeur 1999, 266f.), as well as from PPNA contexts in Jericho (Marshall 1982, 594).

Type 5, Type 6 and Type 7 implements: processing of fibres, weaving?

It is evident, not only from Near Eastern ethnographic sources but also from Bronze Age sites in the region, that sword or pin beaters were used during the weaving process. These tools were mostly made from slightly curved rib sections, some were pointed and some have an additional perforation. Those from Early Bronze Age Arad, (Amiran and Ilan 1992, 73), for example, display an elongated, pointed tip or may be rounded at the end; the edges are most often bevelled and both sides of the beater display a high polish from beating up the weft threads (Amiran and Ilan 1992). Indeed, they resemble some of the Basta Type 1 objects, but in particular the Type 6 and the Type 7 implements (Fig. 13.2, 9).

Before going into further detail, the archaeological record for processing fibres during the 7th millennium BC or even earlier in Near Eastern sites needs to be discussed. There are some simple burial fabrics from Levels VIB and VIA (*c.* 5980–5780 BC) at Çatal Höyük. The textile fibres originally were claimed to be from sheep (Helbæk 1964), but after re-examination they have been identified as flax (*Linum usitatissimum*; Vogelsang-Eastwood 1988). Even without this

re-examination a critical mind would have needed to ask if sheep with a wooly fleece were already known in the region at that time. This topic urgently needs a closer examination. One of the very few hints comes from a sheep figurine from Tepe Sarab, Iran, dating to *c.* 6000 BC (Benecke 1994, 137). However, the existence of an ancient weaving tradition at Çatal Höyük is certain although one should probably not go as far as James Mellaart did (*cit.* in Mallett 1990) in suggesting that there was Neolithic kilim production at the settlement; an idea firmly rejected by Mallett (1990). Wool thread is a prerequisite for all tapestry work so that Mellaart's kilim theory must in any case be rejected.

An even earlier direct proof of primitive weaving comes from Jarmo (Barber 1992, 127) where impressions of plain and basket weave textiles were found on clay dating to 7000 BC. In addition, there are some linen fabrics from Israel, at the site of Nahal Hemar, dating to 6500 BC (Barber 1992, 131; Schick 1989).

This early evidence brings us to another critical point. Quite obviously, all these textile remains must have been produced on a loom. The oldest looms are ground-looms from Neolithic Egypt and Israel (Nicholson and Shaw 2000, 276f.) whereas the invention of warp-weighted looms seems to be from a much later date. The existence of the latter is much easier to prove because the weights of the warp-weighted looms are mostly made out of (burnt) clay and are very likely to survive in the archaeological record. Ground looms do not have loom-weights and are constructed from wood which is very unlikely to survive in the soil. Thus, ground-looms do not produce any artefacts that are directly attributable to them. Consequently, if neither fabrics nor looms are preserved, we have to be content with some bone artefacts which may probably be connected to the weaving process. A meticulous analysis of such bone artefacts deserves major attention.

Again, the bone artefact material from Jericho is of relevance here. Marshall (1982, 572) postulates that there are 93 implements from PPNA levels and 27 from PPNB levels that may be "probable weaving tools". They are interpreted as "shuttles" and "sword beaters". The shuttles are flat implements of a varying length with a perforation, the thin ones being made from ribs, the thicker ones from other skeletal elements (Marshall 1982, fig. 237.5–7). They resemble the flat, Type 6 implements (Fig. 13.2, 5) from Basta which can be connected to weaving activities.

The Type 7 implement from Basta could also be seen in this context. It might have been a pin beater. But the possibility should also be considered that this pointed implement was connected with basketry – even more so because the weaving process seems to have had fore-runners in the form of twining, netting, matting and basketry. The pointed rib implement could easily have been connected with the fabrication of cordage, mats and even solid containers made from plant fibres.

An additional problem in terms of weaving arises from the fact that any direct proof for the cultivation of *Linum usitatissimum* for the production of flax, still is lacking in the Southern Levant during the PPNB and in the botanical record of Basta (Neef 2004), although there is evidence of linen from a cave near the Dead Sea (Neef 2005, 70). The absence of flax from the late PPNB mega-sites may be a matter of preservation conditions and does not necessarily reflect the level of technological knowledge at that time period. It does not seem plausible that imports alone could meet the demands of such a huge population for clothing. Thus, one might expect evidence of weaving utensils.

Concluding remarks

The interpretation of the Basta flat implements is not an easy task since these implements are differently shaped and their morphology implies diverse rather than coherent uses. Although a variety of proposals for their utilisation exists, their function cannot be convincingly explained in every case. This is because there are neither preserved organic finds such as leather and skins, nor baskets, garments or such like at Basta nor do we definitely know whether the primitive containers made from *samagah* were produced using bone implements or whether such flat implements were actually used for plastering floors and walls. However, in this article I have tried to explore possible links between flat implements and every-day techniques practised at the mega-site of Late PPNB Basta. Reflection on the evidence from the bone artefacts themselves and perceived links to all the activities just mentioned, were reviewed. What I learned while going deeper into this topic was that not only is a detailed description and presentation of artefacts absolutely necessary, but also understanding of the economic and cultural background at any given site. Only through such a multi-layered approach, with an intra-site background and including all categories of finds, does such an interpretation gain in reliability.

The arbitrary character of the worked bone assemblage from Basta must be stressed. In terms of the general repertory, it displays traits in common with assemblages from other sites in the Levant. There is a predominance of pointed implements (about 60%), a considerable number of flat objects made from ribs (10%) a fairly large number of various ornamental pieces (about 20%) and many more singular items among which the radius scoops represent the most outstanding objects. However, it must be faced that the relevance of the Basta results, derived from a rather restricted part of the settlement (excavated area: 860 m²), has to be understood with some caution, something that is particularly true for the worked bone assemblage. High taphonomic loss of material and biases to an unknown extent dictate its nature profoundly.

Bibliography

Amiran, R. and Ilan, O. (1992) *Arad, eine 5000 Jahre alte Stadt in der Wüste Negev, Israel.* Neumünster, Karl Wachholtz.

Bar-Yosef, O. and Tchernov, E. (1970) The Natufian bone industry of ha-Yonim Cave. *Israel Exploration Journal* 20, 141–150, fig. 2–4.

Barber, E. (1992) *Prehistoric Textiles.* Princeton, University Press.

Becker, C. (1998) The role of hunting in Pre-Pottery Neolithic pastoralism and its ecological implications: the Basta example (Jordan). *Anthropozoologica* 27, 67–78.

Becker, C. (2000a) Bone and species distribution in Late PPNB Basta (Jordan) – rethinking the anthropogenic factor. In M. Mashkour, A. Choyke, H. Buitenhuis and F. Poplin (eds), *Archaeozoology of the Near East IVA.* Proc. of the 4th International Symposium on the Archaeozoology of southwestern Asia and adjacent areas 32, 196–207. Groningen, ARC-Publicaties.

Becker, C. (2000b) Early domestication in the Southern Levant as viewed from Late PPNB Basta. In L. K. Horwitz, E. Tchernov, P. Ducos, C. Becker, A. von den Driesch, I. Marzin and A. Garrard (eds), *Animal Domestication in the Southern Levant.* Paléorient 25 (2), 70–72.

Becker, C. (2002) Nothing to do with indigenous domestication? Cattle from Late PPNB Basta. In H. Buitenhuis, A. M. Choyke, M. Mashkour and A. H. Al-Shiyab (eds), *Archaeozoology of the Near East V.* Proc. of the 5th International Symposium on the Archaeozoology of southwestern Asia and adjacent areas 62, 112–137. Groningen, ARC-Publicaties.

Becker, C. (2004) On the identification of sheep and goats: the evidence from Basta. In H. J. Nissen, M. Muheisen and H. G. K. Gebel (eds), *Basta I. The Human Ecology.* Bibliotheca neolithica Asiae meridionalis et occidentalis, 219–310. Berlin, ex oriente.

Becker, C. (2005) Jagen und Schlachten vor 9000 Jahren. Ergebnisse aus der Archäozoologie. Exhibition Catalogue "Gesichter des Orients. 10000 Jahre Kunst und Kultur aus Jordanien" edited by *Ausstellungshalle der Bundesrepublik Deutschland/Bonn und dem Vorderasiatischen Museum, Staatliche Museen zu Berlin – Stiftung Preußischer Kulturbesitz/Berlin*, 61–66. Mainz, Philipp von Zabern.

Becker, C. and Kroll, H. (2008) *Das Prähistorische Olynth. Ausgrabungen in der Toumba Agios Mamas 1994–1996. Ernährung und Rohstoffnutzung im Wandel.* Prähist. Archäologie Südosteuropa 22. Rahden/Westfalen, Marie Leidorf.

Becker, C. and Karasneh, W. (in press) The bone industry. Typology, technology, osteology. In C. Becker, W. Karasneh and N. Qadi, (eds), *Basta IV. 3. The bone, ground stone and stone vessel industries* 7–58. Berlin, ex oriente.

Benecke, N. (1994) *Der Mensch und seine Haustiere.* Stuttgart, Theiss.

Campana, D. V. (1989) *Natufian and Protoneolithic Bone Tools.* Oxford, British Archaeological Report S494.

Christidou, R. and Legrand, A. (2005) Hide working and bone tools: experimentation design and applications. In H. Luik, A. M. Choyke, C. E. Batey and L. Lōugas (eds), *From Hooves to Horns, from Mollusc to Mammoth. Manufacture and use of bone artefacts from prehistoric times to the present. Proceedings of the 4th meeting ICAZ Worked Bone Research Group, Tallinn, 26th–31st August 2003.* Muinasaja Teadus 15, 385–396. Tallinn, Insitute of History.

De Contenson, H. (2000) Ramad, site néolithique en Damascène (Syrie) aux VIIIᵉ et VIIᵉ millénaires avant l'ère chrétienne. *Bibliothèque Arch. Hist.* 157. Beyrouth.

Le Dosseur, G. (2006) *La néolithisation au Levant Sud à travers l'exploitation des matières osseuses.* Unpublished theses, University of Paris.

Le Dosseur, G. (2008) La place de l'industrie osseuse dans la Néolithisation au Levant Sud. *Paléorient* 34 (1), 59–89.

Gebel, H. (2004) Central to what? Remarks on the settlement patterns of the LPPNB mega-sites in Jordan. In H. D. Bienert, H. Gebel and R. Neef (eds), *Central Settlements in Neolithic Jordan*. Studies in Early Near Eastern Production, Subsistence and Environment 5, 1–19. Berlin, ex oriente.

Gebel, H., Muheisen, M. and Nissen, H. J. (1988) Preliminary report on the First Season of Excavations at the Late Aceramic Neolithic site of Basta. In A. N. Garrard and H. Gebel (eds), *The Prehistory of Jordan. The state of research in 1986*. 101–134.Oxford, British Archaeological Report S396.

Gebel, H., Muheisen, M., Nissen, H. J. and Qadi, N. (2004) Late PPNB Basta: results of 1992. In H -D. Bienert, H. Gebel. and R. Neef (eds), *Central Settlements in Neolithic Jordan. Studies in early Near Eastern productions, subsistence, and environment 5*, 71–103. Berlin, ex oriente.

Helbæk, H. (1964) Textiles from Çatal Hüyük. *Archaeology* 16 (1), 39–46.

Hermansen, B. D. (1991) Small Finds. In H. J. Nissen, M. Muheisen and H. Gebel (eds), *Report on the Excavations at Basta 1988*. Annual of the Department of Antiquities of Jordan 35, 26–29.

Hermansen, B. D. (1997) Art and ritual behaviour in Neolithic Basta. In H. Gebel, Z. Kafafi and G. Rollefson (eds), *The Prehistory of Jordan, II. Perspectives from 1997*. Studies in Early Near Eastern Production, Subsistence, and Environment 4, 333–343. Berlin, ex oriente.

Hermansen, B. D. (2004) The small finds. In H. Gebel, M. Muheisen, H. J. Nissen and N. Qadi (eds), *Late PPNB Basta: results of 1992*, 95–103. Berlin, ex oriente.

Karasneh, W. (1989) *Bone artefacts from Basta*. Unpublished MA thesis, Yarmouk University, Irbid/Jordan (translated from Arabic).

Kirkbride, D. (1966a) Five seasons at the Pre-Pottery Neolithic Site of Beidha in Jordan. *Palestine Exploration Quarterly* 98 (1), 8–72.

Kirkbride, D. (1966b) Beidha, an Early Neolithic Village in Jordan. *Archaeology* 19, 199–207.

Kuijt, I. (2000a) *Life in Neolithic Farming Communities. Social organisation, identity, and differentiation*. New York, Plenum Press.

Kuijt, I. (2000b) People and space in early agricultural villages: exploring daily lives, community size, and architecture in the Late Pre-Pottery Neolithic. *Journal of Anthropological Archaeology* 19 (1), 75–102.

Legrand, A. (2007) *Fabrication et Utilisation de l'Outillage en Matières Osseuses du Néolithique de Chypre: Khirokitia et Cap Andreas-Kastros*. Oxford, Archaeopress (British Archaeological Report S1678).

Legrand, A. and Sidéra, I. (2007) Methods, means, and results when studying European bone industries. In C. Gates St-Pierre and R. B. Walker (eds), *Bones as Tools: current methods and interpretations in worked bone studies*, 67–79. Oxford, Archaeopress (British Archaeological Report S1622).

Mallett, M. (1990) A weaver's view of the Catal Hüyük controversy. *Oriental Rug Review* 10 (6), 32–43.

Marshall, D. (1982) Jericho bone tools and objects. In K. M. Kenyon and T. A. Holland (eds), *Excavations at Jericho* 4, App. E (British School of Archaeology in Jerusalem 1982) 570–622.

Martin, L. and Russell, N. (1996) Surface material: animal bone and worked bone. In I. Hodder (ed.), *On the Surface: Çatalhöyük 1993–1995*. Çatalhöyük Project Vol. 1. BIAA Monograph 22, 199–214. Cambridge, McDonald Institute for Archaeological Research.

Neef, R. (1997) Status and perspectives of archaeobiological research in Jordan. In H. Gebel, Z. Kafafi and G. O. Rollefson (eds), *The Prehistory of Jordan, II. Perspectives from 1997*. Studies in Early Near Eastern Production, Subsistence, and Environment 4, 601–609. Berlin, ex oriente.

Neef, R. (2004) Vegetation and plant husbandry. In H. J. Nissen, M. Muheisen and H. Gebel (eds), *Basta I. The Human Ecology*. Bibliotheca neolithica Asiae meridionalis et occidentalis 187–218. Berlin, ex oriente.

Neef, R. (2005) Umwelt, Ackerbau und Sammelwirtschaft vor 9000 Jahren – Ergebnisse aus der Archäobotanik. Exhibition catalogue "Gesichter des Orients. 10000 Jahre Kunst und Kultur aus Jordanien" edited by *Ausstellungshalle der Bundesrepublik Deutschland/Bonn und dem Vorderasiatischen Museum, Staatliche Museen zu Berlin – Stiftung Preußischer Kulturbesitz/Berlin* 67–71. Mainz, Philipp von Zabern.

Nicholson, P. T. and Shaw, I. (2000) *Ancient Egyptian Materials and Technology*. Cambridge, Cambridge University Press.

Nissen, H. J., Muheisen, M. and Gebel, H. (1987) Report on the first two seasons of excavations at Basta (1986–1987). *Annual of the Department of Antiquities of Jordan* 31, 79–119.

Nissen, H. J., Muheisen, M. and Gebel, H. (1991) Report on excavations at Basta 1988. *Annual of the Department of Antiquities of Jordan* 35, 13–40.

Olsen, S. L. (2000) The bone artifacts. In A. Moore (ed.), *Village on the Euphrates: from foraging to farming at Abu Hureyra*, 154–162. Oxford, Oxford University Press.

Reese, D. S. (forthcoming) Marine mollusc artefacts (working title). In B. D. Hermansen, H. Gebel and D. S. Reese (eds), with a contribution of K. McNamara. *Basta IV.1. The small finds and ornament industries*. Berlin, ex oriente.

Russell, N. (2001a) The social life of bone: a preliminary assessment of bone tool manufacture and discard at Çatalhöyük. In A. M. Choyke and L. Bartosiewicz (eds), *Crafting Bone: skeletal technologies through time and space*. Proceedings of the 2nd meeting of the (ICAZ) Worked Bone Research Group, Budapest, 31st August–5th September 1999. 241–249. Oxford, Archaeopress (British Archaeological Report S937).

Russell, N. (2001b) Neolithic relations of production: insights from the bone tool industry. In A. M. Choyke and L. Bartosiewicz (eds), *Crafting Bone: skeletal technologies through time and space*. Proceedings of the 2nd meeting of the (ICAZ) Worked Bone Research Group, Budapest, 31st August – 5th September 1999, 271–280. Oxford, Archaeopress (British Archaeological Report S937).

Russell, N. (2005) Çatalhöyük worked bone. In I. Hodder (ed.), *On the Surface: Çatalhöyük 1993–1995*. Çatalhöyük Project Vol. 1. 339–367. BIAA Monograph 22. Cambridge, McDonald Institute for Archaeological Research.

Schick, T. (1989) Early Neolithic twined basketry and fabrics from the Nahal Hemar Cave. Israel. IX. *Rencontres Internationales d'Archéologie et d'Histoire d'Antibes «Tissage, Corderie, Vannerie»*, 20–21–22 Octobre 1988, 41–52. Juan-les-Pins.

Semenov, S. A. (1964) *Prehistoric Technology*. Bath, Adams & Dart.

Stordeur, D. (1981a) La contribution de l'industrie de l'os à la délimitation des aires culturelles: l'exemple du Natoufien. In J. Cauvin and P. Sanlaville (eds), *Préhistoire du Levant*. Coll. Internat. du CNRS 598, 432–437. Paris, CNRS.

Stordeur, D. (1981b) Jericho bone artefacts from PPNA – L'outils d'os pendant la Préhistoire. *La Recherche* 121 (12), 452–465.

Stordeur, D. (1982) L'industrie osseuse de la Damascène du VIIIᵉ au VIᵉ millénaire. In H. Camps-Fabrer (ed.), *L'Industrie en Os et Bois de Cervidé durant le Néolithique et l'Âge des Métaux*, 9–23. Paris, CNRS.

Stordeur, D. (1999) Néolithisation et outillage osseux. La révolution a-t-elle eu lieu? In M. Julien, A. Averbouh, D. Ramseyer, C. Bellier, D. Buisson, P. Cattelain, M Patou-Mathis and N. Provenzano (eds), *Préhistoire d'Os. Recueil d'études sur l'industrie osseuse préhistorique*. Hommage à Henriette Camps-Fabrer, 261–272. Aix-en-Provence, Publications de l'Université de Provence.

Vogelsang-Eastwood, G. (1988) A re-examination of the fibres from Çatal Hüyük textiles. *Oriental Carpet and Textile Studies* 3 (1), 15–19.

Watson, P (1983) Jarmo worked bone. In L. S. Braidwood, R. J. Braidwood, B. Howe, C. A. Reed and P. T. Watson (eds), *Prehistoric Archaeology along the Zagros Flanks*, 347–369. Chicago, Oriental Institute Publications.

CHAPTER 14

Tubular Bone Artefacts in Burial Context at Ajvide, Gotland *c.* 2500 cal BC. Are They Musical Instruments?

Kristiina Mannermaa and Riitta Rainio

Tubular bone artefacts of different size and form are commonly found in Middle Neolithic inhumation burials in Gotland and Öland, Sweden. These were the burials of the people of the so-called Scandinavian Pitted Ware Culture. Small tubular artefacts have commonly been interpreted as beads used in decoration as, in many cases, they appear in clusters by the head region and along the body. Archaeologists discovered a grave (62) at the site of Ajvide in 1998, which contained large numbers of grave goods, among them tubular bone artefacts of an extraordinary character. Based on their appearance, these single or two-piece artefacts with or without pierced holes were interpreted as flutes. Their suitability for sound production, however, has never been studied systematically. In this article, we will discuss the presence and function of the various tubular bone artefacts found in grave 62. We will describe the finds, sort them tentatively and report on possible ethnographic parallels. The article is intended as an introduction to this research project, which seeks to analyze the sound-producing capability of the artefacts and reassess their interpretation as musical instruments. The find contexts of the artefacts, as well as, the grave entity with all other artefacts, will be studied from the perspective of music archaeology.

Keywords
Bone artefacts; Pitted Ware; Gotland; flutes; musical instruments; music archaeology.

Introduction

In the summer 1998, the Archaeological Department of the University of Gotland, lead by Professor Inger Österholm continued an archaeological field school excavation at the Middle Neolithic site of Ajvide, situated on the west coast of the island of Gotland in Sweden (Fig. 14.1). The site had been excavated over many years, during which an extensive activity area with a cemetery including well-preserved skeletal remains came to light and was investigated. By the end of the field season in 1998, an area of about 1600 m² had been excavated and 62 graves investigated (e.g. Burenhult 1997a, 1997b, 2002; Österholm 1998a, 1998b). Many of the graves at Ajvide are richly provided with animal tooth pendants,

pieces of ceramic, stone and bone artefacts and unmodified animal bones – such as skulls and teeth. In 2009, when the field school excavations at Ajvide were paused, a total of 84 graves had been found.

Interestingly, the last grave that was excavated in the field season 1998 – grave 62 – turned out to be different from all the other investigated graves. Initially, at a depth of approximately 12.20 masl, the remains of a skeleton, lying relatively near the surface, started to become exposed out of the dark soil. This was grave 57. Later on, when this grave had been excavated and taken away, another inhumation, grave 62, was found beneath it. As the excavation of this lower grave proceeded, it turned out that the grave not

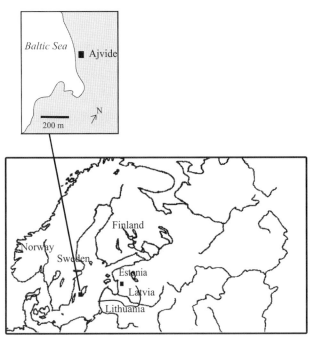

Figure 14.1 Location of Ajvide site, Gotland, Sweden.

only had an extraordinary number of grave goods, but it also included a type of artefact which had never before been found in Gotland or neighbouring areas (Österholm 1998a, 1998b). Moreover, there have been no similar artefacts found in the more recent excavations at Ajvide (Johan Norderäng, pers. comm. 2011). The body in grave 62 had been placed stretched out on its back with head and upper torso towards the south (Fig. 14.2). The head was turned slightly towards the east (Burenhult 2002, 116). According to Petra Molnar (2002, 373), the skeleton belongs to a woman aged between 25–30 years. The cranium of the woman is relatively robust and her stature, about 156–166 cm, is taller than the average woman in this population. The skeleton shows traces of anaemia or some other kind of deficiency, a health problem that has not been recognized in any other skeletons from Ajvide (Molnar 2008, 283).

A total of 70 numbered contexts and nearly 200 individual artefacts were recorded in grave 62 (Burenhult 2002, 116–117). Perhaps the most striking ones were the tubular bone artefacts, 67 in number, that were found lying in different parts of the grave. Some of them had pierced holes in their sides or an additional bone tube at one end (Fig. 14.3). These

Figure 14.2 Grave 62 at Ajvide during excavation in 1998 (photograph: Göran Burenhult).

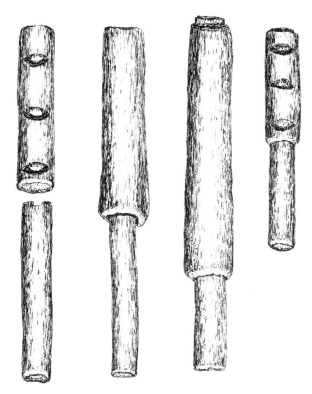

Figure 14.3 Tubular bone artefacts (ID 34705, 34648, 34649, 34704) from grave 62 at Ajvide. Taxonomic identifications and lengths from left to right: ulna of unidentified species, 28 mm; ulna and radius of swan (Cygnus sp.), 98 mm; ulna and radius of swan, 94 mm; ulna and radius of swan, 60 mm (drawing: Sven Österholm).

artefacts which have no parallels in contemporary other graves in Gotland or any other place in Northern Europe, were interpreted as flutes by Österholm (1998a; 1998b) and Göran Burenhult (2002, 116–117). However, their suitability for sound production has not been studied systematically. Apart from the tubular bone artefacts, a find concentration near the right arm of the deceased contained pierced seal (*Phocidae*) and wild boar (*Sus scrofa*) teeth, European hedgehog (*Erinaceus europaeus*) mandibles, pharyngeal bones from the cyprinid fish (*Cyprinidae*) and tarsometatarsus artefacts from the common crane (*Grus grus*) (Burenhult 2002, 116–117; Mannermaa 2008, 9). A clay figurine resembling a swimming water bird or a seal lay at the foot of the grave (Fig. 14.4) (Burenhult 2002, 117; Mannermaa 2008, 11). Near the head were found

a butterfly-shaped pendant from sturgeon (*Acipenser sturio*) bone (Fig. 14.5), a carefully made bone comb (Fig. 14.6) and about 30 pieces of mother-of-pearl of soft shell clam (*Mya arenaria*) or swan mussel (*Anodonta cygnea*) (Fig. 14.7) comprising yet more examples of outstanding craftmanship within the Ajvide population (Österholm 1998a, 1998b). A great number of tools such as scrapers, arrowheads, points and harpoons were also found in the grave. All the finds are listed and described in Table 14.1 and Fig. 14.8.

In this article, we will describe the tubular bone artefacts from grave 62 and discuss their potential functions. These artefacts have earlier been interpreted as flutes and our main approach here is to look at them as musical instruments, that is, artefacts intended or used for sound production. We will

Figure 14.4 Clay figurine (ID 34681) from grave 62 at Ajvide (photograph: Johan Norderäng).

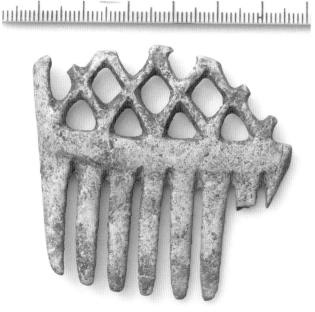

Figure 14.6 Bone comb (ID 34679) from grave 62 at Ajvide (photograph: Johan Norderäng).

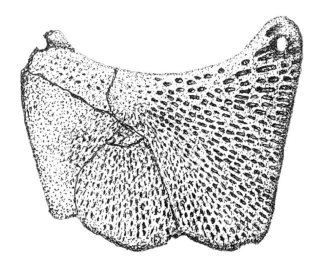

*Figure 14.5 Butterfly pendant (ID 34680) made of the bone plate of the sturgeon (*Acipenser sturio*) from grave 62 at Ajvide. Length about 64 mm (drawing: Sven Österholm).*

Figure 14.7 Worked pieces of mother-of-pearl (ID 34678) from grave 62 at Ajvide (photograph: Johan Norderäng).

Table 14.1 List of the finds in grave 62 at Ajvide. Adapted from Burenhult (2002, 116–118).

ID-NUMBER	ARTEFACT
34644	Bone point
34645	Piece of elk antler
34646	Single tubular artefact with holes
34647	Large two-pieced tubular artefact with holes
34648	Large two-pieced tubular artefact without holes
34649	Large two-pieced tubular artefact without holes
34650	Large single tubular artefact without holes
34651	Large single tubular artefact without holes
34652	Large single tubular artefact without holes
34653	Small single tubular artefact without holes
34654	Small single tubular artefact without holes
34655	Small single tubular artefact without holes
34656	Small single tubular artefact without holes
34657	Small single tubular artefact without holes
34658	Knife made of wild boar tusk
34659	Bone point
34660	Bone point
34661	Fragment of an arrowhead
34662	Small single tubular artefact without holes
34663	Spoon made of wild boar bone
34664	Spoon made of wild boar bone
34665	Find collection:
34666	Bone point (part of ID 34665)
34667	Bone point (part of ID 34665)
34668	Fragment of a harpoon (part of ID 34665)
34669	Fragment of a harpoon (part of ID 34665)
34670	Bird tarsometatarsus artefacts, 2 pcs (part of ID 34665)
34671	Pierced wild boar teeth, 4 pcs (part of ID 34665)
34672	Pierced seal teeth, 39 pcs (part of ID 34665)
34673	Hedgehog jaws (part of ID 34665)
34674	Mini-adze (part of ID 34665)
34675	Small tubular artefacts without holes, 7 pcs (part of ID 34665)
34676	Large single tubular artefact without holes (part of ID 34665)
34677	Single tubular artefacts with holes, 3 pcs (part of ID 34665)
34678	Worked pieces of mother of pearl, c. 30 pcs
34679	Bone comb

ID-NUMBER	ARTEFACT
34680	Butterfly pendant made of sturgeon bone
34681	Clay figurine resembling seal or bird
34682	Double-edged stone axe
34683	Bone arrowhead
34684	Bone arrowhead
34685	Hedgehog jaws
34686	Bone point
34687	Worked bone, burnt
34688	Seal tooth
34689	Hedgehog spines
34690	Hedgehog spines
34691	Bone point
34692	Seal tooth
34693	Pierced wild boar tusk
34694	Bone point
34695	Fragment of harpoon
34696	Small single tubular artefact without holes
34697	Small single tubular artefact without holes
34698	Fragment of a small single tubular artefact without holes
34699	Small single tubular artefact without holes
34700	Large single tubular artefact without holes
34701	Large single tubular artefact without holes
34702	Large single tubular artefact without holes
34703	Large two-pieced tubular artefact without holes
34704	Small two-pieced tubular artefact with holes
34705	Small single tubular artefact with holes
34706	Small single tubular artefact with holes
34707	Small single tubular artefact with holes
34708	Small single tubular artefact with holes
34709	Small single tubular artefact without holes
34710	Seal teeth, 3 pcs
34711	Large single tubular artefact without holes, small single tubular artefact without holes
34712	Tubular bone beads (made of bones of birds and hares)
34713	Wild boar jaw

just describe the tubular artefacts, sort them tentatively and report preliminary observations and possible ethnographical parallels. This article will act as an introduction to our recently launched project aimed at the analysis of the sound-producing capability of the artefacts and reassessment of their interpretation as flutes. We will also consider alternative interpretations including their use in other kinds of wind instruments or musical instruments. The find contexts of the artefacts as well as the grave entity and other graves from the cemetery will be studied from the perspective of music archaeology. This interdisciplinary field of research, also called archaeomusicology or auditory archaeology, seeks to explore ideas related to music and sound on the basis of archaeological materials (e.g. Lund 1979, 1981, 1984/1991, 1988; Hickmann 1997a, 2000, 2007). In order to study prehistoric music or early sound environments, this empirical approach is probably the most accurate and reliable one.

The site and its cultural background

The Ajvide archaeological site, excavated in 1983–1986 and 1992–2009, is situated on the island of Gotland. In the Middle Neolithic, the site was located on the seashore adjacent to a bay that was protected by a small island (Burenhult 2002). The site complex consists of activity areas and 84 graves (Norderäng 2008a). The site was utilized from the Late Mesolithic to the Bronze Age (Österholm 1989, 95), but the main period of activities can be dated to *c.* 3100–2700 cal BC, which corresponds to the Late Middle Neolithic in Swedish prehistoric chronology (Burenhult 1997b, xi; 2002, 32). The burials were dug down through the cultural layer, which indicates that they are slightly more recent. According to twelve radiocarbon dates taken from the burials, the cemetery was used between *c.* 2900–2300 cal BC. Grave 62 dates to *c.* 2500 cal BC (Burenhult 1997b, xx; 2002, 32; Possnert 2002; Norderäng 2008b, Tab. 2).

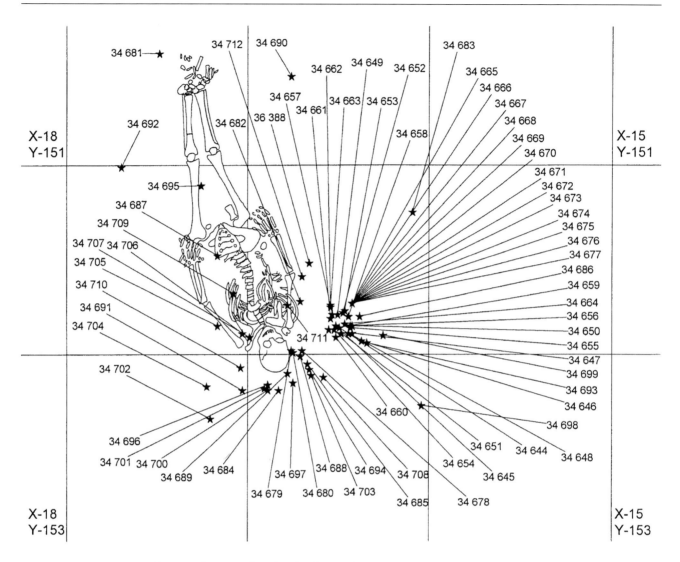

Figure 14.8 Vector drawing and artefact distribution of grave 62 at Ajvide (Burenhult 2002, fig. 108b).

Ajvide belongs to a complex of hunter-gatherer groups called the Pitted Ware Culture who appeared on the coastal areas of south-eastern Sweden, the Åland Islands and the islands of Gotland and Öland *c.* 3300 cal BC (Edenmo *et al.* 1997). The subsistence economy of these coastal groups was based on marine resources, mainly seals and fish (Lidén *et al.* 1995; Storå 2000; Olson *et al.* 2002; Mannermaa & Storå 2006). Since there are no hearths or other clear indications of dwellings to be found at Ajvide, it is possible that the site was not a permanent dwelling site. Instead, it was probably used periodically in connection with hunting, fishing and burial rituals. The actual dwelling site may be located farther inland (Norderäng 2008a, 23; Johansson 2009, 22–28).

Description of different types of the tubular artefacts found in grave 62

Altogether 67 tubular bone artefacts, with or without pierced holes, came to light in grave 62 (Table 14.2). Most of them are concentrated at some distance from the right arm of the deceased while others are found in the vicinity of the skull and by the shoulders, arms and chest. Thus, the artefacts were not necessarily parts of a single unit. All artefacts, however, were made using the same technique: that of cutting off the long bone epiphyses and polishing the ends. This technique is also used for making the beads of Middle Neolithic Ire, Visby and Västerbjers, Gotland (Janzon 1974, 67). All artefacts were measured by us in 2006 and 2011 at the University of

Gotland. The osteological analysis was conducted by K. M. in 2006 and 2011 (cf. Mannermaa 2008). While Burenhult (2002, 116–117) divides the artefacts into 40 flutes and 27 beads, Österholm (1998b, 218) reports only 35 flutes. In the following – to avoid premature interpretation – we will treat each and every piece as a tubular bone artefact and group the material tentatively according to size and structural characteristics.

Tubular artefacts with holes

Ten of the tubular bone artefacts have pierced holes, usually six in number, placed along the bone shaft (Fig. 14.9). Compared to other tubular artefacts, these artefacts are relatively short and broad (Fig. 14.10). The size varies from 28.4 mm to 44.8 mm in length and from 7.4 mm to 11.7 mm in breadth. All the artefacts were made from swan (*Cygnus* sp.) ulna or radius. Although these artefacts resemble flutes,

Figure 14.9 Tubular artefacts with holes (ID 34677a–c) from grave 62 at Ajvide. Taxonomic identifications from left to right: radius? of swan; radius of swan; unidentified (photograph: Johan Norderäng).

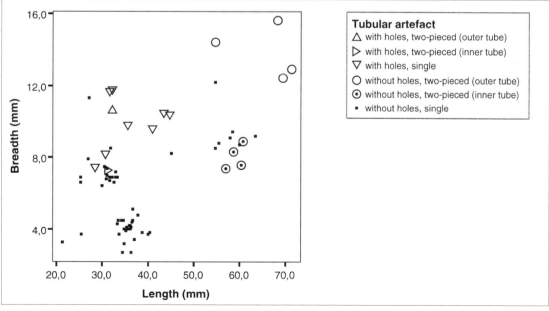

Figure 14.10 Scatter plot of the sizes of tubular artefacts from grave 62 at Ajvide.

Table 14.2. Taxonomic and anatomical identifications and measurements of the tubular bone artefacts in grave 62 at Ajvide. Abbreviations: ID no. = ID (identification) number; Str. = structuring of the tubes of the two-pieced artefacts; Anatom. = anatomical part; sin. = sinister; dex. = dexter; L = length (mm); B = greatest breadth (mm); Burenhult = Burenhult's (2002, 116–117) interpretation of the artefact. NB: Since the identification numbers are not to be found on the actual artefacts, it is debatable whether the numbers given here are correct. The numbering in the table is based on Burenhult's (ibid.) description and the reconstruction of the grave at Gotland Museum.

ID no.	Artefact type	Str.	Animal species	Anatom.	L.	B.	Burenhult
34646	tubular with holes	–	*Cygnus* sp.	radius sin.	35.5	9.7	single flute
34647	tubular without holes	outer	*Cygnus* sp.	ulna sin.	71.3	12.9	large single flute
	tubular with holes	inner	–	–	31.5	7.3	–
34648	tubular without holes	outer	*Cygnus* sp.	ulna sin.	54.8	14.4	large double flute
	tubular without holes	inner	*Cygnus* sp.	radius sin.	58.7	8.3	
34649	tubular without holes	outer	*Cygnus* sp.	ulna sin.	68.3	15.6	large double flute
	tubular without holes	inner	*Cygnus* sp.	radius sin.	60.7	8.9	
34650	tubular without holes	–	*Cygnus* sp.	ulna sin.	54.8	12.2	large single flute
34651	tubular without holes	–	*Cygnus* sp.	radius sin.	63.3	9.2	large single flute
34652	tubular without holes	–	*Cygnus* sp.	radius	58.5	9.4	large single flute
34653	tubular without holes	–	Anatidae	ulna	31.7	6.9	small single flute
34654	tubular without holes	–	*Phalocrocorax carbo?*	ulna	32.6	6.6	small single flute
34655	tubular without holes	–	*Larus* sp.	ulna sin.	33.0	7.2	small single flute
34656	tubular without holes	–	*Cygnus* sp.	radius	31.1	7.4	small single flute
34657	tubular without holes	–	–	ulna	25.2	6.6	small single flute
34662	tubular without holes	–	*Cygnus* sp.	radius sin.	30.8	8.6	small single flute
34675a	tubular without holes	–	*Cygnus* sp.	radius	31.8	8.5	small flute
34675b	tubular without holes	–	*Phalacrocorax carbo?*	ulna	29.9	6.4	small flute
34675c	tubular without holes	–	Anatidae	ulna	32.2	6.9	small flute
34675d	tubular without holes	–	*Larus* sp.	ulna sin.	33.4	6.9	small flute
34675e	tubular without holes	–	*Phalacrocorax carbo?*	ulna	31.7	6.7	small flute
34675f	tubular without holes	–	*Larus* sp.	ulna	32.9	6.9	small flute
34675g	tubular without holes	–	*Cygnus* sp.	radius	30.4	7.5	small flute
34676	tubular without holes	–	*Cygnus* sp.	radius dex.	55.4	8.8	large single flute
34677a	tubular with holes	–	–	–	32.1	11.7	single flute
34677b	tubular with holes	–	*Cygnus* sp.?	radius?	44.8	10.3	single flute
34677c	tubular with holes	–	*Cygnus* sp.	radius	43.4	10.4	single flute
34696	tubular without holes	–	*Larus* sp.	radius	25.5	3.7	small single flute
34697	tubular without holes	–	*Larus* sp.?	ulna	25.2	6.9	small single flute
34698	tubular without holes	–	*Cygnus* sp.	radius dex.	26.9	7.9	small single flute
34699	tubular without holes	–	–	–	–	–	small single flute
34700	tubular without holes	–	*Cygnus* sp.	radius dex.	57.9	9.1	large single flute
34701	tubular without holes	–	*Cygnus* sp.	radius sin.	59.9	8.7	large single flute
34702	tubular without holes	–	*Cygnus* sp.	radius	45.1	8.2	large single flute
34703	tubular without holes	outer	*Cygnus* sp.	ulna	69.4	12.4	large double flute
	tubular without holes	inner	*Grus grus?*	ulna	60.3	7.6	
34704	tubular with holes	outer	*Cygnus* sp.	ulna	32.1	10.7	small double flute
	tubular without holes	inner	*Cygnus* sp.	radius	56.9	7.4	
34705	tubular with holes	–	–	ulna	28.4	7.4	small single flute
34706	tubular with holes	–	*Cygnus* sp.	radius	30.7	8.1	small single flute
34707	tubular with holes	–	*Cygnus* sp.?	ulna sin.	31.7	11.6	small single flute
34708	tubular with holes	–	*Cygnus* sp.	radius dex.	41.1	9.5	small single flute
34709	tubular without holes	–	*Cygnus* sp.	ulna	27.2	11.3	small single flute
34711a	tubular without holes	–	*Cygnus* sp.	radius sin.	54.8	8.5	large single flute
34711b	tubular without holes	–	*Larus* sp.	ulna dex.	31.1	7.0	small single flute
34712a	tubular without holes	–	Anatidae	ulna dex.	36.6	5.1	bead
34712b	tubular without holes	–	Anatidae	ulna dex.	36.5	4.4	bead
34712c	tubular without holes	–	Alcidae?	tibiotarsus?	37.8	4.8	bead
34712d	tubular without holes	–	*Lepus timidus*	metatarsus?	34.9	3.2	bead
34712e	tubular without holes	–	*Lepus timidus*	metatarsus?	37.0	3.4	bead

ID no.	Artefact type	Str.	Animal species	Anatom.	L.	B.	Burenhult
34712f	tubular without holes	–	*Lepus timidus*	metatarsus?	34.8	4.0	bead
34712g	tubular without holes	–	*Lepus timidus*	metatarsus?	36.0	4.0	bead
34712h	tubular without holes	–	*Lepus timidus*	metatarsus?	36.2	4.0	bead
34712i	tubular without holes	–	*Lepus timidus*	metatarsus?	35.7	4.0	bead
34712j	tubular without holes	–	*Lepus timidus*	metatarsus?	35.3	4.1	bead
34712k	tubular without holes	–	*Lepus timidus*	metatarsus?	33.5	4.5	bead
34712l	tubular without holes	–	*Lepus timidus*	metatarsus?	38.7	3.8	bead
34712m	tubular without holes	–	*Lepus timidus*	metatarsus?	40.1	3.7	bead
34712n	tubular without holes	–	*Lepus timidus*	metatars. sin.	35.2	3.9	bead
34712o	tubular without holes	–	*Lepus timidus*	metatars. dex.	35.5	4.0	bead
34712p	tubular without holes	–	*Lepus timidus*	metatarsus?	36.0	4.2	bead
34712q	tubular without holes	–	*Lepus timidus*	metatarsus?	33.6	3.7	bead
34712r	tubular without holes	–	*Lepus timidus*	metatars. IV	21.2	3.3	bead
34712s	tubular without holes	–	*Lepus timidus*	metatarsus?	36.3	4.1	bead
34712t	tubular without holes	–	*Lepus timidus*	metatarsus?	33.4	4.3	bead
34712u	tubular without holes	–	*Lepus timidus*	metatarsus?	34.2	4.5	bead
34712v	tubular without holes	–	*Lepus timidus*	metatarsus?	36.2	4.2	bead
34712w	tubular without holes	–	*Lepus timidus*	metatarsus?	40.5	3.8	bead
34712x	tubular without holes	–	–	–	36.6	4.5	bead
34712y	tubular without holes	–	–	–	34.7	4.5	bead
34712z	tubular without holes	–	–	–	36.4	2.7	bead
34712å	tubular without holes	–	–	–	34.4	2.7	bead

there are holes on both sides of the tubes, which would not be practical for a player. In addition, the shape and size of the holes seem to be rather unsuitable for finger-holes. These details, as well as, the structure and placement of possible sound-holes, blow-holes and use-wear marks on them should be studied systematically before coming to any conclusion. Besides, it should be taken into account that there is a wide variety of wind instruments in the world. Traditional flutes in Spain and France have two or three holes on the backside: two for thumbs and one for a little finger (Brown 1984, 763–764; Schechter 1984, 766; Payno 2002). Furthermore, the artefacts could have functioned as reed instruments, with separate reeds as mouthpieces. Olov Gibson's (pers. comm. 2011) experiment, however, does not support this idea.

Double-pieced tubular artefacts

Five of the tubular artefacts have additional tubes at one end, which makes these artefacts double-pieced (Fig. 14.11). Compared to other tubular artefacts, these tubes are long and broad (Fig. 14.10). The size of the individual tubes varies from 54.8 mm to 71.3 mm in length and from 7.4 mm to 15.6 mm in breadth. Seven single tubes that cluster in the same group could be parts of broken artefacts (Fig. 14.12). Most of the double-pieced artefacts were made from swan ulna and radius. Although the two-piece structure is unusual in the flute family, parallels can be found worldwide, from South Africa to Finland.

For example, in so-called 'slide whistles' the inner tube can be moved to obtain different notes, that is, frequencies of sound (Leisiö 1983, 39, 118–119, 154; Rycroft 1984, 280–281).

Large single tubular artefacts without holes

Nearly 20 of the single tubular artefacts without holes seem to form a group of their own (Fig. 14.13). They are clearly smaller than the tubes of the double-pieced artefacts, but remarkably larger than the artefacts in the final group (Fig. 14.10). Their size varies from 25.2 mm to 33.0 mm in length and from 6.4 mm to 8.5 mm in breadth. The artefacts have been made from the ulna or radius of great cormorant (*Phalacrocorax carbo*), swan, duck (*Anatidae*) or some large species of gull (*Larus* sp.). Interestingly enough, these artefacts can also be interpreted as flutes. In the 1970s, music archaeologist Cajsa Lund (1984/1991, 42–43; cf. Janzon 1974, 74; Lund 1988, 301–302) studied similar bone tubes from Middle Neolithic Ire and Stora Förvar, Gotland. She was able to produce sound by blowing across the ends of the tubes. According to her, this high-pitched sound could have been used to imitate birds and lure them within shooting or catching range. In this case, the structure of the flute is simple and typical for the flute family. However, the structure is so simple that there is no way of distinguishing these artefacts from, for example, large bone beads. A skillful player would probably be able to produce sound by blowing across the ends of the largest beads.

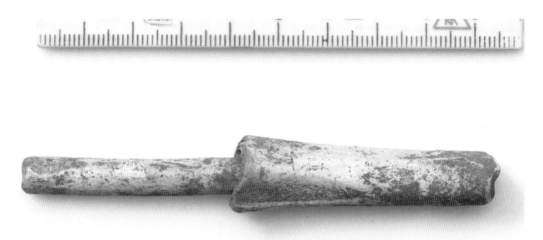

Figure 14.11 Two-pieced tubular artefact without holes (ID 34648) made of ulna and radius of swan from grave 62 at Ajvide (photograph: Johan Norderäng).

Figure 14.12 Single tubular artefact without holes (ID 34651) made of radius of swan from grave 62 at Ajvide (photograph: Johan Norderäng).

Small single tubular artefacts without holes

About 28 single tubular artefacts without holes form the last group; the so-called bone beads (Fig. 14.14). These artefacts are markedly smaller than all the other artefacts, especially in their breadth, which varies from 2.5 mm to 5.1 mm (Fig. 14.10). Such narrow tubes could hardly have been blown as flutes. Eighteen of the artefacts were made of mountain hare (*Lepus timidus*) bones and the remainder from bird bones (Mannermaa 2008, 9). Bone beads are fairly common at Ajvide. They were found in eleven single burials, three multiple burials and one cenotaph – a grave lacking a human skeleton. Most of the artefacts were made from the wing bones of birds, mainly swan, common crane, great cormorant and guillemot (*Uria aalge*) (Mannermaa 2008, 9–10, Fig. 14.9). Beads have been found as single contexts or in clusters of two beads or more. Especially at Ire, larger clusters seem to comprise dress

ornaments, necklaces or headgear (cf. Janzon 1974, 67–74, Figs 14.15–16). An interesting feature is that the beads seem to appear in matching pairs: in a single grave it is often possible to find two identical beads made from the left and right side element of the same individual animal (Mannermaa 2008, 10, Fig. 14.8).

Other possible types of musical instruments at Ajvide

In addition to the potential flutes, other types of finds in Ajvide graves could be studied as potential musical instruments. In grave 62, the find concentration near the right arm of the deceased – apparently a bag or pouch – contains a cluster of tooth pendants: 39 seal teeth and four wild boar teeth with pierced holes in their upper ends (Figs 14.15 and 14.16)

*Figure 14.13 Single tubular artefacts without holes (ID 34675a–g) from grave 62 at Ajvide. Taxonomic identifications from left to right: ulna of gull (*Larus sp.*); radius of swan; radius of swan; ulna of duck (*Anatidae*); ulna of great cormorant (*Phalacrocorax carbo*); ulna of gull; ulna of great cormorant (photograph: Johan Norderäng).*

Figure 14.14 Single tubular artefact without holes (ID 34696) made of radius of gull from grave 62 at Ajvide (photograph: Johan Norderäng).

(cf. Sachs 1928/1965, 8–9; Janzon 1974, 88). This interpretation also involves clustered beads or other tubular artefacts (cf. Lund 1984/1991, 6–7). Wild boar, seal or even European hedgehog mandibles, found in some of the Ajvide graves (e.g. Burenhult 2002, 44, 114–117), could have been used as rasps. In such musical instruments, sound is produced by scraping an uneven surface – for example a row of teeth – with a stick or other rigid objects (Sachs 1928/1965, 16–18). This interpretation was originally suggested by Janzon (1974, 77–78; cf. Lund 1997, 36) for the wild boar mandibles of Ire.

Interpretation of musical instruments in Stone Age archaeology – some general considerations

As expressed above, we do not yet know whether some of the tubular artefacts should be interpreted as musical instruments. However, the idea of flutes at Ajvide is not new nor is it extraordinary or sensational in a global archaeological perspective. Ethnomusicologists have found musical instruments in the most archaic cultures in Africa,

(Burenhult 2002, 116). In graves 1, 2 and 5 similar clusters of tooth pendants seem to form an edging or clothing application at the thighs or hips of the deceased (Burenhult 2002, 43–45, figs 12, 15, 16, 24, 25). When the bearer of this kind of cloth, skirt or apron moved, the pendants would click against one another. In other words, they would function as rattles

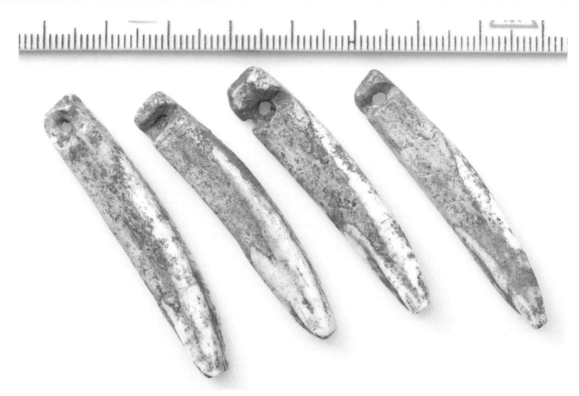

Figure 14.15 Pendants (ID 34671) made of wild boar (Sus scrofa) *teeth from grave 62 at Ajvide (photograph: Johan Norderäng).*

Figure 14.16 Upper part of the skeleton and the concentration of finds near the right arm of the deceased in grave 62 at Ajvide (a reconstruction of the grave at Gotland Museum) (photograph: Kristiina Mannermaa).

Asia and North and South America (Sachs 1928/1965, 1940). Since flutes, rattles and rasps were popular musical instruments in recent hunter-fisher-gatherer societies, they have been regarded as the oldest types of musical instruments deriving from the Stone Age (Sachs 1928/1965, 8–9, 16–18, 1940, 60–64). Although archaeologists have found similar artefacts at many Stone Age sites (e.g. Saint-Pèrier 1930, 65; Seewald 1934, 11–13, T. I: 1–4; Scothern 1986, 75, fig. 2g; Dauvois 1994; Hickmann 1997b, 82; Morley 2003, 37–43; d'Errico *et al.* 2005), these finds have rarely been studied systematically from the music-archaeological point of view. Recent reports on Palaeolithic flute finds are a positive exception to this rule (e.g. Lawson and d'Errico 2002; Münzel *et al.* 2002; Conard and Malina 2008). Potential prehistoric musical instruments should be studied using both musicological and archaeological methods: paying attention to the sound-related structures of the artefacts and use-wear marks that could refer to sound production. In addition, the artefacts should be replicated and the replicas tested in practice.

A couple of recent archaeological reports seem to support the musical interpretation of clustered bone pendants. Mannermaa (2006, 294) and Larsson (2006, 276) have studied use-wear marks on duck humerus and animal tooth pendants in Mesolithic and Neolithic graves at Zvejnieki in Latvia. Based on the use-wear marks on the bone surface and around the holes, the pendants hung on a string and were able to move freely. This means that they were not tightly fastened to the substratum. Experimental studies show that a considerable time of use is needed before such a heavy use-wear can develop on the pendants (Larsson 2006, 276).

When studying such a remote past like the Stone Age, it is impossible to draw a clear line between music and something that is "non-music". Nor is it possible or meaningful to distinguish between musical instruments and more practical sound tools, for example for imitating birdcalls. In our initial study, we will look at a wide variety of sound production: sounds heard in rituals, funerals, feasts, hunting, fishing and daily practices. Moreover, we are interested in all environmental sounds: sounds of birds, mammals, plants, sea and weather. Our aim is to understand how people comprehended these sounds and constructed and responded to their sonic environment. The extremely rich and well preserved osteological material from Ajvide provides favourable prerequisites for this kind of reconstruction. As we have not yet made a precise study on the usage and use-wear marks of the artefacts of grave 62, we cannot say if the hypothesis of their musical function is correct. However, in the future, this approach can provide insights into the function and meaning of the instruments and their sounds as well as the roles of sound in so-called daily life and ritual, including burial practices. This study has the potential for shedding light on the early history of music, for example the relationship of music – i.e. organized sound – to other sound environments.

Conclusions

In this article, we have described extraordinary tubular bone artefacts found in the *c.* 4500 year-old female burial, grave 62, from the Middle Neolithic site of Ajvide in Gotland. Although these artefacts were found in different parts of the grave, most of them concentrated at some distance from the right arm of the deceased, in a possible bag or pouch made of hide. As this concentration also contained clustered animal tooth pendants and mandibles, it is possible that the artefacts formed a kind of sound producing device or devices, like flutes, rattles and rasps. Whatever function the specimens had, it is evident that they were important in the burial practice or rituals connected to it. The woman in grave 62 was not an ordinary person from her community. The selection of unique artefacts that followed her in death can be seen as reflecting her personality, special skills or qualifications, and a special role in the family, tribe or society.

A detailed microscopic study of the tubular artefacts and other specimens has recently begun. Our aim is to analyze use-wear marks on the artefacts to interpret their uses. Manufacturing marks will also be analyzed since we will make replicas of the finds and investigate whether they can be played in practice. Our working hypothesis will be that the tubular artefacts, as well as many other finds in grave 62, may all have musical functions. We know that there are several other lines of interpretation which could be followed, for example the use of the tubular artefacts as necklaces, dress ornaments, buttons or some kind of sewing implements. The evaluation of these hypotheses, however, will demand research projects of their own.

Acknowledgements

We want to thank Göran Burenhult and Johan Norderäng, both from the University of Gotland, for providing us photos and drawings. Antti Halkka and Tarja Sundell, both from the University of Helsinki, are acknowledged for their comments on the previous versions of the manuscript, and Paresh Joshi for the language revision.

Bibliography

Brown, H. M. (1984) Flageolet. In S. Sadie (ed.), *Dictionary of Musical Instruments* 1, 763–764. London, Macmillan.
Burenhult, G. (1997a) Gravarnas vittnesbörd. In G. Burenhult (ed.), *Ajvide och den Moderna Arkeologin*, 52–70. Falköping, Natur och kultur.
Burenhult, G. (1997b) Introduction. In G. Burenhult (ed.), *Remote Sensing. Applied techniques for the study of cultural resources and the localization, identification and documentation of sub-surface prehistoric remains in Swedish archaeology* 1, IX. Hässleholm, Stockholm University (Theses and Papers in Swedish Archaeology 13:a).

Burenhult, G. (2002) The grave-field at Ajvide. In G. Burenhult (ed.), *Remote sensing. Applied techniques for the study of cultural resources and the localization, identification and documentation of sub-surface prehistoric remains in Swedish archaeology* 2, 31–168. Hässleholm, Stockholm University (Theses and papers in North-European Archaeology 13:b).

Conard, N. and Malina, M. (2008) New evidence for the origins of music from the caves of the Swabian Jura. In A. A. Both, R. Eichmann, E. Hickmann and L. C. Koch (eds), *Challenges and Objectives in Music Archaeology: Studien zur Musikarchäologie 6, 13*–22. Berlin and Rahden Westfalen, Deutsches Archäologisches Institut Orient-Abteilung and Marie Leidorf.

Dauvois, M. (1994) Les temoins sonores paleolithiques. In C. Homo-Lechner (ed.), *La Pluridisciplinaritè en Archèologie Musicale,* 1–2, 151–206. Recherche Musique et Danse 11. Paris, Maison des Sciences de l'Homme.

Edenmo, R., Larsson, M., Nordqvist, B. and Olsson, E. (1997) Gropkeramikerna – fanns de? In M. Larsson and E. Olsson (eds), *Regionalt och Interregionalt: Stenåldersundersökningar i Syd-och Mellansverige,* 135–211. Stockholm, Riksantikvarieämbetet (Arkeologiska Undersökningar Skrifter 23).

D'Errico, F., Henshilwood, C. S., Vanhaeren, M. and van Niekerk, K. (2005) Nassarius kraussianus shell beads from Blombos cave: evidence for symbolic behaviour in the Middle Stone Age. *Journal of Human Evolution* 48, 3–24.

Hickmann, E. (1997a) Musikarchäologie: I Begriffsbestimmung Aufgabenfeld. In F. Blume (ed.), *Die Musik in Geschichte und Gegenwart: Allgemeine Enzyklopädie der Musik 6, 929*–935. Kassel, Bärenreiter.

Hickmann, E. (1997b) Rasseln VI: Archäologische Rasseln. In F. Blume (ed.), *Die Musik in Geschichte und Gegenwart: Allgemeine Enzyklopädie der Musik 8, 82*–86. Kassel, Bärenreiter.

Hickmann, E. (2000) Music archaeology – an introduction. In E. Hickmann and I. Laufs (eds), *Saiteninstrumente im Archäologischen Kontext: Studien zur Musikarchäologie 1, 1*–4. Berlin and Rahden Westfalen, Deutsches Archäologisches Institut Orient-Abteilung and Marie Leidorf.

Hickmann, E. (2007) Archaeomusicology. *Oxford Music Online.* http://www.oxfordmusiconline.com/subscriber/article/grove/music/47381 (accessed 13 March 2009).

Janzon, G. O. (1974) *Gotlands Mellanneolitiska Gravar.* Stockholm, Almqvist & Wiksell (Studies in North-European Archaeology 6).

Johansson, N. (2009) *25 År Senare: en Nyinventering av Keramiken på Ajvide.* Uppsats i arkeologi. Högskolan på Gotland.

Larsson, L. (2006) Tooth for a tooth for a grave. Tooth ornaments from the graves at the cemetery of Zvejnieki. In L. Larsson and I. Zagorska (eds), *Back to the Origin. New research in the Mesolithic-Neolithic Zvejnieki cemetery and environment, northern Latvia,* 153–288. Stockholm, Almqvist & Wiksell (Acta Archaeologica Lundensia Series in 8, no 52).

Lawson, G. and d'Errico, F. (2002) Microscopic, experimental and theoretical re-Assessment of Upper Palaeolithic bird-bone pipes from Isturizt, France. In E. Hickmann, A. D. Kilmer and R. Eichmann (eds), *The Archaeology of Sound: Studien zur Musikarchäologie 3,* 119–142. Berlin & Rahden Westfalen, Deutsches Archäologisches Institut Orient-Abteilung & Marie Leidorf.

Leisiö, T. (1983) *Suomen ja Karjalan Vanhakantaiset Torvi- ja pillisoittimet.* Kansanmusiikki-instituutin julkaisuja 12. Kaustinen, Kansanmusiikki-instituutti.

Lidén, K., Nuñez, M. and Nelson, E. (1995) Diet and nutritional stress in the subneolithic population from the Åland Islands. An analysis of stable carbon isotopes and pathological traits. In *Arkælogiske Rapporter/ Esbjerg Museum* 1. Esbjerg, Esbjerg Museum.

Lund, C. (1979) Metoder och problem inom Nordens musikarkeologi. *Svensk Tidskrift för Musikforskning* 61 (1), 95–107.

Lund, C. (1981) Archaeomusicology of Scandinavia. *World Archaeology* 12 (3), 246–265.

Lund, C. (1984/1991) *Fornnordiska Klanger: the sounds of prehistoric Scandinavia.* CD-rom cover text. Musica Sveciae, MSCD 101.

Lund. C. (1988) On animal calls in ancient Scandinavia: theory and data. In E. Hickmann and D. W. Hughes (eds), *The Archaeology of Early Music Cultures: the Third International Meeting of the ICTM Study Group on Music Archaeology,* 292–303. Bonn, Verlag für systematische Musikwissenschaft.

Lund, C. (1997) En storslagen uvertyr: bronslurarna. In G. Andersson (ed.), *Musik i Norden,* 34–50. Stockholm, Kungliga musikaliska Akademien (Kungliga musikaliska akademiens skriftserie 85).

Mannermaa, K. (2006) Bird remains in the human burials at Zvejnieki, Latvia. Introduction to bird finds and a proposal for interpretation. In L. Larsson and I. Zagorska (eds), *Back to the Origin. New research in the Mesolithic-Neolithic Zvejnieki cemetery and environment, northern Latvia,* 289–300. Stockholm, Almqvist & Wiksell (Acta Archaeologica Lundensia Series in 8, no 52).

Mannermaa, K. (2008) Birds and burials at Ajvide (Gotland, Sweden) and Zvejnieki (Latvia) about 8000–3900 BP. *Journal of Anthropological Archaeology* 27, 201–225.

Mannermaa, K. and Storå, J. (2006) Stone Age exploitation of birds on the Island of Gotland, Baltic Sea. *International Journal of Osteoarchaeology* 16, 429–452.

Molnar, P. (2002) Anthropological analysis of the skeletal material from Ajvide, Eksta Sn. Gotland. In G. Burenhult (ed.), *Remote Sensing. Applied techniques for the study of cultural resources and the localization, identification and documentation of sub-surface prehistoric remains in Swedish archaeology* 2, 371–374. Hässleholm, Stockholm university (Theses and papers in North-European Archaeology 13:b).

Molnar, P. (2008) Antropologisk beskrivning av de mänskliga skelettlämningarna från Ajvide. In I. Österholm *Jakobs/Ajvide: Undersökningar på en gotländsk boplatsudde från stenåldern,* 276–286. Hässleholm, Gotland University (Gotland University Press Monograph 3).

Morley, I. (2003) *The Evolutionary Origins and Archaeology of Music.* Doctoral thesis. Electronic edition in 2006. http://www.dar.cam.ac.uk/dcrr (accessed 18.Februrary 2011).

Münzel, S., Seeberger, F. and Hein, W. (2002) The Geissenklösterle Flute: discovery, experiments, reconstruction. In E. Hickmann, A. D. Kilmer and R. Eichmann (eds), *The Archaeology of Sound: Studien zur Musikarchäologie 3,* 107–118. Berlin & Rahden Westfalen, Deutsches Archäologisches Institut Orient-Abteilung & Marie Leidorf.

Norderäng, J. (2008a) *Ajvideboplatsen. Rapport från arkeologisk undersökning 2008 av fornlämning nr. 171 på fastigheten Ajvide 2:1 i Eksta socken, Gotland.* Högskolan på Gotland.

Norderäng, J. (2008b) ^{14}C-dateringar från Ajvide. In I. Österholm *Jakobs/ Ajvide: Undersökningar på en gotländsk boplatsudde från stenåldern,* 296–297. Hässleholm, Gotland University (Gotland University Press Monograph 3).

Olson, C., Limburg, K., Patterson, W., Elfman, M., Kristiansson, P. and Ehrenberg, S. (2002) Reconstruction of fisheries and marine environment: preliminary studies on hard parts of codfish (*Gadus morhua*) from Ajvide, Gotland, Sweden. In G. Burenhult (ed.), *Remote Sensing. Applied techniques for the study of cultural resources and the localization, identification and documentation of sub-surface prehistoric remains in Swedish archaeology* 2, 375–385. Hässleholm, Stockholm University (Theses and papers in North-European Archaeology 13:b).

Österholm, I. (1989) *Bosättningsmönster på Gotland under stenåldern. En analys av fysisk miljö, ekonomi och struktur.* Stockholm, I. Österholm (Theses and Papers in Archaeology 3).

Österholm, I. (1998a) Flöjter, praktkam, pärlemorplattor – nya hantverk från Ajvide på Gotland. *Populär Arkeologi* 3, 34–35.

Österholm, I. (1998b) Intressanta stenåldersfynd vid Ajvide i Eksta. *Gotländskt Arkiv* 70, 218–220.

Payno, L. A. (2002) *Construcción de Instrumentos Tradicionales.* http://www.es-aqui.com/payno/pdf/flabiol.jpg (accessed 02 February 2011).

Possnert, G. (2002) Stable and radiometric carbon results from Ajvide. In G. Burenhult (ed.) *Remote Sensing. Applied techniques for the study of cultural resources and the localization, identification and documentation of sub-surface prehistoric remains in Swedish archaeology* 2, 169–172. Hässleholm, Stockholm university (Theses and papers in North-European Archaeology 13:b).

Rycroft, D. K. (1984) Igemfe. In S. Sadie (ed.), *The New Grove Dictionary of Musical Instruments* 2, 280–281. London, Macmillan.

Sachs, C. (1928/1965) *Geist und Werden der Musikinstrumente.* Hilversum, Frits A. M. Knuf.

Sachs, C. (1940) *The History of Musical Instruments.* New York, Norton.

Saint-Pèrier, R. (1930) *La Grotte d'Isturitz* I. *Archives de l'Institut de palèontologie humaine.* Paris, Masson et Cie.

Schechter, J. M. (1984) Flaviol. In S. Sadie (ed.) *The New Grove Dictionary of Musical Instruments* 1, 766. London, Macmillan.

Scothern, P. M. T. (1986) Presentation of a music-archaeological research project. The musical evidences of the palaeolithic: a palaeo-organological survey. In C. Lund (ed.), *Second Conference of the ICTM Study Group on Music Archaeology* 1, 73–79. Stockholm, Kungl. Musikaliska Akademien.

Seewald, O. (1934) *Beiträge zur Kenntnis der steinzeitlichen Musikinstrumente Europas.* Wien, Anton Schroll.

Storå, J. (2000) Sealing and animal husbandry in the Ålandic Middle and Late Neolithic. *Fennoscandia Archaeologica* XVI, 57–81.

CHAPTER 15

Strict Rules – Loose Rules: Raw Material Preferences at the Late Neolithic Site of Aszód in Central Hungary

Zsuzsanna Tóth

The site of Aszód–Papi földek in Central Hungary lay on the border between the two main cultural complexes of the Late Neolithic (5000/4900–4500/4400 BC), the Lengyel and Tisza Cultures. It has long been suggested by researchers that the people living here controlled local obsidian exploitation and played an important role in the circulation of this and other raw materials and products such as Spondylus or antler. Traces of this role emerge from comparison of the archaeozoological material and the worked osseous assemblage. The archaeozoological material is characteristic of the Late Neolithic in the region with cattle dominating faunal assemblages and an increased importance of game animals. The worked osseous material shows clear preferences for skeletal elements from cervids and caprines and an increased role for red deer antler compared to earlier Neolithic periods. In this paper, I will look at some of the rules governing raw material selection at Aszód-Papi földek in comparison to two other coeval Late Neolithic sites in Hungary and explore why the people living here produced antler tools in such great numbers.

Keywords
Hungary; Late Neolithic; raw material; skeletal element preference; manufacturing rules.

Introduction

Rules and regulations govern behaviour in many aspects of daily human actions. The average Late Neolithic toolkit consists of, more or less, similar tool types and forms. Technological levels and functional needs were widespread and consistent within the Carpathian Basin. The fixed anatomic form of the raw material represents both possibilities and limitations in their transformation into usable working tools. The technology and the basic ideas for working hard osseous materials are common across the Late Neolithic of Hungary as well, something which also explains the similar composition of the toolkits. There are two areas, however where differences emerge between sites in different regions. Comparison of basic tool types shows that percentage contributions of particular types can vary. At some sites one tool type seems to have been preferred over another used in the same tasks. The other big difference lies in the different technical traditions of the people living in these settlements. There are sites where the traditional rules of manufacturing certain tool types from a distinct raw material and skeletal element in a certain way is very strictly followed while at other sites these rules are more loose, allowing the production of certain tool types from much more variable raw materials and skeletal elements. In some cases, the manufacturing process and the techniques may vary as well. In this paper, the hard osseous tools and ornaments from Aszód-Papi földek will be compared to another large, southern Transdanubian site at Alsónyék-Bátaszék – so far the largest settlement and cemetery of the Lengyel Culture found in Hungary, and another slightly earlier settlement at Öcsöd-Kováshalom on the Great Hungarian Plain (Fig. 15.1).

Öcsöd-Kováshalom is a large 'tell-like' settlement (Raczky 2009, 102) with two major phases and six levels (Phase A: lower 6th–4th level level, Phase B: upper 3rd–1st level) with the cultural layers attaining a maximum thickness of 160 cm. The C^{14} dates [5180 (68.2%) 5050–4980 (68.2%) 4850 cal BC based on Raczky 2009, fig. 3, recalibrated with OxCal 4.1 IntCal 09] show that the settlement at Aszód-Papi földek was founded when life at Öcsöd had already come to an end. AMS dates confirm a short lifespan for the settlement at Aszód at 4800 (68.2%) 4720–4790 (68.2%) 4680 cal BC and for the cemetery 4760 (68.2%) 4700–4710 (68.2%) 4640 cal BC (N. Kalicz and Zs. Siklósi: Absolute and relative chronological position of the Aszód-Papi földek Late Neolithic site in the light of new radiocarbon dates. *Theory and Method in Archaeology of the Neolithic (7th–3rd Millenium BC)* Conference. 26–28 October 2010, Mikulov) corresponding to observations based on pottery style, settlement structure and graves. There were several excavation seasons at Alsónyék-Bátaszék (Gallina *et al.* 2010; Zalai-Gaál and Osztás 2009). A large settlement was unearthed here (an estimated area based on survey data over 722,000 m² with 243,180 m² excavated by several teams).

It contains remains of the Early Neolithic Starčevo Culture, the Middle Neolithic Transdanubian Linear Pottery Culture (TLPC), the Late Neolithic and Early Chalcolithic Lengyel Culture as well as finds from the Bronze Age and Celtic period. The Late Neolithic Lengyel Culture was the dominant period at the site. More than 8500 settlement features were recovered, including more than 70 houses. The cemetery contained more than 2400 graves. There are no definitive numbers yet for the features nor any AMS dates at the moment. New results may be expected as the study continues.

Aszód-Papi földek

This *c.* 20 hectares settlement and cemetery from the Late Neolithic Lengyel culture is one of the largest and most important sites of this period in Hungary (Kalicz 1985, 1998, 2006). It has close connections with Tisza Culture sites lying on the Great Hungarian Plain. Although Aszód is situated on the eastern side of the Danube, the settlement culturally belongs to the Transdanubian Lengyel cultural complex. Trade and exchange were very important factors in the settlement's development. The site is characterized by large amounts of obsidian, Spondylus shell and red deer antler. For decades it has

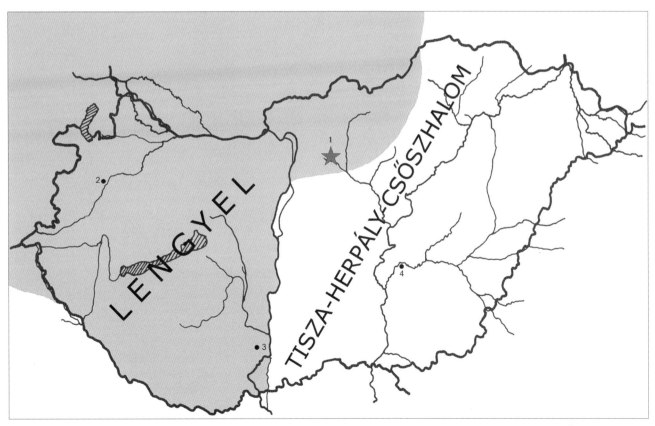

Figure 15.1 Cultural background and archaeological sites. 1) Aszód-Papi földek, 2) Gór-Kápolnadomb, 3) Alsónyék-Bátaszék, 4) Öcsöd-Kováshalom.

been accepted in scholarly discussions that the settlement was founded in order to exploit and exchange various raw materials considered valuable at this time (Kalicz 1985, 69–71).

Obsidian sources may be found on a relatively small territory in the Tokaj-Eperjes Mountains on the present day Hungarian as well as the Slovakian sides of the border. Obsidian was valued as a raw material in neolithic times for the knapped stone industry, and was traded over long distances (Biró 1998, 33–34). Researchers (Biró 1998, 34; Kalicz 1985, 69–70) have long suggested that due to its exceptional setting, Aszód may have been a settlement that specialized in the exploitation and trade in this raw material. Spondylus (Csengeri-Siklósi 2011) came from much more distant territories such as the Black and Aegean Seas. It may be assumed that trade played an important role in the distribution of this socially significant raw material as well. Finally, red deer antler may also have played an important role in the economic organisation of the site. The exceptionally large percentage contribution of antler at Aszód compared with what has been found at other coeval settlements suggests something special was going on here with regard to this important raw material.

At the moment, attempts to reconstruct the economy and the trade/exchange system in the Late Neolithic in the Carpathian Basin are hindered by the relatively small amount of its material culture found and studied from archaeological excavations. It is only possible to guess at the role of other critical commodities such as conserved meat or hide which may have led to more intense hunting activities. Such products could also have been exchanged between territories for other raw materials and goods (Kalicz-Raczky 1987, 122; Vörös 2005, 221). The excellent setting of the site and amount of foreign raw materials and goods found there during excavations underlines the fact that Aszód was an important trade and exchange centre between the western and eastern halves of the country in Late Neolithic times.

Archaeozoology at Aszód-Papi földek

The archaeozoological study was originally carried out by Sándor Bökönyi during and shortly after the excavation seasons. Unfortunately, he died before a detailed study could be published although some of the data, such as the bone size variations and age distribution graphs, are available (Bökönyi 1974, 1988), although his manuscript was lost sometime over the last decades so that details such as the skeletal element percentages in the faunal material are not available. Altogether Bökönyi identified 25,596 bone specimens. The faunal composition displays slightly more wild species (ratio of wild to domesticated animals: 57.12% compared to 42.88%).

Sándor Bökönyi was never able to finish the identification and study of the Aszód material. His study was continued by Zsófia Kovács (unpublished manuscript), who examined and identified a further 6855 specimens including 32 pieces of

river shell and 91 objects belonging to the worked osseous assemblage.

Thus, the two archaeozoological studies yielded a total of 32,419 bone specimens. Wild animals dominate (ratio of wild to domesticated animal: 55% compared to 45% from a NISP=28,739). This may be partly related to the setting of the site in the wooded mid-mountain region where wild species seem to have been more numerous (Choyke 1998; Choyke and Bartosiewicz 2009; Vörös 2005, 221. These so-called mountains do not exceed 300–1000 masl). They are thus also more represented in the archaeological material and played a bigger role in the economy. Among the wild species, the presence of red deer (*Cervus elaphus* L. 1758, 18.10%) is followed by wild boar (*Sus scrofa* L. 1758, 13.24%), aurochs (*Bos primigenius* Boj. 1827, 11.97%) roe deer (*Capreolus capreolus* L. 1758, 4.57%) and wild horse (*Equus ferus gmilini* Ant. 1912) in the assemblage clearly show the importance of wild species exploited for meat over fur-bearing species which number altogether 0.46%, represented by brown bear (*Ursus arctos* L. 1758), grey wolf (*Canis lupus* L. 1758), red fox (*Vulpes vulpes* L. 1758), marten (*Martes* sp.), badger (*Meles meles* L. 1758), hare (*Lepus europaeus* Pall. 1778) and beaver (*Castor fiber* L. 1758). Due to lack of fine excavation techniques some of the smaller fur-bearing species may well be under-represented in the assemblage. Nevertheless, this large diversity in wild species suggests proximity of this settlement to a mosaic-like environment suitable for different species preferring diverse habitats.

Of the domestic species, cattle (*Bos taurus* L. 1758) is the most numerous (30.15%) in the assemblage followed by pig (*Sus domesticus* Erx. 1777, 6.88%), caprines (Ovis/Capra, 1.69%) and dog (*Canis familiaris* L. 1758, 1.37%). This picture broadly corresponds to faunal composition at other Late Neolithic sites in Hungary. On average, Late Neolithic communities were mainly involved with breeding and exploiting cattle followed by pig with only a minor role played by small ruminants. Hunting becomes increasingly important with time. Due perhaps to varied environmental settings, roe deer dominates over red deer at settlements on the Great Hungarian Plain (Kovács and Gál 2009, table 1).

Worked osseous assemblage

The worked osseous assemblage of Aszód was first studied by István Vörös (unpublished manuscript), who identified the species and skeletal elements for 1312 objects. His identification and notes, to which he generously gave me free access, yielded a great deal of information about the assemblage itself and the taphonomic losses it has suffered over the last forty years. Due to intense interest by researchers organising exhibitions, several restoration campaigns and collection movements, a considerable part of the assemblage was lost or went missing. I had the possibility to study an

Table 15.1. Raw material choices for the hide beamers from the sites of Alsónyék-Bátaszék, Aszód-Papi földek and Öcsöd-Kováshalom.

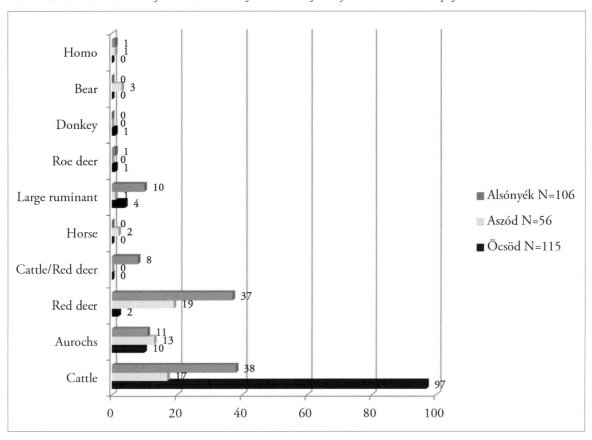

Table 15.2 Skeletal element distribution of hide beamers at the sites of Alsónyék-Bátaszék, Aszód-Papi földek and Öcsöd-Kováshalom.

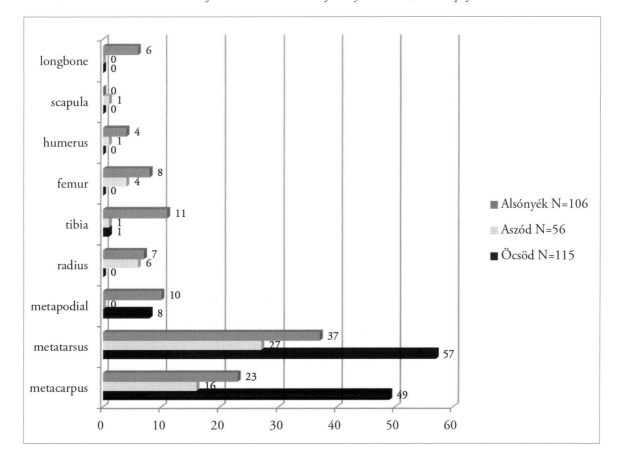

assemblage containing altogether 1123 pieces, the largest so far for this time period. Not many published assemblages exist for comparison in Hungary. One exception is the small collection of Gór-Kápolnadomb (Choyke 2006), a little 'appetizer' from Polgár-Csőszhalom (Choyke 1997b) and Berettyóújfalu-Herpály (Kalicz et al. 2011).

Different methods have been combined to get at as much information as possible for the interpretation of the collection. The typological systematization has been combined with the study of the selected raw material and skeletal element preferences, manufacturing processes and when possible a use-wear study. The typological system used by Jörg Schibler (Schibler 1981) and colleagues for Neolithic lake dwelling materials i.e. Twann (Schibler 1981; Suter 1981), Zürich-Mozartstrasse (Schibler 1987, 1997), Arbon-Bleiche 3 (Deschler-Erb et al. 2004), St Blaise-Bains des Dames (Choyke and Bartosiewicz unpublished manuscript), was very useful. This system can be easily adopted for any prehistoric collection in Europe.

The worked osseous assemblage contains altogether 1123 pieces, 633 pieces (56%) made from red and roe deer antler and 490 pieces (47%) from bone and some from tusk coming from eleven species. (Table 15.3)

The comparison of the archaeozoological material to the worked osseous material regarding species and skeletal element preferences is unfortunately limited because S. Bökönyi's manuscript containing the data from 25,596 pieces, the majority of the material, cannot be found. The comparison between the species could be carried out based on his report to the Hungarian Academy of Sciences containing a faunal list with the exact number of bones identified. The comparison of the species combined with skeletal elements was unfortunately not possible. Thus, a detailed study could only be based upon the assemblage studied by Zs. Kovács although this proved to be too small for statistical evaluation. A χ^2 test was carried out on the whole material regarding animal species. This showed the presence of some species to be homogenous, but other species turned out to be over-represented in the worked osseous assemblage compared to the archaeozoological material. Cattle, aurochs, domestic pig and wild swine were homogeneous (χ^2= 3.166; df= 3; P=0.367) while caprinae, small ruminants (*Ovis/Capra/Capreolus*) and red deer were over-represented in the worked material (χ^2= 309.274; df= 4; P=0.000). The over-representation of caprinae and roe deer is clearly related to the selection of these bones as raw material for the production of awls (Schibler type 1/1; 1/2; 1/3; 1/7). This is especially true for sheep and goat metapodials which are much more numerous in the worked osseous assemblage than their representation in the archaeozoological material (1.69% see above) would suggest. There was clear selection for roe deer metapodials as well, but this seems to be secondary compared to the great importance of sheep and goat bone in tool production. In the case of red deer, the test shows a significant over-representation of raw materials from this

Table 15.3 Composition of the worked osseous assemblage.

Species / Typol.	Bos t.	Bos prim.	Large urgulate	Ursus arctos	Equus caballus	Ovis aries	Capra hircus	Ovis/Capra	Ovis/Capra/Capreolus	Capreolus capreolus	Cervus elaphus	Sus dom.	Sus scrofa	Lepus europeus	Canis/Vulpes	Homo	Unid	Total
Awls	3	–	21	–	–	7	1	137	16	39	16	6	–	1	2	1	5	255
Rib burnishers	5	2	–	–	–	–	–	–	–	–	–	–	–	–	–	–	–	7
Spatulas	–	–	1	–	–	–	–	–	13	–	1	–	–	–	–	–	82	97
Bevel ends	2	2	1	–	–	–	–	–	–	4	2	–	–	–	1	–	–	12
Hide-beamers	17	13	1	3	2	–	–	–	–	–	19	–	–	–	–	1	–	56
Tooth	6	–	–	–	–	–	–	–	–	–	–	–	22	–	–	–	–	28
Waste	3	–	3	–	–	–	–	–	–	–	3	–	–	–	–	–	–	9
Other	–	2	2	–	–	–	–	–	–	–	–	–	–	–	–	–	22	26
Bone																		**490**
Axe/adze	–	–	–	–	–	–	–	–	–	–	191	–	–	–	–	–	–	191
Hammer	–	–	–	–	–	–	–	–	–	–	11	–	–	–	–	–	–	11
Pick	–	–	–	–	–	–	–	–	–	–	12	–	–	–	–	–	–	12
Socket	–	–	–	–	–	–	–	–	–	–	7	–	–	–	–	–	–	7
Punch	–	–	–	–	–	–	–	–	–	2	4	–	–	–	–	–	–	6
Point	–	–	–	–	–	–	–	–	–	13	–	–	–	–	–	–	–	13
Bevel end	–	–	–	–	–	–	–	–	–	2	–	–	–	–	–	–	–	2
Waste	–	–	–	–	–	–	–	–	–	8	364	–	–	–	–	–	–	372
Other	–	–	–	–	–	–	–	–	–	–	19	–	–	–	–	–	–	19
Antler																		**633**

species although it should be stressed that this is because antler artefacts were included in the data.

Awls

Caprinae and roe deer are not really emphatically different in morphological terms, but their metapodials are greatly over-represented in the worked osseous material. They were clearly appreciated as a raw material and kept to produce bi-partitioned awls with either the proximal (Schibler type 1/1) or the distal epiphysis (Schibler type 1/2) removed (Fig. 15.2, 1–2). Awls of all types comprise 52% of the worked bone assemblage. The presence of roe deer is very pronounced among the small ruminant metapodial awls, reflecting a special preference at Aszód for this raw material. A special subtype, slender, quartered awls, occurs here more frequently than at other sites (Choyke and Tóth 2013). Among the small and middle-sized awls, this

'species triad', caprinae and roe deer is most important but more rarely pig bones, fibula (Fig. 15.2, 3) or mandible fragments, hare radii and in one case, a human humerus, were used as well.

This group is the most numerous among all the pointed tools, but the use-wear observations demonstrated that they were multi-purpose tools. Most were used on soft materials, whether leather or textile. A goodly proportion was also utilized on more rigid materials in more forceful actions (i.e. bark) but there may have been other use wear possibilities as well which have not been preserved.

Large ungulate (cattle) awls are almost entirely missing at Aszód in contradistinction to the situation at other Late Neolithic sites such as the proximal metatarsal awl from cattle (Schibler type 1/6) from Gór-Kápolnadomb (Choyke 2006, fig. 2a), where they can be found regularly, although not in great numbers. The large ungulates are only represented in Aszód by red deer metapodials used as raw material. Massive

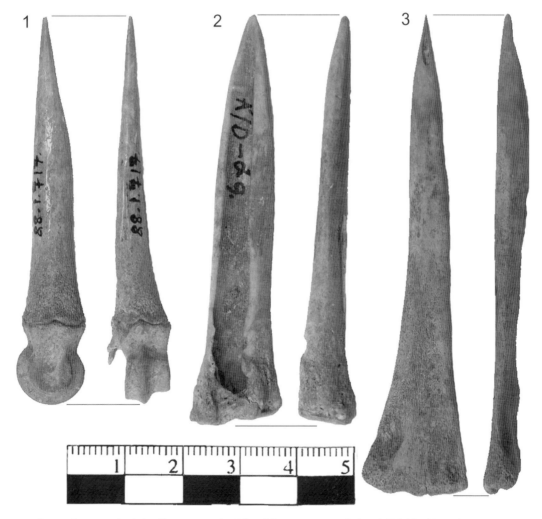

Figure 15.2 Awl types from Aszód, 1) Small ruminant distal-based bipartite metapodial awl (Schibler Type 1/1; Inv. Nr.: 88.1.717), 2) Small ruminant, proximal-based bipartite metapodial awl (Schibler Type 1/2; Inv. Nr.: 88.1.771), 3) Awl made from pig fibula (Inv. Nr.: 88.1.784) (photograph: Zsuzsanna Tóth).

awls, although not very numerous, are almost exclusively made from red deer metapodials.

Rib burnishers

Rib burnishers occur frequently in Late Neolithic worked osseous assemblages. Generally, they are made from large ruminant ribs, especially from cattle or aurochs, either retaining the whole circumference (Fig. 15.3, 1) or split in half (Fig. 15.3, 2). The long, flat shape of the bone makes it very suitable for use as burnishing tools. On other contemporary sites such as Öcsöd, they are represented in large quantities suggesting that they were a common tool type used often in daily life for a variety of different activities. At Aszód this type occurs rarely; only seven pieces were found. It may well be that the task these tools were used for was carried out by morphologically different tool types at the site.

'Hide-Beamers'

This is an easily identifiable tool type occurring in great quantities on most Late Neolithic sites in the region (Fig. 15.4) (Tóth 2013). Based on the form, these objects may be divided into two subcategories, one with two worked surfaces on the medial and lateral sides and another with four sides worked with two additional faces on the dorsal and palmar surfaces (Fig. 15.4, 2–3). Probably, this typological distinction is artificial. In my opinion, they are not real subtypes but represent two stages of the lifetime of the tool's life beginning with (one or) two worked faces and when these faces were exhausted two other faces were created and used until the compact tissue was used up and the tool broke in two at the middle. In addition, there is a category within this tool type of pieces that do not fit into the above-mentioned scheme. They may display irregularities concerning the number and symmetry of the worked surfaces (Fig. 15.4, 1).

Figure 15.3 Rib burnishers, 1) from whole rib (Inv. Nr. 88.1.343), 2) from split rib (Inv. Nr. 88.1.301) (photograph: Zsuzsanna Tóth).

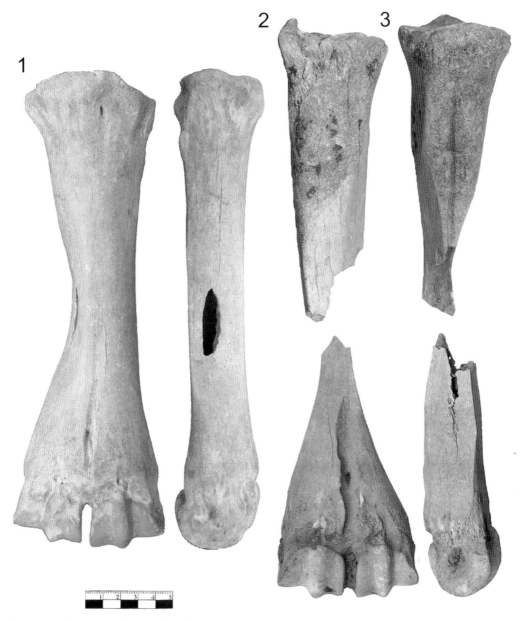

Figure 15.4. Hide beamers 1) complete with worked surface on lateral side (Inv. Nr. 88.1.373), 2) broken in half, proximal end (Inv. Nr. 88.1.231), 3) distal end (Inv. Nr. 80.36.170) (photograph: Zsuzsanna Tóth).

A standardized picture may be drawn regarding their raw material and skeletal element preference. The most preferred raw materials were the metacarpals and metatarsals of large ruminants, particularly cattle and aurochs. This is the average picture that can be seen on all contemporary sites with cattle metapodials being the most common raw material (Tables 15.1–2, i.e. Öcsöd: 84%, Alsónyék: 60%).

At Aszód, however (cattle ratio: 30%), the rules of raw material selection for this tool type are much more flexible. The raw material chosen for this tool is very variable with

skeletal elements from wild species playing a much bigger role (domesticated: 30% wild: 66%) than at other sites. Bovines dominate (54%), although other species are important as well (46%), with a special preference for red deer (33%). Additional species, all large mammals, are more numerous here as well and include brown bear (*Ursus arctus* L. 1758), a wild equid (*Equus ferus gmeilini* Antonius, 1912) and a human bone. The skeletal element preference is generally more colourful (Table 15.2). Besides metapodials (Öcsöd: 99%; Alsónyék: 80%; Aszód: 77%) other long bones (radius, tibia, femur and, humerus) were used to manufacture these 'hide-beamers' as well as a scapula. The raw material and skeletal element choice in hard animal industries has been shown to be dictated as much by cultural tradition as rationales of purported efficiency or availability (Choyke 1997a, 1997b; Choyke *et al.* 2004). Strict rules of preference are often at play.

The manufacturing process was not complicated. The bone was cleaned (at least the diaphysis) and prepared with intense scraping all around. Then the working surfaces were created by scraping. The tool is often renewed by scraping and the life of the tool ends when the central compact tissue is consumed and the tool is broken. There are different suggestions about whether these were hide-processing tools, playing a role in defleshing and dehairing or hide softening (Radin 1923). S. Semenov (Semenov 1964, 185, fig. 99.4) suggested they could have been used as pottery polishers while G. Henriksen wrote that some of these objects were preforms prepared for tool-making, but not yet finished (Henriksen 1974, 11). None of these suggestions have yet been proved or disproved because the continuous rescraping of the working surface(s) of these tools means that no use-wear traces survive.

Antler

Antler tools and waste from their manufacture clearly dominate the Aszód assemblage (56%); antler seems to have been preferred over bone (44%) as a raw material (Table 15.3). Acquisition of the raw material could be maintained by hunting or gathering shed antler. The setting of the site in the mid-mountain region makes both ways plausible and there is evidence in the faunal material for both kinds of acquisition. This raw material was regenerated from year to year and could be easily collected and exploited with some local knowledge of the movements and habits of the local red deer stag population.

Antler was mainly used for tools requiring both flexibility and strength, making these implements suitable for heavy-duty tasks, wood-processing (axes or adzes, hammers and chisels), agriculture (picks, mattocks), mining (picks and mattocks), stone-knapping (hammers, punches and pressure flakers) or hunting and warfare (projectile points). Besides heavy-duty tools, antler was used for producing smaller tools as well (i.e. shafts, harpoons, projectile points) for similar purposes. Antler can be easily shaped and is an attractive looking material closely associated with the qualities of the male red deer (Choyke 2010). Even today it has a special value for a variety of ornaments.

The operational sequence seems to have been highly standardised. First, the antler rack was chopped up into pieces for further tool production. This creates blanks which can then be transformed into tools, mostly into T-shaped axes/adzes (Fig. 15.5, 1), which were manufactured on a large-scale at the site. There are few complete pieces (20 pieces or 3% of all

worked antler), but we have a lot of broken or reused pieces in the assemblage (133 pieces, 21% of the worked antler; Fig. 15.5, 2–3) with characteristic forms.

As seen before, the antler-working was widespread and important at Aszód. This is the largest antler tool assemblage compared to other sites of the Hungarian Late Neolithic. Of course, this may be the result of uneven study, but it also reflects differences between sites as well. On the Great Hungarian Plain (i.e. Öcsöd) antler occurs notably less frequently as a raw material since it would not have been so directly available in great quantities compared to sites in the mid-mountain region (Aszód and Alsónyék). This dominance of antler as a raw material is one reason it has been suggested that Aszód may have played a crucial role, not just in the exploitation and distribution of obsidian but also of antler (as a raw material or in the form of finished tools as products) as well. Aszód is exceptional among the sites lying in similar environments, because here antler occurs exceptionally frequently in the faunal and worked assemblages compared with sites having, more or less, the same potentials for accessing this raw material.

Conclusions

The composition of the archaeozoological and the worked osseous assemblages at Aszód-Papi földek stands out among other contemporary or near contemporary sites in terms of preferences displayed for particular raw materials. This is partly related to the bone manufacturing continuum (Choyke 1997a) representing the degree to which energy was put into the production of a particular object, whether the raw material was selected during butchering or drawn from the remains of meals. The raw material and skeletal element choices made by craftspeople manufacturing the toolkit were connected to long term traditions of how these objects should be made and used. Such traditions are very conservative and change more slowly than the lives of individuals living at the settlements (Choyke 2009). In general, it can be said that worked osseous materials of the Neolithic in Hungary are characterised by the clear dominance of Class I tools corresponding to the planned end of the bone manufacturing continuum (Choyke 2001). Most toolkits are based on well-planned multi-stage manufactured tools, often renewed or reshaped for a new function. The Class I–II and Class II tools (less planned or *ad hoc* tools) are found in negligible quantities at Aszód, all connected to refuse bones. *Ad hoc* tools are common for various awls (8 pieces) or smaller bevel-ended tools (1 piece) where the blank could be easily selected from household food debris.

Thus, the same technological and functional demands can be found on all known Late Neolithic sites in the Carpathian Basin but the rules of raw material selection show significant differences. Öcsöd lies on one end of this line. The populations there seem to have conformed strictly to certain rules of raw material preferences in terms of species and skeletal element

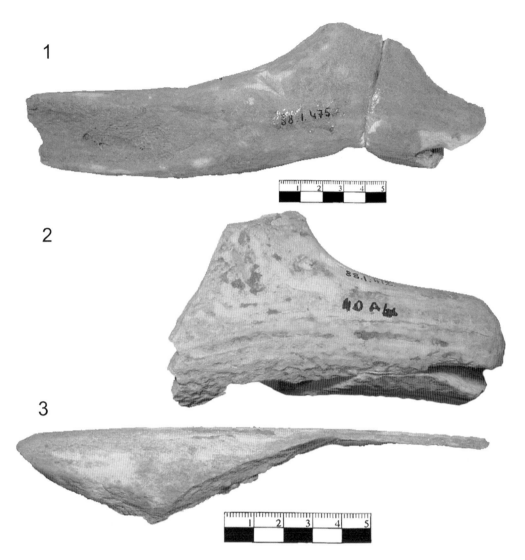

Figure 15.5 Antler tools 1) T-shaped heavy duty tool (Inv. Nr. 88.1.475), 2) back half of the same type (Inv. Nr. 88.1.412), 3) reshaped upper part (Inv. Nr. 88.1.507) (photograph: Zsuzsanna Tóth).

selection. The raw material choices correspond to the basic animal economy, with overwhelming ascendance of cattle and strong traditions concerning the role of small ruminants in tool production. Aszód lies at the other end of bone tool manufacturing. The rules of manufacturing seem to have been looser. While certain tool types remain there is less concern of over what raw materials were chosen in terms of species and especially skeletal element – almost as if they were less interested in their manufacture.

At Öcsöd, where craftspeople paid close attention to bone manufacturing and kept strictly to the rules of technical style, almost all the tools produced belong to the Class I end of the manufacturing continuum. The manufacturing process seems to be highly standardised beginning with raw material and

skeletal element preferences. There were standardised steps and techniques used during manufacture, resulting in tools of approximately the same size, form and quality. This makes the assemblage on the site look fairly uniform. In contrast, at Aszód, craftspeople there were less bound to strict rules of bone manufacturing although, generally, they kept to certain principals of manufacturing, especially as regards production of blanks. However, there were a significantly large proportion of cases when these rules were ignored. For this reason, the worked bone assemblage looks more variable or colourful with notable variations in the raw material and form of certain important tool types.

In contrast to the bone tools however, the treatment of the antler and the techniques used during tool production, utilization and renewal are extremely uniform at Aszód, similarly to the bone tool manufacturing rules at Öcsöd. Division of the antler rack (*débitage*) was carried out each time using the same technique. The partition places are standard, resulting in uniformly shaped blanks and characteristic waste. The technical style of the antler tools is the same so that finished tools do not differ greatly in size and shape. This attention to manufacturing tradition for antler may be connected to the importance of antler tool production at Aszód as a specialised settlement with a large-scale production of antler products for trade.

The sites Aszód and Öcsöd (and possibly Alsónyék) thus differ significantly in the way raw materials were selected as well as in some aspects of manufacturing style within the hard animal industry. From the beginning until the end of the manufacturing process in Öcsöd the common tradition of bone tool manufacturing was strongly respected and followed. The bone tools at Aszód reflect a loosening of these manufacturing traditions especially in terms of species and skeletal element choice. However, manufacturing rules were strictly adhered to in the production of antler tools. This different attitude to the manufacturing of antler objects may be connected to the exceptional role antler played in trade and exchange specialization at this settlement. Simply said, while bone tool production was important for household economies it seems to have played no role, compared to antler, in exchange systems between settlements. In addition, given the role of Aszód as an exchange hub for goods and raw materials, the population itself may have been more mixed or less stable arriving with a variety of somewhat differing bone manufacturing traditions, a circumstance also possibly reflected in more variable pottery styles at this site (Kalicz 2006).

Acknowledgements

I would like to express my warm thanks to Alice Choyke who has followed this work from its very beginning and inspired me with her ideas as well as correcting my linguistic imperfections. To Nándor Kalicz, who invited me to study the worked bone assemblage of Aszód for my PhD thesis. To Zsófia E. Kovács, who made a great and important contribution to this work in her study of the archaeozoological material from Aszód and generously let me use the data from her unpublished manuscript written for the monograph of the site. To Zsuzsanna Siklósi, who informed me about the AMS dates for the site and helped in recalibrating the Öcsöd dates. To István Vörös, who freely gave me his notes on the Aszód worked osseous assemblage for further study. To Pál Raczky, who offered Alice Choyke and myself a chance to study the worked osseous assemblage of Öcsöd-Kováshalom, one of the most important sites from the Late Neolithic of Hungary. To Anett Osztás and Éva Á. Nyerges, who let me peek into the worked osseous assemblage of Alsónyék. This is an extraordinary site from this time period in terms of its size and finds and its study has only just begun.

To László Bartosiewicz and Péter Csippán who offered their time for consultation and help in the species and skeletal element identifications of problematic pieces. And finally to the Hungarian Scientific Research Fund (OTKA Nr. 75677) for their support.

Bibliography

Biró, K. (1998) *Lithic Implements and the Circulation of Raw Materials in the Great Hungarian Plain During the Late Neolithic Period.* Budapest, Hungarian National Museum.

Bökönyi, S. (1974) *History of Domestic Mammals in Central and Eastern Europe.* Budapest, Akadémiai Kiadó.

Bökönyi S. (1988) *Környezeti és kulturális hatások a késő-neolitikus kárpát-medencei és balkáni lelőhelyek csontanyagán. Akadémiai székfoglaló, 1986. január 9. (Environmental and Cultural Influences on the Faunal Materials from Late Neolithic Sites in the Carpathian Basin and Balkans. Talk presented on taking his Academy Seat on January 9, 1989).* Budapest, Akadémiai Kiadó.

Choyke, A. M. (1997a) The bone tool manufacturing continuum. *Anthropozoologica* 25–26, 65–72.

Choyke, A. M. (1997b) Polgár-Csőszhalom-dűlő lelőhely csont-, agancs- és agyartárgyainak vizsgálata (Investigations of the bone, antler and tusk objects from the site of Polgár-Csőszhalom-dűlő). In P. Raczky, T. Kovács and A. Anders (eds), *Utak a Múltba: Az M3-as autópálya régészeti leletmentései (Paths into the Past: rescue excavations on the M3 motorway).* 157–159. Budapest, The Hungarian National Museum and the Archaeological Institute of the Eötvös Loránd University.

Choyke, A. M. (1998) Bronze Age red deer: case studies from the Great Hungarian Plain. In P. Anreiter, L. Bartosiewicz, E. Jerem and W. Meid (eds), *Man and the Animal World. Studies in memoriam Sándor Bökönyi.* 157–178. Budapest, Archaeolingua Kiadó.

Choyke, A. M. (2001) A quantitative approach to the concept of quality in prehistoric bone manufacturing. In H. Buitenhuis and W. Prummel (eds), *Animals and Man in the Past.* 59–66. Groningen, ARC-Publicatie 41.

Choyke, A. M. (2006) Shadows of daily life and death at the Proto-Lengyel site of Gór-Kápolnadomb (A mindennapi élet árnyjátékai: Gór-Kápolnadomb a Proto-lengyeli kultúrában). *Savaria* 30, 93–105. Vas Megyei Múzeuomok Igazgatósága, Szombathely.

Choyke, A. M. (2009) Grandmother's awl: individual and collective memory through material culture. In I. Barbiera, A. Choyke and J. Rasson (eds), *Materializing Memory, Archaeological Material Culture and the Semantics of the Past.* 21–40. Oxford, Archaeopress (British Archaeological Report S1977).

Choyke, A. M. (2010) The Bone is the beast: animal amulets and ornaments in power and magic. In D. Campana, P. Crabtree, S. D. DeFrance, J. Lev-Tov and A. Choyke (eds), *Anthropological Approaches to Zooarchaeology: colonialism, complexity, and animal transformations.* 197–209. Oxford, Oxbow Books.

Choyke, A. M. and Bartosiewicz L. (2009) Telltale tools from a tell: bone and antler manufacturing at Bronze Age Jászdózsa-Kápolnahalom, Hungary. *Tiscium* XX, 357–376. Jász-Nagykun-Szolnok Megyei Múzeumok Igazgatósága, Szolnok.

Choyke, A. M., Vretemark, M. and Sten, S. (2004) Levels of social identity expressed in the refuse and worked bone from the Middle Bronze Age Százhalombatta-Földvár, Vatya-culture, Hungary. In S. Jones O'day, W. Van Neer and A. Ervynck (eds), *Behaviour Behind Bones. The zooarchaeology of ritual, religion, status and identity.* 177–189. Oxford, Oxbow Books.

Choyke, A. M. and Tóth, Zs. (2013) Practice makes Perfect: quartered metapodial awls in the Late Neolithic of Hungary. In A. Anders, G. Kulcsár, G. Kalla, V. Kiss and G. V. Szabó (eds), *Moments in Time. Papers Presented to Pál Raczky on His 60th Birthday*. Ősrégészeti Tanulmányok, 337–352. Budapest, Eötvös Loránd University, L'Harmattan.

Csengeri, P. and Siklósi, Zs. (2011) Reconsideration of *Spondylus* usage in the Middle and Late Neolithic of the Carpathian Basin. In F. Ifantidis and M. Nikolaidou (eds), *Spondylus in Prehistory: new data and approaches. Contributions to the archaeology of shell technologies*. 47–62. Oxford, Archaeopress (British Archaeological Report S2216).

Deschler-Erb, S., Marti-Grädel, E. and Schibler, J. (2004) Die Knochen-, Zahn- und Geweihartefakte. In S. Jacomet, U. Leuzinger and J. Schibler (eds), *Die jungsteinzeitliche Seeufersiedlung Arbon\Bleiche3: Umwelt und Wirtschaft*. Archäologie im Thurgau, Band 12. 277–366. Frauenfeld Departement für Kultur und Erziehung des Kanthons Thurgau.

Gallina, Zs., Hornok, P., Paluch, T. and Somogyi, K. (2010) Előzetes jelentés az M6 AP TO 10/B és 11. számú lelőhelyrészen végzett megelőző feltárásról. Alsónyék-Bátaszék (Tolna megye) 2006–2009. [Vorbericht über die präventive Ausgrabung am Fundortsteil Nr. M6 AP TO 10/B und 11. Alsónyék-Bátaszék (Komitat Tolna) 2006–2009.] *A Wosinsky Mór Múzeum Évkönyve* 32, 7–100.

Henriksen, G. (1974) Maglemosekulturens facetskrabede knogler. *Aarboger for Nordisk Oldkyndighed og Historie*. 5–17. København, Det Kongelige Nordiske Oldskrift-Selskab, København.

Kalicz, N. (1985) *Kőkori falu Aszódon (Neolithisches Dorf in Aszód)*. Múzeumi Füzetek 32. Aszód, Petőfi Múzeum.

Kalicz, N. (1998) *Figürliche Kunst und bemalte Keramik aus dem Neolithikum Westungarns*. Budapest, Archaeolingua (Series Minor 10).

Kalicz, N. (2006) Die Bedeutung des schwarzen Gefäßbemalung der Lengyel-Kultur aus Aszód (Kom. Pest, Ungarn). *Analele Banatului, Seria Arheologie-Istorie*, 14 (1), 135–157.

Kalicz, N. and Raczky, P. (1987) Berettyóújfalu-Herpály. A settlement of the Herpály culture. In L. Tálas and P. Raczky (eds), *The Late Neolithic of the Tisza Region*. 105–125. Budapest and Szolnok, Directorate Szolnok County Museums.

Kalicz, N., Raczky, P., Anders, A. and Kovács, K. (2011) *Preserved by Ancestral Fires. Pictures of an excavation. The Neolithic village at Berettyóújfalu-Herpály*. Budapest, Pytheas.

Kovács, Zs. E. and Gál, E. (2009) Animal remains from the site Öcsöd-Kováshalom. In F. Draşovean, D. L. Ciobotaru and M. Maddison (eds), *Ten Years After: the Neolithic of the Balkans, as uncovered by the last decade of research*. 151–157. Timişoara, Editura Marineasa.

Raczky, P. (2009) Archaeological data on space use at a Tell-Like settlement of the Tisza culture. (New results from Öcsöd-Kováshalom, Hungary).

In F. Draşovean, D. L. Ciobotaru and M. Maddison (eds), *Ten Years After: the Neolithic of the Balkans, as uncovered by the last decade of research*. 101–124. Timişoara, Editura Marineasa.

Radin, P. (1923) *The Winnebago tribe*. Thirty-Seventh Annual Report of the Bureau of American Ethnology to the Secretary of the Smithonian Institution 1915–1916, 33–560. Washington, Government Printing Office.

Schibler, J. (1981) *Typologische Untersuchungen der cortaillodzeitlichen Knochenartefacte. Die neolithischen Ufersiedlungen von Twann, Band 17*. Schriftenreihe der Erziehungsdirektion des Kantons Bern. Bern: Archäologischer Dienst des Kantons Bern, Staatlicher Lehrmittelverlag.

Schibler, J. (1987) XV. Die Hirschgeweihartefakte. XVI. Die Knochenartefakte. In *Zürich-Mozartstrasse. Neolithische und Bronzezeitliche Ufersiedlungen. Berichte der Zürcher Denkmalpflege, Monographien 4, Band 1*. 156–165, 167–175. Zürich. Orell Füssli Verlag.

Schibler, J. (1997) Knochen- und Geweihartefakte. In J. Schibler, H. Hüster-Plogmann, S. Jacomet, C. Brombacher, E. Gross-Klee and A. Rast-Eicher (eds), *Ökonomie und Ökologie Neolithischer und Bronzezeitlicher Ufersiedlungen am Zürichsee. Ergebnisse der Ausgrabungen Mozartstrasse, Kanalisationssanierung Seefeld, AKAD/ Pressehaus und Mythenschloss in Zürich*. 122–219. Zürich, Fotorotar.

Semenov, S. A. (1964) *Prehistoric Technology: an experimental study of the oldest tools and artefacts from traces of manufacture and wear*. Bath, Adams & Dart.

Suter, P. J. (1981) *Die Hirschgeweihartefakte der Cortaillod-Schichten. Die neolithischen Ufersiedlungen von Twann, Band 15*. Schriftenreihe der Erziehungsdirektion des Kantons Bern. Bern, Archäologischer Dienst des Kantons Bern, Staatlicher Lehrmittelverlag.

Tóth, Zs. (2013) Rules and Misrules. 'Hide Beamer' variability in the Hungarian Late Neolithic. In F. Lang (ed.), *The Sound of Bones. Proceedings of the 8th Meeting of the ICAZ Worked Bone Research Group in Salzburg 2011*. ARCHÆOPlus – Schriften zur Archäologie und Archäometrie an der Paris-Lodron Universität Salzburg, Band 5, 251–261. Salzburg, Paris, Universität Salzburg.

Vörös, I. (2005) Neolitikus állattartás és vadászat a Dél-Alföldön (Neolithic animal husbandry and hunting in the Great Hungarian Plain). In L. Bende and G. Lőrinczy (eds), *Hétköznapok Vénuszai*. 203–243. Hódmezővásárhely, Hódmezővásárhelyi Múzeum.

Zalai-Gaál, I. and Osztás, A. (2009) Neue Aspekte zur Erforschung des Neolithikums in Ungarn. Ein Fragenkatalog zu Siedlung und Gräberfeld der Lengyel-Kultur von Alsónyék, Südtransdanubien. In V. Becker, M. Thomas and A. Wolf-Schuler, (eds), *Zeiten – Kulturen – Systeme. Gedenkschrift für Jan Lichardus*. Schriften des Zentrums für Archäologie und Kulturgeschichte des Schwarzmeerraumes, Band 17. 111–139. Langenweißbach, Beier & Beran.

CHAPTER 16

More than Fun and Games? An Experimental Study of Worked Bone Astragali from Two Middle Bronze Age Hungarian Sites

Jacqueline Meier

Dense, compact astragali are ideal raw materials that likely served a variety of functions in the past. Astragali have most often been interpreted as gaming and ritual artifacts at archaeological sites (Gilmour 1997). Building upon previous worked bone studies, a comparison of archaeological wear on astragali and experimentally-produced wear was undertaken to investigate several functional interpretations of these artifacts. Multiple lines of evidence derived from use-wear and experimental studies indicate that astragali were likely used as ceramic burnishers at the Middle Bronze Age sites of Zagyvapálfalva-Homokbanya and Kisterenye-Hársas in Hungary. However, astragali were still potentially multipurpose objects.

Keywords
Bronze Age Hungary; usewear analysis; astragali; experimental archaeology; ceramic burnishing.

Introduction

Ungulate astragali were frequently chosen as raw materials to serve a variety of functions in the past due to their dense, compact structure and aesthetically-pleasing symmetrical shape (Dandoy 2006; Brien 1982). These hind limb bones have most often been interpreted as gaming pieces and religious artifacts, such as divination pieces, at archaeological sites from diverse time periods beginning in the Chalcolithic at sites in the Near East (Gilmour 1997; Dandoy 2006), Mediterranean Europe (Reese 2000) and contact period sites in North America (Lewis 1990). More recent interpretations have suggested that medio-laterally polished astragali functioned as hide softeners (Bejenaru *et al.* 2010) or ceramic burnishers (Choyke and Bartosiewicz 2009; Meier 2009; S. Olsen pers. comm. 9 August, 2009). This paper documents

use wear and experimental studies conducted to test these recent hypotheses. These findings offer new insight into the function of astragali artifacts at the Middle Bronze Age sites of Zagyvapálfalva-Homokbanya and Kisterenye-Hársas in Hungary.

Modified astragali have been recovered from a wide range of time periods and geographic areas and, not surprisingly, have been interpreted in a variety of ways. The modified astragali are frequently flattened on the medial and lateral sides and are often associated with gaming, cultic or ritual activities. This interpretation has been applied to astragalus bones with smoothed sides from the Middle Bronze Age site of Megiddo, Israel and from Alishar Huyuk, Turkey (Gilmour 1997). The traditional interpretation of astragali as game pieces was influenced by classical period sculptures depicting individuals playing knuckle bone games (Newton 1874) and ethnographic studies of astragali games (Lovett *et al.*1901). Flattened astragali have also been called counting objects or tokens of exchange based on contextual information. These include medio-laterally ground astragali found in Iron Age domestic storerooms at Tel Beersheba, Israel (Sasson 2007). Modified astragali have also been interpreted as amulets, such as the drilled astragali found in Late Bronze Age to medieval levels at Gordion in Turkey (Dandoy 2006). The significance of these pieces is attested by the manufacture of amulet copies of the modified bones. For example, flattened and drilled caprine astragali were recovered at the same site as glass and ivory jewelry imitations of flattened astragali in the Classical Greek occupation levels at Heracleia (Brien 1982). Flattened astragali were also found associated with marble replicas in the Central Asian Bronze Age site of Bactria-Margiana (Hiebert 1994).

Modified astragali have been recovered from several sites in Hungary with extensive, ongoing worked bone research programs (Choyke and Schibler 2007). Like in other regions, culturally modified astragali recovered from several Bronze Age sites in Hungary have previously been interpreted as counting, gaming or time-keeping pieces (Bartosiewicz 1999). Medio-laterally abraded and polished astragali recovered from the Bronze Age sites of Jászdózsa-Kápolnahalom and Nagyrév

(Choyke and Bartosiewicz 2009) were interpreted similarly. Twenty-six flattened astragali were also recovered from the sites of Zagyvapálfalva-Homokbanya (Fig. 16.1) and Kisterenye-Hársas. These were studied as part of a Master's thesis on the worked bone assemblages from the two sites (Meier 2009). The worked astragali were selected for the experimental study reported here, because despite widespread interpretations, no experimental wear studies have yet been conducted to test the hypotheses of their functions.

Furthermore, the astragali artifacts studied are of special interest, because they derive from sites that are among the first in Hungary to keep faunal material for study (Bartosiewicz and Gal 2010). The assemblages lack detailed contextual information due to the early date of these excavations and this limits the functional interpretations of the flattened astragali. Moreover, only worked bones were saved during the excavations. Even so, the collection of these bone artifacts marks an important methodological development in the history of Hungarian zooarchaeology and an experimental wear study was conducted to gain more information about the potential of these landmark artefacts.

A total of 26 worked astragali were recovered from Zagyvapálfalva-Homokbanya (Fig 16.1) and Kisterenye-Hársas, 13 from each site. The astragali from the two sites

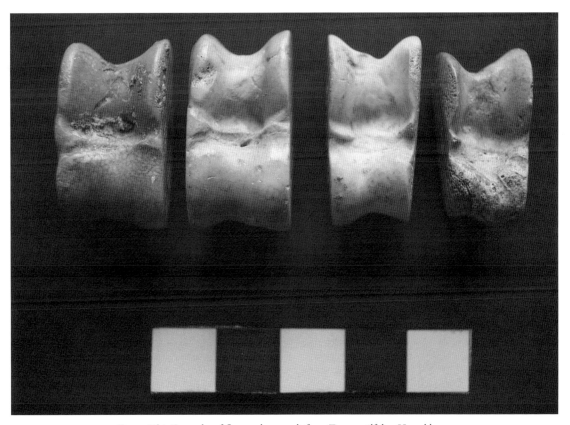

Figure 16.1 Examples of flattened astragali from Zagyvapálfalva-Homokbanya.

originated nearly entirely from sheep and goat, but often could not be identified to taxon because of the high degree of modification on the bones. The Zagyvapálfalva-Homokbanya sample is identified as goat (N=1), sheep (N=3), sheep/goat (N=8) and medium-sized ungulate (N=1), while the astragali from Kisterenye-Hársas were identified as sheep/goat (N=12) and sheep (N=1).

A preliminary usewear study of the astragali artifacts from Zagyvapálfalva-Homokbanya and Kisterenye-Hársas suggests that they were handheld and abraded flat on a coarse granular surface such as ceramic or treated hide (S. Olsen pers. comm. 9 August, 2009; Meier 2009). Hide and ceramic processing industries are evidenced by the presence of hide scrapers made of antler (Bartosiewicz 2009) and burnished ceramic vessels (Guba 2009) on these sites, thus the astragali wear could have developed during their use as tools for either activity. Additionally, unmodified astragali have flat medial and lateral surfaces with convex outer margins that are similar in shape to the beveled edges of many long bone tools typically utilized in these industries in the Bronze Age (Choyke 2000; Christidou and Legrand 2005). Building upon the preliminary analysis of the artifact wear and evidence of site-level industries, an experimental study was developed with the following four objectives:

1. To investigate potential functions of the astragali as scrapers or burnishers by comparing the wear on archaeological specimens to wear produced on experimentally worked astragali.
2. To determine if astragali are efficient tools for ceramic and hide processing.
3. To use experimentation to isolate three factors that affect the appearance of wear on astragali: the type of material worked, the moisture level of the material and duration of use.
4. To determine the most likely combination of factors that produced the artifact wear through comparison of the archaeological specimens and experimentally-produced wear.

Methods

The possible functions of the flattened astragali from Zagyvapálfalva-Homokbanya and Kisterenye-Hársas were investigated by using modern astragali on four different working surfaces. Four domestic goat astragali were used to work each of the following materials for 120 minutes each: moist clay, leather hard clay, soaked deer hide, and dried deer hide. Both the medial and lateral sides of each astragalus were experimentally worked. The reconstruction of the worked materials and the manner in which the astragali were used in the past was based on archaeological evidence and previous experimental bone tool studies (Griffiths 2006; Christidou and Legrand 2005). The methods employed to recreate the past activities in which the artifact wear potentially developed are described to demonstrate the comparability of the resulting wear.

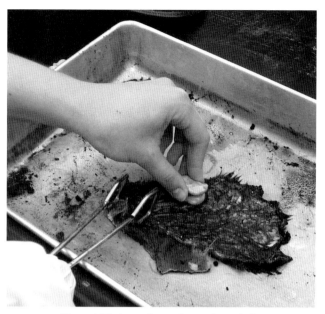

Figure 16.2 Astragalus used to work wet hide.

For the most part, the clay and hide materials were prepared in a manner that best replicated the archaeological materials found at the two sites. The hardness and particle size of ceramic vessels from the two sites were recreated by adding minerals and temper grog to OM Ban Clay. The ceramic chemical formula specifications were derived from analysis of the fabric composition of pots from a nearby (~200 m) cemetery dated within 50 years of the two sites (Orsolya 2009). Coil-built clay cylinders mimicking the shape and diameter of the pots were manufactured and either dried until leather hard or kept moist. Next, deer hind limbs were obtained from the Massachusetts Wildlife Department. Hide was removed from the legs and prepared by soaking in an ash solution (Griffiths 2006) or by defleshing and drying. The wet and dry sections of the two materials were then worked with astragali.

Goat astragali were held as indicated by the circular handling polish on the astragali artifacts (Fig. 16.2) and applied to the material with moderate pressure. The abraded lateral and medial aspects of all experimentally worked bones were examined every 10 minutes at 10×, 20×, 30× and 40× magnification and every 30 minutes at 65× magnification on a Nikon SMZ800 stereomicroscope. Characteristics of the resultant wear were noted in detail.

Results

Preliminary analysis of archaeological wear

The function of the astragali artifacts from the two sites was assessed by comparing the intensity, extent and type of wear present to that on experimentally worked astragali. Both optical and backscatter imaging (Fig. 16.3) were used to observe the wear on the flattened surfaces of the astragali artifacts. Heavy wear and polish was noted macroscopically on the medial and lateral sides of the artifacts. A pattern of diagonally striated wear, with some micropitting and cracking was observed on the magnified surfaces (Table 16.1). There was no evidence that the sides were flattened by cutting. Two circular areas of

handling polish were present on most of the artifacts, which suggests that two fingers gripped the bones by the dorsal and ventral sides as in Figure 16.2. It appears that the abrasive use of astragali on a gritty material resulted in striated wear and considerable volume deformation of the surfaces. This preliminary hypothesis of the artifact function was further investigated using experimental archaeology.

Table 16.1 Description of wear variation by material worked (120 minutes).

TYPE OF MATERIAL WORKED / ARTIFACT WEAR		ASTRAGALI	DRY HIDE	WET CLAY	LEATHER-HARD CLAY	WET HIDE
		Least Grit ⟶ *Most Grit*				
Intensity of Wear		Heavy	Rare	Light	Heavy	Heavy
Extent of Wear		Entire Medial & Lateral Surface	Outer Margins Only	Entire Medial & Lateral Surface	Entire Medial & Lateral Surface	Outer Margins Only
Pitting	*% of Total Wear*	Moderate–High (40–60%)	None	Low (< 5 %)	Moderate (30–40%)	High (> 80%)
	Size	Micropits	N/A	Micropits	Micropits	Micropits and Craters
Striations	*% of Total Wear*	>90%	Few	~50%	>90%	<50%
	Average Length (% of astragalus)	25%	5–10%	50%	10–25%	5–10%
	Outline	Shallow; sharp margins	Shallow	Shallow, sharp margins	Shallow; sharp margins	Deep; broad
	Orientation	Diagonal	Random	Random; curving	Diagonal	Proximal-Distal
Osteons		Few exposed and rounded by polish	Not exposed	Not Exposed	Moderate amount exposed and polished	Many exposed; sharp outline
Polish		Heavy	Light	Moderate	Heavy	Heavy

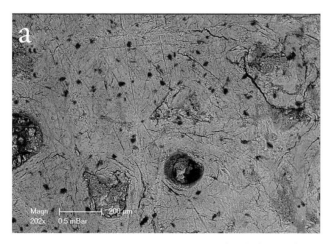 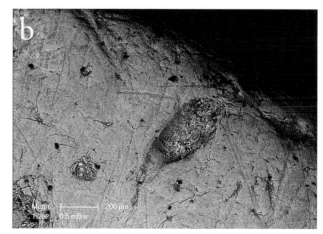

Figure 16.3 BSI images of worked astragali. a) 92.55.7 (Zagyvapálfalva), b) 92.62.28/1 (Kisterenye).

Analysis of experimentally-produced wear

The experiment isolated three variables that potentially influenced wear development on the astragali artifacts: type of material worked (ceramic or hide), moisture of material (wet or dry) and duration of use. Working astragali with different combinations of these variables produced distinct wear patterns (Table 16.1). The intensity and extent of the artifact wear were most similar to wear produced by experimentally working leather-hard clay and wet hide. Additionally, polish of the working surface, presence and orientation of striations, and micropitting were observed on the experimental astragali and compared to the astragali artifacts. The characteristics observed on astragali used to work leather-hard clay were most similar to the artifact wear (Table 16.1). Moreover, the ease of using astragali to work the materials was indicative of their potential functions.

Intensity of wear

Astragali experimentally used to work ash-treated wet hide or leather-hard clay exhibited an evenly distributed reduction of the active tool surface. This flattening and heavy wear was similar to that on the astragali artifacts. Diminution of the surface occurred quickly due to the plasticity and softness of the bone in relation to the hardness of the worked material, the abrasive particles on the surface and the pressure applied to the astragalus during use (Lemoine 1994). The hardness of the worked clay was related to the moisture level (Fig. 16.4). Leather-hard clay flattened the astragali surface to a greater extent than wet clay. In contrast, astragali used to work wet hide had more reduced surfaces than those employed in dry hide working (Table 16.2). In summary, these results indicate that the degree of surface reduction was affected both by the amount of grit and the moisture level of the material.

Extent of wear

The location of wear on the astragali differed according to the type of material worked. The extent of the wear on astragali used to work the cylinders of leather-hard clay was most similar to the extent of wear on the astragali artifacts (Fig. 16.5). Wear was localized on the margins of the astragali used to work wet hide, but evenly covered the entire medial/lateral side of astragali worked on leather-hard clay material. This difference was related to the manner in which astragali were angled to gain leverage against the slick, tough hide material (Fig. 16.6). In contrast, using the entire surface of the bone was more beneficial for working the interior and exterior of the shaped clay.

Table 16.2 Surface reduction of astragali by material worked (30 min).

Material	Clay		Hide	
Moisture Level	Wet	Leather-Hard	Dry	Wet
Reduced Width (average mm)	0.05	0.6	0.04	0.17

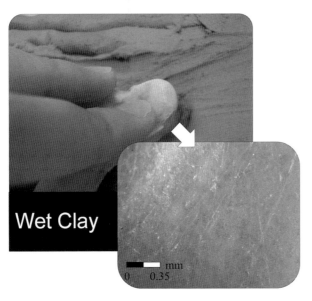
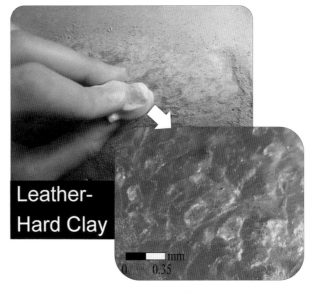

Figure 16.4 Variation in wear due to moisture level. Astragali used to work clay material for 30 minutes. Surface viewed at 20×.

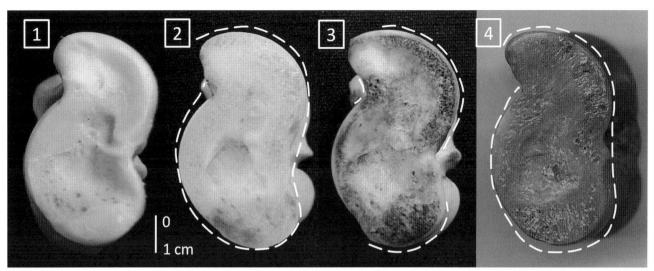

Figure 16.5 Variation in extent of wear. Lateral aspect (1) control astragalus compared to the same aspect that was experimentally worn by (2) working wet hide and (3) burnishing leather-hard clay and an (4) astragalus artifact. Volume deformation of surface indicated by dashed line. Active tool surface is task-specific.

Discussion

Ease of use

Astragali were not effective hide softeners or scrapers when held as indicated by the handling polish. These small bones easily slipped from the hand when moistened by the wet hide and the rounded medial and lateral margins were not sharp enough to remove flesh. In contrast, astragali successfully and efficiently burnished leather-hard clay cylinders. Removal of excess material and smoothing of rough areas was accomplished in a modest amount of time (3 minutes per sq. in/6.45 cm²) and little energy was expended on the work as moderate pressure sufficed for adequate burnishing. Faster burnishing was possible as the working surfaces of astragali were flattened. This effectively resharpened the margins of the abrading medial or lateral side and smoothed the working surface. The results showed that both the medial and lateral sides of astragali effectively functioned as ceramic burnishers.

Summary of wear results

Astragali used to burnish leather-hard clay for 120 minutes exhibited an even reduction of the active tool surface and wear that was similar to the flat surfaces on the artifacts. Volume deformation from hide-working was considerable, but not evenly distributed and thus was dissimilar to the wear on the astragali artifacts. Likewise, wear on astragali used to soften dry hide and smooth wet clay was not similar to the artifact wear. Although the astragali used to work wet clay had a similar pattern of striated wear as the artifacts, the level of volume deformation was not comparable. Similarly, the surface volume was not reduced on the astragali used to soften dry hide and striations were scarce.

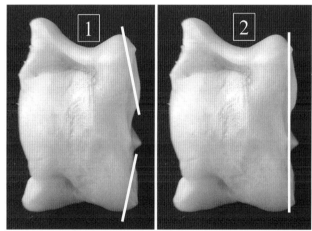

Figure 16.6 Extent of wear by function. Areas of lateral surface flattened by (1) working wet hide and (2) burnishing leather-hard clay indicated by white line on control astragali.

Not only were the astragali used as burnishers efficient and easy to use, but they became more productive as their duration of use increased. The margins of the astragali became sharper with use as working the leather-hard ceramic removed the outmost features of the bone. In contrast, astragali easily slipped from the hand while working wet hide, and were not effective defleshers.

Conclusion

The experimental study indicates that wear on the flat astragali artifacts is most consistent with wear produced when astragali were used as ceramic burnishers. A comparison of artifact and experimentally-produced wear reduces the problem of equifinality, yet astragali were still potentially multipurpose objects. It is also possible that the astragali were smoothed on ceramic surfaces, but not as a part of burnishing. For example, astragali could have been worn on a ceramic surface solely to modify the bones, because astragali with flattened sides have a more random outcome when rolled as dice than unaltered astragali (Lorenson 1947; *in* Lewis 1988). However, the ease of using astragali as ceramic burnishers and the manner that they resharpen with use supports this functional interpretation. Furthermore, the minimum amount of time required to develop the burnishing wear and surface reduction characteristic of the artifacts was 120 minutes (Fig. 16.7), a considerable period to spend modifying astragali for another purpose. Other evidence for ceramic burnishing at the sites

indicates that this process created striations on the surface of vessels (Guba pers. comm). Kiln-firing of the experimentally burnished surfaces and comparison to the ceramic artifact surfaces could further indicate how astragali burnishers modify the surface of ceramic containers. In conclusion, the efficacy and characteristic wear of astragali functioning as ceramic burnishers should be considered in future worked astragali studies.

Acknowledgements

This research would not have been possible without Laszlo Bartosiewicz and Alice Choyke who arranged access to the assemblages and gave guidance. The comments given by Natalie Munro were vital and I am grateful for the advice that she provided throughout this study. Thanks to Szilvia Guba for communication on her study of the Zagyvapálfalva-Homokbanya and Kisterenye-Hársas ceramic material. Comments from Sandra Olsen on the backscatter images influenced the selection of materials worked by astragali. I appreciate the guidance of Patrick Getty on ceramic grain particle size. SEM access for the initial study was made possible by Dr. Catriona Pickard and the University of Edinburgh. Thanks to Frank W. Smith for his support, comments and aid in acquiring materials. Thanks to Dr. Elizabeth Jockusch for use of the Nikon SMZ Stereomicroscope.

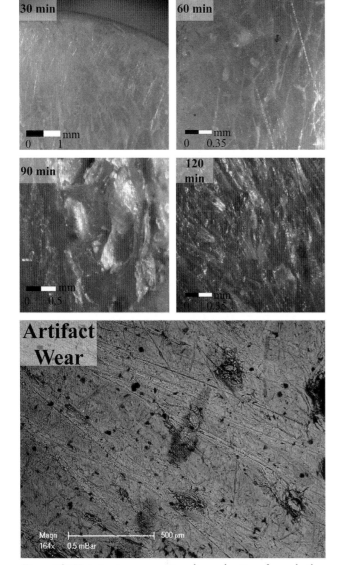

Figure 16.7 Variation in wear on astragali over duration of use as leather-hard ceramic burnishers in comparison to artefact wear (lateral aspect).

Bibliography

Bartosiewicz, L. (1999) A systematic review of astragalus finds from archaeological sites. In A. Vaday (ed.), Pannonia and Beyond. Studies in Honor of Laszlo Barkoczi. *Antaeus* 24, 37–44.

Bartosiewicz, L. (2009) Appendix i. – Bronze Age worked antler remains from Zagyvapálfalva–Homokbánya (Northern Hungary). *Tisicum* XX, 143–146.

Bartosiewicz, L. and Gál, E. (2010) Archaeozoological finds in Hungary. *Patay Pál Festschrift*, 1–16.Nógrád County, Northern.

Bejenaru. L., Monah, D. and Bodi, G. (2010) A deposit of astragali at the Copper Age tell of Poduri-Dealul Ghindaru, Romania. *Antiquity Project Gallery*. http://antiquity.ac.uk/projgall/bejenaru323

Brien, F. (1982) Ear studs for Greek ladies, *Anatolian Studies* 32, 89–92.

Choyke, A. (2000) Refuse and modified bone from Százhalombatta-Földvár. In I. Poroszlai and M. Vicze (eds), *Százhalombatta Archaeological Expedition Annual Report* 1, 97–102. Százhalombatta, Archaeolingua.

Choyke, A., Bartosiewicz, L. (2009) Telltale tools from a tell: bone and antler manufacturing at Bronze Age Jászdózsa–Kápolnahalom, Hungary. *Tisicum* XIX, 357–375.

Choyke, A. and Schibler, J. (2007) Prehistoric bone tools: research in central europe. In C. G. St-Pierre, C. G. and R. B. Walker (eds), *Bones as Tools: current methods and interpretations in worked bone studies*. Oxford, Archaeopress (British Archaeological Report S1622).

Christidou, R. and Legrand, A. (2005) Hide working and bone tools: experimentation, design and application. In H. Luik, A. Choyke, C. Batey and L. Lõugas (eds), *From Hooves to Horns, from Mollusc to Mammoth: manufacture and use of bone artefacts from prehistoric times to the present*, Tallinn, Tallinn Book Printers.

Dandoy, J. R. (2006) Astragali through Time. In M. Maltby (ed.), *Intergrating Zooarchaeology*, 131–137. Oxford, Oxbow Books.

Gilmour, G. (1997) The nature and function of astragalus bones from Archaeological Contexts in the Levant and Eastern Mediterranean. *Oxford Journal of Archaeology*, 16 (2), 167–175.

Guba, S. (2009) Újabb adatok a Zagyva-volgyének kozépso bronzkori történetéhez. *Tisicum XX*, 127–137.

Griffiths, J. (2006) *Bone Tools and Technological Choice: change and stability an the Northern Plains.* Unpublished PhD thesis, University of Arizona.

Hiebert, F. T. (1994) *Origins of the Bronze Age Oasis Civilization in Central Asia.* Cambridge, Harvard University.

Lemoine, G. M. (1994) Use wear on bone and antler tools from the Mackenzie Delta, Northwest Territories. *American Antiquity*, 59 (2), 316–334.

Lewis, B. R. (1988) Old World dice in the Protohistoric Southern United States. *Current Anthropology*, 29 (5), 759–768.

Lewis, B. R. (1990) On astragalus dice and culture contact: reply to Eisenberg. *Current Anthropology*, 31 (4), 410–413.

Lorenson, R. W. (1947) Worked deer astragali from the Angel site. *Proceedings of the Indiana Academy of Science* 57, 31–32.

Lovett, E. (1901) The ancient and modern game of astragals. In E. Lovett, M. L. Dames, D. F. de I'Hoste Ranking, C. Violet Turner, E. Linder and E. C. Sykes (eds), *Folklore* 12 (3), 280–293.

Meier, J. (2009) *Carving out a Niche: a study of worked osseous material from two Middle Bronze Age Hungarian sites.* Unpublished MSc Thesis, University of Edinburgh.

Newton, C. T. (1874) *Synopsis of the Contents of the British Museum. Department of Greek and Roman antiquities: Græco-Roman sculptures.* London, British Museum Press.

Orsolya, V. (2009) *Salgotarjan-bevasarlokozponti es Cinobaňa-i kesı bronzkori temetık fekete bevonatos keramiainak archeometriai osszehasonlito vizsgalata.* Unpublished MA Thesis, Szegedi Tudomanyegyetem.

Reese D. S. (2000) Worked astragali. In J. W. Shaw and M. C. Shaw (eds), *Kommos: an Excavation on the South Coast of Crete Volume IV: The Greek Sanctuary.* 398–401. Princeton, Princeton University Press.

Sasson, A. (2007) Corpus of 694 Astragali from Stratum II at Tel Beersheba, Tel Aviv. *Journal of the Institute of Archaeology of Tel Aviv University* 34 (2), 171–181.

CHAPTER 17

Economic and Social Context of Bone Tool Use, Formative Bolivia

Katherine M. Moore

Bone tool assemblages from three Formative village sites in Bolivia (1800 BC–AD 500) are used to examine economic factors influencing bone tool technology. Wood is scarce in this high altitude region, making the use of bone for tools relatively important. The demand for bone tool raw material, the organization of craft production, and the social and economic significance of several bone tool types are examined for a focused sample of 349 tools recovered with sieving and flotation. While most bone tools were made from the bones of native (mostly domesticated) camelids, bones from dogs, birds, and deer antler may have been chosen for their special properties. Highly selective use was made of several skeletal elements, including the scapulae, ilium, and mandibles. Diversity of craft intensity was typical for most functional categories and craft specialists seem to have made both utilitarian tools (netting and other textile implements) and ornaments. Unfinished tools show household production was general at all three sites. The location of chips and exhausted tools documents activity areas around structures. Tools for weaving as well as basket-making, leather-working and shaping ceramics were common in all sites. Over time there was an increase in the proportion of expediently manufactured tools, though the range of craft activities showed less shift during the same period. The setting of the sites near extensive wetlands around Lake Titicaca is reflected in the importance of tools for fishing; a previously enigmatic scapula tool is suggested here to have been a tool for harvesting lake reeds.

Keywords
Bolivia; Lake Titicaca; Formative Cultures; Kala Uyuni; Sonaji; Kumi Kipa; bone tools; economic archaeology.

Introduction

The Formative sites in the Lake Titicaca basin were some of the first permanent sites in the high plateau (3800 m) of Bolivia. The earliest villages in the southern part of the lake date to *c.* 1800 BCE (Whitehead 1999, 2007) and are located along the contemporary shoreline with extensive shallow marshes. The lakeshore is relatively warm and well watered compared to the colder and arid grasslands of the surrounding plateaus and mountains. Over the course of the Formative, particularly from Middle Formative (500

BC) through the Late Formative (200 BC to AD 500.), the landscape around the sites changed as lake levels fluctuated and new habitats emerged on the exposed lakebed. Survey and excavation (Bandy 2001; Bandy and Hastorf 2007; Hastorf 1999, 2005, 2006; Lemuz 2001) show that villages increased in size and number over time. Important sites in each region included substantial ceremonial spaces. Sunken plazas were the focus of public events involving decorated ceramics and monuments engraved with supernatural figures and animals (Hastorf 2003, Chavez 2002). The economic evidence for these sites yields evidence for hunting, herding, fishing (Moore *et al.* 1999, 2010, Moore 2011), farming and gathering wild plant foods (Bruno 2008; Moore *et al.* 2010). The bone tool technology from three sites is compared here with the zooarchaeological record to link the economic life with the social life of these villages and early centres.

Formative Archaeology of the Taraco Peninsula

Material from sites excavated between 2003 and 2009 is reported here (Fig. 17.1). The first, Kala Uyuni (15 ha), faces the lake to the south and has multiple sectors that date over a period from the Early Formative (Early Chiripa Period) to the Late Formative. A later, eroded classic Tiwanaku settlement covers most of the lower site but few intact deposits have been excavated. The second site, Sonaji (approximately 6 ha), on a low rise facing the lake to the west, has deposits from the Middle Formative and Late Formative, and is also blanketed by later, Tiwanaku deposits. The third site, Kumi Kipa (11 ha) faces the lake to the north-west, and has shallow Late Formative deposits under an eroded Tiwanaku occupation.

Earlier research recognized the importance of Formative tool technology. Bennett (1936, 443) noted of his work at Chiripa "bone artifacts are abundant in the Chiripa levels" and that bone tools were less abundant in later, Tiwanaku levels. Browman (2008 ms) noted in regard to the bone tool assemblage from excavations at Chiripa in the 1970s that the Middle Formative levels that he studied from the central mound of the site seemed dominated by weaving tools. Of the more than 1200 worked bone pieces in that sample, weaving and netting tools predominated, followed by scrapers and other forms.

Excavation and recovery techniques were designed to collect as unbiased and complete a sample of worked bone as possible. Archaeologists identified a few worked bones but the majority (93%) of worked bone pieces were found after animal bone samples from 6mm mesh sieves had been washed and sorted. Modification was recorded with the aid of a 10x hand lens, based on the presence of at least one surface that had been significantly modified. Abraded and glossy surfaces were not used as evidence of modification, since the animal bone scrap had many rounded and shiny surfaces from weathering, burning, and mineralization. Use polish and striae

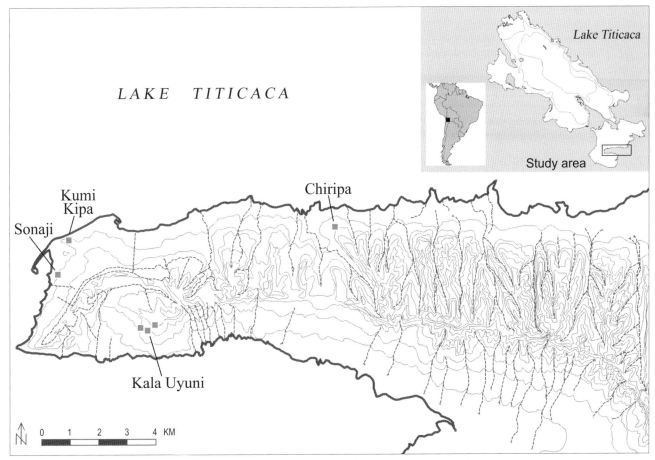

Figure 17.1 Map of Taraco peninsula showing location of sites in study in southern Lake Titicaca basin.

were examined with a low-power (40×) microscope. Battering or repeated light cutting of unmodified bone surfaces were noted but are not included here, though this may exclude some pressure and percussion flakers from the sample.

Many waste pieces and indeterminate edges were included in this sample compared to museum collections or samples based on hand collection. This allows a comprehensive assessment of bone-working, use, and discard at these sites. Bone tools were assigned to general morphological categories based on an earlier study at the site of Chiripa (Moore 1999). Evidence from wear traces, polish, ethnographic analogy, and archaeological context are used to link these shapes to the function and possible social significance of the objects. Traces of burning, rodent damage, erosion and mineralization were recorded using the same taphonomic scheme as the zooarchaeological remains.

A small portion of the site was examined using flotation recovery collected on 1 mm mesh (about 1% of the total sediment excavated). These samples are a check on screen bias and provide a glimpse of bone tools in the microartifactural record. For example, screening and hand collection yielded a sample of bone artifacts in which 20–30% of finds were complete tools or ornaments; while flotation produced an assemblage where only 10% of the pieces were complete, and 40% were tiny chips off the working edges of other tools.

The zooarchaeological record from the three sites provided a baseline to evaluate the selectivity and intensity of bone tool production as well as likely important craft activities. Most comparisons are between the Late Formative tools (N=349 objects) at three sites. In a preliminary examination of change over time, 884 pieces from Kala Uyuni are compared. The most common animals used in the region were *Lama* (wild and domesticated camelids) and *Vicugna* (the related wild vicuña). The remains of fish and birds were also common, but deer, canids, felids, and rodents were relatively rare. Domesticated camelids were widespread by Formative times, and specialized forms for wool and cargo had begun to emerge. Spinning, weaving, and harnessing animals are considered likely domestic activities along with other crafts and food preparation. Hunting wild camelids, deer, and birds was incidental; but fishing was routine and important, likely involving reed-bundle boats, nets, and traps. The domestic architecture consisted of mud brick walls on masonry footings, or lighter, perishable walls. Ceramic technology, style, and distribution have been intensively studied, and are the best evidence for the organization of craft function and the social practices at the three sites (Steadman 2007; Roddick 2009).

Selectivity of Raw Material

Most bone tools were made from bones of large mammals, either camelid or deer (antler only). Bird long bones were occasionally used (3% of the tools sampled). A few objects in other samples were made from dog bones, otherwise no bones of smaller mammals, rodents or fish were used for tools. Given the low diversity of animal species used and the importance of camelids in the Titicaca basin, interpretations of the selectivity of taxa for tool manufacture are limited. Camelid bone was abundant and commonly used. Deer antler, though, was rare (17 fragments of any deer bone or antler at the three sites combined during the Late Formative) and very commonly worked into hammers, picks, and other heavy tools. The special working qualities of antler seem to have been so prized that every antler dropped must have been gathered for tool use. At Kala Uyuni, four antler tools were made compared to scant evidence for one deer carcass; Kumi Kipa has a single scrap of unworked antler; at Sonaji there was one antler tool compared to an MNI of one carcass. Worked fragments made up 29% of all finds of deer. A similar measure of selectivity of bird bone in tool making shows a different pattern. Birds, typically rare, were more important during Late Formative than any other period (Moore 2011). Even so, only about 5% of bird bones were used to make tools at Kala Uyuni, about 1% at Sonaji, and none at Kumi Kipa, showing that a desire for bird bones for tool manufacture did not increase hunting. In a related study using more samples, selectivity of rare canid bone for bone artifacts was high, ranging from 13–23% of all canid bones modified.

Selectivity of skeletal element

The most common skeletal elements used to make tools were camelid/large mammal long bones, scapulae, and ribs. Ribs and long bones cannot easily be quantified, but abundant scapulae (14.7% of 359 tools), mandibles (9.1%), and ilia (6.1%) can be compared to their abundance in the animal bone assemblage. The intensity of selection on a particular element was calculated for these elements (Table 17.1), showing different selectivity of particular elements and differences in selectivity between sites. When the incidence of skeletal elements used as tools are compared to their representation in the animal bone scrap, the most intense use of bone elements at the site was at Kala Uyuni. The assemblage at Kumi Kipa showed the least intensive use of animal parts, compared to the bones of the animals used as food. At all three sites, the use of mandibles was similarly selective, but the selectivity of use of ilium and

Table 17.1 Selectivity of skeletal element (%). Selectivity is expressed by the number of skeletal elements made into tools divided by the total number of that element (worked and unworked) in the deposit.

Skeletal element	Kala Uyuni	Kumi Kipa	Sonaji
Scapula	33.0	18.9	32.4
Ilium	34.2	0	17.2
Mandible	13.5	12.2	13.2

scapula differed widely. In particular, one-third of all camelid ilia at Kala Uyuni were made into scrapers, but no ilium scrapers were used at Kumi Kipa, even though approximately 26 ilia from 13 adult animals were available for use.

Organization of bone tool manufacture and use

A limited number of craft techniques were used to produce the bone tools from the Taraco sites. Many pieces had been so modified in finishing or use that initial shaping traces had been obscured. Some pieces had such irregular outlines that their original shape could have been produced during cracking of bone to release marrow, with no further shaping. Others were made on blank prepared by grooving and snapping. A few pieces indicated that the bone had been flaked to produce a simple blank before further shaping by grinding. Whittling to shape bone tools can be distinguished from grinding based on the traces of wavy striae on the shaped surface from whittling versus linear parallel traces left on bone tools as they are pushed across a grinding slab (Olsen 1984). Based on these criteria, whittling was a very rare technique, but grinding was very common. Grinding slabs were common finds on these sites.

Shaped bone tools were most often made by grooving and snapping (31% of tools and waste). The stone tools used for engraving grooves could have been simple chert and quartzite flakes, based on experiments. No burins were found in the lithic assemblage (Bandy 2005), nor any metal tools. Fine stone drills or flake tools must have been available to perforate beads and the eyes of needles and shuttles. Though engraving and pyroengraving of figures are found on bone objects from later periods at these sites, the only decoration noted in the Late Formative sample was grooves, notches and dot-and-circle patterns. These embellishments were restricted to a small number of carefully finished pieces, and indicate the maker had thinned the preliminary blank from perhaps 6 mm to less than 2 mm (presumably by careful grinding) before applying the design. Subtle differences in the numbers and locations of these marks may be related to personal ownership or identity, even though they are not openly representational

Choyke (1997) suggested a schema of manufacturing intensity to organize observations of craft organization of bone tools in which the percentage of the bone surface that has been removed is a key variable. As a first step the tools,

blanks, and waste pieces were been assigned to ordered groups of manufacturing intensity. The dominant group at each site was expedient tools with less than 10% of the surface altered during manufacture (Table 17.2). The most elaborate tools (those with more than 80% of the original surface removed) are contrasted with the expedient tools. Craft intensity was unevenly distributed between the three sites, with more than twice as high a proportion of tools in the most intensively worked category at Kumi Kipa compared to Sonaji. This intensity is established during manufacture, and does not correlate directly to the function or the social meaning of a particular piece. The highest scores for manufacturing intensity were shared by textile production tools and beads.

The intensity of use of a tool is estimated by how heavily it is worn, whether use continued after chipping or reorienting the use surface, and where it was discarded. None the tools in this sample were found in obvious caches or included in grave fill, though burials were found at each site. Life history variables are summarized in Table 17.3 and Figure 17.2, comparing the progress of manufacture and use of each piece. First, the proportion of waste, unfinished pieces and pieces that broke during manufacture are similar at each site, suggesting that bone tool manufacture took place at each at similar rates, rather than being concentrated at one community. Most tools at each site showed clear signs of wear. Similar proportions at each site had been reused at another angle or had worn so thin that their working edges broke through. Though the manufacturing intensity variable suggested a different intensity of craft in the small sample from Kumi Kipa, the use and discard experience of tools there show few differences compared to the other sites.

Table 17.2 Manufacturing intensity of bone tools in Late Formative sites; expedient tools contrasted with intensively manufactured tools.

SITE	MAX. PORTION OF BONE TOOL SURFACE MODIFIED					
	20%	40%	60%	80%	100%	Site totals
Kala Uyuni	162	19	5	6	21	213
Kumi Kipa	25	5	2	1	9	42
Sonaji	62	14	5	3	6	93
Total	249	38	12	10	36	348

Table 17.3 Life history of bone tools for three Late Formative assemblages.

SITE	PRE-USE	USED	REUSED	BROKEN	WORN	EXHAUSTED	INDET.	SITE TOTAL
Sonaji	15	27	3	7	21	4	1	46
Kala Uyuni	33	71	6	7	85	13	2	217
Kumi Kipa	7	11	2		21	4	1	46

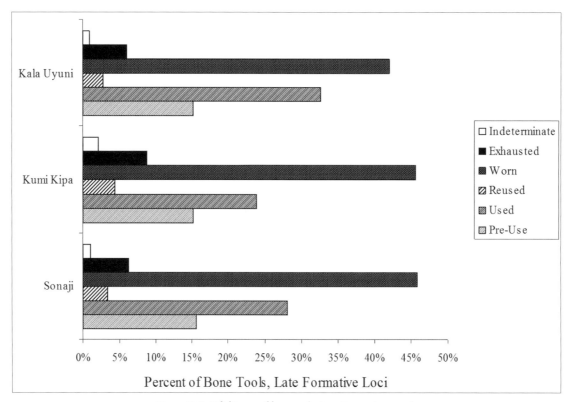

Figure 17.2 Life history of bone tools, Late Formative sample.

Table 17.4 Archaeological contexts of bone tools around Late Formative structures and occupation areas, Kala Uyuni, 2009 season.

Archaeological Context	10%	20%	30%	40%	50%	60%	70%	80%	100%	Total
Walls and Wall fall	3	–	–	2	–	–	–	–	–	5
Middens	3	–	–	1	–	1	–	–	1	6
Occupation Surfaces, floors	14	9	7	3	1	–	1	1	2	38
Pits and Features	3	1	1	1	–	1	–	–	1	8
Fill, Secondary deposits	10	6	1	–	–	–	–	–	–	17
Total	32	16	9	7	1	2	1	1	4	74

Discard and taphonomy

The discard of bone tools in specific archaeological context was compiled for a sample at Kala Uyuni around several structures and associated surfaces excavated in 2009 (Table 17.4). Despite the complex histories of these deposits, most of the bone tools were found in surfaces and features, linking their use to the deposit in which they were found. Of the 38 tools from the surfaces, 5 were discarded during the process of manufacture, 4 were chips broken off use edges (and presumably very close to the locus of use), 20 were discarded after breakage, and 9 were lost or discarded when they were still complete. On a

household level, it appears that bone tools were in a continuing cycle of manufacture, use, loss, and discard. The few intensively finished tools were kept close to the locus of use, and did not get swept up in middens, fill, or among wall fall. Waste pieces (not separated in this table) were most common in middens and pits, and much less common on living surfaces.

The taphonomy of bone tools varied with archaeological context in a similar fashion to the other animal bone scrap. The polish and compressed wear surfaces on bone tools offered protection from weathering in some of the reworked deposits, indicating that some tools were abandoned on exposed surfaces once their use life was over. Bone tools were burned more often than the other bone scrap (9.9% for tools and 4.5% for scrap in study of 171 tools and 14,274 bones from all periods of the 2009 season at Kala Uyuni) opening the question of whether exposing a bone tool to fire was a deliberate practice, either to alter its appearance or working properties, or to "finish" its working life. While deliberate burning may have occasionally occurred (an engraved zoomorphic amulet from a post-Formative deposit at Kala Uyuni was burned a shiny, even black, for example), it appears that bone tools were more often exposed to heat as a result of the close association of bone tool use with household spaces and ordinary burning for cooking and craft production. Several examples of bone tools that had already been highly weathered before they were burned shows that burning often affected unassociated objects discarded in nearby deposits.

Archaeological context for bone tool types

Bone tools are common in the Andes but have received little attention compared to ceramics and textiles. In an earlier study of the Chiripa bone tools I concentrated on the shape of the working edge of the tools (Moore 1999). Here, I modify those types by considering wear traces on the working edges, manufacturing intensity, and evidence for other craft activities. Functions associated with the diversity of bone tool morphological types were assigned based on analogies to metal tools, to bone tools still in use in the Andes, or to bone tool types known from other parts of the world. In a few cases (Julien 1985) observations of working surfaces have been used to clarify the assignment of tools into types. In Table 17.5 morphological types have been combined into functional categories with broader economic significance.

Antler

Antler is rare in these sites, though apparently highly prized; the few antler fragments were cut waste pieces or fragments of heavy tools to be used either as hammers or as heavy picks in agriculture (Bermann 1994, 104).

Scrapers

This broad category includes rounded and bevelled end scrapers on long bone shaft fragments, ribs, and scapula blades and several types of much broader scrapers. Tools categorized as scrapers show longitudinal and oblique use striae and often have high polish. They are similar to classic hide scrapers and smoothers, though their heavy wear and high rate of breakage suggest that they were used for many purposes involving hard materials and considerable force, perhaps as chisels and levers. Many have multiple surfaces and edges. The surface taphonomy of one long bone scraper from Kala Uyuni suggests that some of these long bone tools may have been hafted with an adhesive, others were simply held in the hand, based on their small size and uniform polish.

Long bone scrapers, rib end scrapers, and narrow scrapers made on scapula blades are ancient in the history of the Andes (Buc 2010; Craig 2005; Hernhahn 2004; MacNeish *et al.* 1983; Cardoza 1984 ms; Hurtado de Mendoza 1987; Lynch 1980; Rick 1980; Scheinsohn 2010), but broad scrapers, with working edges as wide as 15 cm (Fig. 17.3), appear to be a tool type that arose in the Formative, the early ceramic-using period of this region (Shimada 1982, 1985; Wing 1972). For one type, the curved edge of a trimmed camelid ilium blade was worn to a bevel on a hard, abrasive surface. For scapula scrapers, a similar curved, bevelled working edge was prepared on the proximal, vertebral border of the scapula blade (distinct from the tool mentioned below made on the caudal border). The shape and size of these scrapers, their trace evidence for a hard material and appearance in the Formative make it plausible that they are ceramic scrapers. They are similar in shape and size to modern "potter's ribs" of wood and plastic used to open and control vessel shapes in pottery making. Also suggestive is that two of the ilium scrapers (not included in this sample since they were found in mixed contexts) have rounded white grains of mineral lodged in the trabecular bone of the working edge, residue from the material being worked. Similar curved edges on worked pottery shards at the Taraco sites have been identified as tools for shaping and finishing pottery (Roddick 2009, 212). The wide bone scrapers may have overlapped in function with these tools. Concentrations of such worked shards generally overlap with bone scrapers at Kala Uyuni and Sonaji.

Table 17.5 Distribution of bone tool functional types for Late Formative assemblages.

	ANTLER	SCRAPERS	AWLS	IMPLEMENTS	GRINDER	PLANT PROCESSING	BEADS, ORNAMENTS	TEXTILE IMPLEMENTS	TOGGLES	INDET.	TOTAL
Kumi Kipa		19	2	9		1	1	4	3	7	46
Kala Uyuni	3	86	17	26	4	10	23	20	2	26	217
Sonaji		34	9	29		4	10	8	1	1	96
Total	3	139	28	64	4	15	34	32	6	34	359

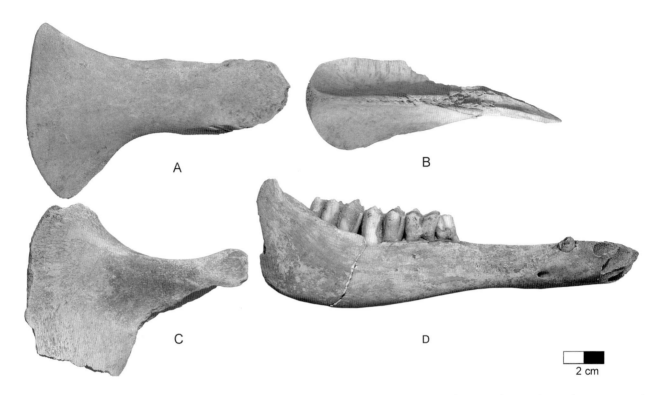

Figure 17.3 Broad scrapers, all camelid bone from Kala Uyuni. A. Ilium scraper, locus 9134. B. Scapula scraper, locus 9048. C. Ilium scraper Kala Uyuni, locus 9121. D. Mandible scraper, locus 9238.

The most common type of all scrapers in this sample was made from camelid mandibles (24% of 137 scrapers). Two types are found: one apparently earlier and distributed in at least two widely separated parts of the Formative Andes, and one produced later and closely associated with the Tiwanaku state that expanded out of the Titicaca basin after AD 500 The earlier type is made on the trimmed body of a camelid mandible with a broad, curved working edge formed across the angle of the ascending ramus; the portion with the cheek teeth served as the handle. They have a bevelled edge and striae indicating abrasive working material. Use-wear progressed extensively into the body of the mandible and they often broke open during later stages of use. Mandible body scrapers are known from the early Formative of the Titicaca Basin and from the Formative of the northern part of Peru (Shimada 1982, 1985), a distance of at least 1500 km, but few comparable Formative assemblages (Chavez 1977; Rick 1980; Steadman 1995; Wing 1972) are known from the regions in between to suggest a common source or pattern. The mandible body scrapers may have shared the ceramic shaping function suggested for the ilium and scapula scrapers, based on their working edge, but it is interesting to note that a preliminary study of food residues from tools at Kala Uyuni (Logan 2006, 57) identified a tuber starch

grain on one of these tools, suggesting a food processing role. The tooth row making up the handle of these tools would have been obvious to the worker and onlookers; the life history of the animal would be readable from the teeth and may have been part of the social and economic identity of these scrapers.

The other type of mandible scraper used the coronoid process and condyle as the handle with a curved working edge cut from the angle of the bone (the cheek portion was discarded). The mandible ramus scraper is associated with Tiwanaku IV–V sites (Goldstein 2005; Park 2001; Capriles 2003). Bermann (1994, 187) notes that at the Taraco site of Lukermata, many finished and unfinished mandible scrapers were found in domestic contexts. Goldstein has suggested (2005, 199) that this specific tool might have been a significant part of Tiwanaku identity as the influence of Tiwanaku styles and iconography spread beyond the Titicaca basin. Three examples of the ramus scraper were found in Late Formative context at Kala Uyuni, suggesting deep roots for this tradition. Further work on the context and wear on the mandible scrapers may suggest if one form replaced the other (Gladwell 2007, 84; M. Warwick pers. comm. 2010; Beaule 2002, 186) or if the apparent relationship between the two types is coincidental.

Awls

These pieces include narrow pointed long bone tools (5–10 mm wide), pointed tools on other blanks, and narrow (3–5 mm wide) and intensively modified pieces that have been called "pins" in other assemblages. All of the awls have worn surfaces and wear traces that suggest use on soft material in a direction parallel to the long axis of the bone. Ethnographic analogy is consistent with these traces in suggesting that they were heavily used in basketry as well as working with hides and textiles. Basket containers would have been likely very important in ancient times, as they have been in traditional communities in the region today.

Implements

This is a residual category of broken pieces that lack enough features to be included in either the scraper or awl category but show the shape and wear traces of one of those tools. Most of them are made of long bone and show smoothing or wear on one or more edges.

Grinders

These relatively rare pieces are small bones, such as a first phalanx or a distal humerus, that have been evenly ground to produce a blunt, even working surface. Some could be pestles or grinders, or possibly bottle stoppers. Their rough surface, with the outer layer of the bone worn away, shows little trace of the use of the object. Gladwell (2007, fig. 14) describes a similar piece from Khonkho Wankane and Webster (1993, 297) lists several similar objects from the site of Tiwanaku.

Plant processing tools

These serrated tools were made on a blank made on the caudal border of a scapula (Fig. 17.4). The blade and spine of the scapula was removed by grooving and a series of small teeth were cut into on the remnant edge of the blade (the infraspinous fossa). Their conspicuous serrated edge recalls other types of notched scapula tools from North America and the Near East that have been interpreted as rasps or tally devices (Watson and LeBlanc 1990; Zuckerman *et al.* 2007), however most of those examples were made by grooving a thick rounded surface, not a thin, knife-like edge. Tools from similar pieces in Neolithic Europe have been interpreted as flax hackles or hide fleshers (Northe 2003). The Taraco scapula tools are similar to those in the thinness of the blade and wear. Julien (1985, 219) illustrates serrated scapula tools from preceramic contexts in Junin, Peru (*c.* 5000 BC) and based on wear traces and replication suggests that they are hide scraping tools. The details of those tools do not match the Taraco tools exactly. The working edge of the Taraco scapula tools takes on a high polish while the "saw" teeth wear to rounded stumps. The polish does not invading the spaces between the teeth (Fig. 17.5). Use striae run parallel to the working edge, suggesting a stroking or cutting motion, not a scraping motion perpendicular to the working edge. Kidder (1985) replicated a very similar scapula tool based on models from Chumash and Paiute collections in North America (Wheat 1967, 41). Kidder confirmed that the thin teeth were ideal for cutting handfuls of fresh aquatic reeds. This suggested material is a plausible match for the wear traces on the Taraco tools and for the distribution of the similar tools in the Andes near lakes and other wetlands. Traditional uses for these reeds include

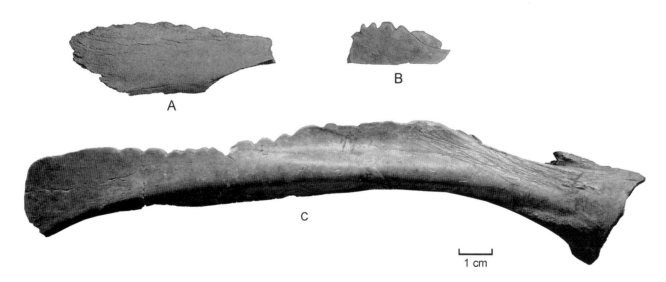

Figure 17.4 Plant processing tools from camelid scapulae. A. Kala Uyuni Locus 9148. Broken edge, note highly weathered surface. B. Kala Uyuni Locus 9092. C. Chiripa, Locus 1253. Complete saw; note grooves from manufacture covered with handling gloss at glenoid.

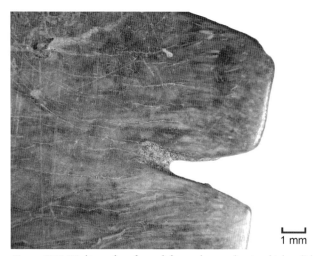

Figure 17.5 Working edge of camelid scapula saw showing high polish, longitudinal wear, and lack of wear between teeth. Kala Uyuni, Locus 9092. Same piece as Fig. 17.4 B (photograph: Alan Farahani).

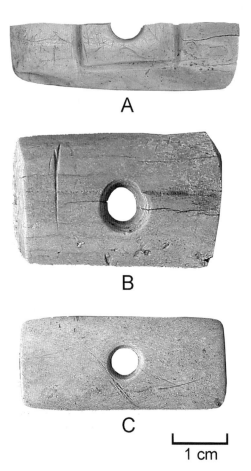

Figure 17.6 Bone toggles showing plain and engraved surfaces, all from Kumi Kipa. A. Broken toggle with engraved decoration, Locus 6607 B. Unfinished toggle with traces of snapping to produce blank on left, incomplete engraving, Locus 6612 C. Toggle with no decoration, Locus 6668.

fuel, material for making boats and housing, fodder, and food (Portugal 2002).

Textile processing tools

Bone tools associated with textile production are almost universal in the Andes, predating the domestication of camelids. Textiles were made from both wool (from camelids) and plant fibers. In the Taraco sample, textile-working tools include those for netting (gauges), weaving (picks and shuttles), and sewing (needles). Other indirect evidence for the importance of textile production for the Formative period are occasional ceramic spindle whorls, the presence of small camelids similar in size and proportion to today's alpacas, depictions of clothing and cordage; and, in nearby regions, preserved fiber and textile fragments (Dransart 2002, 231). One of the most important textiles in the Taraco sites would have been nets for fishing in the lake (Moore 2011). Looping and twining and backstrap weaving of narrow strips would have been common in the region (Conklin 1985), Weaving picks (*wichuña*) can be quickly made from a metapodial (a modern weaver made one in ten minutes (Miller 1979, 78). The high degree of polish on these tools indicates prolonged curation and reuse. Even in the modern Andes, weaving picks have been one of the most persistent uses of animal bone (Flores Ochoa 1979, 99; Stevenson 1974), and individual tools are likely to be used for many decades. In contrast, the shuttles and net gauges represent extremely detailed and controlled craftsmanship, based on a reconstruction of their manufacture from blanks.

Toggles

These flat, rectangular, objects were perforated in the center by drilling and are occasionally decorated with engraved lines, notches, or small dots (Fig. 17.6). While some become highly polished, it is not clear that they are implements rather than ornaments or other personal objects. Little abrasion has smoothed the central holes, weakening the suggestion that they might be fasteners (toggles) for llama harnesses or clothing. They have been classified as pendants (Bennett 1936, 444) and beads (Gladwell 2007, fig. 15) A thin gold plaque from a burial at Sonaji had the same general size and outline (Hastorf 2006, 57), but the bone toggles have been found on surfaces or in pit fills, not in burials. Other, more expedient perforated tools made from sections of ribs and phalanges are also classified as toggles.

Beads and ornaments

Flat stone beads and shell beads are known primarily from burials, bone beads were used as well. A distinctive Andean bone bead was made by grooving tubes from the midshafts of camelid first phalanges. More pieces of waste from dividing the phalanx into multiple beads were found than beads themselves at Kala Uyuni (3 beads/8 waste) and Sonaji (1 bead/8 waste), suggesting that bead making was a common activity. Bird long bones were made into beads using the same groove-and-snap technique; about half of all bone beads found were made from bird bone. Most of the beads reported here came from outside of burials and are larger than the beads from burials, suggesting that ornamentation of clothing or hair may have been common, but different than ceremonial or mortuary traditions.

Indeterminate fragments

A residual category of manufacturing waste and fragments of working and lateral edges of tools, so small that the original form cannot be determined.

Discussion

Bone implements were intrinsic to daily practice in the villages of the Taraco peninsula. They carry some limited evidence for style themselves, but were used to make ceramics, textiles, and other craft items with socially and ideologically conspicuous form, colour and decoration. Specifically, the broad scrapers appear to be linked to both the work of ceramic production and to the creation of particular shapes and sizes of ceramic vessels. This introduction of a new shape and size of tool,

and selection of a bone to use as a new blank, reflects the significance of emerging pottery production across a broad region. The intensity of production of the scrapers themselves, most noticeable at Kala Uyuni and Sonaji, suggests how important these scrapers were. The mandible body scrapers may have had a role in food preparation as well as signalling the identity of herd animals. Similarly, the central role of textiles to body image, social position, craft activities, and the landscape of animal production would be encapsulated in bone weaving tools made from the skeletons of the wool-producing animals. The serrated scapula saws emphasize the role of the role of the lake marsh in daily life, as do the net gauges. It has been difficult to pinpoint specific household activity areas in the production of ceramics or stone tools. Similarly, the production of bone tools appears to have been a common event around the structures at Kala Uyuni, not an activity restricted to a few locations.

One measure of the impact of increasing political centralization in the region would be changing organization of craft activities such as bone tool production. Manufactured with locally abundant bone scrap and stone and produced in individual households, the production of bone tools might be difficult to control from the outside. Few differences can be seen in the distribution of bone tools and manufacturing waste between the Formative and Post-Formative (Tiwanaku) samples in the Taraco sites, though disturbance of the upper layers of the sites means that samples are not truly comparable (Fig. 17.7). A noticeable difference in a preliminary consideration of

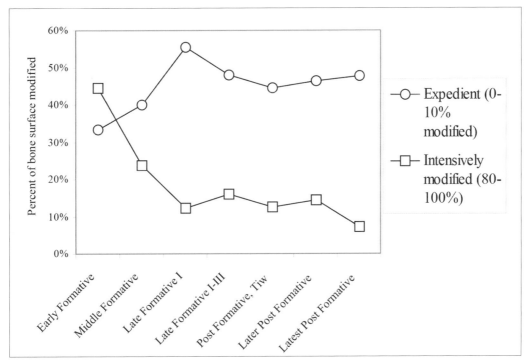

Figure 17.7 Changes in the proportion of expedient and intensively modified tools at Kala Uyuni, all periods (Early Formative to latest Post-Formative (Tiwanku) deposits).

all the periods at Kala Uyuni is the decline in manufacturing intensity over time, from a high of 44% of all tools in the Early Formative in the most intensively worked category (based partly on the importance of finely made net gauges), declining to a low of 7% in the latest post-Formative component. Both the decline of fishing in the late periods and the decline in intensity of craft in the Taraco sites contribute to this pattern. Despite the decrease of craft intensity, similar proportions of functional types and tool life histories are seen in the Post-Formative as the Formative levels.

The Tiwanaku economy is thought to have been supported by intensive animal production and textile manufacture in the Titicaca Basin, however, bone tool evidence for textile production apart from net-making shows no change (7.6% for the Formative / 7.8% for the post-Formative deposits) at Kala Uyuni. Though the population of the Taraco peninsula experienced striking shifts in social networks and shared ideology over this period, the world of household craft production seems to have been resistant to re-organization. A tightly bound cycle of animal production, food production, raw material selection and craft production is represented by the use of bone tools. The social world that this technology represents, with its impressive set of skills, knowledge, and shared meanings would have worked to make this aspect of prehistoric life deeply conservative.

Acknowledgments

Fredrik Hiebert prepared Figures 17.1, 17.3, 17.4 and 17.6. Alan Farahani took the micrograph in Figure 17.5. I would like to acknowledge the assistance of the Taraco archaeological project staff members, particularly director Christine Hastorf, Maria Bruno and Andrew Roddick.

Bibliography

Bandy, M. S. (2001) *Population and History in the Ancient Titicaca Basin.* Unpublished doctoral dissertation, University of California Berkeley.

Bandy, M. S. (2005) Analysis de artefactos liticos de siete temporadas de excavacion en cuatro sitios de Taraco y Santa Rosa. In C.A. Hastorf (ed.), *Taraco Archaeological Project: Report of the 2005 excavations at the sites of Sonaje and Kala Uyuni,* 95–98. Report submitted to the Directorate Unidad Nacional de Arqueologia de Bolivia.

Bandy, M. S. and Hastorf, C. A. (eds) (2007) *Kala Uyuni: an early political center in the southern Lake Titicaca Basin. 2003 excavations of the Taraco Archaeological Project.* Contributions of the Archaeological Research Facility, 64. University of California, Berkeley.

Beaule, C. D. (2002) *Late Intermediate Period Political Economy and Household Organization at Jachakala, Bolivia.* Unpublished doctoral dissertation, University of Pittsburgh.

Bennett, W. C. (1936) Excavations in Bolivia. *American Museum of Natural History Anthropological Papers* 35, 329–507.

Bermann, M. (1994) *Lukurmata: household archaeology in Prehispanic Bolivia.* Princeton, Princeton University Press.

Browman, D. L. (2008 ms) Bone tools from Chiripa. In C. Hastorf, M. S. Bandy, and L. Steadman (eds), *Recent Archaeology at Formative Chiripa 1998–2006 Excavations of the Taraco Archaeological Project at Chiripa.*

Buc, N. (2010) *Tecnologia Osea de Cazadores-Recolectores del Humedal del Parana Inferior (Bajios Riberenos Meridionales).* Unpublished doctoral thesis, Universidad de Buenos Aires.

Bruno, M. C. (2008) *Waranq Waranqa: ethnobotanical perspectives on agricultural intensification in the Lake Titicaca Basin (Taraco Peninsula, Bolivia).* Unpublished doctoral disssertation, Washington University, St Louis.

Capriles, J. E. (2003) *Entre el Valle y la Peninsula: variabilidad en la utlizacion de recursos faunisticas durante Tiwanaku (400–1100) en el sitio Iwawi, Bolivia.* Unpublshed licenciatura thesis, Universidad Mayor de San Andres, La Paz.

Cardoza, C. R. (1984 ms) *Bone Tools from the Panaulauca Area.* Unpublished manuscript, author's files.

Chavez, S. (2002) Identification of the camelid woman and feline man themes, motifs, and designs in Pucara style pottery. In W. Isbell and H. Silverman (eds), *Andean Archaeology II: art, landscape and society* 36–70. New York, Springer.

Chavez, K. M. (1977) *Marcavalle: the ceramics from an Early Horizon site in the valley of Cusco Peru, and implications for South Highland socio-economic interaction.* Unpublished doctoral dissertation, University of Pennsylvania.

Choyke, A. M. (1997) The bone tool manufacturing continuum. *Anthropozoologica* 25–26, 65–72.

Conklin, W. (1985) Pucara and Tiahuanako tapestry: time and style in a sierra weaving tradition. *Ñawpa Pacha* 21, 1–43.

Craig, N. M. (2005) *The Formation of Early Settled Villages and the Emergence of Leadership: a test of three theoretical models in the Rio Ilave, Lake Titicaca Basin, Southern Peru.* Unpublished doctoral dissertation, University of California, Santa Barbara.

Dransart, P. Z. (2002) *Earth, Water, Fleece and Fabric: an ethnography and archaeology of Andean camelid herding.* London, Routledge.

Flores Ochoa, J. A. (1979) *Pastoralists of the Andes: the alpacas herders of Paratia.* R. Bolton (translator), Philadelphia, Institute for the Study of Human Issues.

Gladwell, R. R. (2007) Industrias de herramientas de hueso del periodo Formativo Tardio en Khonkho Wankane (Bolivia). *Nuevas Aportes* 4, 79–90.

Goldstein, P. (2005) *Andean Diaspora: the Tiwanaku colonies and the origins of South American empire.* Gainesville, University Press of Florida.

Hastorf, C. A. (ed.) (1999) *Early Settlement at Chiripa, Bolivia: research of the Taraco Archaeological Project.* Contributions of the Archaeological Research Facility 57, University of California Berkeley.

Hastorf, C. A. (2003) Community with the ancestors: ceremonies and social memory in the Middle Formative at Chiripa, Bolivia. *Journal of Anthropological Archaeology* 22, 305–332.

Hastorf, C. A. (ed.) (2005) *Projecto Arqueologico Taraco: informe de las excavaciones de la Temporada del 2004 en los sitios de Kumi Kipa, Sonaji y Chiripa.* Report submitted to the Directorate Unidad Nacional de Arqueologia de Bolivia.

Hastorf, C. A. (ed.) (2006) *Taraco Archaeological Project: report of the 2005 excavations at the sites of Sonaje and Kala Uyuni.* Report submitted to the Directorate Unidad Nacional de Arqueologia de Bolivia.

Herhahn, C. L. (2004) *Moving to Live: a pastoral mobility model for the South Central Andes.* Unpublished doctoral dissertation, University of California Santa Barbara.

Hurtado de Mendoza, L. (1987) Cazadores de las punas de Junin, Cerro de Pasco, Peru. *Estudios Atacameños* 8, 198–243.

Julien, M. (1985) L'Outillage Osseux. In D. Lavallee, M. Julien, J. Wheeler and C. Karlin (eds), *Telarmachay. 1. Chasseurs et pasteurs préhistoriques des Andes,* 215–235. Paris, Edition recherche sur les Civilisations, Travaux de l' Institutes français d'etudes Andines.

Kidder, N. (1985) The scapular saw, a Stone and Bone Age project. *Bulletin of Primitive Technology,* 28–29.

Lemuz, C. (2001) *Patrones de Asentamiento Arqueológico en la Península de Santiago de Huatta, Bolivia.* Unpublished licenciatura thesis, University Mayor de San Andres, La Paz.

Logan, A. L. (2006) *The Application of Phytolith and Starch Grain Analysis to Understanding Formative Period Subsistence, Ritual, and Trade on the Taraco Peninsula, Highland Bolivia.* Unpublished M.A. Thesis, University of Missouri, Columbia.

Lynch, T. S. (1980) *Guitarrero Cave: early man in the Andes.* New York, Academic.

MacNeish, R. S., Vierra R. K., Nelken-Turner A., Lurie R. and Garcia Cook A. (1983) *Prehistory of the Ayacucho Basin, Vol. IV: the preceramic way of life.* Ann Arbor, University of Michigan.

Miller, G. (1979) *An Introduction to the Ethnoarchaeology of the Andean Camelids.* Unpublished doctoral dissertation, University of California, Berkeley.

Moore, K. M. (1999) Chiripa worked bone and bone tools. In C. A. Hastorf (ed.), *Early Settlement at Chiripa Bolivia: research of the Taraco Archaeological Project.* Contributions of the Archaeological Research Facility 57, 73–93. University of California Berkeley.

Moore, K. M. (2011) Grace under pressure: responses to changing environments by herders and fishers in the Formative Lake Titicaca basin, Bolivia. In N. Miller, K. Moore and K. Ryan (eds), *Sustainable Lifeways: cultural persistence in an ever-changing environment,* 244–272. Philadelpha, University of Pennsylvania Museum

Moore, K. M., Bruno M. C., Capriles J. and Hastorf C. A. (2010) Integrated contextual approaches to understanding past activities using plant and animal remains from Kala Uyuni (Lake Titicaca, Bolivia). In A. M. Van Derwarker and T. M. Peres (eds), *Integrating Zooarchaeology and Paleoethnobotany: a consideration of issues, methods, and cases,* 173–203. New York, Springer.

Moore, K. M., Steadman, D. W. and deFrance, S. (1999) Herds, fish, and fowl in the domestic and ritual economy of Formative Chiripa. In C. A. Hastorf (ed.), *Early Settlement at Chiripa Bolivia: research of the Taraco Archaeological Project.* Contributions of the Archaeological Research Facility 57, 105–116, University of California Berkeley.

Northe, A. (2003) Notched implements made of scapulae-still a problem. In A. Choyke and L. Bartosiewicz (eds), *Crafting Bone: skeletal technologies through time and space,* 179–183. Oxford, Archaeopress (British Archaeological Report S937).

Olsen, S. L. (1984) *Analytical Approaches to the Manufacture and Use of Bone Artifacts in Prehistory.* Unpublished doctoral dissertation, University of London Institute of Archaeology.

Park, J. E. (2001) *Food from the Heartland: the Iwawe site and political economy from a faunal perspective.* Unpublished M.A. thesis, Simon Fraser University.

Portugal Loayza, J. (2002) *Los Urus: approvechimento y manejo de recorsos acuaticas.* La Paz, Lidema.

Rick, J. W. (1980) *Prehistoric Hunters of the High Andes.* New York, Academic.

Roddick, A. (2009) *Communities of Pottery Production and Consumption on the Taraco Peninsula, Bolivia, 200 BC to 300 AD.* Unpublished doctoral dissertation, University of California Berkeley.

Scheinsohn, V. (2010) *Hearts and Bones: bone raw material exploitation in Tierra del Fuego.* Oxford, Archaeopress (British Archaeological Report S2094).

Shimada, M. (1982) Zooarchaology of Huacaloma: behavioral and cultural implications. In K. Terada and Y. Ohuku (eds), *Excavations at Huacaloma in the Cajamarca Valley, Peru, 1979 Report of the Japanese Scientific Expedition to Nuclear America,* 303–336. Tokyo, University of Tokyo Press.

Shimada, M. (1985) Continuities and change in patterns of faunal resource utilization: Formative through Cajamarca periods. In K. Terada and Y. Onuku (eds), *The Formative Period in the Cajamarca Basin, Peru: excavations at Huacaloma and Layzon, 1982,* 289–310. Tokyo, University of Tokyo Press.

Steadman, L. H. (1995) *Excavations at Camata: an early ceramic chronology for the Western Titicaca Basin, Peru.* Unpublished doctoral dissertation, University of California Los Angeles.

Steadman, L. H. (2007) Ceramic Analysis. In M. S. Bandy, and C. A. Hastorf (eds), *Kala Uyuni: an early political center in the Southern Lake Titicaca Basin. 2003 excavations of the Taraco Archaeological Project.* Contributions of the Archaeological Research Facility 64, 67–112. University of California, Berkeley.

Stevenson, I. N. (1974) *Andean Village Technology.* Oxford, Pitt Rivers Museum.

Watson, P. J. and LeBlanc, S. A. (1990) *Girikihaciyan: a Halafian site in southeastern Turkey.* Monograph 33, Institute of Archaeology, University of California, Los Angeles.

Webster, A. D. (1993) *The Role of Camelids in the Emergence of Tiwanaku.* Unpublished doctoral dissertation, University of Chicago.

Wheat, M. (1967) *Survival Arts of the Paiutes.* Reno, University of Nevada.

Whitehead, W. T. (1999) Radiocarbon dating. In C. A. Hastorf (ed.), *Early Settlement at Chiripa Bolivia: research of the Taraco Archaeological Project,* Contributions of the Archaeological Research Facility 57, 17–21. University of California Berkeley.

Whitehead, W. T. (2007) Radiocarbon dating. In M. S. Bandy and C. A. Hastorf (eds), *Kala Uyuni: an early political center in the southern Lake Titicaca Basin. 2003 excavations of the Taraco Archaeological Project.* Contributions of the Archaeological Research Facility 64, 13–17. University of California, Berkeley.

Wing, E. (1972) Utilization of animal resources in the Peruvian Andes. In S. Izumi and K. Terada (eds), *Andes 4: excavations at Kotosh, Peru.* 327–352. Tokyo, University of Tokyo Press.

Zuckerman, A., Kolaska-Horwitz, L., Lev-Tov J. And Maier A. M. (2007) A bone of contention? Iron Age IIA notched scapulae from Tell es-Sâfi/Gath, Israel. *Bulletin of the American Schools of Oriental Research* 347, 57–81.

New Methods of Materials Identification

Exotic Materials Used in the Construction of Iron Age Sword Handles from South Cave, UK

Sonia O'Connor

The Late Iron Age weapons cache from South Cave in East Yorkshire, UK, includes five high status iron swords with copper alloy sheaths and remarkably well preserved handles in an unprecedented range of organic materials. These include horn and antler but also cetacean bone, cetacean ivory and elephant ivory. The identification criteria for these materials are given, the importance of integrating the identification and conservation processes is discussed and the origins and possible significance of the materials used are explored.

Keywords
Sword; handle; Iron Age; cetacean; elephant; bone; antler; ivory.

Introduction

In 2002, a unique cache of Late Iron Age weapons was discovered by metal detectorists at South Cave in East Yorkshire, just to the north of the estuary of the River Humber (Fig. 18.1). The cache included a bundle of 33 iron spearheads surrounded by five iron swords in copper-alloy scabbards, finely worked with Celtic motifs, deposited in a pit cut into the fill of a ditch enclosing an Iron Age settlement in the territory of the Parisi (Evans 2006). The cache is of major importance, significantly increasing the quantity of archaeologically excavated Iron Age weaponry from Britain.

The cache had remained safe, only 30 cm below the current ground surface, until a change of crop to potatoes led to deep ploughing of the field causing severe damage to the uppermost swords and fragmentation of the surviving handles (Fig. 18.2). The cache was excavated by the Humber Archaeology Partnership and lifted by conservators from the York Archaeological Trust (YAT), who also undertook the initial conservation treatment to stabilise the finds. Subsequently, their study and conservation for publication

and display was carried out by the staff of the Museum of London Archaeology (MOLA) and the cache is now exhibited at The Treasure House, East Riding Archives and Local Studies, Beverley, East Yorkshire, UK. The publication of the cache (Evans *et al.* forthcoming) will include specialist contributions on the associated pottery finds, metallurgical analysis of the scabbards, the evidence for mineral-preserved organic (MPO) remains in the corrosion of the scabbards and spearheads, and the identification of the materials of the sword handles.

Immediately after the swords were recovered, the author was engaged by YAT to identify the materials of the handles in order to inform the initial conservation process necessary to ensure the continued survival of the finds. During the later stages of their conservation, the author was invited to undertake a further examination of the fragments, for MOLA, and was able to confirm and refine the preliminary identifications (O'Connor in Evans *et al.* forthcoming). Horn, antler, cetacean bone, cetacean ivory and elephant ivory were all identified. This paper illustrates the benefits of integrating identification with conservation, describes the criteria used in the identification of the materials, and explores the implications of these findings in terms of the provenance of the swords, how the materials might have been acquired and, perhaps, the reasons behind the choices made.

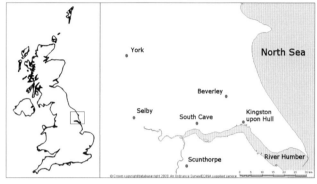

Figure 18.1 Location map of South Cave, North Humberside, UK. Right-hand map © Crown copyright/database right 2009. An Ordnance Survey/EDINA supplied service.

Description and dating of the South Cave swords

Each sword (RF16, RF17, RF18, RF40 and RF41), and indeed each spearhead, is different in shape and detail, the copper-alloy scabbards are decorated in repoussé work and cast openwork, one has panels of silver and another has fields of red and blue glass enamel. All five swords were recovered with the remains of their handles. Unfortunately, they were discovered too late to be described in detail in Stead's opus on British Iron-Age swords and scabbards (Stead 2006) and are only briefly mentioned in an addendum, but they all belong to his Group F, 'Later Swords and Scabbards in the North'. The swords and spearheads will be fully described in Evans *et al.* (forthcoming).

Sherds of Dressel Type 20 amphora, used to line and cap the pit led Evans (2006) to suggest a date of deposition in the third quarter of the 1st century AD. Further work on the full ceramic assemblage (Doherty in Evans *et al.* forthcoming) and the metallurgical study of the scabbard alloys (Northover in Evans *et al.* forthcoming) also suggests a mid to late 1st century date for this event. Stylistic dating is difficult as the

Figure 18.2 The South Cave cache in situ showing the shattered handles of the uppermost swords. © York Archaeological Trust.

chronology of these Celtic motifs is not well understood but the conservation work has revealed much evidence of wear and repair of the scabbards and Northover's metallurgical study also indicates the presence of older components. It is quite likely then that the swords pre-dated the Roman occupation of this area. Evidence indicates that the spears, at least, were wrapped in a hide or fleece (Cameron in Evans *et al.* forthcoming). It is possible that the weapons were hidden to put them out of reach of the invading forces with a view to retrieving them later or ceremonially buried to show they were 'put beyond use'. Halkon (2010, 27) suggests that the cache may have been buried in response to the *lex Julia Vi publica* (Digest 48. 6, 1) which forbade the carrying of arms. However, without further evidence, the intended purpose of the cache remains a matter of speculation.

Terminology and construction of British Iron Age sword handles

The terminology used here for the parts of the handle is that used by Stead (2006, 9) and alternative terms, found elsewhere in the literature (e.g. Rynne 1981), are given in parenthesis. Typically, there are three main elements to British Iron Age sword handles (hilts). The lowest element is the guard (hand guard, hilt guard or quillon), which sits immediately above the metal hilt end (hilt guard) of the blade, and is usually similar in width to the hilt end. Above this is the grip (hand grip), shaped to sit comfortably in the clenched hand. The grip may be constructed from one or several tubular sections, sometimes interspersed with metal washers. Finally, the handle terminates in a pommel which is wider than the grip and prevents the sword from sliding forwards out of the hand. All these elements are perforated through the centre to accommodate the blade's tang, which is generally rectangular or oval in section and tapers away from the blade. The top end of the tang, protruding from the top of the pommel, may be bent over or capped with a metal button (knop) to secure the handle in position.

Integration of conservation and materials identification

To be efficient and effective, the conservation of archaeological finds must be fully integrated within an archaeological project. Question Oriented Conservation (originally termed Problem Oriented Conservation) is a strategy for maximising information gain and minimising intervention, whilst ensuring the integrity and long-term survival of cultural artefacts (O'Connor 1996). Key to the success of this approach is planning and liaison between the conservators, archaeologists and all the other specialists throughout the project. Following this model, the identification of the wet and shattered materials of the South Cave sword handles was fully integrated within the conservation programme and to the benefit of both parties.

It is important that the lifting of the swords and handle fragments was achieved by YAT conservation staff without the aid of consolidants or adhesives. The detached fragments and three uppermost swords were individually lifted and supported using specially padded boards and boxes. The remaining two swords and the bundle of spearheads were recovered in a single soil block, held in compression by elasticated bandage, supported by a rigid, external jacket of plaster bandage, then undercut with metal sheeting and lifted on a rigid board. After radiography, the soil block was excavated in the conservation laboratory. Recognising the organic nature of the sword handles these were sprayed with a 1:1 solution of pure water and industrial methylated spirits, packed wet in suitably padded closed plastic boxes and kept in dark, refrigerated conditions to prevent them from drying out or developing fungal or other micro-organism growths (Paterson *et al.* 2003).

Examining the handle remains at this point allowed the author to observe the characteristics of the fracture patterns, break surface textures and other deterioration features without an obscuring layer of consolidant. It was also possible to access aspects of the handle components that would later be hidden by the processes of conservation and reconstruction of the swords (Fig. 18.3). Some of the external surfaces were still obscured by sediments or corrosion, and stained green or brown with copper and iron corrosion products respectively. Even so, it was possible to provide preliminary identifications of the osseous materials involved and to gain a clearer idea of their state of preservation. After discussion with the conservators the author removed sediments from the surfaces of the components, using water and soft fine brushes, following which it was possible to confirm the presence of ivory, bone, antler and horn components on various of the sword handles. However a more detailed examination was inhibited by the fragility of the material and great care had to be taken not to lose the relationship of adjacent fragments.

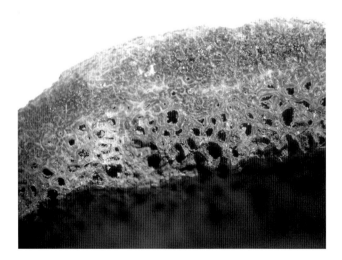

Figure 18.3 Transverse fracture through the antler grip of sword RF18. Field c. *15 mm wide (photograph: Sonia O'Connor).*

Armed with these identifications, the conservators were able to develop a strategy for the remedial conservation of the handle remains that took into account the needs of the different material types and their states of preservation. Drying the material carried the risk of further delamination of the shattered pieces, especially the ivory, so the handles were carefully cleaned of sediment, consolidated with a colloidal dispersion of an acrylic resin (Primal WS-24), followed by slow air-drying (Paterson *et al.* 2003). In this stabilised state the swords were then stored in dry conditions whilst funding for the study, publication and display of the cache was under consideration. Despite YAT's involvement in the initial conservation work, the commercial archaeology context required competitive tendering for the subsequent work, and this contract was awarded to MOLA, where the final stages of the conservation of the swords were undertaken.

At MOLA the fragments of the handles were joined together (with HMG Paraloid B72) so that the forms and details of the surviving components could be studied and drawn. At this point the author was invited to refine the identifications of the materials. The consolidating resin had made the surfaces rather reflective and adhesive obscured

previously visible aspects but it was now easier to handle the components, to appreciate their size and shape and to map the position, extent and grain direction of the materials involved (Table 18.1 and Fig. 18.4).

The last stage of the conservation process was the re-attachment of the handle fragments to the tangs and the swords themselves. This involved some reconstruction of missing areas, to ensure physical stability (Goodman in Evans *et al.* forthcoming) which inevitably has hidden some of the evidence that had been crucial to providing confident identifications of the materials.

Techniques of identification

Most of the identification guides for animal hard tissues make no mention of horn or other keratinous materials, such as baleen, but are focussed on osseous structures, particularly ivories and other materials used in their imitation (Penniman 1952; Espinoza and Mann 1992). These guides largely describe the natural surface morphology and structures revealed in thin or polished sections of 'typical' specimens, of relatively

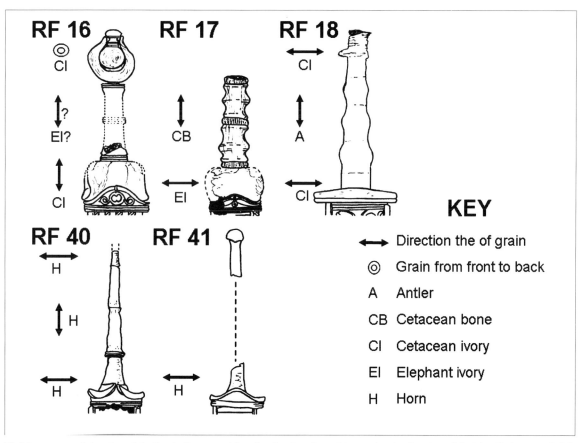

Figure 18.4 Reconstructed drawing of the South Cave sword handles showing the position and grain direction of the identified materials (after Evans et al. forthcoming).

Table 18.1 Description of the South Cave swords and handle remains.

RECORDED FIND number (RF) AND ACCESSION NUMBER	DESCRIPTION AFTER STEAD (2006)	ORGANIC MATERIALS OF THE HANDLES		
		HILT GUARD	*GRIP*	*POMMEL*
RF 16 ERYMS 2005.99.1	Sword: Group F, Hilt: Type viii Scabbard: Type Y Suspension loop: Type 6 Chape: Type h	Cetacean ivory, sperm whale	Ivory, possibly elephant (RF 20)	Cetacean ivory, sperm whale
RF 17 ERYMS 2005.99.5	Sword: Group F, Hilt: Type crown-shaped Scabbard: Type Y Suspension loop: Type 6 Chape: Type h	Elephant ivory (RF 22)	Cetacean bone (RF 22 and 26)	Not surviving
RF 18 ERYMS 2005.99.8	Sword: Group F, Hilt: Type vii Scabbard: Type Y Suspension loop: Flat and rectangular Chape: Type g	Cetacean ivory, sperm whale	Antler beam	Cetacean ivory, sperm whale
RF 40 ERYMS 2005.99.9	Sword: Group F, Hilt: Type viii Scabbard: Type Y Suspension loop: circular Chape: Type g	Horn	Horn	Horn
RF 41 ERYMS 2005.99.10	Sword: Group F, Hilt: Type viii (crown shaped) Scabbard: Type Y Suspension loop: circular Chape: Type h	Possible horn/or wood (not examined by author)	No surviving material recorded	No surviving material recorded

fresh material. This limits their usefulness when examining worked objects that cannot be sectioned or whose physical appearance or properties have been altered during manufacture, decoration, wear or decay. The author addressed some of these deficiencies in a paper describing the criteria used in the identification of osseous and keratinous archaeological objects from York (O'Connor 1987) and Krzyszkowska (1990) covers ivory objects from Near Eastern sites.

The fragments of the South Cave sword handles were examined by eye and under a low power binocular microscope, using incident light at a variety of angles to help illuminate the detailed textures and structures. The identifications of the materials are based on macroscopic and microscopic features observed through comparison of those seen in materials of known species, in various states of preservation and working. Here the identification of each of the materials of the sword handles is discussed (see also Fig. 18.4).

Horn

Horn is mostly composed of the protein keratin which is very susceptible to fungal degradation. It can survive in desiccated environments and, occasionally, in waterlogged, anoxic deposits, such as acid bogs. However, where horn is in intimate contact with corroding metal, traces of it may be preserved in environments where organic materials do not otherwise survive. The solutions formed by corroding copper alloy objects are biocidal so they inhibit the biodegradation of organic materials such as horn. In addition, if these solutions, and those formed by corroding iron, gradually infuse the organic material and then precipitate within it, they can form persistent moulds or casts of its structure. These are termed mineral preserved organic (MPO) remains. Normally only that part of the organic material closest to the metal is preserved; the extent of the remains and the quality of detail depending very much on the relative rates at which the metal is corroding and the organic material is decaying.

All the iron tang fragments of sword RF40 are covered in a thin layer of MPO horn. In the least well preserved areas the horn is very fibrous in appearance and, at first, easily mistakable for decayed wood although it lacks features particular to wood such as ray cells. The horn on the grip is better preserved and under low magnification shows the characteristic fine, corrugated, lamellar sheet structure of horn (Fig. 18.5). The long axis of the horn is parallel to the direction of the corrugations. The corrosion has also penetrated deeply into the junctions between the components of the handle preserving evidence of its construction. The grain direction of the horn pommel and of the guard is horizontal (i.e. across the tang) whilst the grain in the grip runs vertically. A copper alloy washer separates the grip from the guard and a sharp junction half-way along the grip indicates that it was made from two cylinders of horn. The horn is most probably cattle: it is unlikely at this period that sheep would have yielded sufficient solid horn of this size, though horn from a large male goat may have done so. The pommel and guard would have been cut from solid horn tips but the grip might have been worked from the portion of horn directly below the tip which has a wider external diameter and a narrow, tapering hollow that could be utilised to house the tang of the blade.

Figure 18.5 MPO horn remains from the grip of sword RF40. Field c. 5 mm wide (photograph: Sonia O'Connor).

There were also reported to be traces of a possible horn or a fine-grained wood at the base of the tang of sword RF41 (Paterson *et al.* 2003). The grain of the material ran across the tang and probably related to its guard. Unfortunately, this sword was not submitted to the author for examination and the identification of these MPO remains is unconfirmed.

Antler and bone

Objects of antler and bone can be very difficult to tell apart when only the modified surface of the compact tissue is visible. A distinctly ordered and lamellar vascular structure indicates bone, but if the structure appears more chaotic it might be bone or antler and may perhaps only be differentiated from a section though the thickness of the material. Working on the sword handles whilst they were still in fragments proved very advantageous as it was possible to examine fracture surfaces that approximated to both longitudinal and transverse sections of the osseous materials.

Before conservation, the fragmentary state of the handle of sword RF18 enabled the grip to be identified as red deer antler but it was only after it had been painstakingly re-assembled that it was possible to fully understand its construction. Figure 18.3 shows a transverse break that reveals the relatively unordered structure of the antler cortex and the characteristic spongy medulla, which has been cut away in the centre to accommodate the iron tang. Corrosion from the tang has stained the antler enhancing the visibility of features within these structures. The characteristics of the cortex/medulla transition and the diameter of the grip (approximately 30 mm) suggest that this is either the beam or large tine of red deer. Although incomplete, the grip appears to be made up of several tubular sections of antler, slotted over the rectangular section tang and shaped to form probably three smoothly rounded cordons to fit between the fingers.

Cetacean bone

Surprisingly, only one handle component from the five swords was made of bone; the grip of sword RF17. This is formed from two similar sized cylinders of bone separated from each other and from the pommel and guard by raised, decorated, copper alloy washers. Both sections of the grip have concave mouldings either side of a central rounded cordon. Bone grips reported elsewhere (Rynne 1983; MacGregor 1985, 165–167; Stead 2006) appear to be tubes formed from the shafts of longbones. With longbone grips the structure of the bone is organised concentrically around the tang, which is housed in the bone's marrow cavity. Instead, it can be seen in Figure 18.6 that in this grip the longitudinal lamellar structure of the bone runs through from one side of the handle to the other, indicating that it was shaped from a solid block of tissue with a width and thickness of at least 30 mm. In addition, the histological structures of the bone are on a scale too large to be from a longbone of a large mammal such as cattle or horse. The transverse break section in Figure 18.6 also shows that the bone is largely remodelled by secondary osteon structures. Taken together, this evidence indicates that this grip has been cut from the jaw bone of a relatively large cetacean such as sperm whale (*Physeter macrocephalus*).

Elephant Ivory

The guard of sword RF17 is very fragmentary and much of its worked surface is missing. The cracking of its finely laminated structure and the lack of evidence for a vascular system show this to be an ivory. The longitudinal axis of the tooth runs horizontally across the tang. The surviving area of worked surface at one end of the shoulder of the guard, shown in Figure 18.7, approximates to a transverse section. Here, intersecting lines form the Schreger pattern characteristic of elephant ivory. Despite the rounded shape of this surface, decay has enhanced the visibility of the pattern, producing a texture of nested, inverted 'V' shapes. The Schreger pattern is produced by the regular organisation of the dentinal tubules,

found in all ivory from extant and extinct elephant, including mammoth, but this ivory guard has neither the density nor dark colouration often seen in fossilised terrestrial or marine specimen material. Instead it has the friability, cracking and decay typical of archaeological ivory preserved in wet burial conditions. This does not entirely rule out subfossil mammoth ivory from permafrost conditions, but a more likely explanation is that it was contemporary elephant ivory. It has been shown possible to distinguish modern elephant from mammoth through accurate measurements of the angles of intersection of the Schreger pattern lines (Espinoza and Mann 1991, 10–2), but this is not feasible where, as in this case, the surface is small and far from flat.

The grip of sword RF16 is ivory and is separated from the pommel and guard by copper alloy washers. Very little of it survives, as the central portion of the tang is missing, but the fracture surfaces show slight, regular parallel corrugations. Similar corrugations are revealed when elephant ivory delaminates concentrically. However, on its own, this evidence is not sufficient to confirm the identification of this ivory as elephant.

Figure 18.6 Transverse fracture through cetacean bone grip of sword RF17. Field c. 10 mm wide (photograph Sonia O'Connor).

Figure 18.7 Schreger pattern typical of elephant ivory visible over the rounded shoulder of the guard of sword RF17 (photograph: Sonia O'Connor).

Cetacean Ivory

No other ivory has a tell-tale feature as characteristic as the Schreger pattern of elephant ivory. Instead identification relies on finding a number of features that together support one conclusion. This includes an estimation of the overall size and shape of the object, the fineness, regularity and path of the laminations (both longitudinally and transverse to the axis of the tooth), the distribution of bands indicating variations in the mineralisation of the dentine and irregular patterning of the dentine. Using such criteria, both the guards and pommels of swords RF16 and RF18 have been identified as cetacean teeth, specifically sperm whale ivory.

Sperm whale teeth are conical and often solid for much of their length and the dentine is thickly covered in a layer of cementum. The cross-section is most circular towards the tip of the tooth, developing into a rounded oval lower down and often becoming narrower and flatter towards the base. Mature males produce the largest teeth, often in excess of 1 kg in weight and diameters of *c.* 150 mm have been recorded (Hillson 1986, 54). A pair of 19th century teeth in the collections of the Hull Maritime Museum are each *c.* 200 mm in height and weigh 1.23 kg and 1.30 kg respectively, despite being trimmed flat at the base (West and Credland 1995, 59–60).

Killer whale (*Orcinus orca*) is another large-toothed whale found around the British coast but, with a maximum height *c.* 120 mm (Watson 1981, 214), their teeth are too small and slender to have been made into these pommels and guards. Killer whale teeth also have a slight longitudinal groove on one or both sides (Espinoza and Mann 1992, 16) which should be visible as an undulation in the layers of the tooth and was not observed in any of the pieces.

The pommel of sword RF16 is in the form of a ball surrounded by a penannular collar or crescent carved from a single large piece of sperm whale ivory, from the solid tip of the tooth (Fig. 18.8). The tooth is oriented horizontally, with the axis of the tooth running through the ball from one face to the other, the concentric cracks between lamellae reflecting the oval cross-section of the tooth. A small, off-centre dimple on one side of the ball probably marks the top of the pulp cavity. The textured and longitudinally grooved cementum covering of the tooth survives on the edge of the pommel.

The guard of sword RF16 is oval in cross-section and is also carved from a single large piece of ivory, at least 60 mm wide. The long axis of the tooth is coaxial with the sword, with the tip uppermost. Features, such as the fine laminations and bands of varying mineralisation particularly apparent in areas that have been stained green by the corroding copper alloy hilt end (Fig. 18.9), and the overall size and shape of the guard are consistent with this also being sperm whale tooth. The green staining has also helped pick out an isolated whorled structure. This is a section through a spheroidal feature often formed down the centre of mature sperm whale teeth (Fig. 18.9).

The pommel and guard of sword RF18 are very much less well preserved but the fineness of the laminations and character of the cracking suggests that both are sperm whale ivory. The pommel is cut from a solid piece of a large whale tooth with the grain running transversally. The guard is a

Figure 18.8 Front and side view of the sperm whale ivory pommel of sword RF16 (photograph: Sonia O'Connor).

Figure 18.9 Detail of sperm whale ivory from the guard of sword RF16 showing bryozoan etching (top) and whorled structures in the ivory (lower right). Field c. *20 mm wide (photograph: Sonia O'Connor).*

Figure 18.10 The finely lamellar sperm whale ivory of the guard from sword RF18. Field c. 10 mm wide (photograph: Sonia O'Connor).

longitudinal section from one side of a large cetacean tooth Fig. 18.10). As in sword RF16, corrosion from the copper alloy hilt end has enhanced the visibility of the bands of varying mineralisation.

Discussion

The swords from the South Cave cache are remarkably well preserved and present materials and combinations of materials not reported elsewhere. Stead (2006) catalogues 275 La Tène period (4th century BC into the Roman period) swords from British sites. Some of these consist of only scabbards or fittings, but even where the tangs have survived there is little evidence for the materials of the handles. A few have cast metal handles and 43 are reported as having evidence of organic handle elements, mostly in the form of MPO remains on the tangs or other metal handle fittings such as washers or sheathing. Where preservation has been good enough to allow more precise identification, horn has been identified on 11 swords, wood on nine (although only two are identified to species so some of these could also be horn), bone on two and antler on two. Apart from the Bryher Sword (Stead

2006, 171; catalogue no 87) from the Isles of Scilly, all the swords with horn handle elements come from Yorkshire, north of the Humber. Like South Cave sword RF40, some of these handles are entirely of horn but two, from the East Riding of Yorkshire (Stead, 2006, 195–6; catalogue nos 210 and 211), also have antler components. None of the handles described by Stead has elephant or cetacean ivory or cetacean bone components.

In the use of osseous materials, particularly cetacean bone and ivory, the South Cave sword handles seem to have a greater affinity with those found further north, in areas not covered by Stead. In Rynne's (1983) brief survey of La Tène sword and dagger handle elements from Ireland and Scotland, the materials are identified as antler or bone/antler, the distinction not having always been determined. However, the pommel recognised by Rynne from the Broch of Burrian, North Ronaldsay, Orkney, was subsequently confirmed by MacGregor (1974, 76–78 and fig. 9, 127) as cetacean bone. In addition, pommels and hilt guards in cetacean bone and ivory are found on other sites from Atlantic Scotland, for instance the bone pommel and guard from Scalloway in Shetland (Sharples 1998, 158–159) and the ivory guard from Gurness (Hedges 1987, 88 and 111, fig. 2.37). Several sword or dagger handle elements in both cetacean bone and ivory from Mine Howe in Orkney have also been examined by the author, although not yet published. The pommels from Dungarvan, Co. Waterford, Ireland, the Broch of Burrian, North Ronaldsay, Orkney and North Uist, Hebrides, described by Rynne, and the pommel from Scalloway, are stylistically similar to the ball and crescent of South Cave Sword RF16.

Evidence from Bronze Age dagger finds shows that the use of cetacean material in the handles of cutting-edge weapons was a long-standing tradition. Mark Maltby is reassessing the classification of Early Bronze age dagger pommels (Maltby forthcoming). He and the author confirmed identifications of pommels in Hull and Sheffield museums. Those from Garton Slack and Garrowby, on the Yorkshire Wolds, appear to be cetacean bone (O'Connor forthcoming.). Examination of photographs by the author of other pommels in this study suggest that in total eight of the 21 pommels may be cetacean bone. In addition, the author has confirmed that the Late Bronze Age dagger pommel from the Gristhorpe burial, near Filey, North Yorkshire is cetacean bone (Melton *et al.* 2010), and that from the Early Bronze Age cist burial at Forteviot, Perthshire (Driscoll *et al.* 2010), as very decayed cetacean ivory. Two other ivory pommels are described by Hardaker (1974). The pommel from Ashgrove Methilhill, Fife (corpus no. 1), is identified as sperm whale, whilst that from Leicester (corpus no. 24), is simply termed ivory (Hardaker 1974, 7 and 21 respectively).

Marine ivory continues to be a material of significance in later swords. Ellis Davidson (1998, 181) mentions a number of instances in the Norse and Irish sagas of swords with ivory handle components, including the sword Legbiter that had a walrus ivory guard and the sword Footbiter, described in *Laxdæla Saga* as 'a great weapon and good, with hilt formed of walrus ivory'. Solinus's writing in the third century mentions the Irish 'who cultivate elegance adorn the hilts of their swords with the tusks of great sea-animals' (translation by Joyce; Mallory 1981, 104). Whale bone too continues in this role, examples including the 5th or 6th century sword guard from excavations at Collierstown, Co. Meath, Ireland (Riddler and Trzaskap-Nartovski 2009) and the 9th or 10th century Viking, five-lobed, whale bone sword pommel from Coppergate, York (MacGregor *et al.* 1999, 1945).

Roman army equipment, more or less contemporary with the South Cave swords, was not entirely standardised and local forms were often adopted, perhaps along with local recruits, both from occupied territories and those beyond the frontiers. Swords from Hod Hill, Waddon Hill, Roecliffe, Newstead and Camelon, are seen by Bishop and Coulston (2006, 82) as examples of this practise, producing a fusion of the Roman short sword design and La Tène type features.

In contrast with the British Iron Age evidence, however, cetacean bone and ivory are not reported on Roman Swords. Most surviving Roman sword handle grips are bone, generally horse or cattle metapodials (MacGregor 1985, 165). These long-bone grips can have octagonal, rhomboidal or a barrel-shaped profile (Bishop and Coulston 2006, 78–83; MacGregor 1985, 165–166). Wood is the most common alternative to bone, although ivory also occurs. Guards and pommels have also been found in wood, bone and ivory Bishop and Coulston 2006, 78). Antler hilt guards have also been recorded (Chapman 2005, 10–11 and plate A swords). Horn is rarely mentioned but there is evidence of its use on Roman daggers (Scott 1985) and knives. Again, this may be due to a combination of poor preservation and misidentification of MPO horn remains as wood, and perhaps, early conservation techniques that often involved the removal of surface corrosion and the evidence it contained.

When discussing Roman ivory objects, unfortunately, texts mostly do not specify the species. In the author's experience, British Roman ivory objects are almost invariably elephant ivory, but the term 'ivory' on its own in publications and collection catalogues frequently indicates that the species was not, or could not be assigned. As Carnap-Bornheim (1994) points out, the surfaces where the Shreger lines might be seen, for instance the ends of the grip, are obscured by both the pommel and guard where handles are complete. This emphasises that identification is best undertaken prior to or during conservation and reconstruction. This difficulty in identifying the exploitation of ivories from other species is compounded by the common habit of subsuming ivory within the category of 'bone' objects in archaeological reports. However, a brief literature survey for this paper has revealed no records of non-elephant ivory in the construction of Roman sword handles.

Acquisition of the cetacean bone and ivory

There is scant evidence for whaling in the UK before the 17th century but plenty of evidence for the use of cetacean bone for often very specific types of objects (MacGregor 1985, 31). Until the Viking period, objects from large cetacean have a distribution largely restricted to the North of Britain. MacGregor (1974) argues that the quantity of cetacean bone finds from Late Iron Age sites in northern and western coastal Scotland suggests that acquisition had gone beyond the utilisation of occasional strandings. He suggests that material acquisition must have at least involved active inshore hunting of smaller whales. It is possible that the Humber estuary might also have provided opportunities for corralling smaller cetaceans in bays or for driving them ashore in the shallows and other early historic whaling techniques, as described by Clark (1947).

Sperm whales, however, are unlikely to have been hunted around the shores of the British Isles at this time, not only because of their immense size but because shallow coastal waters are not their normal habitat. Their primary prey, cephalopods, mostly live in the deep oceans of the world and sperm whales entering the North Sea, for instance, are very liable to starve and ultimately die of dehydration. For reasons not fully understood, the incidence of strandings around the British Isles has risen at a rate of 14% per year since 1970 (Goold *et al.* 2002). Since 1990, there have been 132 stranding, the majority being on the Scottish coast (Zoological Society of London 2011) including 11 stranded at Backaskaill Bay, Sanday on 7 December 1994 (Kompanje and Reumer 1995). But strandings are not just a recent phenomenon and records for the countries boarding the North Sea go back at least to the early 16th century (Smeenk 1997) and it is reasonable to suppose that occasional stranding have always occurred. However, the hilt guard of South Cave sword RF16 has small irregular holes cut deep into surviving areas of its worked surface that seem to indicate another taphonomic pathway (Fig. 18.9). The branching network with expanding tubular structures are typical of bryozoan etching and suggests that the whale died and rotted on the sea bed where the tooth became detached and was eventually washed up and collected from the strand line of a beach.

Acquisition of the elephant ivory

The use of elephant ivory might at first seem the most surprising material to find incorporated in a La Tène sword. Apart from Caesar's campaigns in 55 and 54 BC, it was only in AD 43 that the Roman conquest of Britain really began. Progress north was intermittent and may have been arrested at the southern bank of the River Humber for perhaps some 20 years. In AD 69, with civil unrest amongst client tribes on this frontier, the Roman army advanced northwards, finally crossing the River Humber into the domain of the Parisi *c.*

AD 71. However, during the frontier period, *c.* AD 47–70, the Humber was only the border of the Roman tax world and not an impermeable barrier. Trade continued across the river and a trading site was established on the northern shore at Redcliff, less than 10 km from South Cave, linking the Parisian elite to all that the material culture of the Roman world had to offer (Creighton 1990, 193).

A piece of elephant ivory large enough to produce the guard for South Cave sword RF17 could have been of considerable value and might represent gift exchange between the Roman authorities and an influential Parisian leader. MacGregor (1985, 39) takes the lack of Roman ivory working waste in Britain as an indication that elephant ivory was imported as finished objects and it is possible that the guard on sword RF17 was a Roman form acquired largely complete and just requiring fitting. However, the lack of ivory working waste could be due to issues of recovering finely divided material. There was clearly a long tradition of cetacean ivory working already established in the British Isles at this time, and the elephant ivory could equally well have been worked locally.

Significance of material choice.

The use of horn and antler for handle components can be explained in purely utilitarian terms but the more exotic materials need further consideration. Certainly the use of both cetacean and elephant ivory would have indicated something of the status and wealth of the owner, which is also apparent from the quality, materials and decoration of the scabbards. On the pommel of sword RF17, the colour contrast and difference in reflectance of the dentine and cementum would have been very striking and clearly identifiable as sperm whale tooth to anyone familiar with the material. When freshly cut the dentine of the central ball would have been pale yellow and the surrounding cementum white (Penniman 1952, 28), like the sun nestling in a crescent moon. The elephant ivory, however acquired, might have been merely considered by the craftsman as a useful substitute for sperm whale ivory! However, if the Schreger pattern on the guard of sword RF16 was as evident in its original polished state as it is now in the decayed remains, this elephant ivory may have been prized in its own right. Imported as luxury material from their Roman neighbours, elephant ivory would have communicated sophistication, exclusivity and connections with the new and rising power in the south.

The selection of cetacean bone for the grip of sword RF17 also requires consideration. Cetacean jaw compact tissue has to be drilled or cut out to accommodate the sword's tang. Whilst this may be less convenient than using sections of antler beam or the hollow shaft of a large long-bone, it might produce a better initial fit and be less likely to work loose on the tang with use. The coarser structure of cetacean bone may also initially provide a more non-slip surface but wear in the hand would soon impart a polish.

It is worth speculating that perhaps the use of both cetacean ivory and bone in these sword handles had a more symbolic, perhaps even an empowering function. Glimpsed at sea, the natural history of the larger off-shore whales would have been unknown; pure mystery. Beached, their huge carcasses still draw crowds and inspire awe today. In the past they could have easily become the focus of legends, a gift of the sea providing meat to eat, fat, oil and bone to burn, skins for clothing and lashings, flexible sheets of baleen or teeth and bone to fashion into objects. It has been suggested that whales were a significant element in Neolithic symbolism (Whittle 2000). That their economic value was historically significant is attested to by the description, in the *Icelandic Saga of Grettir the Strong*, of rival communities fighting over a stranded carcass and British records, from as early as the 12th century, detailing ownership rights to strandings and swingeing fines for illicit removal of parts of these whales (Clark 1947, 90). Ownership might be granted to senior clerics or noblemen, although the whale's tongue might be reserved for royalty.

A stranded sperm whale in particular would have presented a formidable sight at up to 20 m in length and 38,000 kg in weight (Watson 1981, 171). All the recorded sperm whale strandings in the North Sea are males (Smeek 1997), females seldom moving more then 40° from the equator (Watson 1981, 174). On beaching they have been known to produce a roar audible for several kilometres (*ibid.*, 175). In photographs of strandings, and in even the earliest of pictorial recordings, the two most prominent features are the jaw hanging open to reveal upward of 48 huge teeth and the large, protruding genitals (Fig. 18.11). Embodying such obvious and potent symbols of masculine power it is, perhaps, not so surprising that the bones and teeth of the whale should be used in the fabrication of weapons of status and war.

Conclusions

The handles of the South Cave swords are remarkably well preserved and present materials and combinations of materials not reported elsewhere on British Iron Age swords. Given that so few sword handles have survived from this period, it is not surprising that there are so few parallels but they do exhibit traits otherwise only seen in swords from the North of Britain. Both horn and antler would have been readily available materials but in Iron Age Britain whale bone, whale ivory and elephant ivory were rare commodities signifying status and power. The use of cetacean bone and ivory for cutting-edge weapons was long-established, perhaps imbuing the weapon, or its owner, with the power of the beast. The use of elephant ivory signalled contact with the Roman empire to the south of the River Humber and perhaps the assimilation of Roman values, or possibly it was simply viewed as a convenient substitute for its cetacean counterpart.

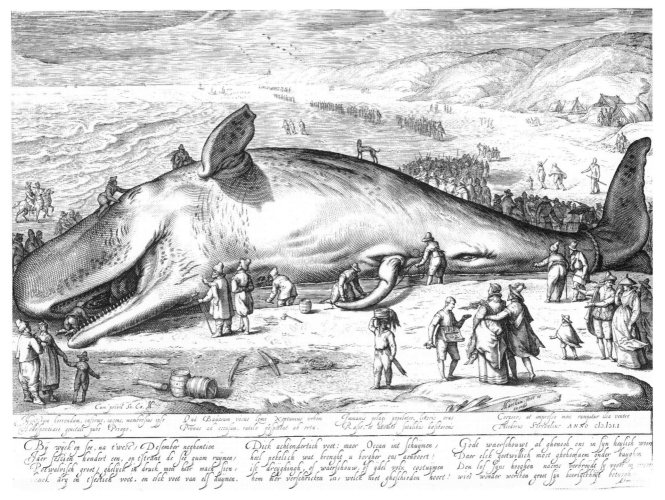

Figure 18.11 Sperm whale stranding on the Dutch coast near Beverwijk, dated 1601. The size of the whale is greatly exaggerated and the Latin caption mentions the genitals, which are in the process of being measured. © Trustees of the British Museum.

Acknowledgements

My thanks go to Dave Evans for information relating to the discovery of the cache, the conservation staff of the York Archaeological Trust and Museum of London Archaeology (MOLA) for copies of their conservation reports, David Marchant, East Riding Council for images of the swords and Nicola Powell and Michael Marshall of MOLA for sight of the cache publication in draft and for providing additional information and commenting on this paper. I also thank Professor Martin Millet for sharing his thoughts on the nature of the Roman frontier at the River Humber. Fraser Hunter for information relating to recent finds from Scotland and the Northern and Western Isles and for access to the material from Gurness and Mine Howe, Orkney. Alison Sheridan for inviting me to examine the remains of the dagger pommel from Forteviot. Ian Riddler for alerting me to the find from Collierstown. Julie Bond for sharing her knowledge of Anglo-Saxon swords and Joseph Botting, then Assistant Curator of Natural Sciences (Geology), Leeds Museums and Galleries and now Young International Fellow, Nanjing Institute of Geology and Palaeontology, for the identification of the bryozoan etching. The research reported here has been carried out under a 3 year post-doctoral fellowship, *Cultural Objects Worked in Skeletal Hard Tissues*, funded by the Arts and Humanities Research Council and the Engineering and Physical Sciences Research Council, through their Science and Heritage Programme. This project will evaluate, validate and develop the criteria and techniques used in the identification of differently preserved archaeological material and objects from historical collections.

Bibliography

Bishop, M. C. and Coulston, J. C. N. (2006) *Roman Military Equipment from the Punic Wars to the Fall of Rome* (2nd edition). Oxford, Oxbow Books.

Chapman, E. M. (2005) *A catalogue of Roman Military Equipment in the National Museum of Wales*. Oxford, Archaeopress (British Archaeological Report 388).

Clark, G. (1947) Whales as an Economic Factor in Prehistoric Europe. *Antiquity* 21 (82), 84–104.

Creighton, J. (1990) The Humber frontier in the first century AD. In S. Ellis and D. R. Crowther (eds), *Humber Perspectives: a region through the ages*, 182–198. Hull, Hull University Press.

Driscoll, S., Brophy, K. and Noble, G. (2010) The Strathearn Environs and Royal Forteviot project (SERF). *Antiquity* 84, 343 March 2010, http://www.antiquity.ac.uk/projgall/driscoll323/ (accessed 20 September 2011)

Ellis Davidson, H. (1998) *The Sword in Anglo-Saxon England*. Woodbridge, Boydell Press.

Espinoza, E. O. and Mann, M.-J, (1992) *Identification Guide for Ivory and Ivory Substitutes* (2dn edition). World Wildlife Fund and Conservation Foundation.

Evans, D. (2006) Celtic art revealed. *Current Archaeology* 203, 572–577.

Evans, D., Marshall, M., *et al.* (forthcoming) A first century AD hoard of weapons from South cave, East Yorkshire. *Britannia*.

Goold, J. C., Whitehead, H. and Reid, R. J. (2002) North Atlantic sperm whale, *Physeter macrocephalus*, strandings on the coastlines of the British Isles and eastern Canada. *Canadian Field-Naturalist* 116 (3), 371–388.

Halkon P. (2010) Britons and Romans in an East Yorkshire Landscape, UK. *Bollettino di Archeologia on line,* volume speciale E / E10 / 3, accessed at http://151.12.58.75/archeologia/bao_document/articoli/3_HALKON.pdf (accessed 11 September 2012)

Hardaker, R. (1974) *A Corpus of Early Bronze Age Dagger Pommels from Great Britain and Ireland*. Oxford, British Archaeological Report 3.

Hedges, J. (1987) *Bu, Gurness and the Brochs of Orkney, Part II,* Oxford, British Archaeological Report 164.

Hillson, S. (1986) *Teeth*. Cambridge, Cambridge University Press.

Kompanje, E. J. O. and Reumer, J. W. F. (1995) Strandings of male sperm whales *Physeter macrocephalus* Linnaeus, 1758 in Western Europe between October 1994 and January 1995. *Deinsea* 2, 89–94.

Krzyszkowska, O. (1990) *Ivory and Related Materials: an illustrated guide* London, Institute of Classical Studies (Classical Handbook 3, Bulletin Supplement 59).

MacGregor, A. (1974) The Broch of Burrian, North Ronaldsay, Orkney. *Proceedings of the Society of Antiquaries of Scotland* 105, 63–118.

MacGregor, A. (1985) *Bone Antler Ivory and Horn. The technology of skeletal materials since the Roman period*. London, Croom Helm.

MacGregor, A., Mainman, A. J. and Rogers, N. S. H. (1999) *Craft, Industry and Everyday Life: bone, antler, ivory and horn from Anglo-Scandinavian and Medieval York*. York, Council for British Archaeology/Archaeology of York AY17/12.

Mallory, J. P. (1981) The Sword of the Ulster Cycle. In B. G. Scott (ed.), *Studies on Early Ireland. Essays in honour of M. V. Duignan*, 99–114. Belfast, Association of Young Irish Archaeologists.

Maltby, M. (forthcoming) A revised classification for British Copper and Early Bronze Age daggers and knives, and classification of Early Bronze Age dagger and knife pommel-pieces. In A. Woodward and J. Hunter and D. Bukach (eds), *Ritual in Early Bronze Age Grave Goods*. Oxford, Oxbow Books.

Melton, N., Montgomery, J., Knüsel, C. J., Batt, C., Needham, S., Parker Pearson, M., Sheridan, A., Heron, C., Horsley, T., Schmidt, A., Evans, A., Carter, E., Edwards, H., Hargreaves, M., Janaway, R., Lynnerup, N., Northover, P., O'Connor, S., Ogden, A., Taylor, T., Wastling, V. and Wilson, A. (2010). Gristhorpe Man: an Early Bronze Age log-coffin burial scientifically defined. *Antiquity* 84 (325), 796–815.

O'Connor, S. (1987) The identification of osseous and keratinaceous materials at York. In K. Starling and D. Watkinson (eds), *Archaeological Bone, Antler and Ivory*, 9–21. London, United Kingdom Institute for Conservation (Occasional Paper 5).

O'Connor, S. (1996) Developing a conservation strategy in a rescue archaeology environment. In *Preprints, Archaeological Conservation and its Consequence. IIC 16th International Congress, 1996, Copenhagen*, 133–136. London, International Institute for Conservation.

O'Connor, S. (forthcoming) Appendix IV Identification of Bronze Age pommels and other osseous objects. In A. Woodward and J. Hunter and D.Bukach (eds), *Ritual in Early Bronze Age Grave Goods*. Oxford, Oxbow Books

Paterson, E., Spriggs, J. and Vere-Stevens, L. (2003) *Conservation Laboratory Assessment Report: RSC2002, East Yorkshire weapons cache*. Unpublished archive report, York Archaeological Trust.

Penniman, T. K. (1952) *Pictures of Ivory and other Animal Teeth, Bone and Antler*. Oxford, University of Oxford (Pitt Rivers Museum Occasional Papers on Technology 5).

Riddler, I. and Trzaska-Nartowski, N. (2009) Appendix 13 Bone objects, in R. O'Hara. *Report on the Archaeological Excavations of Collierstown 1, Co Meath*. M3 Clonee-North of Kells Motorway Scheme, Ministerial Directions No. A008/015, accessed at http://www.m3motorway.ie/Archaeology/Section2/Collierstown1/file,16721,en.pdf (accessed 14 February 2012).

Rynne, E. (1981) A classification of pre-Viking Irish iron swords. In B. G. Scott (ed.), *Studies on Early Ireland: essays in honour of M. V. Duignan*, 93–97. Belfast, Association of Young Irish Archaeologists.

Rynne, E. (1983) Some Early Iron Age Sword-Hilts from Ireland and Scotland. In A. O'Connor and D. V. Clarke (eds), *From the Stone Age to the 'Forty–Five*, 188–196. Edinburgh, John Donald.

Scott, I. R. (1985) Daggers. In W. H. Manning *Catalogue of the Romano-British Iron Tools, Fittings and Weapons in the British Museum*, 152–159. London, British Museum.

Sharples, N. (1998) *Scalloway. A Broch, Late Iron Age Settlement and Medieval Cemetery in Shetland*. Oxford, Oxbow Monograph 82.

Smeenk, C. (1997) Strandings of sperm whales *Physeter macrocephalus* in the North Sea: history and patterns. In T. G. Jacques and R. H. Lambertsen (eds), *Sperm Whale Deaths in the North Sea, Science and Management, Bulletin de L'Institut Royal des Sciences Naturelles de Belgique, Biologie* 67 (supplement), 15–28.

Stead, I. M. (2006) *British Iron Age Swords and Scabbards*. London, British Museum.

Von Carnap-Bornheim, C. (1994) Some observations on Roman militaria of ivory. In C. van Driel-Murray (ed.), *Military Equipment in Context. Proceedings of the Ninth International Roman Military Equipment Conference, Leiden. Journal of Roman Military Equipment Studies* 5, 27–32.

Watson, L. (1981) *Sea Guide to Whales of the World*. London, Hutchinson and Co.

West, J. and Credland, A. G. (1995) *Scrimshaw: the art of the whaler*. Beverley, Hull City Museums and Art Gallery and Hutton Press.

Whittle, A. (2000) 'Very like a whale': menhirs, motifs and myths in the Mesolithic-Neolithic transition of northwest Europe. *Cambridge Archaeological Journal* 10 (2), 243–259.

Zoological Society of London. (2011) The mighty fall. *Wildabout* (summer), 10.

Chapter 19

An Introduction to ZooMS (Zooarchaeology by Mass Spectrometry) for Taxonomic Identification of Worked and Raw Materials

Oliver W. Hounslow, Joanna P. Simpson, Lauren Whalley and Matthew J. Collins

In this review we describe the principle behind a new method to identify the origin of worked bone, antler and ivory; ZooMS, short for Zooarchaeology by Mass Spectrometry. The method exploits the fact that the dominant organic component of these tissues is the fibrous protein collagen, which comprises (with water) almost half the volume of intact material. ZooMS is a sensitive technique that extracts the collagen molecules, cuts them into peptides using an enzyme which cleaves at specific residues, and then detects the mass distribution of the resultant peptides. While most peptides in mammalian collagen remain the same (due to the slow evolution of this molecule), differences in mass highlight differences in sequence that can be used to help identify the organism in question. ZooMS is a technique in its infancy, and the number of species for which we have collagen fingerprints or sequences is small, but growing primarily on the back of genome sequencing initiatives. The strengths and limitations of ZooMS and the other common molecular identification method (DNA) are compared and contrasted.

Keywords
Protein; collagen; Mass Spectrometry; species identification; ZooMS.

The problem with identification

How useful are low molecular methods in the identification of worked bone? When bone is largely intact, attributes such as size, morphology and surface features provide clues to species origin (Hillier and Bell 2007). Most identification is, however, comparative and the lack of available reference collections limits the number of skilled professionals available for analysing samples. Even the technique is heavily reliant on personal judgement, and thus is susceptible to variance and dispute (O'Connor 2000). One of the major problems with the morphological comparison method is that many commonly found elements lack discriminating features.

The working of bone often removes morphological features that would have once allowed species identification, This results in researchers becoming increasingly reliant on microscopic features to discriminate tissues such as bone, ivory and antler (Ashby 2009), which identify differences in histology (Greenlee and Dunnell 2010; Martiniakova *et al.* 2007). Microscopic methods have shown the ability to discriminate between land (mammalian/avian) and marine (fish) species; coupling of this technique with Near Infra-Red (NIR) microscopy has enabled further discrimination between land and avian species and has been used widely within the field of animal feed analysis (van Raamsdonk *et al.* 2007). If bone is heated or burnt, this will result in morphological distortion, but analysis can be undertaken with difficulty using electron microscopy (Imaizumi *et al.* 2002; Cattaneo *et al.* 1999).

Due to the problems attendant upon these techniques there has been a long-standing interest in molecular based identification, which utilise DNA and protein in bone. These may be applied to bones that no longer have distinguishing features as a result of either post depositional effects or due to human modifications. In this (mini-) review we will discuss the latest of these dubbed Zooarchaeology by Mass Spectrometry (ZooMS) and consider this method in the wider context of alternative approaches.

Molecular based methods for identification

DNA

All cells contain DNA, some of which may remain trapped within bone in a manner that continues to elude researchers. Using this DNA, the species from which the bone originated can be identified (Bar-Gal *et al.* 2003; Haile *et al.* 2007; Newman *et al.* 2002; Loreille *et al.* 1997). The method is very powerful, in particular in the light of new methods for sequence analysis (Knapp and Hofreiter 2010), however when examining bones that may have have derived from common domesticates, there is a higher risk of contamination. It is thought that this contamination can occur during the synthesis of certain reagents used in the process such as dNTPs (Leonard *et al.* 2007). Leonard *et al.* observed that extraneous cow, goat, pig and chicken DNA had been routinely amplified under a range of PCR conditions in four separate labs (2007, 1363). She estimated that up to 50% of all amplified ancient DNA results could in fact be false positives as a result (2007, 1365).

Protein

The dominant components of worked bone are mineral and protein/water. In volume terms the two components are largely equivalent, but the proportion of protein/water falls over time, and collagen is estimated to be lost by between 2–7 Ma in temperate latitudes (Buckley and Collins 2011). Recently more than 100 proteins were found in a 40,000 year old permafrost mammoth bone (Cappellini *et al.* 2012), however of these proteins by far the most common is collagen. The survival of collagen while other proteins degrade allows for the selective enrichment of collagen, making it easier to extract, isolate and purify, and ultimately provide species-specific markers on the protein (Schmidt-Schultz and Schultz 2004).

Collagen, the most abundant proteins in animals (Shoulders and Raines 2009), is the major organic stress-bearing component of connective tissues such as cartilage, tendon and ligament;

also bones and teeth. It is the unique structure of collagen, and the abundance in which it is present in the living system which makes it valuable to bioarchaeologists.

Collagen is a fibrous protein made up of three polypeptide chains, of similar sizes. The way in which these polypeptides can be arranged creates multiple variations of the protein. Type I collagen is the main protein found in bone tissue and consists of two identical chains of alpha-1 and a chain of alpha-2 which wind together to form a right handed triple helical structure (Soulders and Raines 2009). These triple helices are organised into fibrils, which themselves are bundled into higher order fibres (*ibid.*). Bone collagen is further strengthened by the growth of minerals into the fibrils (Neudelman *et al.* 2010) resulting in compression of the triple helical bonds. This mineral 'strait-jacket' both protects the collagen from microbial attack (Nielsen-Marsh *et al.* 2000) and also physically stabilises the helix by restricting mobility (polymer-in-a-box) (Covington *et al.* 2008).

Post-mortem degradation of biomolecules

Post-mortem degradation of biomolecules (including collagen and DNA) in bone increase with time and can be a result of a number of different pathways such as biodegradation (Collins *et al.* 2002). DNA seems to decay through random chain scission which results in a predictable range of fragment lengths (Poinar *et al.* 2006; Deagle *et al.* 2006). The relative rates of the various types of DNA damage and the way in which they accumulate is still poorly characterised (Gilbert *et al.* 2003; Willerslev and Cooper 2005).

Collagen degradation is less well understood, but is believed to occur at a slower rate than DNA in temperate burial environments (Nielsen-Marsh 2002), with successful extractions being carried out from samples of greater than a million years in age (Buckley *et al.* 2011; Buckley and Collins 2011).

Collagen degradation had been modelled in the same way as DNA (Rudakova and Zaikov 1987; Riley and Collins 1994; Collins *et al.* 1995), Dobberstein *et al.* (2009) argue that this is in fact wrong. Their study of the diagenesis of collagen indicated a stable amino acid profile and C:N ratio where the yield was above 1% (Dobberstein *et al.* 2009). It is proposed that this may be a result of the polypeptide remaining intact, even in bones with low levels of collagen. Such results indicate that hydrolysis of collagen is not in fact random, but that the acid-insoluble bone collagen fraction is either present as intact alpha chains or absent (Dobberstein *et al.* 2009). These results indicate that collagen remains mostly intact in bones with even low yields, demonstrating that degradation is perhaps less of an issue when working with collagen, giving it value above DNA as there is a higher chance that collagen will persist in archaeological samples.

ZooMS

The concept behind ZooMS was to develop a method which offers cheap and fast discrimination of otherwise unidentifiable remains (Buckley *et al.* 2010). The method works with our knowledge of degradation; targeting collagen, which is effectively purified over the long term due to the selective retention of this protein in older bone samples (Buckley *et al.* 2008a, 1763; Collins *et al.* 2010, 6). Collagen itself degrades to release soluble peptides and these are isolated by either acid treatment or mild heating in a buffer designed to protect the mineral phase (Fig. 19.1). The extracted collagen is digested and analysed to produce a peptide fingerprint. It is this fingerprint which can then be used to infer species identification though the absence or presence of discriminating peptides (Buckley and Kansa 2011; Steen and Mann 2004). Figure 20.1 illustrates the steps involved in undertaking high throughput ZooMS screening of whole bone beads to identify the animal origin.

Methods of extraction

Two methods have been used to extract the collagen from bone samples. The original technique is more reliable, but is destructive, using hydrochloric acid to dissolve the mineral component of the bone to leave a collagen pellet (Buckley *et al.* 2009). The collagen pellet in the bottom of the tube is rinsed and then gelatinised at 65°C in 50 mM ammonium bicarbonate. In a modified version of the method, the acid

step is not used (van Doorn *et al.* 2011), instead, the sample is warmed twice in 50 mM, ammonium bicarbonate buffer (pH 8.0) at 65°C for one hour. The solution from the first extract is discarded as the first heating step removes contaminant proteins and other molecules such as lipids that may be in the bone, while the second step extracts soluble collagen that is not associated with bioapatite in the bone.

Subsequent analysis

Regardless of the choice of extraction method, the rest of the analytical process is the same. The solubilised collagen is fragmented using the digestive enzyme trypsin, which cleaves at lysine and arginine. Together these two residues make up approximately one in every 12 amino acids in collagen. As the average mass of a collagen amino acid is 90 Daltons (Da), the average mass collagen tryptic peptide 12 amino acids in length is 1,060 Da. However the lysine and arginine residues are not evenly distributed, and trypsin does not always cut at every residue. This results in a mix of tryptic peptides ranging from >3000 Da to <500 Da. Peptides less than <500 Da in size fall in to a region which contains lots of small artefact peaks and are therefore excluded from the analysis.

The absolute mass of each peptide in the mixture from a particular sample is analysed using Matrix-assisted laser desorption/ionization Time of Flight Mass Spectrometry (MALDI-TOF). This is a rapid analytical technique in which a UV laser is used to desorb the peptides, these peptides are

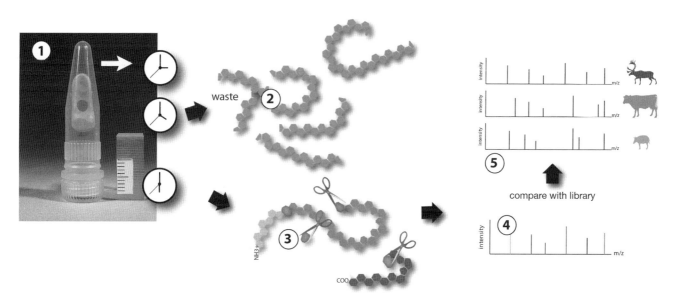

Figure 19.1 High throughput ZooMS screening of bone beads. (1) The sample is soaked overnight in buffer solution (50 mM ammonium bicarbonate, pH 8.0) at room temperature. This initial soak is then discarded. (2) Collagen is extracted though heating in buffer solution for one hour at 65°C. (3) The extract is then treated with trypsin, and the digests purified on a ZipTip. The resulting peptide mixtures are analysed by matrix assisted laser desorption ionization mass spectrometry (MALDI-MS), and the spectra compared with those of known species (photograph: Sonia O'Connor).

then accelerated and their mass measured by their time-of-flight; the smaller masses travelling faster, and therefore reaching the detector before heavier masses. The distribution of masses reflects the sequence of the collagen. Although the amino acid sequences which make up all Type I collagen are similar, there are variations between species. It is these variations which can be detected by measuring the mass of the tryptic peptides.

Identification

Comparison of an unknown sample with either spectra from known species or masses predicted from known collagen sequences are then used to match the observed profile of masses. The problem at present is that the ZooMS method can only identify species that have already been identified by the method. In this way it is analogous with problems noted in other zooarchaeological methods and is highly dependent on the extent of the available reference material, but unlike classical zooarchaeology there are as yet no substantive reference collections of sequences. However, this is being rapidly addressed by large scale genomic sequencing programs such as the 1000 Plants and Animals reference genome project which aims to generate reference genomes for 1000 economically and scientifically important plant/animal species in the next two years.

Example application: pig pins

One promising use of ZooMS is its use as a tool to identify or pick out samples that show a level of uncertainty in identification of their material origin (Fig. 19.1). This high throughput cost effective technique enables archaeologists to scan large amounts of material and pick out samples with atypical or damaged morphology, as well as samples such as human bones fragments which are too small or damaged to be recognised by eye.

During investigation of an early medieval site at Burdale near Wharram Percy in Yorkshire, a number of bone pins were identified, some of which were believed to come from pig fibulae, so called pig-pins. These have a long narrow triangular outline and a perforation at the thicker wider top end. The Burdale excavation explored socio-economic transitions and intensification of agriculture in the early medieval period, and therefore the origin of animal based materials excavated on the site is of importance.

These pins are termed 'pig fibula pins' due to their preliminary morphological identification. The use of this material to make these long thin pins is common and it was not surprising to find that four of the six samples were confirmed by ZooMS as being of pig origin, However out of the two remaining pins, one was identified as being of ruminant origin, the other was found to have masses which

were consistent with cattle/sheep/goat and deer. Although this identification can seem ambiguous and does not narrow down identification to a particular species, it does highlight that it is unlikely these two pins were made from pig material.

Cost

The cost of DNA sequencing has fallen rapidly over the past decade or so. In 1995 the cost per base pair was around US\$1, this fell to US\$0.1 in 1998 with improvements which were made to sample sequencing (Chan 2005, 16). Between 1998 and 2005, the price dropped 100 fold again to around US\$0.01, which Chan attributes to the 'public and private race to complete the human genome' (2005, 16). The price of sequencing is expected to fall further still as the use of next-generation- sequencing becomes more routine. Even so, the low cost of carrying out collagen-peptide identification is one of its major advantages, with the average analytical costs being less than €15 per sample (varies by batch size) (Collins *et al.* 2010). It is worth noting, however, that the use of next-generation sequencing, including barcoded and targeted sequencing, could help to minimise the effect of sample contamination in DNA studies (Knapp and Hofreiter 2010). If the possibility of amplification of contaminant DNA could be removed or minimised, this combined with the other advantages of DNA sequencing could mean that it may be favoured over the use of ZooMS as a simple, minimally destructive means of identifying worked bone, antler and ivory.

Limitations of ZooMS

In comparison to DNA, collagen analysis avoids many of the limitations associated with contamination. This is because the analysis is conducted directly from the bone (Buckley *et al.* 2009, 2010) and therefore avoids an amplification step, which is known to be a major source of contamination for traditional DNA studies. Collagen also has a highly characteristic motif that is usually sufficiently variable to enable meaningful comparison between distant taxa, if enough sequence is obtained (Buckley *et al.* 2008b). However the analysis is not immune to problems of contamination. Possible sources include the use of animal glue for conservation and the introduction of extraneous proteins to a sample (Buckley *et al.* 2008c). The way in which samples are collected and stored is likely to impact on the type of further analysis that can be carried out.

Another limitation of the ZooMS protocol is the availability of collagen within the bone. Poor preservation of the bone can lead to loss of protein. This loss of protein is particularly prevalent in acidic conditions which open up the structure and permit enzymolytic attack (Nielsen-Marsh *et al.* 2000) or in situations where the bone has been repeatedly flushed, for example in well drained sediments with a fluctuating water table.

A yet greater limitation of ZooMS is the slow rate of evolution of the target protein, collagen (Buckley *et al.* 2010; Collins *et al.* 2010). In the case of goats, this means that the genus *Capra* can be sorted from *Ovis* (sheep) but cannot distinguish between the remains of a domestic goat and a wild ibex (Buckley *et al.* 2010, 14). This is due to the slow evolution of collagen chains (Collins *et al.* 2010, 8); comparisons carried out by Buckley *et al.* (2010) across a range of caprine species (*Capra ibex, C. aegagrus, C. hircus*) revealed that the marker for goats (*m/z* 3093) was established in the ibex (*C. ibex*) before the emergence of the suggested ancestors of the domestic goat (*C. aegagrus* and *C. falconeri*). Whilst this does not pose a problem in areas outside of the geographic and temporal ranges of ibex and the initial domestication of goats, respectively, it could limit the use of ZooMS in regions where the geographic ranges of early domesticated goats and their wild counterparts overlapped, such as the south Levant (Smith 1998). Likewise ZooMS is not able to discriminate other closely related species such as red deer and elk. Furthermore if the spectra are poor and few peptides are observed, the discrimination can be limited. As the database grows the number of unique markers declines, for example the mass currently used to discriminate goat from sheep is also found in reindeer, a useful mass for pig *m/z* 1453 is also found in camel and vicuna. This may not be a problem if the question surrounds bone fragments in which these alternative species do not overlap, but as animals migrate or domestic animals are moved, the problem over species overlap will increase.

DNA analysis has a marked advantage over ZooMS in that many species have been sequenced notably for specific regions of the mitochondrial genome. For example the Consortium for the Barcode of Life (http://www.barcodeoflife.org/) aims to have DNA barcoded some 500,000 species by 2015. As a result, DNA based methods for identification are applicable to a much wider range of species than ZooMS and will always achieve higher resolution (in the future, to populations and even individuals). A further limitation of ZooMS, is that although the cost per sample is relatively low, the method requires access to a mass-spectrometer, limiting the number of laboratories in which the analysis can be carried out.

Finally, although the new alternative method for ZooMS is termed non-destructive (van Doorn *et al.* 2011), one must take into account the effects of soaking and heating the samples, which were previously dry. For example, during ZooMS analysis of bone beads, cracking was observed on several of the beads which may have been due to the rehydration of the collagen chains, and expansion of the beads as they were soaked in the ammonium bicarbonate solution. A further problem is that if the samples are not fully dried fungal growth can occur. A study by Von Holstein *et al.* (2014) analysing collagen extracted from bone combs found that the ZooMS method did not cause any observed modifications to the samples.

Conclusion

Working often destroys or masks morphological and microscopic features used to identify species. The relatively low cost of ZooMS and minimally destructive extraction protocol opens species identification to a wider range of samples than was previously viable. Fragments of bone that would be impossible to identify by the usual zooarchaeological methods and are not important enough to justify the expense of DNA sequencing can be analysed using ZooMS (Collins *et al.* 2010). Since ZooMS is still in its relative infancy the main drawback of the protocol is the size of the database, to which the spectra can be compared, which limits the number of species that can be successfully identified. A further area of research will be to establish the extent to which soaking bones and heating at 65°C may modify worked bone, and whether the process is more or less damaging in well preserved or heavily degraded material. A key future development will be the ability to sample material directly in the museum, shipping the extracts (not the samples) to the laboratory.

Acknowledgements

All authors contributed equally to the review. We would like to thank Martin Slater, Stacie Sachs and Stephen Butler for their assistance in testing the limits of the application of ZooMS. We are grateful to Nienke Van Doorn and Marc Wadsley for their continuing work in developing the ZooMS technique. A special thanks is for Sonia O'Connor, for providing the photograph used in Figure 1. We would also like to acknowledge Simone Haeberle, Steven Ashby and Pál Raczky for providing materials for analysis.

Bibliography

Ashby, S. P. (2009) Combs, contact and chronology: reconsidering hair combs in early-historic and Viking-Age Atlantic Scotland. *Medieval Archaeology* 53, 1–33.

Bar-Gal, G. K., Ducos, P. and Horwitz, L. K. (2003) The application of ancient DNA analysis to identify Neolithic caprinae: a case study from the site of Hatoula, Israel. *International Journal of Osteoarchaeology* 13 (3), 120–131.

Buckley, M. and Collins, M. (2011) Collagen survival and its use for species identification in Holocene-lower Pleistocene bone fragments from British archaeological and paleontological sites. *Antiqua* 1 (1), 10.4081/antiqua.2011.e1

Buckley, M. and Kansa, S. W. (2011) Collagen fingerprinting of archaeological bone and teeth remains from Domuztepe, South Eastern Turkey. *Archaeological and Anthropological Sciences* 3 (3), 271-280.

Buckley, M., Anderung C., Penkman, K., Raney, B. J., Götherström, A., Thomas-Oates, J. and Collins, M. J. (2008a) Comparing the survival of osteocalcin and mtDNA in archaeological bone from four European sites. *Journal of Archaeological Science* 35 (6), 1756–1764.

Buckley, M., Collins, M. and Thomas-Oates, J. (2008b) A method of isolating the collagen (I) alpha 2 chain carboxytelopeptide for species identification in bone fragments. *Analytical Biochemistry* 374 (2), 325–334.

Buckley, M., Walker, A., Ho, S. Y., Yang, Y., Smith, C., Ashton, P., Thomas-Oates, J., Cappellini, E., Koon, H., Penkman, K., Elsworth, B., Ashford, D., Solazzo, C., Andrews, P., Strahler, J., Shapiro, B., Ostrom, P., Gandhi, H., Miller, W., Raney, B., Zylber, M. I., Gilbert, M. T., Prigodich, R. V., Ryan, M., Rijsdijk, K. F., Janoo, A. and Collins, M. J. (2008c) Comment on "protein sequences from mastodon and *Tyrannosaurus rex* revealed by mass spectrometry". *Science* 319 (5859), 33.

Buckley, M., Collins, M., Thomas-Oates, J. and Wilson, J. C. (2009) Species identification by analysis of bone collagen using matrix-assisted laser desorption/ionisation time-of-flight mass spectrometry. *Rapid Communications in Mass Spectrometry* 23 (23), 3843–3854.

Buckley, M., Kansa, S. W., Howard, S., Campbell, S., Thomas-Oates, J. and Collins, M. (2010) Distinguishing between archaeological sheep and goat bones using a single collagen peptide. *Journal of Archaeological Science* 37 (1), 13–20.

Buckley, M., Larkin, N. and Collins, M. (2011) Mammoth and mastodon collagen sequences; survival and utility, *Geochimica et Cosmochimica Acta* 75 (7), 2007–2016.

Cappellini, E., Jensen, L. J., Szklarczyk, D., Ginolhac, A., Da Fonseca, R. A. R., Stafford, T. W., Holen, S. R., Collins, M. J., Orlando, L., Willerslev, E., Gilbert, M. T. P. and Olsen, J. V. (2012) Proteomic analysis of a Pleistocene mammoth femur reveals more than one hundred ancient bone proteins. *Journal of Proteome Research* 11, 917–926.

Cattaneo, C., Dimartino, S., Scali, S., Craig, O. E., Grandi, M. and Sokol, R. J. (1999) Determining the human origin of fragments of burnt bone: a comparative study of histological, immunological and DNA techniques. *Forensic Science International* 102 (2–3), 181–191.

Chan, E. Y. (2005) Advances in sequencing technology. *Mutation Research* 573, 13-40.

Collins, M. J., Riley, M. S., Child, A. M. and Turner-Walker, G. (1995) A basic mathematical simulation of the chemical degradation of ancient collagen. *Journal of Archaeological Science* 22 (2), 175–183.

Collins, M. J., Nielsen-Marsh, C. M., Hiller, J., Smith, C. I., Roberts, J. P., Prigodich, R. V., Wess, T. J., Csapò, J., Millard, A. R. and Turner-Walker, G. (2002) The survival of organic matter in bone: a review, *Archaeometry* 44 (3), 383–394.

Collins, M., Buckley, M., Grundy, H. H., Thomas-Oates, J., Wilson, J. and Van Doorn, N. (2010) ZooMS: the collagen barcode and fingerprints. *Spectroscopy Europe* 22 (2), 11–13.

Cooper, A. and Poinar, H. N. (2000) Ancient DNA: do it right or not at all. *Science* 289 (5482), 1139.

Covington, A. D., Song, L., Suparno, O., Koon, H. E. C. and Collins, M. J. (2008) Link-lock: an explanation of the chemical stabilisation of collagen. *Journal of the Society of Leather Technologists and Chemists* 92 (1), 1–7.

Deagle, B., Eveson, J. P. and Jarman, S. (2006) Quantification of damage in DNA recovered from highly degraded samples: a case study on DNA in faeces. *Frontiers Zoology* 3, 11.

Dobberstein, R. C., Collins, M. J., Craig, O. E., Taylor, G., Penkman, K. E. H. and Ritz-Timme, S. (2009) Archaeological collagen: why worry about collagen diagenesis? *Archaeological and Anthropological Science* 1, 31–42.

Gilbert, M. T. P., Willerslev, E., Hansen, A. J., Barnes, I., Rudbeck, L., Lynnerup, N. and Cooper, A. (2003) Distribution patterns of postmortem damage in human mitochondrial DNA. *American Journal of Human Genetics* 72 (1), 32–47.

Greenlee, D. M. and Dunnell, R. C. (2010) Identification of fragmentary bone from the Pacific. *Journal of Archaeological Science* 37 (5), 957–970.

Haile, J., Holdaway, R., Oliver, K., Bunce, M., Gilbert, M. T. P., Nielsen, R., Munch, K., Ho, S. Y. W., Shapiro, B. and Willerslev, E. (2007) Ancient DNA chronology within sediment deposits: are paleobiological reconstructions possible and is DNA leaching a factor? *Molecular Biology and Evolution* 24 (4), 982–989.

Hillier, M. L. and Bell, L. S. (2007) Differentiating human bone from animal bone: A review of histological methods. *Journal of Forensic Sciences* 52 (2), 249–263.

Imaizumi, K., Saitoh, K., Sekiguchi, K. and Yoshino, M. (2002) Identification of fragmented bones based on anthropological and DNA analyses: case report. *Legal medicine (Tokyo, Japan)* 4 (4), 251–256.

Knapp, M. and Hofreiter, M. (2010) Next Generation Sequencing of Ancient DNA: requirements, strategies and perspectives. *Genes* 1, 227–243.

Leonard, J. A., Shanks, O., Hofreiter, M., Kruez, E., Hodges, L., Ream, W., Wayne, R. K. and Fleischer, R. C. (2007) Animal DNA in PCR reagents plagues ancient DNA research. *Journal of Archaeological Science* 34 (9), 1361–1366.

Loreille, O., Vigne, J. D., Hardy, C., Callou, C., Treinenclaustre, F., Dennebouy, N. and Monnerot, M. (1997) First distinction of sheep and goat archaeological bones by the means of their fossil mtDNA. *Journal of Archaeological Science* 24 (1), 33–37.

Martiniakova, M., Grosskopf, B., Omelka, R., Dammers, K., Vondrakova, M. and Bauerova, M. (2007) Histological study of compact bone tissue in some mammals: a method for species determination. *International Journal of Osteoarchaeology* 17 (1), 82–90.

Newman, M. E., Parboosingh, J. S., Bridge, P. J. and Ceri, H. (2002) Identification of archaeological animal bone by PCR/DNA analysis. *Journal of Archaeological Science* 29 (1), 77–84.

Nielsen-Marsh, C. (2002) Biomolecules in fossil remains. *The Biochemist* 24 (3) (June), 12–14.

Nielsen-Marsh, C. M., Hedges, R. E. M., Mann, T. and Collins, M. J. (2000) A preliminary investigation of the application of differential scanning calorimetry to the study of collagen degradation in archaeological bone, *Thermochimica Acta* 365 (1–2), 129–139.

Nudelman, F., Pieterse, K., George, A., Bomans, P. H. H., Friedrich, H., Brylka, L. J., Hilbers, P. A. J., With, G. De, and Sommerdijk, N. A. J. M. (2010) The role of collagen in bone apatite formation in the presence of hydroxyapatite nucleation inhibitors. *Nature Materials* 9, 1004–1008.

O'Connor, T. P. (2000) *The Archaeology of Animal Bones*, 36–40. Austin (Texas), TAMU Press.

Poinar, H. N., Schwarz, C., Qi, J., Shapiro, B., Macphee, R. D. E., Buiges, B., Tikhonov, A., Huson, D. H., Tomsho, L. P., Auch, A., Rampp, M., Miller, W. and Shuster, S. C. (2006) Metagenomics to palaenogeomics: large-scale sequencing of mammoth DNA. *Science* 311 (5759), 392–394.

Riley, M. S. and Collins, M. J. (1994) The polymer model of collagen degradation. *Polymer Degradation and Stability* 46 (1), 93–97.

Rudakova, T. E. and Zaikov, G. E. (1987) Degradation of collagen and its possible applications in medicine, *Polymer Degradation and Stability* 18 (4), 271–291.

Schmidt-Schultz, T. H. and Schultz, M. (2004) Bone protects proteins over thousands of years: extraction, analysis, and interpretation of extracellular matrix proteins in archeological skeletal remains. *American Journal of Physical Anthropology* 123 (1), 30–39.

Shoulders, M. and Raines, R. T. (2009) Collagen structure and stability. *Annual Review of Biochemistry* 78, 929–958.

Smith, B. D. (1998) *The Emergence of Agriculture.* New York, Scientific American Library.

Steen, H. and Mann, M. (2004) The ABC's (and XYZ's) of peptide sequencing. *Nature Reviews Molecular Cell Biology* 5, 699–711.

Van Doorn, N. L., Hollund, H. and Collins, M. J. (2011) A novel and non-destructive approach for ZooMS analysis: ammonium bicarbonate buffer extraction. *Archaeological and Anthropological Sciences* 3 (3), 281-289.

Van Raamsdonk, L. W. D., von Holst, C., Baeten,V., Berben,G., Boix, A. and de Jong, J. (2007) New developments in the detection and identification of processed animal proteins in feeds. *Animal Feed Science and Technology* 133 (1–2), 63–83.

Von Holstein, I. C. C., Ashby, S. P., van Doorn, N. L., Sachs, S. M., Buckley, M., Meiri, M., Barnes, I., Brundle, A. and Collins, M. J. (2014) Searching for Scandinavians in pre-Viking Scotland: molecular finger printing of Early Medieval combs. *Journal of Archaeological Sciences* 41, 1–6. http://dx.doi.org/10.1016/j.jas.2013.07.026

Willerslev, E. and Cooper, A. (2005) Ancient DNA. *Proceedings of the Royal Society B: Biological Sciences* 272 (1558), 3–16.

CHAPTER 20

Some Comments on the Identification of Cervid Species in Worked Antler

Steven P. Ashby

"…Variation in antler construction combines in the least reliable manner all the effects of sexual, developmental and individual variation that can be imagined" (Webb 2000: 62)

Research into objects of worked antler is characterised by a certain inconsistency of approach to raw material identification, particularly regarding identification to species level. Some workers routinely record species, while others do not, and it is apparent that a number of diagnostic criteria have been used, albeit often implicitly. This paper makes no claim to resolve this situation, but in outlining some of the potentials and many confounds of various microscopic and macroscopic techniques, the author hopes to inspire cautious enquiry into raw material exploitation, and to encourage further research into the introduced phenomena. Recently developed biomolecular approaches have the potential to transform the way we think about this material, but at present we are still reliant on sampling techniques that may not always be appropriate for application to the material in question. They may, however, provide an excellent complement to zooarchaeological approaches.

Keywords
Antler; artefacts; species; deer; combs; worked bone; raw material identification; microscopy; macrostructure.

Introduction

This article emerges from exploratory work undertaken in the course of the author's doctoral research at the University of York. It began in an attempt to address a long-standing question in Scottish archaeology: that of pre-Viking Age contact between northern Scotland and Scandinavia (see Barrett 2003; Myhre 1993). A key piece of evidence relates to the identification of certain combs of 'pre-Viking' form as being made from reindeer antler (*Rangifer tarandus*): a species alien to the British Isles since early prehistory (Clutton-Brock and MacGregor 1988). This issue has been investigated at length elsewhere (Weber 1992, 1993, 1994; Ballin Smith 1995; Ashby 2006, 2009), but given that the means by which antler may be identified to species are not well known, the present paper provides an opportunity to introduce the issue of identification in a little further detail.

Initial work in this field (Weber 1992, 1993, 1994; Ballin Smith 1995) stated that it was possible to confidently identify the antler in combs to species level (i.e. *Cervus elaphus* vs *Rangifer tarandus*). This research was dependent on the identifications of an experienced zooarchaeologist, Rolf Lie, curator of the zoological museum at the University of Bergen. Unfortunately, detailed accounts of Dr Lie's identification criteria have not been published, and this has led to some scepticism amongst archaeologists of Atlantic Scotland (see Graham-Campbell and Batey 1998, 23; Smith 2000, 185). The key information we have is as follows:

> "… the combs show very clearly the spongy structure characteristic of reindeer antler. In this spongy part the pores are larger; elsewhere the bones are very solid with nearly invisible pores. The antler of red deer has at its base a spongy part similar to that of the bones; elsewhere it looks very solid and heavier than reindeer antler. Elk antler has for the most no spongy parts; it is very hard and has a glassy look." (Lie 1993)

This is a useful start, but clearly further empirical work is needed. Independent of the work published by Weber, a number of specialists have published short statements on identification methods (see Ambrosiani 1981, 102–109; Carlé *et al.* 1976; Ilkjaer 1993, 316–319; Stephan 1994). Most notably, Dr Lyuba Smirnova (2005, 9–15), a Russian archaeologist studying worked bone and antler from medieval Novgorod, recently devised a macroscopic system for the recognition of red deer (*Cervus elaphus*), reindeer (*Rangifer tarandus*), and European elk (*Alces alces*) antler. This proved effective in the recognition both of waste products and of finished combs (Smirnova 2002). However, while Ambrosiani, Smirnova *et al.* outlined their identification criteria in some detail, these methods have yet to be subjected to independent investigation. One objective of the present author's doctoral research was to critically consider these approaches and to build upon the insights they provided, in order to develop a new, systematic protocol for the identification of worked antler to species, and to offer some suggestions for further work. This paper provides some reflections on these issues.

The experience with antler fragments and manufacturing waste that Smirnova gathered in the course of her original Ph.D research (Smirnova 1997) helped lay the groundwork for the identification of antler to species in simple and composite combs; a task she undertook as part of a second thesis (Smirnova 2002, subsequently published as Smirnova 2005). Smirnova was kind enough to demonstrate her approach, some elements of which have been adapted and incorporated into the methods discussed below (embellished with observations from the author's personal collection and the reference material at the British Museum (Natural History)). It should be noted that the following material does not contain the findings of controlled investigations or quantitative analyses. Rather, it provides a number of observations which may prove useful as rules-of-thumb, or as starting points (null hypotheses?) for finer-grained zoological analyses.

Gross and surface morphology

It is now appropriate to briefly highlight the basic differences in gross antler morphology between the three cervid species at the centre of this paper. Such information is invaluable in the

study of craft debitage, semi-manufactures, and other waste material, as well as a prerequisite for the study of finished objects. In what follows, the key morphological characteristics of red deer (*C. elaphus*), reindeer (*R. tarandus*) and elk (*A. alces*) antler are outlined (Fig. 20.1).

The antlers of the red deer (*C. elaphus*) are highly variable, but can be defined briefly by the presence of a few characteristics, most notably a marked branching and lack of palmation. However, in rare cases, *C. elaphus* may also develop palmation in the crown. In the British Isles this trait is generally, though not exclusively, related to interbreeding with Sika (*Cervus nippon*), a cervid that was recently introduced to Britain (for a detailed discussion see Lowe and Gardiner 1975).

Continental red deer antlers may reach 120 cm in length, and have up to 20 points, but in Scotland 90 cm and 14 points would be considered good development (Krzyskowska 1990, 60). The beam has a much greater radius than that of reindeer (*R. tarandus*), but fragments could be confused with elk (*A. alces*) where evidence of tines or palmation is not preserved. However, the pedicle, consisting entirely of compact bone, is much longer in red deer than in elk, and the shape of the bony coronet is oval, whereas in elk it is roughly circular (Smirnova pers. comm.), with a 'beaded' surface texture.

The surface of red deer antler is usually very rough, and marked by deep channels, though there is some variability between (and even within) the antlers of *Cervus* individuals. For instance, upper tines are often smoother than the main beam, perhaps due to brushing (rubbing against vegetation in order to accelerate the shedding of velvet) (Krzyskowska 1990, 60). Nonetheless, where present, the rough outer surface is diagnostic (see Fig. 20.2). Unfortunately, it is usually removed prior to the manufacture of objects (see MacGregor 1985, 58), but may occasionally be preserved even in worked artefacts.

The antlers of *A. alces* lack a brow tine, and tend to have a large round burr (see Fig. 20.1). Most notably, they are large and heavily palmated, reaching up to 2m in span (Huffman 2003). Though less palmated examples are known (see Saether and Haagenrud 1985, 985), they are nonetheless distinctive

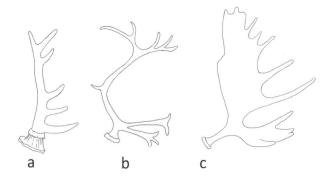

a   b   c

Figure 20.1 Gross morphology of (a) Cervus elaphus, *(b)* Rangifer tarandus, *male, (c)* Alces alces *(drawings: Hayley Saul).*

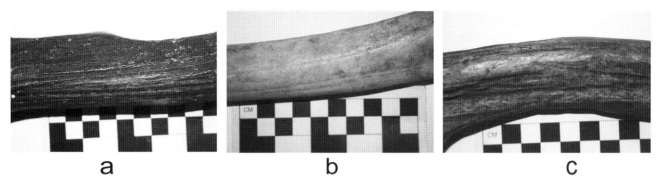

Figure 20.2 Surface texture of (a) Cervus elaphus, *(b)* Rangifer tarandus, *(c)* Alces alces *(photographs: S. Ashby).*

in form, size, and weight. The surface of elk antler features broad guttering, but this can be differentiated from red deer antler, principally by means of scale (Fig. 20.2).

Reindeer (*R. tarandus*) antlers are quite distinctive (Fig. 20.1). They are markedly asymmetrical, relatively thin in cross-section, and have a characteristic rough, outer surface (which is grey in fresh material). The males also bear distinctive 'snow shovels' for brow tines. Also of note is the fact that *R. tarandus* pedicles may be less than 5mm long (Lie *et al.* 2003, 335). The antlers of male and female reindeer are easily distinguished, bull antler being much more elaborate and massive than cow antler. Nonetheless, there is variation within sexes, and it is possible that a rack from a young male may be confused with that of a mature female. More importantly, however, the antlers of reindeer as a whole are sufficiently distinctive so that they are very unlikely to be mistaken for those of another species. The natural outer surface of reindeer antler is somewhat less rough than that of red deer or elk. It lacks the distinctive channelling, although isolated grooves are occasionally present (Fig. 20.2).

Macrostructure and small-scale variation

In objects, the task of isolating consistently preserved distinctive features is obviously more difficult. Occasionally, it is impossible to categorically differentiate elk and red deer, but Smirnova claims that in her experience it is always possible to identify reindeer antler, providing that a variety of criteria are investigated in combination (see Smirnova 2002, 19). Polish, texture, dimensions and compact structure can be valuable clues, but none of these properties are sufficiently diagnostic to be used as anything more than supporting criteria.

Identification of the raw materials used in highly worked objects such as dress pins and composite combs can prove challenging, as in many cases all traces of porous material and surface texture have been systematically removed as part of the manufacturing process. However, in the less closely-worked areas of artefacts, one may occasionally discern small zones

Figure 20.3 Macrostructural preservation in archaeological material: a) core and core-compacta margin revealed in longitudinal section, on reverse of an early-medieval comb connecting plate from Burdale, Yorkshire: probably C. elaphus; *b) core preserved in transverse section on back edge of an early-medieval comb toothplate from Birka, Sweden, indeterminate species (photographs: S. Ashby, courtesy Julian D. Richards (a) and Statens Historiska Museet (b)).*

of visible macrostructure, and these often prove valuable in material characterisation and identification. On single-sided composite combs, for example, inspection of the back surface (the surface running along the upper edge of the comb at approximately 90° to the front face of the connecting plate) is frequently instructive. This area may render visible the rough interior surfaces of the toothplates clamped between connecting plates. Breakages also facilitate identification, as they often reveal the cross-sections of connecting plates in which distinctive features of internal macrostructure may be visible (Fig. 20.3). In particular, one may observe the distinctive characteristics of (1) outer areas of compact antler; (2) porous core, composed of cancellous tissue; and (3) the margin between these two zones.

Compact antler

Both Ambrosiani (1981, 103) and Smirnova (2005, 11) have suggested that the compact material that makes up the outer portion of an antler contains certain diagnostic features. Smirnova has suggested that there are species-diagnostic differences in the degree of 'organisation' of blood vessels in the compacta which has implications for the roughness of the texture. Similarly, Ambrosiani points out that elk antler preserves the 'black thread' traces of blood vessels in its compacta, which is itself less 'regular' than that seen in red deer antler. However, this author found it difficult to characterise either modern or archaeological material in this way, and no diagnostic characteristics could be identified under low magnification (up to 10×). To a certain degree the compact structure of red deer antler does seem more regular and organised than that of reindeer, but this is not easily quantified, and the degree of overlap is so marked that any attempt to delineate a fixed watershed between the two species would be something of an arbitrary contrivance. Moreover, the compact structure of elk was very difficult to observe (even at a magnification of 10×, with a movable light source). All in all, I found that the structure of compact tissue in modern antler could not be readily used as a means of species differentiation. It is possible that diagenetic staining would render identification more straightforward, and future investigations involving quantitative image analysis might facilitate more precise characterisation of the antler compacta of different species, but at the present time, there appears no justification for the application of this methodology in isolation.

Porous core and 'transition zone'

A number of researchers (e.g. Ambrosiani 1981; Smirnova 2005) have noted distinctive features of the porous core and its margin with outer compact antler in red deer, reindeer, and elk. Notwithstanding the fact that these phenomena are not easily quantified, they offer potential as diagnostic criteria that could be recorded on a qualitative basis, providing that the protocols of recording were sufficiently rigorous, and undertaken with the use of a reference collection. They thus merit further investigation herein.

To summarise, the porous core of elk antler is very distinctive, containing fine, elongated pores that are often only clearly visible with the aid of a microscope. In material previously seen by the author, palmated areas evidenced a distinctive spongy core, in which the porosity was clearly visible, but nonetheless markedly finer than that typical for red deer (Fig. 20.4a). No attempt at quantification was made; this is perhaps an area that would merit further investigation. In the material examined in the present study (which was relatively small in size, and not well-palmated), the core was very finely porous throughout, such that individual pores were not easily identifiable with the naked eye (Fig. 20.4b). Indeed, in the distal areas such as the tines of *A. alces* antler, the core areas themselves were invisible without magnification. This is no doubt the phenomenon to which Penniman (1952, 37) refers when he notes that "elk seems to be closer-grained than reindeer".

Red deer and reindeer antler are relatively easily distinguished from elk, as the pores are much rounder in *Cervus* and *Rangifer* than in *Alces*. Reindeer antler core is typically very fine, but the primary difference between *Cervus* and *Rangifer* lies in the gradation to compacta. In reindeer this is extremely gentle and diffuse with a semi-porous zone (no doubt Lie's 'spongy structure'), while the boundary is much more discrete in red deer (Smirnova 2002) (Fig. 20.5).

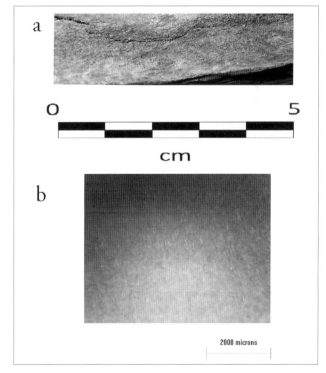

Figure 20.4 Core structure in Alces alces: *a) open, spongy structure visible in palmated areas; early medieval material from Birka, Sweden; b) finer structure in relatively unpalmated modern material (photographs: S. Ashby, (a) courtesy Statens Historiska Museet).*

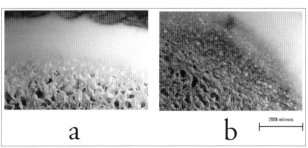

Figure 20.5 Core-compacta transition in a) Cervus elaphus, *b)* Rangifer tarandus. *Modern material (photographs: S. Ashby).*

These criteria have been shown to be useful in the study of antler waste and artefacts (Smirnova 1997, 2002); they were, after all, developed in order to be of use in the analysis of archaeological material. One might hope that the application of such criteria to other corpora should prove possible; given that the techniques appear to have been effective as aids in the study of highly worked objects such as composite combs, one may suppose that they might be easily applied to a wide range of other objects (such as handles, pegs, vessels, toggles, buckleplates and strap-ends), if not to very highly-worked pieces such as decorative pins. Nonetheless, Smirnova's criteria are grounded in personal experience rather than empirical testing. More importantly, given that these techniques were developed through the study of, and in preparation for, the recording of material from Novgorod, it may be that the particular preservation quality of the material from this corpus lends itself to fine-grained analysis. Thus, we should consider whether Smirnova's criteria (or her application of confidence qualifiers) may require modification in order to account for differences in preservation at other sites. In particular, it is important to consider the possibility of distinctive macrostructures being generated (or influenced) by factors other than species. In the following, I review existing literature on the relationship between antler growth and a number of variables: individual maturity; sex, environment, and phase of antlerogenesis. I then offer some preliminary thoughts on the potential of these (and other) variables to confound attempts to identify species on macrostructural grounds.

Existing work on the process of antler growth

The key factors likely to affect antler growth and development are discussed below. These factors are inter-related, rather than being truly independent variables. For example, the relationship between environment and nutrition must be a close (but complex) one, and it may also be that different sexes respond to malnutrition in different ways (see for instance Clutton-Brock 1989, 2; Horwitz and Smith 1990).

Individual confounds

Many physical attributes of deer vary considerably between individual animals (Mitchell *et al.* 1977, 41). For example, the age of the animal from which antler was taken may have an influence. Age is related to overall morphology, as antler size and complexity increase until a peak is reached (at around 9–11 years in *C. elaphus*), before the beginning of a slow decline known as 'going back' (see Mitchell *et al.* 1977, 39, table 8). Clearly then, we must consider the possibility that age also affects internal structure.

Related to this is the developmental stage of the antler itself. As antler grows afresh each year, its gross morphology goes

through a period of change (see MacEwen 1920; Chapman 1975, 135–141). Thus, antler taken from deer via hunting may vary in its properties depending upon the point in the antler cycle at which the animal was slaughtered. In practice, it could be argued that this is unlikely to present a major problem, as in Western Europe at least, most archaeological deposits of manufacturing waste consist very largely of shed antler, and therefore represent a roughly uniform state of annual development. However, given the ambiguity as to the proportion of original waste build up that these deposits represent, it is worth considering this variable more closely. It is also notable that waste deposits from medieval Novgorod, Russia, are dominated by antler from butchered animals (Smirnova 1997, 139), and one might expect a similar phenomenon to prevail in medieval Norway, where reindeer hunting is evidenced both historically and archaeologically (chiefly in the form of extensive trapping systems and associated activity sites) (see Indrelid and Huftammer 2011; Jordhøy 2008).

In most species of deer, only males normally bear antlers. However, in reindeer these structures are present in both males (bulls), and females (cows). The reason for this is unclear (although see Li *et al.* 2003), but it nonetheless represents another component of morphological – and possibly structural – variation that must be accounted for. Hormonal cycles affect bone growth in many taxa (e.g. Horwitz and Smith 1990), and hormones clearly have an important role in antlerogenesis (Harrison Matthews 1971, 376–377; Chapman 1975; Goss 1995). Thus, in female reindeer it is possible that pregnancy and lactation may have an effect on antler formation, though a search of the zoological literature uncovered few studies of such phenomena. Penniman (1952, 35–36) does consider such influences to be important in the formation of antler, but his evidence is rather anecdotal. Nonetheless, it is a variable that must be borne in mind when considering any differences between the antlers of individual female reindeer.

Hormones are of course also important agents in the development of male deer, and as castration is known to have an impact on the overall growth of antlers, it may also affect internal structure and histology (see for instance MacEwen 1920, 32, 104–105; Bubenik 1990, 281–283; Goss 1995; Kierdorf *et al.* 1995, 38–39). This should therefore be taken into consideration, but again Penniman (1952, 35–36) appears to be one of only a few scholars to have considered the importance of such phenomena to the antiquarian or archaeologist. Nonetheless, although there are anthropological accounts of castration being employed by present day reindeer pastoralists (see Took 2004, 7–8), I know of no record of early medieval deer castration, and any such level of park management seems unlikely to have developed in Europe prior to the second millennium AD at the earliest. Indeed, archaeological analyses of prehistoric and medieval reindeer exploitation have stressed the importance of wild animals as opposed to domestic stock (e.g. Hambleton and Rowley-Conwy 1997; papers in Jackson and Thacker 1997), and although there are ethnohistoric allusions to the herding of 'tame' reindeer (Ross 1940, 20–21), I have yet to find explicit historical references to castration, while Odner (1985, 5) claims that the 'subsistence pattern of reindeer-herding belongs to the Post-Reformation Period'(see Storli 1993, and associated comments).

Disease and trauma can also affect antler morphology. Apart from direct damage to the antlers and pedicles themselves (MacEwen 1920, 23–26), abnormality occasionally seems to be related to genital damage or under-development. The swept-back morphology of cromie antlers (*ibid.*, 27–31), and the soft, unmineralised overgrowths that characterise perruque heads (Page 1971, 39; Luxmoore 1980, 59–60) may form in this way. Furthermore, parasites such as liver fluke may affect antlerogenesis. Corkscrew antlers are often thought to be related to such endoparasitic infestation (Luxmoore 1980, 60), though some studies have refuted this, and it has been suggested that they are the result of a 'hereditary disturbance in calcium metabolism' (see Chapman 1975, 151). All in all, it seems that the subject is not well understood, and while some pathological malformation may be identifiable, less clear cut cases might be relatively common and not recognised as abnormal (cf. King and Ulijaszek 1999, 175–176; Eveleth and Tanner 1990, 191–192).

Population-level confounds

There is also a great deal of variation at the inter-population level. Comparative studies of populations across the globe have demonstrated that there is much variation in antler size and gross morphology within *Cervus elaphus*; notably there is a north-west to south-east increase in both body and antler size across Europe. While some of this variation may be genotypic, it seems likely that at least some component of antler development is environmentally linked (Mitchell *et al.* 1977, 2–3; Luxmoore 1980, 61; Clutton-Brock 1989, 13, 71). Indeed, environment has been demonstrated to have an effect on the growth and development of antler (Asleson *et al.* 1997; Schmidt *et al.* 2001), and it is notable that many of the relatively small red deer of Britain live in areas of atypical habitat. In Scotland they tend to occupy exposed, highland areas with poor soils, and young animals removed and reared away from this environment have been seen to reach greater sizes (Mitchell *et al.* 1977, 5, 9; Clutton-Brock 1989, 2). Moreover, Scottish red deer populations from woodland and park habitats have been reported to grow larger antlers than those that occupy the hills (Whitehead 1964; Mitchell *et al.* 1977, 41; Clutton-Brock 1989, 59).

It may be that nutrition has a very marked impact on antler formation (see, for example, Azorit *et al.* 2002; Kruuk *et al.* 2002), particularly as antlers have a low growth priority relative to other elements of a deer's body (Clutton-Brock 1989, 62;

see also Chapman 1975, 141–145). However, the relationship between nutrition and antlerogenesis is not well understood. Asleson *et al.* (1997) found that protein restriction had no consistent effect on the number of points, degree of spread, main beam length or circumference in their sample population of white-tailed deer (*Odocoileus virginianus*). However, it is likely that other nutritional components, such as calcium and phosphorous, are important in antler growth (Chapman 1975, 141; Mitchell *et al.* 1977, 9; see also Goss 1995; Asleson *et al.* 1996; Kierdorf *et al.* 2000).

It has been suggested that red deer stags with extremely well-developed antlers and supernumary points may owe such morphology to a high plane of nutrition (see for example Chapman 1975, 152; Whitehead 1964, 62). Controlled experimental work has shown that an increase in nutritional plane at a formative period may lead to accelerated and amplified antler growth (Arman 1971, cited in Mitchell *et al.* 1977, 44; Clutton-Brock 1989, 59, 62). Contrary to popular sporting belief (see, for example, Luxmoore 1980, 60), it has also been postulated that the reason for the hummel's lack of antlers is not genetic, but relates to poor nutrition in the early stages of life, and a consequent failure to grow pedicles (Clutton-Brock 1989, 62; Lincoln and Fletcher 1984). Chapman (1975, 132) has also noted that harsh environmental conditions may lead to delayed pedicle formation.

Nutrition is thus clearly important, but reaching a consensus is difficult, as much of the evidence is anecdotal, while laboratory experiments do not always adequately account for the effects of weather and outside activity (Mitchell *et al.* 1977, 10). This is a problem, as while climate clearly affects the availability and quality of food in an area (see Clutton-Brock 1989, 79–83, 135–136), it may also have a more direct effect on deer development. Temperature and weather conditions impact metabolism, as well as activity and shelter-seeking behaviour, which in turn have implications for energy consumption and heat stress (Mitchell *et al.* 1977, 16–17; see also Clutton-Brock 1989, 59, 89–91). Population density and competition for resources may also conceivably be important (Mitchell *et al.* 1977, 19, 45; Schmidt *et al.* 2001; Clutton-Brock *et al.* 1984; but see Clutton-Brock 1989, 113; Azorit *et al.* 2002). The effect of such phenomena on an animal's condition and performance, and in particular how stress might impact antler growth, are relatively poorly understood.

Exposure to sunlight may be an important factor, as photoperiod is known to be an important consideration in the hormonal and behavioural cycles of deer (Goss 1969; Chapman 1975, 148; Mitchell *et al.* 1977, 3). Indeed, this factor is bound up with that of nutrition, as the deer's food intake seems to fluctuate seasonally (Mitchell *et al.* 1977, 9; Luxmoore 1980, 20–26; see also Muir and Sykes 1988). Indeed, it may be that inter-population differences in nutrition are lost beneath this seasonal imprint.

In certain situations it appears that red deer may hybridise with Sika deer (*Cervus nippon*). This has been observed in captivity and in the wild, in various countries, most notably in the Lake District of northern England (Lowe and Gardiner 1975) and the Scottish highlands (McNally 1969; Clutton-Brock 1989, 173–175). Indeed, some have raised concerns as to the long-term genetic purity of Scottish stock as a whole (Clutton-Brock 1989, 177). However, it is difficult to assess the level of interbreeding, given the inadequate documentation of introductions and translocations, and the lack of understanding of the consequences of hybridisation in deer (Mitchell *et al.* 1977, 2; see also Whitehead 1964, 371–395).

A number of other variables may be considered to be of interest, although their influence is arguably marginal. For instance, it might be claimed that shed antler and antler from butchered individuals progress through a variety of taphonomic pathways, perhaps relating to the period during which they are exposed to the elements, or to the closing of blood vessels (recall that Ambrosiani [1981, figs 54–57] noted that blood vessels were still visible in elk antler years after shedding). However, it seems unlikely that such influences would have a significant effect on internal structure, and, given the constraints placed on this research by its origin as a component of a much wider doctoral research project, they are not explored in depth here. Moreover, in what follows, it has only been possible to consider in detail some of the questions discussed above, although it is hoped that this represents a useful first research step.

Characterising antler

In order to test the techniques defined by Smirnova, and to identify any further useful criteria, or problems, a small qualitative investigation was undertaken of the macrostructural variation in the three species of interest. A collection of modern antler was subjected to microscopic and 'by eye' analysis (see Tables 20.1 and 20.2). In the context of this study, it was not possible to control for the factors of age, pathology, or environment to any realistic extent given the nature of the materials available and the ethical constraints of modern zoological research. Nonetheless, some level of control was achieved, and the results are of some interest, while further verification of the techniques of identification has been established through blind test replications (detailed in Ashby 2009). In what follows, the key characteristics of *C. elaphus*, *R. tarandus*, and *A. alces* antler are described, with particular attention paid to the degree to which identifying criteria may be characterised as diagnostic. The discussion incorporates reference to both published literature and the author's own investigations. Table 20.2 summarises the observed impact of each variable upon phenomena that offer potential for use in identification, and the following text treats the same issues in a more discursive manner.

Morphological position

The first influence upon macrostructure relates to the possibility of variation within a single antler, based on morphological position. With this in mind, a like-for-like analysis of material was undertaken. Thus, the form, dimensions, and macrostructural phenomena of material taken from the burrs of *C. elaphus* antler were compared with their expression in basal and upper beam sections, with tine bases and tips, and with palmated areas. The same procedure was applied to samples of reindeer and elk antler.

In all three species, one may discern some infilling at the burr, causing a somewhat diffuse core-compacta boundary (this appears to have been previously noted by Rolf Lie; see above). However, elsewhere in the antler, the boundary between core and compacta is consistent, and though the quantity of useable compacta diminishes as the beam as a whole thins, the ratio of core to compacta thickness does not appear to change significantly in areas other than the tine tips (Figs 20.6–20.8).

Age/Size

Comparison of burrs from old and young animals of each species (and then for basal beams, upper beams, tine bases and tips, and palmated areas) allowed the investigation of patterning according to size/maturity. Unfortunately, it was not feasible to attribute individual age on the basis of antler size or morphology; given the complexity of life-long antler development, such estimates are known to be simplistic and problematic. However, by dividing the sample into broad categories (in accordance with evidence for a clear bimodality in size distribution, based on antlers for which total length was known; see Ashby 2006, appendix 3), and calibrating this with a number of antlers from animals of known age and shed at a known date, it was possible to categorise the material according to 'development classes'.

In red deer, no consistent macrostructural differences are apparent between poorly and well developed antlers. In the sample examined, there was no macrostructural difference between the two groups; such phenomena are simply present on different scales. The very coarse porosity visible in the cores of some large, well-developed antlers is not present in more poorly developed specimens, but the fundamental structure is identical. Moreover, the discrete boundary between core and compacta is a constant.

In reindeer, although some antlers belonging to the 'poorly developed' category have a finely porous core, in these cases they are still distinguishable from that of elk, chiefly because the semi-porous transition zone is always present. Comparing those reindeer of known age (two antlers from the same 7-year old male, and three antlers from three 4-year old female individuals), macrostructure is consistent between the two divisions, notwithstanding obvious differences in size and gross morphology. While superficial characteristics

Table 20.1 Modern antler used in investigation.

ANTLER REF. NO.	SOURCE	SPECIES	SEX	AGE (YEARS)	DEVELOPMENT CATEGORY
1	Raby Castle	Red Deer	M	Unknown	Good
2	Raby Castle	Red Deer	M	Unknown	Good
3	Raby Castle	Red Deer	M	Unknown	Poor
4	Raby Castle	Red Deer	M	Unknown	Poor
5	Raby Castle	Red Deer	M	Unknown	Poor
6	Raby Castle	Red Deer	M	Unknown	Poor
7	Cairngorm Reindeer Centre	Reindeer	M	Unknown	Poor
8	Cairngorm Reindeer Centre	Reindeer	F	Unknown	Good
9	Cairngorm Reindeer Centre	Red Deer	M	Unknown	Poor
10	Marwell Zoo	Reindeer	M	7	Poor
11	Marwell Zoo	Reindeer	M	7	Poor
12	Paradise Wildlife Park	Reindeer	F	4	Poor
13	Paradise Wildlife Park	Reindeer	F	4	Poor
14	Paradise Wildlife Park	Reindeer	F	4	Poor
15	Skanes Djurpark	Elk	M	2–3	Poor
16	Skanes Djurpark	Elk	M	2–3	Poor
17	Skanes Djurpark	Elk	M	Unknown	?
18	Skanes Djurpark	Elk	M	Unknown	?
19	Skanes Djurpark	Elk	M	Unknown	?
20	Skanes Djurpark	Elk	M	Unknown	Poor
21	Skanes Djurpark	Elk	M	Unknown	?
22	Selsey Lodge	Red Deer	M	3	Poor
23	Cairngorm Reindeer Centre	Red Deer	M	Unknown	Poor
24	Cairngorm Reindeer Centre	Reindeer	M	Unknown	Good
25	Cairngorm Reindeer Centre	Reindeer	F	Unknown	Poor
26	Highland Wildlife Park	Reindeer	M	Unknown	Good
27	Highland Wildlife Park	Reindeer	M	Unknown	Good
28	Highland Wildlife Park	Reindeer	F	Unknown	Good
29	Highland Wildlife Park	Reindeer	F	Unknown	Good
30	Highland Wildlife Park	Reindeer	F	Unknown	Good
31	Highland Wildlife Park	Red Deer	M	Unknown	Good
32	Highland Wildlife Park	Red Deer	M	Unknown	Good
33	Highland Wildlife Park	Red Deer	M	Unknown	Good
34	Donington Park	Red Deer	M	Unknown	Good
35	Donington Park	Red Deer	M	Unknown	Good

Table 20.2 Summary of results.

VARIABLE	VISIBLE EFFECT UPON COMPACTA-CORE TRANSITION	OTHER PERCEIVED EFFECTS
Morphological Position	Infilling at burr	Dimensions
Age	None	Dimensions, morphological complexity, compacta mottling
Sex	None	Dimensions, complexity
Environment	None	Dimensions, complexity
Pathology	None	?

of young antlers are distinctive (notably a darker mottling in the compacta), structure and relative proportions show no consistent differences.

In elk, antler exhibits a dark ring around the edge of the core area, probably relating to the extent of blood vessels. A limited sample meant that it was impossible to test the degree to which this was subject to age-related variation, but superficial phenomena such as these are anyway of limited utility to the archaeologist, and macrostructural phenomena are of greater interest. As it stands, there is no reason to suspect that age has any major effect on core structure, but further work is necessary before it may be accepted without reservation as a criterion of identification.

Sex

Females grow antlers only in reindeer. Reindeer cow antler is, in the main, smaller, and less strongly built than bull antler. It has a smaller cross section, and is frequently both much shorter in length and less complex in morphology than the antler of mature males. However, like-for-like investigation of burrs, basal beams, upper beams, tine bases and tips, and palmated areas for this species show that ratios of core to compacta thickness are similar in male and female examples, while the transition from porous core to compacta seems to be diffuse in both.

Environment

To note the effect of variations in environmental conditions such as climate, nutrition and population pressure, and genetic influences such as isolation, interbreeding and hybridisation, antler material was next compared according to its provenance. Comparison of material from individual sources failed to demonstrate the existence of consistent patterns relating to particular parks. Consideration within a wider frame of reference made it clear that in this sample Scottish examples tended to be relatively large and well-developed in terms of gross morphology. This may simply result from the sampling strategy of the collectors from whom material was acquired, though it is more likely an artefact of differences in habitat and mode of captivity. Notwithstanding any insecurity regarding the root of this disparity in gross morphology and overall development, it is significant that this is not echoed in internal macrostructure.

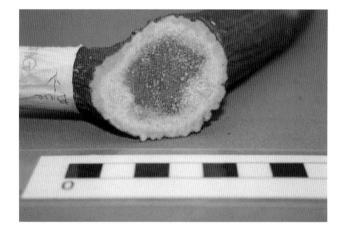

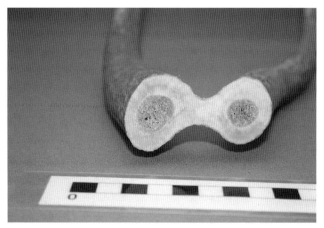

Figure 20.6 Macrostructure at various points along the length of a single Cervus elaphus *antler. Modern material (photographs: S. Ashby).*

Concerning reindeer, the English sample size was small, but examples from Scotland nonetheless seem much more complex in terms of gross morphology than those in southern England. This may relate to environmental factors, as it is generally acknowledged that the area in which the animals can roam in the highlands of Scotland is greater than the restricted parkland available to English populations. Once again, however, internal macrostructure is identical in English and Scottish material.

Thus, there is no evidence of geographical variation in the macrostructure of British red deer or reindeer antler. Furthermore, no significant structural differences were noted between British and Swedish-sourced reindeer antler. This is of course only a preliminary, qualitative investigation, and sample sizes are small with little control, but there is little evidence to suggest that geographical provenance has any important bearing on internal macrostructure in the antler of these species. Detailed investigation of this phenomenon in elk antler material was not possible in these investigations, but would benefit from research.

It is also important to assess the impact of hormonal or pathological influences upon antler growth. There is an extensive literature on this (see also below), and, given the ethical implications of undertaking such work today, it is neither possible nor desirable to further pursue this avenue through controlled investigation. In the sample used in the present study, no significant malformation, pathology, or symptoms of hormonal disturbance were noted, but it is of course possible that any such insult could impact upon macrostructural phenomena.

Antlerogenesis

It is conceivable that antler macrostructure is not immutable, and that it is subject to seasonal variation, just as antler morphology develops through the year. In shed antler, this does not cause a problem, as all such material represents the material completion of the annual cycle of antler growth. However, antler from butchered animals may be taken from the deer at any point in its period of development, such that the 'age at death' of a given antler may introduce a confound to any attempt to identify it to species. The single example of butchered antler in the collection (red deer no. 23, date of kill unknown) displayed a very distinctive surface texture, with a deep surface colour and a marked, consistent surface channelling. More important, though, is the fact that the internal macrostructure seemed identical to that

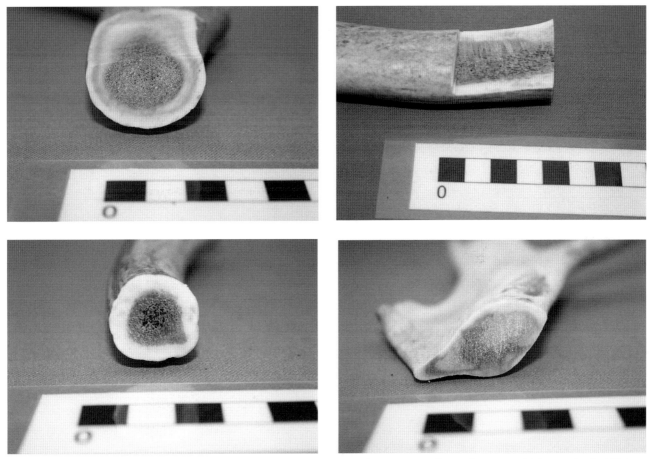

Figure 20.7 Macrostructure at various points along the length of a single Rangifer tarandus *antler. Modern material (photographs: S. Ashby).*

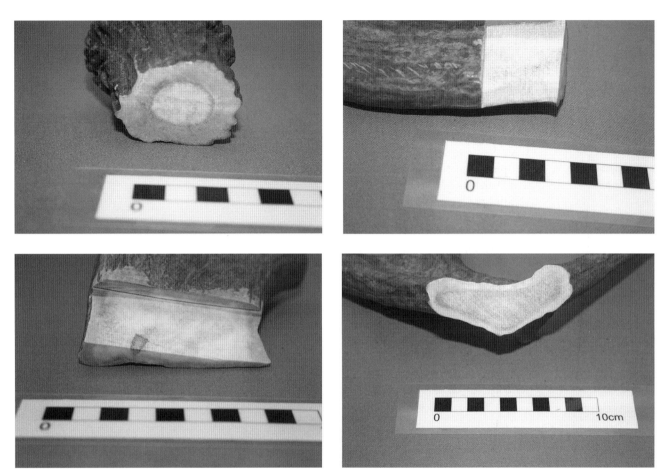

Figure 20.8 Macrostructure at various points along the length of a single Alces alces *antler. Modern material (photographs: S. Ashby).*

of shed antler. Obviously, it is impossible to categorically state that macrostructure does not develop or change during antlerogenesis; such a statement would necessarily be based on controlled analysis of antler representing known stages of development. Such investigation more properly lies within the remit of zoology and biology, rather than archaeology, and there is a wide literature on the relationship between antlerogenesis and various environmental and other constraints (e.g. Asleson *et al.* 1996, 1997; Azorit *et al.* 2002; Kierdorf *et al.* 2000, 1995; Lincoln and Fletcher 1984; MacEwen 1920; Smith 1998). Nonetheless, nothing in the present investigations (limited as they are) or existing literature suggests that species-level distinction on macrostructural grounds would be seriously undermined by antlerogenic confounds.

Discussion

In sum, it seems that our basic identification criteria stand up at least to this base-level analysis. Characterisation of surface texture provides a reliable manner of differentiating species,

as red deer, reindeer, and elk textures are diagnostic. However, such features are not frequently preserved in artefacts, and other criteria must often be utilised.

Diagnostic features within the structure of antler compacta could not be confidently identified, casting doubt on the suggestion that the structure of compact tissue in modern antler may be easily used as a criterion for species distinction, at least in the context of currently available methods and materials. Conversely, the nature of the porous core seems reliable as a distinguishing criterion. For example, the fine porosity of elk antler core material is distinctive, and the apparent absence of visible porosity in the tines of elk antler is particularly diagnostic (see Smirnova 2005, 11). However, differentiation between the cores of red deer and reindeer is more difficult, as no consistently observable characteristics are apparent (although, as above, quantification via image analysis may ultimately prove valuable). Thus, the presence of a semi-porous transition zone in reindeer and its absence in red deer show the greatest potential at present. Problems with this criterion include the possibility of confusion between the semi-porous zone in reindeer and the core itself in distal areas of elk antler, such as the tines. If the preserved areas of core and core-compacta margin are sufficiently large, the two species may be distinguished. However, if only vestiges are preserved in artefacts and the morphology of the core itself is not visible, then there is potential for uncertainty.

Given that the presence or absence of a 'transition' zone is a matter of degree rather than one of absolutes, there is of course the possibility of occasional inaccurate identification, and for this reason identification should be restricted to material in which macrostructural phenomena are both very well preserved and clearly visible. Furthermore, any identification made solely on the basis of this criterion should be qualified by the term 'probable'. With these caveats in mind, it may be instructive to discuss the limits of certainty in a little more detail. On reflection, the misidentification of red deer antler as reindeer is conceivable, as the cut of an antler object may render small areas of marginal core material visually similar to the semi-porous transition zone characteristic of reindeer. In contrast, where the core-compacta margin is clearly discrete, one can have some confidence that the material in question is red deer antler (or, depending on scale, elk). Superficially then, the mistaking of red deer for reindeer seems a more likely problem than the converse.

Palmate areas of elk antler have a coarser porosity than that present in the tines, and one which – when only present in small quantities – could be mistaken for the peripheral areas of red deer or reindeer core. Where worked fragments of such palmated material are the subject of study, identification must be one of probability rather than one of absolutes. Thus, a small reference collection is essential in differentiating species, and one must always err on the side of caution. Identifications should be qualified with terms such as 'probably', and supporting criteria should be used where possible (e.g. size of component, surface texture, compacta structure etc.).

Another difficulty is created by the fact that near the burr of all species, resorption from the pedicle may take place, resulting in a sort of secondary infilling. Should this be seen in red deer antler, it may be mistaken for the semi-porous zone in reindeer. Again, this should only occur if sufficient morphology is not preserved, as the phenomena may be obscured in small fragments, or in those that have been cut obliquely across the edge of the core area. However, consistent recurrence of semi-porosity in many objects would, on the basis of probability, suggest the use of reindeer antler, as the resorption phenomena occur only at the antler base and pedicle.

Thus, all in all, a tripartite system of identification seems appropriate (Fig. 20.9). Where the gross external morphology or outer surface texture of the antler are preserved, a *definite* species identification may be provided. Where surface texture is not present, but core or transition zone macrostructure is well-preserved and visible, a *probable* identification should be made. Criteria such as component size, compacta structure, texture and colour may be used to support such assertions, but are insufficient criteria for identification in their own

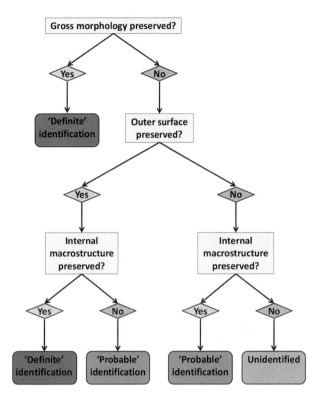

Figure 20.9 A schematic representation of the approach to antler identification suggested here (S. Ashby).

right. Thus, where gross morphology, surface texture, or core-compacta macrostructure are not preserved, an *indeterminate* assignation should be made. In many cases, a characterisation of a material as *indeterminate antler* (rather than bone) is all that may be achieved, and in many cases even this is not possible (see O'Connor 1987, 1999).

Conclusions

On the basis of a qualitative assessment of modern material, it has been suggested here that the zooarchaeological basis for the species-level identification of antler is fundamentally sound, subject to a number of important caveats. In the absence of any large-scale study of the impact of these potential confounds, the most powerful measures of the validity of this methodology come in the form of blind-testing of modern material (Ashby 2009, 18–20), and in the calibration of these methods using biomolecular (proteomic or genetic) techniques (see von Holstein *et al.* in prep; see *Postscript*). Nonetheless, it is argued here that the application of these identification criteria are justified in the characterisation of large or well preserved fragments. In smaller, more highly-worked, or taphonomically degraded pieces, these base-level methods may be of utility, but are best exploited as part of an initial, evaluative assessment undertaken in advance of more rigorous characterisation procedures, such as those that exploit genetic or biomolecular technologies.

Postscript: next generation approaches

Ultimately, it is of course desirable to move beyond 'probable' identifications. Recent developments in biomolecular archaeology now allow some measure of certainty in their identifications, and sampling methods are now minimally destructive, so for the first time such techniques constitute a viable alternative to macroscopic identification.

To provide a little detail, the development of a peptide mass fingerprinting method known as *ZooMS* (Zooarchaeology by Mass Spectrometry) constitutes a significant breakthrough in rapid, minimally destructive, high-throughput analysis of organic materials (Buckley *et al.* 2009). This method facilitates species-level identification of any material containing collagen (the principal protein in bone and antler). Collagen is extracted by demineralisation, trypsinated, fractionated, and analysed by time-of-flight mass spectrometry, and the resultant fingerprint may then be compared to a reference library of previously analysed species. In this way, combs that might not be readily identified on macroscopic grounds can nonetheless be precisely characterised. The rapid rate of throughput possible, together with the small size of samples required (1 mg) means that large numbers of specimens might be analysed, while the technique's use of collagen (which is extremely robust) means that analyses are rarely seriously inhibited or undermined by taphonomic constraints.

A recent application of this approach in the analysis of samples from Scottish Iron Age, Viking-Age and medieval comb teeth yielded promising results (von Holstein *et al.* 2014), and showed the technique to have a higher success rate than either genetic (aDNA) analysis or the macroscopic approach outlined above. However, such analyses, no matter how minimally destructive, may not be applicable in all cases, and, given their relative effectiveness at different scales, it is likely that it is in a judicious combination of these techniques that the most effective way forward will be found.

Acknowledgements

This paper relates the findings of research undertaken as part of a project funded by the AHRC. The paper has benefitted from the thoughts and encouragement of James Barrett, Alice Choyke, Matthew Collins, Sonia O'Connor, Terry O'Connor, Julian D Richards and Isabella von Holstein. Thanks also to Rob Symmonds, for stimulating discussion on the potential relationship between photoperiod, nutrition, and antler growth. For providing antler material, I gratefully acknowledge the help of the staff of the following institutions: Cairngorm Reindeer Centre, Highland Wildlife Park, Marwell Zoological Park, Paradise Wildlife Park, Raby Castle Deer Park, Selsey Lodge Deerpark, and Skanes Djurpark. Particular thanks are due to Michael Ashby, who prepared the samples for these investigations, and to Lyuba Smirnova, whose input and advice was invaluable in the early stages of this research, and who, had the author been able to contact her, would certainly have improved this paper through further useful comments and contributions. All errors remain the author's own.

Bibliography

Ambrosiani, K. (1981) *Viking Age Combs, Comb Making and Comb Makers in the Light of Finds from Birka and Ribe.* Stockholm, Stockholm Studies in Archaeology 2.

Ashby, S. P. (2006) *Time, Trade and Identity: bone and antler combs in Northern Britain c. AD 700–1400.* Unpublished PhD thesis, Department of Archaeology, University of York.

Ashby, S. P. (2009) Combs, contact and chronology: reconsidering hair combs in Early-Historic and Viking-Age Atlantic Scotland. *Medieval Archaeology* 53, 1–34.

Asleson, M. A., Hellgren, E. C. and Varner, L. W. (1996) Nitrogen requirements for antler growth and maintenance in white-tailed deer. *Journal of Wildlife Management* 60 (4), 744–752.

Asleson, M. A., Hellgren, E. C. and Varner, L. W. (1997) Effects of seasonal protein restriction on antlerogenesis and body mass in adult male white-tailed deer. *Journal of Wildlife Management* 61 (4), 1098–1107.

Azorit, C., Analla, M., Carrasco, R. and Munoz-Cobo, J. (2002) Influence of age and environment on antler traits in Spanish red deer (*Cervus elaphus hispanicus*). *Zeitschrift Fur Jagdwissenschaft* 48 (3), 137–144.

Ballin Smith, B. (1995) Reindeer antler combs at Howe: contact between late Iron Age Orkney and Norway. *Universitetets Oldsaksamlings Årbok 1993/94*, 207–211.

Barrett, J. H. (2003) Culture contact in Viking Age Scotland. In J. H. Barrett (ed.), *Contact, Continuity, and Collapse: the Norse colonization of the North Atlantic*, 74–111. Turnhout, Brepols.

Bubenik, G. A. (1990) Neuroendocrine regulation of the antler cycle. In G. A. Bubenik and A. B. Bubenik (eds), *Horns, Pronghorns, and Antlers*, 265–297. New York, Springer-Verlag.

Buckley, M., Collins, M., Thomas-Oates, J. and Wilson, J. C. (2009) Species identification by analysis of bone collagen using J. matrix-assisted laser desorption/ionisation time-of-flight mass spectrometry. *Rapid Communications in Mass Spectrometry* 23 (23), 3843–3854.

Carlé, P., Sigurdh, D. and Ambrosiani, K. (1976) *Preliminary Results of Proton-Induced X-Ray Analysis of Archaeologic Antler Findings.* Stockholm, Annual Reports from Research Institute of Physics.

Chapman, D. I. (1975) Antlers – bones of contention. *Mammal Review* 5 (4), 121–172.

Clutton-Brock, T. H. (1989) *Red Deer in the Highlands.* Oxford, BSP Professional Books.

Clutton-Brock, J. and MacGregor, A. (1988) An end to medieval reindeer in Scotland. *Proceedings of the Society of Antiquaries of Scotland* 118, 23–35.

Clutton-Brock, T. H., Guinness, F. E. and Albon, S. D. (1984) Individuals and populations: the effects of social behaviour on population dynamics in deer. *Proceedings of the Royal Society of Edinburgh* (B) 82, 275–290.

Eveleth, P. B. and Tanner, J. M. (1990) *Worldwide Variation in Human Growth.* Cambridge, Cambridge University Press.

Goss, R. J. (1969) Photoperiodic control of antler cycles in deer.1: phase shift and frequency changes. *Journal of Experimental Zoology* 170, 311–324.

Goss, R. J. (1995) Future directions in antler research. *Anatomical Record* 241 (3), 291–302.

Graham-Campbell, J. and Batey, C. E. (1998) *Vikings in Scotland: an archaeological survey*. Edinburgh, Edinburgh University Press.

Hambleton, E. and Rowley-Conwy, P. (1997) The Medieval reindeer economy at Gæccevaj'njar'ga 244B in the Varanger Fjord, North Norway. *Norwegian Archaeological Review* 30 (1), 55–70.

Harrison Matthews, L. (1971) *The Life of Mammals*. London, Weidenfeld and Nicolson.

Horwitz, L. K. and Smith, P. (1990) A radiographic study of the extent of variation in cortical bone thickness in Soay sheep. *Journal of Archaeological Science* 17, 655–664.

Huffman, B. (2003) *Ultimate Ungulate Fact Sheets*. Retrieved 24th July 2003, from http://www.ultimateungulate.com/Artiodactyla/ Alces_alces.html.

Ilkjaer, J. (1993) *Illerup Ådal: 3. Die Gurtel – Bestandteile und Zubehor, Textband, Jysk Archaeologisk Selskab, Jutland Archaeological Science Publications* 25 (3). Aarhus, Moesgård Museum, Aarhus Universitet.

Indrelid, S. and Hufthammer, A. K. (2011) Medieval mass trapping of reindeer at the Hardangervidda mountain plateau, South Norway. *Quaternary International* 238 (1–2), 44–54.

Jackson, L. J. and Thacker, P. T. (eds) (1997) *Caribou and Reindeer Hunters of the Northern Hemisphere*. Aldershot, Ashgate Publishing (Worldwide Archaeology Series).

Jordhøy, P. (2008) Ancient wild reindeer pitfall trapping systems as indicators for former migration patterns and habitat use in the Dovre region, southern Norway. *Rangifer* 28 (1), 79–87.

Kierdorf, U., Kierdorf, H.and Boyde, A. (2000) Structure and mineralisation density of antler and pedicle bone in red deer (*Cervus elaphus* L.) exposed to different levels of environmental fluoride: a quantitative backscattered electron imaging study. *Journal of Anatomy* 196, 71–83.

Kierdorf, U., Kierdorf, H. and Knuth, S. (1995) Effects of castration on antler growth in fallow deer (*Dama dama* L.). *Journal of Experimental Zoology* 273, 33–43.

King, S. E. and Ulijaszek, S. J. (1999) Invisible insults during growth and development: contemporary theories and past populations. In R. D. Hoppa and C. M. Fitzgerald (eds), *Human Growth in the Past: studies from bones and teeth*, 161–182. Cambridge, Cambridge University Press.

Kruuk, L. E. B., Slate, J., Pemberton, J. M., Brotherstone, S., Guiness, F. and Clutton-Brock, T. (2002) Antler size in red deer: heritability and selection but no evolution. *Evolution* 56 (8), 1683–1695.

Krzyszkowska, O. (1990) *Ivory and Related Materials: an illustrated guide* London, Institute of Classical Studies (Classical Handbook 3, Bulletin Supplement 59).

Lie, R. (1993) Appendix. In B. Weber (ed.), *Norwegian Reindeer Antler Export to Orkney, Universitetets Oldsaksamlings Årbok 1991/1992*, 161–174.

Lie, C., Clark, D. E. and Suttie, J. M. (2003) Deer pedicle height, tissue interactions and antler evolution. *Deer* 12 (6), 333–338.

Lincoln, G. and Fletcher, T. (1984) History of a hummel part VII. Nature vs. nurture. *Deer* 6, 127–131.

Lowe, V. P. W. and Gardiner, A. S. (1975) Hybridisation between red deer (*Cervus elaphus*) and sika deer (*Cervus nippon*) with particular reference to stocks in N.W. England. *Journal of the Zoological Society of London* 177, 553–566.

Luxmoore, E. (1980) *Deer Stalking*. Newton Abbot, David and Charles.

MacEwen, W. (1920) *The Growth and Shedding of the Antler of the Deer: the histological phenomena and their relation to the growth of bone*. Glasgow, Maclehose, Jackson and Co.

MacGregor, A. (1985) *Bone, Antler, Ivory and Horn: the technology of skeletal materials since the Roman period*. London, Croom Helm.

McNally, L. (1969) A probable red deer/sika hybrid. *Deer* 1, 287–288.

Mitchell, B., Staines, B. W. and Welch, D. (1977) *Ecology of Red Deer: a research review relevant to their management in Scotland*. Cambridge, Institute of Terrestrial Ecology.

Muir, P. D. and Sykes, A. R. (1988) Effect of winter nutrition on antler development in red deer (*Cervus elaphus*) – a field study. *New Zealand Journal of Agricultural Research* 31 (2), 145–150.

Myhre, B. (1993) The beginning of the Viking Age – some current archaeological problems. In A. Faulkes and R. Perkins (eds), *Viking Revaluations*, 182–204. London, Viking Society for Northern Research.

O'Connor, S. (1987) The identification of osseous and keratinaceous materials at York. In K. Starling and D. Watkinson (eds), *Archaeological Bone, Antler and Ivory*, 9–21. London, United Kingdom Institute for Conservation (Occasional Paper 5).

O'Connor, S. (1999) The preservation, identification and conservation of the finds. In A. MacGregor, A. J. Mainman and N. S. H. Rogers (eds), *The Craft, Industry and Everyday Life: bone antler, ivory and horn from Anglo-Scandinavian and Medieval York*, 1898–1901. York, Council for British Archaeology/Archaeology of York 17/2.

Odner, K. (1985) Saamis (Lapps), Finns and Scandinavians in history and prehistory. Ethnic origins and ethnic processes in Fenno-Scandinavia. *Norwegian Archaeological Review* 18 (1–2), 1–13.

Page, F. J. T. (ed.) (1971) *Field Guide to British Deer*. Oxford, Blackwell.

Penniman, T. K. (1952) *Pictures of Ivory and Other Animal Teeth, Bone and Antler*. Oxford, Pitt-Rivers Museum (Occasional Papers on Technology 5).

Ross, A. S. C. (1940) *The Terfinnas and Beormas of Ohthere*, Leeds School of English Language Texts and Monograph 7. Kendal, Titus Wilson.

Saether, B.-E. and Haagenrund, H. (1985) Geographical variation in the antlers of Norwegian moose in relation to age and size, *Journal of Wildlife Management* 49, 983–986.

Schmidt, K. T., Stien, A., Albon, S. D. and Guinness, F. E. (2001) Antler length of yearling red deer is determined by population density, weather and early life history. *Oecologia* 127, 191–197.

Smirnova, L. (1997) Antler, bone and ivory working in Nerevsky and Lyudin ends of Medieval Novgorod: evidence from waste analysis. In G. De Boe and F. Verhaeghe (eds), *Material Culture in Medieval Europe: papers of the 'Medieval Europe Brugge 1997' conference*, 137–146. IAP Rapporten 07.

Smirnova, L. (2002) *Comb-making in Medieval Novgorod (950–1450): an industry in transition*. Unpublished PhD Thesis, University of Bournemouth.

Smirnova, L. (2005) *Comb-Making in Medieval Novgorod (950–1450). An industry in transition*. Oxford, Archaeopress (British Archaeological Report S1369).

Smith, A. N. (2000) Material culture and North Sea contacts in the fifth to seventh centuries AD. In J. C. Henderson (ed.), *The Prehistory and Early History of Atlantic Europe*, 181–188. Oxford, Archaeopress (British Archaeological Report S861).

Smith, B. L. (1998) Antler size and winter mortality of elk: effects of environment, birth year, and parasites. *Journal of Mammalogy* 79 (3), 1038–1044.

Stephan, E. (1994) Die Materielbestimmung der "Bein" schnallen aus Bopfingen, Pfullingen und Gruibingen. In D. Quast (ed.), *Merowingerzeitliche Funde aus der Martinskirche in Pfullingen, Kreis Reutlingen. Fundberichte aus Baden-Wurttemberg* 19, 592–660.

Storli, I. (1993) Reply to comments on Sami Viking Age pastoralism – or "The Fur Trade Paradigm" reconsidered. *Norwegian Archaeological Review* 26 (1), 41–48.

Took, R. (2004) *Running with Reindeer: encounters in Russian Lapland.* London, John Murray.

Von Holstein, I. C. C., Ashby, S. P., van Doorn, N. L., Sachs, S. M., Buckley, M., Meiri, M., Barnes, I., Brundle, A. and Collins, M. J. (2014) Searching for Scandinavians in pre-Viking Scotland: molecular finger printing of Early Medieval combs. *Journal of Archaeological Sciences* 41, 1–6. http://dx.doi.org/10.1016/j.jas.2013.07.026

Webb, S. D. (2000) Evolutionary history of New World cervidae. In E. S. Vrba and G. B. Schaller (eds), *Antelopes, Deer, and Relatives: fossil record, behavioural ecology, systematics, and conservation*, 38–64. New Haven and London, Yale University Press.

Weber, B. (1992) Norwegian exports in Orkney and Shetland during the Viking and Middle Ages. In R. A. Hall, R. Hodges and H. Clarke (eds), *Medieval Europe 1992, Preprinted Papers Volume 5: exchange and trade*, 159–167. York, Medieval Europe 1992.

Weber, B. (1993) Norwegian reindeer antler export to Orkney. *Universitetets Oldsaksamlings* Årbok 1991/1992, 161–174.

Weber, B. (1994) Iron Age combs: analyses of raw material. In B. Ambrosiani and H. Clarke (eds), *The Twelfth Viking Congress: developments around the Baltic and the North Sea in the Viking Age*, 190–193. Stockholm, The Birka Project.

Whitehead, G. K. (1964) *The Deer of Great Britain and Ireland.* London, Routledge & Kegan Paul.